Other best-sellers by the author:

Paul Williams

MERLIN
PUBLISHING

First published in 2008 by
Merlin Publishing
Newmarket Hall, Cork Street,
Dublin 8, Ireland
Tel: +353 1 4535866
Fax: +353 1 4535930
publishing@merlin.ie
www.merlinwolfhound.com

1st Edition ISBN 978-1-903582-83-1
2nd Edition ISBN 978-1-903582-88-6

A CIP catalogue record for this book is available from the
British Library.

10 9 8 7 6 5 4 3 2 1

Typeset by Gough Typesetting Services
Cover Design by Graham Thew Design
Cover image courtesy of www.istockphotos.com © Nicholas Monu
Printed and bound by CPI Cox & Wyman, Britain

CONTENTS

Dedicated to the innocent victims of organised crime
and the Gardaí who's job it is to quell
the madness and solve the crimes.

Also to the members of the Irish Army Bomb Squad
who risk their lives every day to defuse
gangland plans for mass murder.

ACKNOWLEDGEMENTS

This is the sixth book I have written about organised crime in Ireland in the past 13 years. And this one, like the others, could not have been done without the help, trust and assistance of a lot of people, most of whom would prefer not to be thanked publicly for various reasons. To them all, I would like to express my deepest thanks for their help and their trust. My thanks also go to the victims and the families of the many victims who shared their stories. And also to a handful of underworld informants who helped spill the beans on some of the nastiest hoodlums contained between the covers of *Crime Wars*.

2008 was my 21st year working as a journalist for the *Sunday World* newspaper, an organisation that I can truly say I am honoured and privileged to be a part of. It was the year that despite all the odds in a hugely competitive marketplace, the *Sunday World* officially became the biggest selling newspaper on the entire island. I would like to say congratulations to all those who achieved this extraordinary distinction. I would also like to thank my employers for their incredible support – and patience – in allowing me to take the time to write another book. My deepest thanks and appreciation go to Managing Director Gerry Lennon, Deputy Managing Director Dave Ringrose, Editor Colm MacGinty, Managing Editor Neil Leslie and my News Editor – who had the dubious task of actually training me to be a journalist in the first place – John 'Dot' Donlon. In certain quarters Donlon is known as 'Bram Stoker' – for creating a monster!

My thanks also go to my picture editor, Gavin McClelland, for his hard work and my colleagues, photographers Padraig

O'Reilly, Liam O'Connor and Charlie Collins of Collins Photo Agency. Special thanks to my researcher Mairead Whelan. My gratitude also goes to Diarmuid McDermot of the Ireland International News Agency and Tomás MacRuarí of CCC. Nuacht.

Thanks as always to Merlin Publishing and especially my publisher, Chenile Keogh, editor Aoife Barrett, Julie Dobson and Ciara McNamara. My gratitude also goes to my long-suffering legal adviser Kieran Kelly – the 'Consiglieri' – of Fanning Kelly and Company Solicitors. And lastly my deepest gratitude and love goes to my wife and children – Anne, Jake and Irena – for their affection and support without which life wouldn't be worth living.

INTRODUCTION

There was no formal declaration or announcement to alert the Irish public that hostilities had begun. Gangland just seemed to slide towards a state of all-out war without prior warning. Since the beginning of the new Millennium, organised crime has seen a dramatic upsurge in Ireland – and brought with it an unprecedented level of violence and bloodshed. At the heart of it all is a burgeoning drug trade which is now conservatively valued at €1 billion a year.

On a per capita basis, the Republic of Ireland now ranks amongst the most violent societies in Western Europe. Three years ago there were more actual gangland murders recorded in Dublin than there were in London – a city with a population at least 13 times larger. The drug trade has bred life into a new generation of ruthless criminal godfathers who have no regard for human life. As we enter the final half of the first decade of the new Millennium, the gangsters have shown that there are no longer any boundaries beyond which they are not prepared to go. In this new era of savagery and barbarism, anything goes.

Criminals are now equipped with the very latest and most sophisticated firepower available. Whole gangs regularly travel to Eastern Europe and the US to train in the use of firearms. And that has been reflected in the accuracy of the hit men on the streets. In August 2008, a major international Garda investigation, involving police forces in three countries, busted a huge gunrunning plot which was being orchestrated by Brian Meehan, the killer of Veronica Guerin, from the comfort of his prison cell. In the past eight years the gangland murder rate has claimed 130 lives and there are no indications that there will be any let up in the bloodshed. Hundreds of people – both innocent and not so innocent – have been seriously injured. These days, Gardaí have a list of at least 40 criminals throughout the country at any one time who are classified as potential gangland targets. The average criminal godfather in modern Ireland has a limited life expectancy – if he is lucky or cute enough, he may live a bit longer.

The introduction of the bomb as a tool of war for criminals in Limerick and Dublin is a disturbing example of how far the warring hoodlums are prepared to go. In the ten months up to October 2008, Irish Army Bomb Squads have had to deal with almost 80 suspect devices – including improvised explosive devices and military spec hand grenades – around the country. The experts admit that it is only a matter of time before one of these lethal weapons will claim several innocent lives and leave many more maimed. Ironically the Bomb Squads are busier now than they were at the height of the Northern Troubles which were resolved in the closing days of the twentieth century.

The underworld has ensured that one conflict was replaced by another. One of the most worrying trends we have seen in recent years is the number of completely innocent people who have been deliberately gunned down by the godfathers. *Crime Wars* exposes the background to the horrific murders of the innocent such as Baiba Saulite, Anthony Campbell and Brian Fitzgerald – all of whom were purposely gunned down when they crossed paths with the hoods.

Crime Wars investigates the changing – and very ugly – face of organised crime in modern Ireland. The book reveals the background stories to some of the most horrendous crimes and murders of the past eight years. It exposes the secret worlds of godfathers Martin 'Marlo' Hyland and Christy Griffin. *Crime Wars* exposes the brutal, sadistic world of Murder Incorporated, the blood-thirsty McCarthy/Dundon mob in Limerick and tells the chilling story of the notorious Grand Canal murders which coincided with the first days of the new decade and century. And it tells the macabre story of the notorious Finglas mob who, according to the more superstitious in gangland, perished as a result of a gypsy's curse.

Crime Wars is the story of organised crime in modern Ireland – and it doesn't make for pleasant reading.

Paul Williams
October 2008

ONE

THE CANAL BUTCHER

The new Millennium was just nine days old and Ireland was still recovering from the party of the century. The country was in the process of unwinding after the frenetic build up to 2000 which had been anticipated with equal measures of excitement and trepidation. The doomsday prophets had been in full cry in the dying days of the 20th Century. They preached that the very future of mankind lay in the balance, as we prepared to step into the great unknown – to cross the threshold of a new century and millennium. The much hyped Y2K syndrome threatened to melt down the world's computer networks, with devastating consequences for life as we knew it. Across the globe security forces and emergency services had been placed on red alert as we braced ourselves for Armageddon. In Ireland thousands of public servants were at their work stations prepared for a valiant effort to save the country from disaster. All Garda and Army leave had also been cancelled. As the clocks struck midnight across the world, however, it all proved to be much ado about nothing. All that changed was the date. And then the party got into full swing. Anxiety was replaced with optimism, hope and a major hangover. But Ireland's criminal underworld was determined to put an end to the celebration. The dark side of Ireland's new prosperity was a dramatic increase in drug abuse and that meant a boom time for organised crime. Gangsters had unleashed a new war to replace the one that had just been resolved in the North. No amount of diplomacy and political negotiation would bring about a ceasefire in this conflict that continues to plague the streets of Irish towns and cities. A ruthless thug was about to give us a taste of the bloody depths to which villains would stoop in the new age.

On the afternoon of Sunday, January 9, 2000, a couple took advantage of the calm weather and went for a walk by the banks of the Grand Canal to clear their heads. Their stroll took them near Aylmer Bridge at Kearneystown, in the County Kildare countryside. They strolled along the tow path where once, in a much more innocent age, horses pulled cargo-laden barges between Dublin and the rest of the country. After 200 years the lumbering boats gave way to progress and inched along the canal for the final time in 1960. For many years, the once vital transport route and its banks had become overgrown and the area was used as an illegal dumping ground. In recent times, however, it had been cleaned up and transformed into a picturesque amenity for walkers and boating enthusiasts. The Celbridge Paddlers Canoe Club was situated nearby. The Local Authority had stopped the practice of illegal dumping. But not everyone had heeded the 'Dumping Prohibited' signs.

Suddenly the couple spotted what looked like a human hand pointing up from the dark, freezing water. The husband used a stick to prod what he at first thought was a shop mannequin, floating just beneath the water. On closer examination he realised that it was a naked body, lying face up in the still canal. He noticed a human face and male genitalia. With chilling symbolism the body's right arm wore a tattoo of the Grim Reaper, which had been partially eaten away by animals.

The shocked couple were joined by other horrified walkers who raised the alarm. They had just discovered one of the most grisly murders in the blood-soaked history of gangland. In what could have been a macabre scene in a Stephen King horror movie, the corpse of the murdered young man beckoned from his watery grave as if he wanted the world to avenge his gruesome end.

When emergency services arrived, firemen pulled the body from the water. There was a gaping gunshot wound to the right cheek. The area was immediately sealed off by Gardaí and Crime Scene Investigators were called in. Gangland's first victim of the new Millennium was laid on the canal bank and covered in a body bag. A scene of a crime tent was erected to preserve any evidence that could bring the attention-seeking corpse some kind of justice.

When dawn broke the following morning, the Gardaí began the task of unravelling the mystery of what looked like an underworld execution. They conducted a painstaking search for clues in the canal and the vegetation that crowded the banks on either side. Then a police diver, who was looking for a murder weapon, made another shocking discovery. Garda Brian Breathnach was 20 minutes into his search of the murky canal bed when he spotted a second body. It was lying face down in just over a metre of water, a short distance from where the first body had been found. This body was fully clothed and the diver could make out that it had severe head injuries.

When the corpse was pulled out, the man's face was unrecognisable. He had been shot through the nose and a large exit wound had shattered the left side of the scalp. Their bodies were brought to the morgue at Tallaght hospital for post-mortem and forensic examination. On closer examination the CSI discovered a second gunshot wound to the chest. An autopsy would later reveal that the men had been dead for several days. The cold water had delayed decomposition.

Reports of the gruesome crime shocked and stunned the country. The double murder dominated news coverage and was even covered by other news organisations around the world. It was one of the worst gangland atrocities ever seen in Ireland at the time. It served to symbolise gangland's vision of the future. In the new Millennium life would be cheaper than ever before. Murder had become an essential tool in the corporate strategy of organised crime. In the first days of the New Year the storm clouds were gathering. On the same day that the first body was found, the *Sunday World* carried a front page story about a missing 17-year-old heroin addict called Patrick Lawlor, from Ballyfermot in West Dublin. He had vanished exactly a year earlier in January 1999. The story reported how Gardaí feared that the young man had been murdered and buried in an unmarked grave. The Lawlor story added to the magnitude of the Grand Canal slaughter.

As Gardaí launched an investigation their first job was to identify the two bodies. They knew that neither of the bodies could have been that of Patrick Lawlor because intelligence sources had revealed that the young addict had been dead for a year. (Patrick Lawlor's body was subsequently discovered buried in January 2002 along another stretch of the Grand Canal near Ballyfermot. It emerged that he had been beaten to death during a row with two other drug addicts who were involved in the distribution of heroin. One man was later convicted of the lesser charge of concealing the body.) It was clear that the Grand Canal bodies were the victims of a gangland execution. Officers began to check their lists of missing persons – particularly missing people with connections to the criminal underworld.

It didn't take long to come up with names. A week earlier the mothers of two young men, who were also from Ballyfermot, had separately reported their sons missing. Kathleen Murray, the mother of 19-year-old Patrick 'Whacker' Murray, contacted the local Garda station on the morning of December 30. The following evening, on New Year's Eve, 21-year-old Darren Carey's mother, Noeleen, told the Gardaí at Kilmainham Station that her son was missing.

Within hours of the discovery of the second body Gardaí had officially identified both men. Patrick Murray's father, Paul, had the heart-breaking task of identifying the first body found as that of his son. The families of the two men had been involved in a desperate search for Patrick in the days before the discovery. Later that evening Darren Carey's uncle had the equally traumatic duty to perform. The extensive injuries to the young man's face made identification difficult. He recognised his nephew's moustache, hair and eyebrows. Darren Carey also had distinctive scars on his knee and elbow which he had sustained in a motorbike crash some years earlier. The uncle also recognised a bracelet with the name Darren inscribed on it. To confirm the identity beyond all doubt Gardaí also ran a check on his dental records.

State Pathologist, Dr Marie Cassidy, found that both men

had been shot in the head with a shotgun. The blast had fractured Patrick Murray's right cheekbone. The shotgun pellets had sliced through the brain tissue and become embedded on the inside of the skull. The large amount of soot around the entry wound in the head indicated that he had had been shot at point blank range. Death had been instant. The body was then dumped in the cold water which had helped to preserve it. There were no other injuries on the body to indicate that Patrick Murray had been beaten or restrained before his murder. Nor did he have any defensive injuries. Darren Carey had also been shot twice at close range – in the chest and head – with a shotgun.

Dr Cassidy felt that Carey had first been shot in the head, with the blast aimed through the bridge of the nose. A large exit wound shattered the base of the skull. The second shot had been aimed at the left side of the chest. The pathologist found evidence of bleeding and bruising on both injuries which suggested that Darren Carey had not died immediately after the shooting. The absence of water in the lungs, however, proved that he was dead when his body was dumped into the canal. Forensic experts found traces of blood and bone tissue on the opposite bank to where the body was found. DNA analysis later confirmed that the tissue belonged to Carey. It was clear that the dead men had been shot on the opposite bank and the bodies had floated to the other side.

The investigation of the Grand Canal murders would be the largest underworld manhunt since the murder of journalist Veronica Guerin four years earlier. The level of public revulsion and shock at the crimes ensured that the probe got top priority. Only once in gangland history had there been a double execution before 2000. In December 1995, drug dealer Eddie McCabe and an innocent young mother who was in his company, were both shot after they were ambushed by gangsters in Tallght, South Dublin. The line of the canal doubled as the border between the Garda Dublin Metropolitan Region (DMR) and the Carlow/Kildare Division. As the bodies were on the south side of the canal, primary responsibility for the investigation automatically fell to the Carlow/Kildare Division. It was under the command of Chief Superintendent Sean Feely and Supt Thomas Neville.

An incident room was set up at Divisional Headquarters in Naas Station, County Kildare. Scores of officers were drafted in to spearhead the operation with back-up from the District Detective Units in Ballyfermot and Clondalkin, the National Bureau of Criminal Investigation (NBCI) and the Technical Bureau. On the ground, the investigation was co-coordinated by the NBCI. Assistant Commissioner Tony Hickey and Det Supt Pat Brehony had overall command. Hickey had led the Veronica Guerin investigation. Both he and Brehony were among the country's most respected detectives.

Once identification of the Grand Canal bodies had been confirmed, Gardaí began searching for a motive and they soon found it. All enquires led back to the drug trade. The ensuing investigation would lift the lid on the sordid underbelly of the criminal drug rackets.

Detectives soon discovered that the outrage had nothing to do with some high-powered criminal conspiracy involving big players. On December 3, 1999, Patrick Murray and another Ballyfermot youth, 18-year-old Gary Kelly, had been arrested at Dublin Airport. After they arrived on a flight from Amsterdam, Customs officers had caught them carrying a kilo of heroin between them, worth over IR£170,000 (€215,900) on the streets. Intelligence sources also identified Darren Carey as one of the organisers of the shipment. He, and another man, had organised the deal as part of a plan to set up their own drug trafficking network. The Customs seizure had cost them a lot of money. But why had Carey been murdered? And why had Murray been singled out for death and Kelly left untouched? The search for answers led directly to Carey's boss, who was the main player in the conspiracy.

He was well known to the police as an extremely violent and dangerous thug who controlled a large heroin dealing operation. Within a few days Gardaí had a prime suspect for the Grand Canal murders. He became gangland's most talked about monster. In media reports he earned the sobriquet, The Canal Butcher, and his picture, which had been purposely blurred out for legal reasons, appeared on several front pages. To the police, reporters, criminals and the people he had terrorised in

Ballyfermot for many years, he was better known as 24-year-old Mark Desmond.

* * * *

One experienced detective who spent most of his service working the beat in Ballyfermot, one of Dublin's largest working class suburban sprawls, had always expected Mark Desmond to make a name for himself – for all the wrong reasons. "From the time he was a kid he was showing seriously violent tendencies. He really was a very nasty character who bullied and terrorised his neighbourhood. Everyone was afraid of him. We knew of several incidents in which he had beaten or sliced people up over petty disputes. He had shot at people, he tried to burn their houses and even a horse," the officer recalled. "Desmond preyed on young drug addicts, who he used as slaves in his heroin business. They lived in constant terror of the man which is why it was impossible for us to get anyone to give evidence against him in court. He was psychotic and he left us in no doubt that he could easily shoot one of us."

Mark Desmond was born in March 1975. He idolised his father Denis 'Dinny Boy' Desmond, a man with a ferocious reputation as a brute who acted as an enforcer for various criminal gangs. Mark's admiration for his father was not diminished by the many savage beatings he had suffered from his father's fists when he was a child. Dinny Boy Desmond was known to settle all arguments, even petty disputes, with his fists. He was also involved in protection rackets around the city in the '70s and '80s and worked as a doorman in various pubs and clubs.

"No one went past Dinny Boy because he could kill you with his bare hands. He couldn't walk from Ballyer (Ballyfermot) to O'Connell Street without being in at least one fight," recalled another cop who knew him well.

However Dinny Boy, who had a string of convictions for assaults, never featured in Garda intelligence reports as a major player in the burgeoning organised crime business. He was more of a hired heavy for the gangsters and racketeers

who didn't want to hurt their own fists. So too was his younger
brother Laurence 'Lar' Desmond. Lar had several convictions
for assault, malicious wounding and possession of offensive
weapons. Mark Desmond's father was a passionate pigeon
fancier and he helped establish a pigeon club near his home in
Ballyfermot. It was through the pigeon club that he became a
close friend of Martin Cahill, the General, one of gangland's
most infamous celebrities. He was also a friend of Christy
Dutton from Ballyfermot, one of Cahill's most trusted associates
and partner in many armed heists. For several years before the
General's murder in August 1994, Dinny Boy was a regular
visitor to Cahill's home at Cowper Downs in Rathmines.
Cahill bought his bird seed from Desmond. The two friends
also travelled to pigeon races in the UK where they purchased
birds, often paying sums up to IR£20,000 (€25,400) each. Dinny
Boy's son grew up in awe of the shadowy godfather. In his eyes
Martin Cahill was a true hero. He tried hard to emulate his role
model and wanted to become the new General.

Mark Desmond was the third of four children – two boys
and two girls – who grew up in the family home on Landen
Road in Ballyfermot. Locals recalled that it was anything but
a happy home. The whole family suffered the brunt of Dinny
Boy's fists when he was drunk or in a bad mood. Desmond's
parents were separated for several years but he continued to
live with his father. There was no doubt that he inherited his
father's predilection for violence. As a child he was a talented
boxer, with a promising career in the sport but he dropped it.
Instead he used his 'talents' to push his weight around and beat
up anyone who annoyed him. He used his father's reputation,
and the family's connection with the General, to push people
around. When he left school at the age of 13, Mark Desmond
could barely read and write. He never worked at a job in his
life. His only attempt at making an honest crust was when he
volunteered to undertake clinical tests for new drugs. As a
result he earned the nickname the Guinea Pig among his peers
– although they tended not to call him that to his face.

In the early 1990s, Desmond was a member of a group
of vicious young thugs, most of them from Ballyfermot and

Clondalkin, who gained notoriety as the M50 gang. The teenage tearaways specialised in robbing high-powered cars to indulge in the inappropriately termed "joy riding". This involved extremely dangerous high speed nocturnal jousts with the police on the new motorway which had opened on the west side of the capital in 1992. The gang also used stolen jeeps to carry out ram raids on business premises in the countryside. Several members of the gang were killed when they crashed stolen vehicles. Desmond's volatile nature singled him out from the rabble and he tended to be more of a loner in the gang. Instead, he preferred to surround himself with younger, vulnerable kids who he could easily bully and exploit. At the same time Desmond began dabbling in the drug trade. In 1991, at the age of 16 he and two associates ambushed a local teenage drug gang, forcing them to hand over their stash of heroin and cash at gunpoint. The drug pushers were too afraid of the teen mobster to seek revenge. In a short time they were given no choice but to work for the Guinea Pig.

Mark Desmond notched up his first recorded criminal conviction, for attempting to break into a car, when he was 18. He was also making a name for himself as a vicious thug. Detectives investigating serious assaults and robberies were hearing a lot about the teenager. During the robbery of a car in Westmanstown, Lucan in 1994, when the owner tried to stop Desmond, Mark stabbed him in the knee and forehead with a screw driver. While making his escape from pursuing Gardaí, he drove the stolen car at speeds of up to 100 miles per hour around Ballyfermot and Clondalkin. He then rammed three police cars, before crashing the stolen vehicle. A bench warrant was issued for his arrest when he failed to turn up in court for an adjournment hearing. Desmond regularly failed to honour his bail conditions. The night before his trial was due to go ahead, Desmond organised for an associate to give him a minor flesh wound in the leg with a pen gun. It was an old trick first used by his hero, the General. He claimed he had been the victim of a gangland attack. In 1996, he was finally convicted of the robbery and jailed for 18 months. He was also disqualified from driving, as he was on numerous occasions. But it didn't stop the gangster getting behind the wheel.

Around the same time he was suspected of doing an armed robbery at the McDonalds restaurant on Kylemore Road in Ballyfermot in February 1994. During the heist a member of staff was tied up at gunpoint and money was taken from the safe. Some years later the Guinea Pig approached an employee at the McDonalds outlet and actually bragged about the incident. He told the young woman that he had probably "kicked" her mother around during the heist and also claimed he had threatened to rape the male employee he tied up. He had no time either for the code observed by so-called Ordinary Decent Criminal's, that a hood left his neighbours in peace. Desmond organised an armed robbery at the local Ballyfermot United Social Club, during which terrified staff were held at gunpoint while the takings were snatched. He was never charged with these crimes.

In January 1995, Desmond discovered that another local youth, 19-year-old Mark McLoughlin, had been selling 'Nap' tablets. These are prescription drugs used to ease the pain of the terminally ill. Naps were popular as a heroin substitute, whenever the drug was in short supply. Gangs like the M50 crew stole the drugs from pharmacies around the country. The Guinea Pig heard that McLoughlin had been using his name to threaten customers who didn't pay up. McLoughlin had also wrongly blamed Desmond for breaking into a car in Ballyfermot. On the evening of January 5, Desmond and two other associates – aged 14 and 16 – called to the house on Ballyfermot Road where McLoughlin was staying. Desmond hit McLoughlin across the head with a bottle and then tied him up with a rope.

Desmond and his accomplices brought McLoughlin to Glencree in the Dublin Mountains. His bindings were taken off and Desmond instructed his associates to beat their captive. They then stripped McLoughlin and tied him to a tree. Desmond whipped him across his back with copper flex. His terrified associates would later describe how Mark liked inflicting pain. The thugs then drove away, leaving their naked and injured victim wandering on a mountain road in the freezing night air. McLoughlin was saved by a passing motorist who brought him to Loughlinstown Hospital in South Dublin. McLoughlin later identified his attackers to the Gardaí and Desmond and his accomplices were arrested. The officer in charge of the case, Detective Sergeant Gabriel O'Gara, had recently been posted to Ballyfermot Garda station. He quickly identified Desmond as a very dangerous criminal and he spent the next seven years trying to put him behind bars.

Desmond denied any involvement in the crime when questioned but his younger associates admitted what they had done. With enough evidence Det Sgt O'Gara charged Desmond with the false imprisonment and assault of McLoughlin on January 7, 1995. Desmond was remanded in custody for three weeks. Gardaí had previously objected to bail on the grounds that Desmond would interfere with witnesses and they wanted the victim to tell the court what had happened to him.

On January 25, he was released on bail when McLoughlin failed to turn up in court. McLoughlin later told the detectives that he had been offered IR£1,000 (€1,270) by Dinny Boy Desmond not to turn up. McLoughlin then fled the country. He died a few months later of a drug overdose while in police custody in England. The charges against Desmond were dropped as a result.

He was also suspected of taking part in a number of armed robberies with other members of the M50 gang, in which shots were fired. During one of those robberies the gang showed that they had no qualms about shooting a cop. On the night of March 5, 1995, three masked raiders, armed with sawn-off shotguns and a pistol, tried to hold up a businessman. He was making a night lodgement at the AIB branch on Capel Street in Dublin's north inner-city. Thirty-two-year-old Garda Peter O'Connor, who was a member of the unarmed North Central Divisional Task Force, arrived at the scene with two colleagues and tackled one of the robbers. As the father of two young children grappled with the thug, another raider shot him in the knee with a sawn-off shotgun. As the officer fell to the ground in agony, the raider put the shotgun to his head and threatened to kill him.

The raiders then held his colleagues back by threatening to shoot them as they jumped into a stolen getaway car. As

the gang sped off, the injured Garda narrowly escaped being
run over by the car when he rolled out of the way just in
time. The officer's leg was saved after several hours of surgery
but he was left seriously maimed. Garda O'Connor and his
colleagues, Sergeant Seán Ward and Garda Marcus Hand,
were subsequently awarded Scott medals for their "exceptional
courage and heroism". Over 13 years later, Garda O'Connor
still had 57 pellets in his leg and there was a possibility that his
leg would still have to be amputated as a result of the injuries.
Despite this the brave officer returned to work. In January 2008,
he was awarded almost €1 million in compensation by the
High Court for his horrific ordeal. Desmond and several other
associates were questioned about the incident but Gardaí had
insufficient evidence to bring them before the courts.

The Guinea Pig grew up with utter contempt for the police
and let them know it at every possible opportunity. He regularly
threatened to kill officers who crossed him and, on a number
of occasions, followed individual Gardaí to their homes in
an attempt to intimidate them. Whenever he was questioned
about a crime Desmond would do everything to distract – and
repulse – officers. He would sit across the table from the cops
laughing and taunting them. One detective recalled his typical
behaviour: "He would be totally unpredictable, a real bastard
to deal with, just like Martin Cahill. He would throw himself
on the ground and begin screaming and taking off his clothes.
Desmond would pick his nose and then eat it in front of you.
He would offer to share it with his interrogators in the hope
that someone might get sick. He would fart and belch and spit.
Then he progressed to rubbing his own shit across his face. He
was a complete animal."

Desmond rammed police cars and organised ambushes.
This was done by parking a stolen car in a pre-arranged location
and then "tipping off" the Gardaí about it. When officers
arrived to recover the vehicle, they would be showered with
stones, missiles and petrol bombs. Other stolen cars were then
used to surround the police cars and repeatedly ram them.
Several officers were injured and had to be hospitalised. In
Hallowe'en 1995, Ballyfermot erupted in one of the worst riots

ever seen in Dublin which had been carefully planned by the local criminals including Desmond. A young child was seriously injured during the disturbances when a petrol bomb blew up at his feet, engulfing him in flames. The six-year-old's father was throwing the bomb at the time. Several high-powered cars had been stolen specifically for use in ramming Garda cars and vans. Strips of wood, filled with six inch nails, were laid across roads to puncture the tyres of emergency vehicles. The police were forced to baton charge their way into Gallanstown Lawns to allow an ambulance in to rescue the severely injured child.

In 1996, the criminal underworld went through dramatic changes after the murder of Veronica Guerin. The unprecedented police counter offensive changed the order of things in gangland. Thugs like Desmond were happy to fill the vacuum left after several criminals were put out of business. In the last years of the 20th Century a new type of drug gang had begun to emerge. Most gang members were aged in their teens or early 20s and, even more than their predecessors, they displayed a disturbing propensity for extreme violence. After a drop in the murder rate for a few years after the Guerin murder, by 1998 the number of gang-related murders had begun to steadily increase.

Desmond at first followed in his father's footsteps and became a heavy for Derek 'Dee Dee' O'Driscoll. 'Dee Dee' was from Croftwood Park in Ballyfermot and was a year older than the Guinea Pig. O'Driscoll supplied heroin and later ecstasy to Desmond who sold it on his patch. Dee Dee and Desmond were regarded as members of a wider gang controlled by Finglas hoodlum PJ Judge, who was known by Gardaí and criminals alike as the Psycho. Judge, who controlled a huge heroin and ecstasy operation, had been responsible for a reign of terror, including at least three murders. He was the most feared killer in gangland until his murder in December 1996. *(See Chapter Four.)* The Psycho's untimely death – six months after the Guerin murder – created a vacuum in the underworld. It was quickly filled by O'Driscoll and his associates on one side of the River Liffey and the Westies on the other. Both groups of young madmen lived up to the Psycho's violent legacy.

In Blanchardstown, West Dublin, Stephen Sugg and Shane

Coates and their gang, alias the Westies, emerged as the most feared and violent drug dealers in the country. They had adopted a "no nonsense" approach to doing business – anyone who owed them as much as IR£100 (€127) for drugs was severely beaten and tortured. If anyone dared try to deal drugs on their patch he or she was tortured, beaten or shot dead. Soon the Westies had been elevated to the top of the Garda 'Most Wanted List'. Similar gangs had also sprung up in Finglas, south of the River Liffey in Clondalkin and south-west in Crumlin and Drimnagh.

Ballyfermot dealer, O'Driscoll had been well known to the local Garda drug squad and was suspected of being an organiser of the 1995 Hallowe'en riots which raged around the Gallanstown area of Ballyfermot. He had come to attention as a close associate of Judge and that gang's bag man, Packie Moore. Packie used a milk round on the Northside of the city to launder drug money. 'Dee Dee' was also aligned to George 'the Penguin' Mitchell who had become one of the biggest drug traffickers in the country. One of O'Driscoll's criminal convictions related to a bizarre animal cruelty case. It followed a drug squad raid on Dee Dee's house in 1996 when officers found a lot more than just drugs. When cops entered they found the drug dealer's pet jaguar 'Princess' tucking into a pig's head in the darkened garage. They also found an African Serval. Both creatures were cooped up in dreadful conditions, in wire mesh cages with no natural light. The animals were seized and later handed over to Dublin Zoo. At the time O'Driscoll claimed that he bought the exotic pets to protect himself against rival drug dealers! When District Judge Gillian Hussey sentenced the heroin dealer to three months in prison she told him: "If either of those animals had got out, I don't want to contemplate what might happen. As an animal lover I am sickened by the way they were locked up, which can only suggest a depraved mind."

Desmond's pal also made the headlines as a result of the Veronica Guerin murder investigation, when it was discovered that he had been paying bribes to a corrupt Garda called John O'Neill, who was based at Tallaght Garda Station. O'Neill, who had been decorated for bravery, was exposed after he was spotted secretly meeting with members of the Gilligan gang. It later emerged that he had been taking money from gang members Paul Ward and Brian 'The Tosser' Meehan. This was in return for information and help in obtaining documents for passports in the names of gang members. When he was caught, O'Neill also came clean about being on the pay roll of O'Driscoll and another Ballyfermot drug dealer called Tony Long.

O'Driscoll and the gang had been delighted with their "acquisition". When 'Dee Dee' was arrested on the corruption charges he admitted secretly filming a meeting with the cop during which he and Long handed him IR£5,000 (€6,350).

"I needed collateral. The banks take your house deeds. I only took a fuckin' picture. He (O'Neill) came to me looking for a few bob and I wouldn't like to see one of your men stuck, you know, good citizen and all of that," he sniggered at the detectives sitting across the table in the interview room.

O'Driscoll and Long eventually pleaded guilty to paying bribes to the Garda and were fined IR£45,000 (€57,150) each or else face 12 months behind bars. Long, who was aged 42 at the time of the offence, decided to pay while Dee Dee decided to hold onto his ill-gotten cash. As a result a warrant was issued to have him committed to prison to serve his sentence. O'Driscoll went into hiding in Portugal where he lived with Packie Moore in a large villa he had purchased with drug money. From there they continued to run their drug distribution network in Ballyfermot, with the help of Mark Desmond.

The Guinea Pig had rapidly emerged as one of the top new kids on the block. He had a natural talent for the new methods being used to run the drug trade. Like the Westies, he took pleasure in inflicting pain. He controlled much of the heroin being sold on a patch that included Lower Ballyfermot and St Michael's Estate in nearby Inchicore. St Michael's Estate was a high rise Corporation flat complex which had become run down and neglected. It became a popular centre for the wholesale dealing of heroin, making life utterly miserable for the residents who were trying to give their kids a decent upbringing. Heroin addicts from all over the city descended on the complex every day to buy their 'gear'.

Desmond waged a campaign of terror on his patch. He controlled a large group of young hopeless drug addicts who were totally dependent on him for their daily fix. These addicts were forced to sell Desmond's drugs to pay for their own habits. Many of these individuals were as young as 15 years of age and they became his glorified slaves. A number of them, both male and female, would later claim to Gardaí that he had sexually assaulted and raped them. The girlfriend of one of Desmond's dealers described how the Guinea Pig seemed to get a "rush" whenever he witnessed her being beaten by her boyfriend. If anyone stepped out of line they were severely beaten, stabbed or shot. The same treatment was meted out to anyone with the temerity to encroach on his patch.

The Gardaí could do little to stop Desmond unless they caught him in actual possession of a gun or drugs. But he had picked up a few tips from his dead hero. His former associates described how he always wore socks over his hands whenever he handled drugs, guns or money, to prevent leaving finger or hand prints. Most of the time he used his army of terrified lackeys to move drugs and money from one location to another. This reduced his risk of being caught. If his slaves were caught none of them would dare admit who owned the 'gear'. Desmond never rewarded any of his 'workers' for their frightened silence. Anything they lost, either cash or drugs, would have to be replaced.

One young drug addict, who had direct experience of life with the Guinea Pig, described his approach. "He was a complete mad man and he loved to hurt people. When I lost stuff to the police I kept me mouth shut and took the rap. But then he [Desmond] came around and beat fuck out of me. He sliced me up with a Stanley blade and told me that I now owed him several thousand pounds and I would have to work if off for him. He was a fuckin' animal and no one would ever tell the police about him," the victim revealed in an interview for this book.

During the Garda investigation into the Grand Canal murders, Desmond's brother summed up Mark's personality. "I have nothing to do with my brother, he is a header, a loner, a fucking psycho," he told cops. Desmond's younger sister described Mark as a "mad bastard" with a violent temper. She described how once, when he was in a "bad mood", he had smashed up the home of their mother, Elizabeth.

Desmond's girlfriend, Jennifer Devine, with whom he had a baby son in 1999, also told police about the horrendous physical and verbal abuse she had suffered when her lover was in a similar mood. She was 16 when she started a long term relationship with Desmond in 1997 after his release from prison on the Lucan car theft charge and the same year Dinny Boy Desmond died. Mark was six years her senior. On one occasion he put a shotgun to her head and threatened to kill her if he ever caught her smoking heroin in the house. He also once threw her down the stairs because she objected to one of his drug dealer pals calling to their home. Everyone the cops interviewed during the investigation gave similar descriptions of a one-man crime wave, who instilled terror in anyone who crossed him.

After O'Driscoll left Ballyfermot, the Guinea Pig had become a much more significant player in the heroin business. He was supplied with 'gear' by Tony Long and O'Driscoll which he then sold on his own patch in Lower Ballyfermot and St Michael's Estate. At one stage he rented a house in Maynooth where he lived with Jennifer Devine and ran his operation from there. One of his partners was Noel 'Fat Boy' Foy, a nephew of the General's brother-in-law, John Foy. Fat Boy, who was born in 1980, got his nickname because he was bordering on obese. The addicts who ran the street operation were also terrified of Foy.

In a two year period between 1998 and the time of the Grand Canal murders, Mark Desmond built up a significant drug dealing operation. The fear instilled in the drug dealers and the opposition ensured the trade controlled by Desmond and Foy expanded rapidly. The two young hoodlums were extremely careful and continued to ensure that they had no contact with the actual product. Garda drug units on the ground knew what was going on but could do little unless they caught them in actual possession. Desmond was utterly paranoid about anyone informing on him and he regularly threatened to blow people away if they opened their mouths. The mind-boggling catalogue of violence from the one man crime wave increased dramatically. There were many examples of his brutality.

In July 1998, a young addict who had been selling heroin for Desmond fell into arrears of IR£250 (€320). On the night of July 20, Desmond smashed the windows at the home of the addict's innocent parents. He also smashed up his father's car. The next day Desmond sent a message to the terrified parents telling them that the family home would be burned down if he wasn't paid. Although financially hard pressed, the couple paid their son's drug debt. The young addict was later forced to leave the country in fear of his life.

Twenty-eight year-old Thomas Healy had allowed his house at O'Moore Road to be used by John Regan, one of Desmond's dealers. Regan used to cut up Desmond's heroin for sale on the street in the house. The drugs were delivered to the house a few times each week by a kid on a mountain bike. But Regan had then committed the cardinal error of attempting to go out on his own. On the night of August 5 Mark Desmond arrived at the house armed with a shotgun and demanded to know Regan's whereabouts. His former 'employee' had just bolted out through the back door. Desmond ran out after him and fired a shot to warn Regan. Then he left.

The following day Desmond summoned Healy to his Uncle 'Lar's' house on Lally Road. Healy was terrified of the Guinea Pig and knew better than to disappoint his 'master' by not turning up. The paranoid thug had decided to target a door man at the Blue Banana night club at the Jensen Hotel in Clondalkin. Desmond maintained that the doorman had sided with Regan in an argument which he claimed had begun over Regan's former girlfriend, 19-year-old Rachel Stephens. The mother-of-one was the best friend of Desmond's girlfriend, Jennifer Devine. Desmond was said to have been "besotted" by Stephens, whose brothers had also been involved in boxing. The two families were old friends.

Healy agreed to drive the Guinea Pig to the club. Such was his fear of Desmond that he agreed to use his own car in the shooting which could be easily traced afterwards. Around 11pm on the night of August 6, 1998, Healy and Desmond drove to the Blue Banana. Desmond had a shotgun hidden under a blanket. As they got closer, the Guinea Pig put on a balaclava and surgical gloves. He told Healy to stop the car with the passenger window, facing the night-club door. Desmond said he wanted to frighten the doorman. He fired two shots and ordered Healy to drive off. As they made their escape, Desmond laughed "like it was a joke" Healy would later tell investigating detectives. Healy abandoned his car and reported it stolen.

Four days later Det Sgt O'Gara's team arrested John Regan and the doorman who had been targeted by Desmond. The officers found the pair in a flat in Inchicore on August 10. The doorman was armed with a sawn-off shotgun. The pair later admitted that they had stolen the gun from Desmond and had intended shooting him before he made another attempt on their lives. Regan revealed how he and his friends had been hassled and bullied by Desmond. The Guinea Pig had also beaten him up and smashed his car.

The following day Thomas Healy was arrested. During questioning he confessed to his role in the Blue Banana incident. He also told detectives about the shooting incident involving Regan. Healy agreed to make a statement outlining Desmond's role in the shootings.

Detectives had also arrested the Guinea Pig. Unlike his terrified associates, he was anything but co-operative and refused to answer any questions. Then, to get his point across, he smeared his own excrement over his face and spread it on the walls and furniture of the police station. The following day he was brought before the District Court where he was charged with causing criminal damage to Clondalkin Garda Station. The event made its way into the national newspapers. The story was accompanied by an extraordinary picture of a grinning Desmond, his face covered in excrement, being escorted by three officers dressed head to toe in special protective suits and face masks. He was released on bail and immediately set about getting himself out of trouble.

On August 15, Thomas Healy arrived at Ballyfermot Station to withdraw his original statements implicating the

Canal Butcher. He told officers that an associate of Desmond, Gordon Marsh, had met him two days earlier with a message. Marsh, who had been a champion boxer, was also involved in the drug business. He was told to withdraw his statement or get out of the country. If he didn't, he would be taken into the mountains and shot. Healy was terrified. He was not prepared to testify against the thug and another case against Desmond was dropped.

In another incident Gordon Marsh also fell foul of the Guinea Pig when he began dealing heroin on his own. In December 1998, Desmond shot Marsh in the legs in Inchicore. Initially Desmond's former associate made a statement identifying Desmond as the shooter. He withdrew his statement, however, when detectives asked him to formally identify Desmond in a line-up.

After Marsh retracted his statement, Desmond threatened him that he would not be so lucky if he opened his mouth again. "The next time I shoot you, I'll shoot you in the head," the Guinea Pig promised him.

Another associate who had stolen drugs from Desmond also ran into trouble. When the Guinea Pig couldn't find the man, he took out his anger on the associate's girlfriend by giving her a severe beating. He also smashed up the man's home and smeared graffiti on the walls, telling his target that he was a dead man.

The mother of another teenager warned Desmond to stay away from her son when she discovered he was selling heroin for Desmond. The Guinea Pig later threatened to kill the teenager, accusing him of being a "rat". After that the teenager was too terrified to leave his home.

In June 1999, Desmond heard that another young drug dealer had been "boasting" that he was a friend of the Guinea Pig. The 22-year-old, who also lived in Maynooth, had made the same mistake as Nap dealer Mark McLoughlin three years earlier. He used Desmond's name to remind some of his own customers about the consequences of ripping him off. Desmond beat up the drug dealer and told him that he had to pay him IR£200 (€254) per week for the privilege of using his name.

After the first payment, Desmond reduced the tariff to IR£100 (€127) on the condition that he kept drugs for him. The young dealer agreed to mind heroin and amphetamine after he was threatened. A week later Desmond summoned his new "friend" and told him to take a tin containing IR£20,000 (€25,400) worth of heroin and mind it for him. Later Desmond offered the dealer IR£100 (€127) to move the drugs for him. When the dealer refused Desmond said he would have to get someone else to do it for him and left. However he arrived back later that night and beat up the dealer. He held a Stanley blade to his victim's throat and told him that he was never to refuse to carry drugs for him again. "This is what happens to people that disobey me," he warned the drug dealer, who managed to escape and call the Gardaí. Later that night detectives seized Desmond's drugs but could not take the case any further against him.

A youth who sold heroin for Desmond over a two year period from 1998, had been collecting between IR£1,000 (€1,270) and IR£2,000 (€2,540) per day. At the height of the operation the young drug addict reckoned Desmond was selling up to nine ounces of heroin per day. Each ounce was valued at between IR£1,800 (€2,286) and IR£2,000 (€2,540). When the youth ripped off Desmond for IR£1,900 (€2,400), he rewarded the disloyalty by smashing a broken bottle into his face and hands. The youth was left seriously scarred and his father later beat up Desmond. In an act of retaliation, the Guinea Pig poured petrol on a horse owned by the youth's father and set the animal ablaze.

When another one of his dealers was ripped off Desmond made him pay up the money he had lost. Then he smashed up the home of one of the guys who had ripped the dealer off in the first place. He too was forced to pay up, with Desmond making a tidy profit in the process.

In the early hours of October 10, 1999, Noel Hanlon was shot in the neck by an intruder who broke into the house on O'Moore Road in Ballyfermot where he rented a room. Hanlon, who had no connection with criminal activities or drugs, was lucky to be alive after the attack. Even though the shooter was wearing a balaclava Hanlon had no doubt who had shot him

– Mark Desmond. Hanlon's crime was that he had discovered
Desmond and one of his dealers wrapping heroin in the
bathroom of the house shortly after Hanlon moved in. The
dealer had also been staying in the house at the time. Hanlon
threw them out.

On the night of October 9, Hanlon had returned home and
spotted Desmond standing outside the house with another local
youth. The pair said they were looking for the other resident of
the house, the man who had been wrapping heroin deals with
Desmond before. Hanlon told them that the man wasn't in and
the pair went away. Around 4am Hanlon was awoken by the
noise of someone breaking into the house downstairs. When
he went to investigate, he confronted a man carrying a shotgun
who he believed to be Desmond. In a scuffle the gun was fired.
Hanlon was hit in the right side of the neck, causing him serious
injury. He would have taken the full force of the blast had he
not managed to deflect the weapon at the last second.

Desmond had always had a fascination for firearms and
at different stages possessed a cache of shotguns, pistols and
machine guns. Desmond 'bought' stolen guns from criminals
in return for heroin. Among his customers was a group of
drug addicts from Athlone in County Westmeath. On October
1, 1999 the group of criminals stole two shotguns and a rifle
equipped with a telescopic sight when they burgled a house in
Drumraney, near Athlone. One of the shotguns, a Churchill,
was valued at IR£10,000 (€12,700). Later that day they brought
the guns to Desmond in Ballyfermot and exchanged them for
money and heroin. They delivered other guns, one of which
had been stolen in Waterford, to the Guinea Pig on at least two
other occasions. Desmond had shown that he was more than
prepared to use them and didn't seem to care where he opened
fire either. A month after the Hanlon shooting, two 15-year-
old youths who had been working for Desmond were walking
past his house on Lally Road. They spotted Desmond standing
outside the house with a shotgun in his hands. He fired a shot
at the pair as they walked past a car parked on the street, across
from the house. The vehicle took the full brunt of the blast. As
the two teenagers ran for their lives Desmond shouted "rats"

and fired a second shot over their heads. Associates would later tell detectives that he had up to ten guns at his disposal. One individual revealed how Desmond regularly test-fired weapons by firing them at the Garda Boat Club from a rock in Memorial Park beside the River Liffey.

Meanwhile Desmond's drug business was expanding all the time. Together with Noel 'Fat Boy' Foy he decided that in order to make real money they should begin smuggling their own heroin in from Amsterdam. They could buy it cheaper there and cut out the middle men, like Dee Dee O'Driscoll, who was still supplying them. By this stage, 21-year-old Darren Carey was also involved in the drug operation. His father Stephen "Hatcher" Carey, who was estranged from his mother, was living in Surrey, England, where he was known to have criminal connections. Darren was living with Sinead Kenny with whom he had a baby son. She was the daughter of another well known drug trafficker called Martin Kenny. Better known as The Pony, Kenny was an aging villain. He had been part of the first generation of Dublin hoods to get involved in the heroin trade. He was a close associate and friend of the notorious Dunne brothers from Crumlin. The Dunnes, particularly Larry and Shamie, were credited with first introducing heroin to Ireland in 1980.

In November 1999, Desmond, Carey and Foy decided to make their move. On November 13, the Guinea Pig travelled to Amsterdam to establish a connection for the heroin. When he returned, the drug dealers began looking around for people to do the dirty work of smuggling the drugs. Patrick Murray was 19 and had begun selling drugs for Carey and Desmond on a small scale, dealing mainly in hashish. Murray had worked as a labourer in a factory with Carey when they first met. He was not a drug addict. Other drug dealers had stolen Murray's stash and he had fallen into debt as a result. He owed Desmond IR£3,000 (€3,810) and was told that if he brought heroin back to Dublin, his bill would be halved. Murray in turn recruited his friend Gary Kelly, an 18-year-old from Colepark in Ballyfermot, to travel with him on the drug smuggling assignment. Murray had promised to pay Kelly for the run.

The two teenagers were brought to a meeting with Desmond
who explained what they were to do. Flights had been organised
and he instructed them to get passports.

On the morning of November 19, Murray and Kelly took
the first flight to Schipol Airport in Amsterdam. Carey had
given them a bundle of Dutch Guilders worth around IR£15,000
(€19,000).

When they arrived in Holland, they met Mark Desmond
who had travelled to the 'Dam', as it is known by criminals,
with his cousin Jonathan Desmond the previous day. Jonathan
Desmond, the youngest son of John Desmond, Dinny Boy's
brother, was two years younger than his cousin. A barman by
profession, he was described as an impressionable young man
who was totally ruled by his dangerous cousin.

The following day Desmond went with his cousin and
Murray to meet what one of them later described as a "big black
bloke" who represented a Turkish heroin dealing gang. The
drug dealer then drove the three Dublin men to an apartment
complex. Inside they met two Turkish men, one of whom
produced a half kilo of heroin. Turkish criminals control much
of the heroin supply in Western Europe, smuggling it directly
from Afghanistan. Desmond handed over 20,000 Guilders in
cash.

The following day, November 21, Gary Kelly returned to
Dublin alone with the heroin and got through Customs without
being detected. Desmond then flew back to Dublin leaving his
cousin and Murray in Holland. A second delivery of heroin
had been cancelled when a member of the Turkish gang was
arrested. Desmond ordered Jonathan and Patrick to wait for
the next delivery.

Back in Dublin, Darren Carey collected the heroin from
Kelly who then returned to the 'Dam'. There he joined Murray
and Jonathan Desmond. Carey and Mark Desmond also
returned to oversee the next part of the deal. In order to avoid
attracting too much notice they took separate flights. The gang
again met with the Turks. This time they were brought to an
apartment in Rotterdam where they produced two packages,
each containing a half kilo of heroin. Jonathan Desmond

counted out 40,000 Guilders on his cousin's instructions and handed it over to the drug dealers. The value of the heroin on the street was in the region of IR£176,000 (€224,000).

On Thursday, December 2, Desmond and the other gang members flew back to Dublin leaving Murray and Kelly behind. When they arrived back in Dublin, Carey was taken aside and questioned by Customs. He was also searched. The Drug Unit attached to Ballyfermot Station had requested that Desmond, Carey and their other known associates be 'flagged' passing through the Airport. They were becoming known as big players and the cops had intelligence that they were planning to smuggle heroin directly from the 'Dam'.

Mark Desmond phoned his hapless couriers from Dublin Airport and told them to return to Ireland by boat, via the UK. The Guinea Pig had also been stopped and searched on his flights in and out of the country in the weeks before. He was worried about the amount of attention they were receiving. The two couriers, however, decided to take their chances and fly. They had been left stranded in Holland by Desmond, with very little money and were anxious to get home as quickly as possible. The two men had been in regular contact with friends at home and in one call Murray had been obviously crying. He told his girlfriend that Desmond had beaten him up and that he was terrified of the man. The Guinea Pig beat up Patrick Murray in a hotel room and hit him in the eye with a wad of money – for spending too much money! Desmond was as miserly as he was violent. "He is mad enough to kill you," he told her. Kelly told a friend on the phone that they had been left to walk around Amsterdam with no money. He too appeared to be scared of the drug trafficker.

Before they took the flight the pair concealed the parcels of heroin under their clothes. On the morning of Friday, December 3, the plan ran into problems which would have dire consequences for the two young men.

Murray and Kelly were spotted as soon as they stepped off the flight from Holland. Incoming flights from Schipol International Airport are always closely scrutinised. Important intelligence can be gleaned about the movements of suspected

criminals, even if they are not carrying contraband. Murray
and Kelly didn't look a bit like international underworld
crime figures. They fitted the description of a typical pair of
downtrodden drug mules. Customs officers, Kevin Murtagh and
Rose Wiseman, detained them for a drug search. The packages
of heroin were found and the pair admitted what was inside
them. They were then arrested by Gardaí and taken to Santry
Garda Station.

The Ballyfermot Drug Squad was contacted and they went
to Santry to interview the two prisoners. While in custody,
Murray claimed that he had made the drug run to pay off a
debt he owed for cannabis. Gardaí specifically questioned them
about Desmond and his gang. They wanted to know if the drugs
belonged to them.

The two teenagers were later charged under the Misuse of
Drugs Act and remanded in custody. On December 7, Murray
was released when his family raised the IR£3,000 (€3,810) bail
money. The following day Kelly was also released for the same
amount.

Desmond was with his cousin and Darren Carey in the
National Boxing Stadium in Dublin when the arrests were
made. When he heard the news he flew into a rage. Jonathan
Desmond would later recall that Carey and his cousin were
worried that they could be arrested next and that the two
couriers might have spilled the beans. They decided to "get
offside" so that they could plan their next move without any
nasty interruptions from the local drug squad. The three went
to the Glenview Hotel in the Glen of the Downs in County
Wicklow where they stayed for the next two nights. Carey and
Desmond appeared to be worried about the situation and they
waited until Murray and Kelly were released from custody
before deciding what to do next.

On the same day Murray was released, Desmond
summoned him to a meeting at his Uncle Lar's house at Lally
Road. Darren Carey brought 19-year-old Murray to the house.
Jonathan Desmond was also present. Murray was obviously
terrified and didn't know what was about to happen to him.
He was taken to the side of the house where he was questioned

by the Guinea Pig and Carey about what had happened in the
Airport and what questions the police had asked him. Desmond
roared abuse at Murray calling him a "lazy bastard" for not
travelling through the UK. He interrogated Murray about what
he had told the police.

Murray said the detectives had been asking about Desmond
and referred to him by his nickname, the Guinea Pig. He said
he had taken responsibility for the seized drugs and begged
Desmond to believe that he had given no other information.
The Guinea Pig informed his doomed courier that he now owed
him IR£30,000 (€38,100). Then he let him go.

After his arrest Gary Kelly told his girlfriend that he had
no choice but to bring the drugs into the country. He said it
was "either that or my life". On the day of his release Kelly
was also summoned to meet with Desmond and Carey at the
Liffey Valley Shopping Centre, near Lucan in Dublin. Jonathan
Desmond was also there when the group met in Carey's car.
Carey demanded to know why they had not gone through
England as instructed. Kelly said that they just wanted to get
home. Desmond was furious and quizzed him about what had
happened with the cops. Kelly assured Desmond that he had
not mentioned any names. Desmond told him to keep his head
down. Then he added a warning: "Keep your mouth shut and
do your time and you'll be ok. I don't take prisoners."

When Kelly got out of the car, Carey asked Desmond if he
believed him. "He'd better not open his mouth or I'll blow his
head off," said Desmond, as he watched Kelly walk away.

In the meantime Desmond had been trying to help his old
pal, Dee Dee O'Driscoll. 'Dee Dee's' brother, Anthony 'Harpo'
O'Driscoll, was facing a trial for possession of IR£200,000
(€254,000) worth of heroin. The 18-year-old had been caught
with the 'gear' in February 1996. Desmond had approached
another local man, on Dee Dee's behalf, and offered him
IR£10,000 (€12,700) to take the rap instead with an additional
IR£1,000 (€1,270) per week while he was inside. The hood had
refused the offer and Dee Dee O'Driscoll had decided to return
from Portugal to Ballyfermot over Christmas. He planned to
"sort out" the problem with the help of the Guinea Pig. He was

still living in the Algarve, avoiding the 12 month jail sentence
he'd been sentenced to for bribing corrupt cop John O'Neill.
Gardaí had been keeping an eye out for him. As soon as he
turned up, he was nabbed and landed in prison. (Three months
later, in March 2000, his brother was jailed for six years on
the drugs charges.) Despite these distractions, Desmond had
not forgotten about the pressing problem of the drug bust in
Dublin Airport. In his paranoid, warped mind he had decided
to make someone pay for what had happened. Desmond was
an extremely volatile and unpredictable character.

Patrick Murray had seemed at ease following his initial
meeting with Desmond after his release from custody. He spent
Christmas with his family and attended some parties with his
friends and girlfriend. According to his mother Kathleen, the
drug bust was a wake-up call in his life. He had decided to take
the rap for the drugs and then get his life in order.

"When Patrick was arrested on December 3 it was the first
time he was ever in court. He said that he had done the crime
and was prepared to do the time," Kathleen would later reveal
in an interview with the *Sunday World*. "After his arrest he had
decided to change his life. He said he had been praying to his
granny and granddad and said he was going to go back to school
and get himself a trade."

Darren Carey meanwhile, had celebrated his twentieth
birthday on Christmas Day with his mother Noeleen, his
girlfriend and son at her home at Islandbridge Court in
Kilmainham. Carey was very close to his mother and had been
very excited about the arrival of his son, Dean, a few months
earlier. Between Christmas and the New Year, he and Sinead
Kenny planned to move from his mother's place to a rented
house in Clondalkin. His friends later recalled that he didn't
seem to be himself and that there was something worrying him.
When an associate told him Desmond had also asked him to
do a drug run, Carey had advised: "Don't do it...just look at
the mess I've got myself into with him."

For his part, Desmond marked the season of peace and
goodwill with violence. On the Sunday before Christmas, he
threw a party to mark the Christening of his child in Mother

Redcaps pub in Central Dublin. The party was attended by members of his family and friends, including Darren Carey. On Christmas night he went to a party in the home of his uncle Gerard Desmond, with his cousin Jonathan. Around 3am the following morning, Mark Desmond stabbed Jonathan Desmond in the arm with a kitchen knife, seriously injuring him. He had been taunting his cousin for most of the night before the unprovoked attack. Jonathan Desmond was rushed to St James' Hospital where he was detained for treatment for four days.

A few days later Desmond ordered Carey to forget about the festivities and set up a meeting with Patrick Murray to "sort out" the drug bust issue.

On the afternoon of December 28, Darren Carey phoned Gary Kelly. He was looking for Patrick Murray. The two friends had been playing a computer game for most of the previous few days, in the home of another friend. Kelly handed the phone to Murray. Carey told him that he and Desmond wanted to meet him at Desmond's grandmother's house on Lally Road at 7.45pm.

Later that day Murray and Kelly took a cab and travelled to Ronanstown and Ballyfermot Stations to "sign on" as part of the conditions of their bail. After that they went back to their respective homes for a short time.

That evening, Murray left his home at Colepark Drive and said goodbye to his father and brother. He went back to Kelly's house at 7.45pm and asked him to walk with him to his meeting. Murray was very nervous and uneasy about the meeting and he told Kelly that he didn't want to go. He was terrified. Kelly was also uneasy about what was happening and felt that the arrangement was "strange". Both of them had been arrested with the drugs but the feared psychopath only wanted to meet one of them. They knew that something bad was going to happen.

Kelly later told detectives that he expected his pal to get a "hiding". Murray got more nervous as he got closer to his appointment with the unknown. Kelly felt very "wary" just being in the area. As they waited, the night air chilled the troubled young men. Kelly's instinct for self-preservation urged him to leave. He told Murray that he wanted to go back to his mother's house to collect his baby. Murray used Kelly's phone to contact Carey and tell him he was there. "They don't want to see you anyway," Murray sighed, as Kelly left.

Patrick Murray was never seen alive again.

Gary Kelly became concerned when Darren Carey called him later that night to say that Murray had not turned up for the meeting. Carey told him he would contact Desmond to find out if he knew anything. It later emerged that Carey had been missing between around 8pm and 12.45pm on the night Murray vanished.

The following morning Darren Carey was overheard by his girlfriend talking on the phone about Murray. After the call he told her that the teenager had not been seen since the previous night.

Later that day, Carey and a friend dismantled his son's cot to bring it to the new house. Around 7pm on the evening of December 29, he and Sinead Kenny went back to Kilmainham. Carey told her to go inside, that he wanted to make a phone call. A few minutes later he asked Sinead if she minded if he went out for a short while. He promised that he would be back in a few minutes.

About 45 minutes later she phoned Carey to see where he'd got to. She recalled that his voice was stressed and it sounded like he was in a car. He said he would be back soon. She rang again 40 minutes later but the phone wasn't answered. On her third attempt the phone went completely dead.

It was the last time anyone had contact with Darren Carey.

Kathleen Murray was overcome with a sense of dread as soon as she discovered that Patrick was missing. She and her family had spent much of the day of December 29 frantically looking for him. She later recalled: "From the minute he went missing I just knew in my heart that he was dead."

The following morning she reported her son missing to the Gardaí.

The Carey family were going through similar trauma after the sudden disappearance of Darren.

Significantly the first person to offer an explanation for the disappearance of both men was Mark Desmond. He claimed that Carey had "gone to England" to get away from his girlfriend. Murray, he said had probably done a runner over the drug charge. After a few days Desmond, and his closest associates, then circulated a rumour that the two men had been kidnapped by the terrorist group the Irish National Liberation Army (INLA). The INLA, which had once proclaimed to be involved in a war against British occupation, was nothing more than another criminal gang. The previous October the INLA had been involved in a ferocious showdown with another criminal group when INLA member Patrick Campbell had been hacked to death. The melee, which involved about 15 men, became known as the 'Ballymount Bloodbath'. As a result the organisation was exposed as a criminal gang, which was heavily involved in drug trafficking and protection rackets in Dublin and the subsequent investigation smashed the INLA. Desmond obviously thought they'd make suitable scapegoats.

Desmond claimed that the INLA had put up IR£25,000 (€31,750) as part of the investment money for the Amsterdam heroin deal and they wanted pay back. He said that Murray and Carey were being held for ransom in either Galway or Sligo.

When they heard the rumours Patrick Murray's father Paul went to Sligo with other members of the family to search for his son. Desmond then told people that the INLA were now demanding IR£58,000 (€73,660) for their safe return.

On January 3, Darren Carey's father, Stephen 'Hatcher' Carey, arrived in Ireland. He immediately began making his own enquiries. On the same day he met Mark Desmond. He later told detectives that Desmond assured him that his son did not owe money for drugs and had not been in danger. Over the following days Garda intelligence also collated sightings of 'Hatcher' meeting with a number of major gangland and subversive figures. He stayed in different hotels around the city.

In the meantime, Mark Desmond unexpectedly found himself spending a night in a prison cell. By this stage local detectives were aware that something serious was going on but hadn't yet got to the bottom of it. They knew that the two men were missing and that it involved the Guinea Pig. On January 6, Desmond, who was disqualified from driving, was spotted on a motorbike in Ballyfermot by a Garda patrol. He was chased and arrested for dangerous driving. He was later charged and remanded in custody. The following day he was released from Mountjoy Prison, when his Uncle 'Lar' put up the bail money.

On Saturday, January 8, Desmond and Noel Foy met with Hatcher Carey at the Ibis Hotel in Clondalkin. Hatcher later told the Gardaí that the Guinea Pig said he had no knowledge of the circumstances surrounding his son's disappearance. Then the following afternoon walkers spotted the body of Patrick Murray floating in the Grand Canal. Desmond decided to get "off-side" and went back to stay for two nights in the Glenview Hotel in the Glen of the Downs, County Wicklow. The following day, January 10, Gardaí found Darren Carey's body.

Mark Desmond had some serious explaining to do.

Two

UNRAVELLING THE MYSTERY

The double murders stand out in gangland's blood-soaked history as symbolic of a new era. The young desperados had crossed the Rubicon and set a chilling precedent. The gruesome crime caused fear and revulsion across the country. The investigation was the one of the largest undertaken in the history of the State and compared with the manhunt that followed Veronica Guerin's execution. Significantly the investigation was led by the same man, Assistant Commissioner Tony Hickey. Other officers who would play key roles in the mammoth enquiry were Detective Superintendent Pat Brehony, Detective Inspector Padraig Kennedy, who had also been involved in the Guerin investigation, and Detective Sergeants Ashley O'Sullivan and Gabriel O'Gara. At least 40 officers were involved in the probe which uncovered an astonishing catalogue of brutal crimes. It lifted the lid on the appalling reality of life for young people caught up in the murky drug culture. The Grand Canal slaughter focused attention – for a short period at least – on the hopeless plight of hundreds of young people who found themselves enslaved to the likes of Mark Desmond.

Within 24 hours the Garda investigation team, which was based at an incident room in Naas station in County Kildare, had established the identities of the two men and a likely motive for their murders. Officers then began the painstaking job of piecing together the mystery. They compiled the last known movements and sightings of the murdered men. Family and friends were interviewed. Det Insp Kennedy and Det Sgt O'Gara, both of whom were based in West Dublin were called in to assist in the investigation because of their extensive knowledge of Desmond and the other personalities involved in the unfolding plot. Det Sgt O'Sullivan, who had only recently moved to the Carlow/ Kildare Division, was also well acquainted with the main players. He was previously a member attached to the drug unit in the Kilmainham and Kevin Street districts where Desmond plied his trade. They had already established that the Guinea Pig was a major drug dealer in the west of the city. Desmond had featured in several investigations and each time had used intimidation and violence to thwart efforts to have him jailed. They were up against a formidable adversary. Detectives began the process of interviewing scores of drug addicts and dealers who were working for Desmond, now nicknamed the Canal Butcher by the media.

Over the next nine months over 50 people were arrested and questioned and scores of others were interviewed. Hundreds of statements were taken, metres of phone records were analysed and traced, hours of surveillance work was done, alibis were cross-checked and informants were quizzed. The investigators began to uncover a terrifying story.

Desmond had been careful to keep his head down in the days after the bodies were found. Despite his reading difficulties, he scrutinised every word that was written about the case. Most of the coverage was about his activities and it made him very nervous. On the evening of January 12, the remains of Patrick Murray were removed to the Church of the Assumption in Ballyfermot. Rachel Stephens, Desmond's family friend, was among the hundreds of mourners who attended the sombre ceremony. The pale, frightened faces of many of Patrick's young friends, who were also mixed up in the drug world, were easily picked out amongst the crowd.

Afterwards 19-year-old Stephens returned to her family home. Desmond, who was a regular visitor to the house, was slouched in a chair with his face buried in *The Star* and *Evening Herald* newspapers. When the murders were mentioned, Desmond remarked that they must have been connected to the heroin seizure. He was trying hard to hide the fact that he was a man under intense pressure. The dogs on the street knew that he was now the prime suspect. Stephens' mother asked the same question the large team of detectives were asking everyone in Ballyfermot at that moment – if the murders were over the drug seizure then why had Gary Kelly been spared? Kelly had earlier attended the removal service at the church.

"Kelly didn't owe money out," Desmond replied nonchalantly, from behind the newspaper.

Stephens' parents went out for a drink sometime later. When he was alone with Rachel, Desmond referred to the newspaper articles about him as a "load of shit". Her family and friends had noticed that Desmond was infatuated with the young mother but had never made a move to start a relationship with her. Despite his attempt to put on a brave face, he appeared rattled and nervous. Desmond told her he'd decided to leave town.

Later on he left the house and went to his girlfriend's place. His sister Melissa and his cousin, Denise Desmond, helped him to pack his clothes. The two women then drove the Canal Butcher to Belfast. Sitting in the passenger seat he instructed his sister to drive along selected back roads to avoid bumping into the police. His sister later told detectives that they hardly spoke during the two hour journey. That night he tried to catch a flight to London but was too late. He booked one for the next day instead.

The following morning, as Desmond flew to Stanstead Airport, Patrick Murray was laid to rest. Family friend Father Charlie Hoey who presided over the funeral, appealed to the many young people who had known Patrick not to allow themselves to be used by drug dealers. "They will never bring you happiness and only care about lining their own pockets," he told the congregation.

Two days later Darren Carey was also buried, following an equally heart-breaking funeral in Inchicore. After the funeral his father, Stephen 'Hatcher' Carey, left the country and returned to the UK. He had spoken with the Gardaí on a number of occasions before the funeral. He confirmed to them that he had initially been told that the INLA were holding his son and Patrick Murray hostage. He said he met the "Chief of Staff" of the INLA and the IRA and had been assured that neither gang had been involved in his son's death.

From his own enquiries he said it was his belief that his son had been murdered on the evening of December 29. He believed that it was at that stage that Darren had learned of Murray's murder. He said his son "may have been asked" to dispose of the body but panicked and was shot as a result. Officers were perplexed when Hatcher Carey then told them that he would need "public proof" that Desmond had been involved in the murder. They didn't know what he meant by this.

When Mark Desmond arrived in London, he went to stay in an apartment at an address at Randolph Street in London NW1 where a relation of Darren Carey had also lived. He remained in the UK for almost two months. Back in Dublin the investigation team was tipped off about their target's whereabouts and contacted their colleagues across the Irish Sea. Detectives were anxious to keep tabs on Desmond's movements so that they knew where to find him if he was going to be charged. They also hoped that he would be forced to return to Ireland if he was hassled by the UK police. One of the senior officers involved in the investigation, Detective Superintendent Tony Sourke, had cut his teeth as a young cop in Ballyfermot. He knew every criminal who ever came from the area. He still had impressive contacts and was able to use them to keep tabs on the prime suspect. Det Supt Sourke learned that a relative of Darren Carey had plotted to have Desmond murdered in London. In the end the plotter abandoned the idea.

On January 21, Hatcher Carey phoned a member of the investigation team and told him that he now believed that Mark Desmond had been one of three people involved in the murders. Gardaí found this as puzzling as his previous comments on "public proof", however, because intelligence sources revealed that the Canal Butcher had met with relations and associates of Hatcher Carey since arriving in London. It was considered strange that Desmond's relationship with Carey had not been adversely affected by the murder allegations.

Two days after that call, on January 23, a man spotted a double-barrelled shotgun in bushes while out walking in the Nangor Road area of Clondalkin. He brought the weapon to Clondalkin Garda Station. It was the Churchill shotgun, stolen by the Athlone thugs and sold to Desmond the previous October. Although they didn't yet know it, the police had just taken possession of the murder weapon. It was a breakthrough. On the same day the *Sunday World* ran a front page interview with Noel Hanlon, who had been shot in the neck by Desmond in October 1999. In the article the Canal Butcher's victim stated that he was in no doubt about who had shot him. He had decided to go public with the story as a result of the Grand Canal outrage.

Meanwhile the London Metropolitan Police discovered that they had an outstanding arrest warrant for Desmond for a traffic offence he had incurred on a previous visit to the city. On Saturday, January 29, a team of armed police officers raided the flat at Randolph Street to execute the outstanding warrant for the Guinea Pig. When officers entered a bedroom in the flat, they found Desmond lying, fully-clothed under the bedcovers. When asked was he Mark Desmond he said he was Mark Hennessy and produced a false Irish driving licence in the same name. Desmond was perspiring and uncomfortable as the police continued to quiz him. During a search of the bedroom Sgt John Gait spotted a copy of the previous week's edition of the *Sunday World* on a locker beside Desmond's bed. The front page carried the headline 'Canal Killer' and was accompanied by a photograph of Desmond with his face partially obscured. Despite this, the officers could still see the remarkable resemblance between the picture and the uncomfortable looking Mr Hennessy, sweating in the bed. The cops arrested him and took him to Kentish Town police station on suspicion of having a forged driver's licence.

Two days later, Desmond appeared at Highburgh Corner Magistrates' Court where he was charged with the outstanding traffic offence and also under the British Forgery and Counterfeiting Act. Two members of the murder investigation team, Detective Gardaí Pat Flynn and Brian Woods, were sent to attend the court, to assist in identifying the most wanted man in Ireland. Desmond promptly pleaded guilty to the offences and was fined Stg£600. The court took into account the two days he had been incarcerated and let him go. Desmond smirked at the two Dublin detectives as he walked out a free man.

Several days later he contacted this writer in the *Sunday World* and invited us to interview him in London. He said he was anxious to put his side of the story across and denied involvement in the murders. We arranged to meet in Leicester Square, Central London but the Guinea Pig changed his mind and didn't turn up. He phoned this writer again and arranged to meet the following day. He said he would be wearing a leather jacket and dark glasses, with a rolled up newspaper under his arm. Again Desmond never showed.

At the same time, he was experiencing money problems and made contact with his relations who wired him a small amount of cash. Desmond also instructed his sister to call to the home of one of his heroin dealers, Derek Adams, to get money he said was owed to him. Adams had already wired IR£500 (€635) to Desmond but it wasn't enough. 'A long-term heroin addict himself, 30-year-old Adams was older than most of the other dealers working for the Guinea Pig. He sold up to an ounce of heroin every few days worth IR£1,800 (€2,286). Shortly before Christmas, Adams had been caught in the process of flushing three ounces of the drug down the toilet when the local drug squad raided his home. The Canal Butcher phoned Adams' girlfriend from London and told her the drug dealer would be "taken out in a box" if he didn't pay up IR£8,000 (€10,160). He had also sent a message to Noel 'Fat Boy' Foy looking for money but Foy claimed he had none to give him. In the meantime people were beginning to talk to the police.

Desmond had rendered assistance of sorts to the Gardaí when he decided to make a run for it. His physical absence meant that a lot of his victims were more inclined to talk to the police. The newspaper interview with Noel Hanlon was further evidence of this. There was also genuine revulsion over the murders and many criminals, who would have otherwise remained tight-lipped, shared what they knew. The same scenario prevailed during the Guerin investigation. Detectives resurrected all the cases against Desmond which they had been forced to drop due to intimidation. They found that the victims were more co-operative than before. Files were opened on a number of other serious criminal cases against Desmond which had surfaced as a result of the investigation. Investigators were astonished at the amount of chaos and mayhem Desmond had inflicted on the lives of the people he dominated.

On the evening of Tuesday, February 15, the investigation team made another significant breakthrough in the case when they arrested Jonathan Desmond for questioning. Detectives had already interviewed Mark Desmond's cousin informally and they knew that he had a lot to tell them. He was harbouring a serious grievance against his unstable cousin because of the stabbing incident at Christmas. The officers were aware that he was part of Mark Desmond's inner circle and he had come to their attention before. Jonathan had been questioned by detectives when he arrived at the home of Derek Adams while the drug search was in progress in December.

Jonathan told Gardaí that he was sickened by the murders of the two men. Over the following two days, Desmond gave the officers extensive details of his trips to Amsterdam with his cousin, Murray, Carey and Kelly. He gave them the background to the two heroin deals which had ultimately led to the arrests of Kelly and Murray in Dublin Airport. Then he gave officers the first real evidence against their prime suspect. He told them where Desmond had hidden a number of firearms. They were under a shed, in a garden a few doors away from his Uncle Lar's house, on Lally Road. Jonathan said the Guinea Pig had shown him two shotguns and a rifle with a telescopic sight attached. There were also a number of cartridges with the weapons. He said Desmond bragged about having the weapons near him to protect himself and his child.

On the morning of February 17, Gardaí searched the garden at the rear of the unoccupied house. Under a Barna shed they found the three weapons and a small amount of ammunition, including a number of used cartridges. Follow-up forensic examination revealed that the discharged cartridges

found at Lally Road had been fired by the Churchill shotgun
found three weeks earlier in Clondalkin. Ballistics experts had
also confirmed that the Churchill gun had been used in the
murders of the two men. The same cartridges had been used
to kill Murray and Carey. Ballistics also confirmed that the
same weapon and cartridges had been used in the shooting of
Noel Hanlon. Jonathan Desmond said he recognised the seized
weapons when detectives showed them to him back at Naas
Garda Station. He also recognised the Churchill shotgun.

On February 16, Gary Kelly had also been detained
for questioning. He gave detectives a number of statements
outlining his involvement in the heroin smuggling operation.
He had also described the meeting he had with Darren Carey
and Mark Desmond after his release from prison in December.
He gave details about the last time he had seen Murray alive
and his belief that Murray had been murdered as a result of his
planned meeting with Desmond. Kelly said he believed that he
too might have ended up in the icy, cold waters of the Grand
Canal if he had stuck around that night.

A week later detectives finally unlocked the mystery of
what had happened the murdered men. Rachel Stephens was
arrested at her home by Det Sgt Ashley O'Sullivan. She was
taken to Naas Garda Station where she was detained under
the provisions of the Offences Against the State Act. Under
the legislation a suspect could be held for a maximum of 48
hours.

During the early stages of her interrogation, she admitted
knowing that Desmond was a heroin dealer in Ballyfermot and
that he had worked for Dee Dee O'Driscoll. She had witnessed
him cutting up deals of heroin and also handling quantities
of speed and ecstasy. She said she was terrified of the Guinea
Pig and described how he threatened to shoot his girlfriend
Jennifer Devine with a shotgun after he caught them smoking
heroin one night. Stephens told detectives that Desmond had
phoned her from England and asked her to collect IR£8,000
(€10,160) for him from Noel Foy and post it to him in London.
She hadn't done so. Stephens said that Desmond asked her if
she had heard anything about him raping another girl to take

money off her drug debt. The officers got the impression that Rachel Stephens knew a lot more but that she was too afraid to share the information. They asked her if there was anything else she wanted to tell them.

"Listen, I'm afraid, I can't tell you. You don't know what Mark will do to me if he finds out," she replied.

Stephens revealed that she believed Desmond had been involved in the murders of Carey and Murray because Murray had been caught with his drugs. She also knew that he bought new clothes around the time the two men disappeared. This had been corroborated by other witnesses. Investigators believed that he had dumped his own clothes to destroy a forensic link with the crimes. She said that on the night that Murray and Kelly were arrested in Dublin Airport, Desmond had called to her home. He told her the drugs were his and he was furious that they had not returned to Ireland by the route he'd instructed them to take. "He said they would have to pay for it one way or the other," she told Det Sgt O'Sullivan. Stephens was reluctant to go any further at that point.

On the second day of her detention she asked to be given a pen and paper in her cell. Over night Rachel Stephens had decided to write down everything she knew about the murders.

During several hours of subsequent interviews, she then revealed details of an extraordinary conversation she had with Desmond, on the night he fled to Belfast. She had been left alone with him after her parents had gone out for a drink to the local pigeon club. Stephens talked to him about the newspaper coverage which clearly pointed to his involvement. When she asked him why the two men had been murdered, she described how Desmond started "spilling it out" as if he couldn't hold onto his secret any longer.

He told her Murray owed him IR£3,000 (€3,810) and that the run to the 'Dam' was to offset this debt. It was "too much money to be let away with". Desmond complained bitterly that he and Noel Foy had lost one million pounds as a result of the seizure. He claimed that Carey had been ripping him off behind his back. Carey had been holding back drug money and sold guns behind Desmond's back which he hadn't paid for.

Stephens then claimed that he told her: "They thought they were ripping me off and getting away with it, but nobody will rip me and Noely off – we're the main men."

Desmond then told Stephens that he could not "do the job" [murder the two men] on his own. She claimed Desmond at first said he took Murray to a disused shack in the Dublin Mountains where he had interrogated him. He had been helped by Carey and Foy. Carey had then left Desmond with Murray on his own. During his interrogation of the terrified teenager Desmond said that Murray had "ratted" Carey out to him, claiming that Carey had been ripping him off. Desmond had summoned Carey to join them. When he arrived, the Canal Butcher had started interrogating him too. Then, according to Stephens, Desmond said that the two men had "ratted up" each other to "get out of being killed". She claimed Desmond said he and Foy then decided to murder the two men. The four drove to the Grand Canal at Aylmer Bridge in Carey's car as Mark said he had damaged the front wheel of his car while driving in the Dublin Mountains. Desmond told her he shot Murray while Foy held Carey. Then he said he shot Carey. Foy had taken away Carey's car and burnt it out on Lynches Lane in Ronanstown, a quiet cul de sac where thieves regularly abandoned stolen vehicles. Desmond told her that if she opened her mouth he would "kill me stone dead".

Arrangements were made by Garda Headquarters to offer protection for Rachel Stephens and Jonathan Desmond by considering their eligibility for joining the Witness Protection Programme. A short time after his release Jonathan Desmond left the country and went to the UK for his own protection.

* * * *

As the enquiry continued, the investigation team uncovered a catalogue of other serious crimes allegedly committed by the Guinea Pig. Among the allegations was a disturbing series of sex attacks. On January 17, 2000, detectives had interviewed a friend of Desmond's girlfriend, Jennifer Devine. The 19-

year-old woman told the officers how she regularly observed Desmond beating Devine. She corroborated Stephens account of the night he had also threatened to shoot Devine and Rachel Stephens with a shotgun, after catching them smoking heroin. She then told them about an incident that occurred the previous November after she had been out with Jennifer Devine. Later that night she was in Desmond's house when he returned with another thug who his girlfriend didn't want in the house. When Devine objected, Desmond chased her up the stairs where she locked herself in the bathroom. The Guinea Pig forced open the door and kicked his screaming girlfriend down the stairs. He accused her of smoking heroin again. Then he beat her with a sweeping brush. She managed to run out the front door to get away from him. He ran after her but he didn't catch her.

When Desmond couldn't catch his girlfriend, he decided to take out his frustration by beating up two men who just happened to be walking by on the street outside. The young woman and Desmond's associate coaxed him back into the house. When he went back into the house his child was crying and the pal left. Desmond was on his own with the young woman. Suddenly, she claimed, he began trying to have sex with her. When she refused he pushed her onto a sofa and, she claimed, he anally raped her. When he had finished she described how he wiped himself in a piece of baby's clothing. She said he had "an evil smile on his face"." When he finished he called a cab and left his crying victim and his child behind. The woman made a formal complaint about the rape and signed a detailed statement.

A week later, detectives were interviewing an 18-year-old woman who had sold heroin for Desmond. The drug addict claimed that on the night of August 22, 1998, she had collected heroin from Desmond at Memorial Park in Inchicore as she usually did. He had brought her for a take away and later on, in his car, he had raped her. Throughout the ordeal she had tried to stop him and was crying. When it was over she told him he had hurt her to which he replied: "You know you wanted it." Then he warned her not to tell anyone about what had happened. Six months after her meeting with the detectives the young woman withdrew her statement of complaint about the rape. At first she made a vexatious complaint against the investigating Gardaí claiming that her complaint had been made up. Later, however, she admitted that she had made up the complaint against the police. The real reason she had dropped her complaint was that she was terrified of Desmond and one of his relations had approached her and asked about her allegations. She told Gardaí that she felt too afraid and intimidated to proceed any further.

As the intensive inquiry continued, detectives interviewed a 22-year-old drug pusher who had also worked for Desmond. When he was 16, the drug addict had participated in the abduction of Mark McLoughlin with Desmond. While he was being interviewed the young man became extremely upset about something else that had happened to him. But each time it came to talking about the alleged rape, the man found it too difficult to relate. Eventually, after postponing his interviews on a few occasions, the man told his horrifying story. He alleged that Desmond had raped him a number of times. The first time he claimed it happened was in the summer of 1994 when he was 15 and Desmond was four years older. They had burgled a house near where Desmond lived. Afterward they went back to 'Dinny Boy' Desmond's pigeon loft, behind the family home. The man claimed that Desmond suddenly threatened him with a machete he was carrying and forced him to undress. The victim claimed he was then raped. When it was over he said he was in pain and on the verge of crying. Afterward, he asked Desmond why he had done it. He said the Guinea Pig acted as nothing had happened and replied: "I just did it."

On another occasion the young man claimed that Desmond had again tried to rape him. He alleged that Desmond slashed him with a sword across his back when he refused. In the summer of 1996 he also claimed he was travelling in a car with the Guinea Pig in the Ballyfermot Industrial Estate where they had burgled a bicycle warehouse. He claimed that Desmond stopped the car, threw him across the car bonnet and again raped him. He warned his victim to keep his mouth shut.

A number of other teenage addicts also told stories of alleged rape attempts.

* * * *

In the meantime, the investigation team had established a source close to Desmond who kept them informed of his movements. They also used electronic surveillance to track their target, with the help of the English police. On Wednesday, March 8, they were tipped off that Desmond intended travelling home to Dublin. Word was filtering back to the Guinea Pig that a lot of people had been talking to the police. He decided he needed to be on the ground to shut them up in person. He was also cash strapped. He had a few people to see about money he was owed. There were plans to put a few of them in hospital. The Garda information revealed that the drug dealer intended to fly into Belfast and then take the train to Dublin, to avoid Garda attention. The previous day, Melissa Desmond had purchased an excess fare train ticket. She had it transferred to Belfast to be picked up by her brother, under an assumed name.

The investigation team decided to arrest and detain Desmond on foot of outstanding warrants for road traffic offences, for dangerous driving and driving without insurance in January 2000. They were confident that the offences were serious enough to warrant a custodial sentence. They had enough ammunition to successfully object to bail. With the Butcher behind bars, they could then buy time to finalise their investigation files for the Director of Public Prosecutions. In addition to the two murders, they had another 12 investigation files relating to the other offences. The investigating team felt that his victims and other witnesses would be more forthcoming with statements, if the main source of their fear was safely locked up. An urgent request for assistance was transmitted to their colleagues at Stanstead Airport, along with a recent picture of the gangster. At 4.10pm a man passed through the Police Control area to catch the Belfast flight. He showed his boarding card to Det Sgt Douglas Benford. It was in the name of an A Dowling. Desmond was allowed to board the flight. As soon as he disappeared through the door of the aircraft, the officer contacted the murder hunt HQ in Naas.

A surveillance team was mobilised and sent to Dundalk

to meet the Belfast train. In Belfast an RUC officer monitored Desmond after he got off the plane and made his way to Central Station. Back in Dundalk, the undercover cops boarded a train but couldn't find their target – he was on the later train. It was then decided to lay in wait for Desmond at Connolly station.

At 10pm Mark Desmond was surrounded by armed officers, as he stepped off the train. He was arrested and taken to the Bridewell Garda Station. The following morning, March 9, Desmond was brought before Kilmainham District Court in handcuffs. His hulking frame and shaved head added to the sense of menace he projected. He grinned and stared at people in the court room. He was remanded in custody on the three charges of dangerous driving and driving without insurance. A large force of Gardaí was drafted in to protect Desmond from an angry crowd of the dead men's relatives and friends.

On April 5, Desmond again appeared under tight security in Kilmainham Court, where he pleaded guilty to the three charges. Judge Gillian Hussey sentenced him to three months for dangerous driving and disqualified him from driving for 30 years. Desmond also pleaded guilty to the charge of causing criminal damage in Clondalkin Garda Station, when he smeared his own excrement around the place. For that, he received a suspended 12 month jail sentence. Desmond was due for release on June 11.

The investigation team decided to arrest the Butcher on the day of his release. In the meantime they continued to compile their case against him. Interim reports were sent to the DPP and there were regular meetings to discuss the prospect of charging Desmond with the murders, firearms, drugs and rape offences. In the intervening period, he made a number of applications for bail on the grounds that he intended appealing the severity of his three month sentence. But the investigation team successfully opposed each application on the grounds that Desmond had a history of doing a runner.

The investigation into the background of the stolen guns recovered in Ballyfermot led officers to the Athlone-based gang of drug addicts who had sold them to the Guinea Pig. In May, a total of 12 people, including one woman, were arrested and questioned about the theft of the guns. Several of them admitted selling the weapons to Desmond in return for heroin in October 1999. They also made statements and indicated that they would testify for the State against the murder suspect.

Detectives had also focused on the activities of a taxi company which was based in Ballyfermot. It was discovered that several drug dealers, including Desmond and his associates, regularly used the services of the company to deliver their drugs. There was less likelihood of being stopped and searched by Gardaí while travelling around in a taxi. Some drivers referred to "dirty work and clean work". The cab company referred to the drug dealer passengers as "JWT" jobs. JWT was the name of a legitimate travel company and the abbreviation was used as a code by the cabbies for the dirty work. A "JWT" meant a trip which could last hours, as the dealer visited customers and dealers around the city. A total of six drivers were arrested and questioned by the murder investigation team under the Offences Against the State Act. After that, 34 drivers attended an open meeting to discuss the arrests. It was decided to draw up a list of known drug dealers and bar them from using the company's services. Drivers were warned that they would be sacked if they picked up anyone whose name was on the list.

Desmond knew that the heat was coming down on him and he expected to be arrested for the canal murders. He instructed his legal team to contact the investigation team and demand that any interviews conducted with him should be electronically recorded. Desmond had claimed that an unidentified officer had threatened to "stitch" him up by making up an admission of guilt for the murders, when the Canal Butcher was arrested. The allegation was found to be false and a ploy designed to thwart the investigation. At the time, the Department of Justice had commenced the process of installing video and audio recording facilities in Garda interview rooms around the country. However there were still only a few stations in the Dublin area which had the equipment already in place. Investigators decided to conduct their interviews with Desmond in Tallaght Garda Station as it was one of the first stations to have the facility in Dublin. Although they were not required by law to accede to the request, the officers were happy to have the interrogation recorded to avoid any further allegations. They didn't want to give Desmond any opportunity to taint their inquiry. The Canal Butcher would also be less likely to smear his faeces around the place, if it was to be recorded for subsequent viewing by jurors with sensitive stomachs.

At 12.20pm on the afternoon of June 12, Desmond was released from Mountjoy Prison. As he walked through the prison gates, detectives were waiting for him. Det Sgt Gabriel O'Gara formally arrested Desmond under the Offences Against the State Act for possession of firearms with intent to endanger life at Aylmer's Bridge between December 28, 1999 and January 10, 2000. At Tallaght Garda Station Desmond refused to allow a doctor take a blood sample.

Over the following 48 hours, he refused to answer any questions put to him. He spent most of the time slumped in his chair, with his tee-shirt pulled over his head. He would also close his eyes and pretend to be asleep. He would occasionally smile. The statements of the various witnesses were put to the thug but he refused to even acknowledge the presence of the officers in the room. He was also questioned about the allegations of rape which had been made. Desmond now had a clear insight into the growing number of allegations that were piling up against him.

In the meantime Detective Superintendent Pat Brehony of the NBCI met with the DPP to discuss the case. The investigation team believed they had established why and how the murders had taken place. The motive for the murder of Patrick Murray was twofold. He had failed to travel back to Ireland as instructed and Desmond blamed him for the seizure of the drugs. Desmond also feared that Murray would testify against him, to save himself. A conviction for the heroin seizure would most likely be a long one. The Canal Butcher had already threatened to murder Murray and his family should he decide to inform. The investigators believed that Murray had been shot dead a short time after he went to meet with Desmond, on the evening of December 28. The murder, they believed, had been committed somewhere other than the

Grand Canal. It had probably been witnessed by Carey, who then panicked. There was phone evidence that Carey had made several attempts to contact Desmond the following day. On the following evening Carey, they believed, had travelled to the Grand Canal with Desmond and possibly 'Fat Boy' Foy to dump Murray's body. Carey was then shot because he had been ripping off Desmond and it was feared he might go to the police about the murder. They had also established a clear link through witnesses and forensics between the stolen firearms, the murders and Desmond. The DPP gave the go ahead to formally charge Mark Desmond, with the murders of Patrick Murray and Darren Carey.

The next morning, June 14, the Canal Butcher was released from his Section 30 detention and immediately re-arrested by Det Sgt John McManus. He formally charged Desmond with the two murders.

When the charges were read out to him, Desmond replied: "Not guilty." As Det Sgt Gabriel O'Gara placed handcuffs on Desmond to take him to a waiting squad car, he turned to the cop and snarled: "I'll get you for this O'Gara. I'll break your fuckin' back." It was the first time the dangerous criminal had spoken since his arrest two days earlier.

He was then taken under armed guard, in a convoy of police cars to appear before Tallaght District Court.

The arrest had again attracted intense media attention and the same hostile crowd had also congregated at the court. As the mobster was brought into the building, the crowd began shouting and hurling abuse at the suspected double killer. Desmond refused to answer or acknowledge the court, when asked his name by Judge James McDonnell. The judge wanted to establish his identity and whether he needed free legal aid. Desmond still refused to answer and looked up at the ceiling. The Judge said he could not continue.

As Desmond was leaving court Noeleen Carey and another relation of Darren Carey called him a "scumbag" and a "murdering bastard".

Desmond turned back to Noeleen Carey and told her: "Do you see youse, when I get out, youse are next. I'll sort youse out."

The day after Desmond's arrest outside Mountjoy Prison, detectives had also arrested Noel 'Fat Boy' Foy. The 19-year-old was serving a jail sentence in St. Patrick's Institution for young offenders. He was arrested on the suspicion that he was in possession of firearms with intent to endanger life at Aylmer Bridge, Kearneystown between December 28, 1999 and January 10, 2000. Rachel Stephens had implicated Foy in the murder plot but there was little other evidence against him. Gardaí, however, were satisfied that he was a close associate and business partner of Desmond.

When asked if he had anything to say about the reason for his arrest, Foy was less than helpful. He told the officers: "I have nothing to say about it, sure how would I know anything about that. You won't get anything out of me. I don't have to account for my movements and I will only answer questions if I feel like it." Foy claimed that he "hardly knew the chap" when asked about his partner-in-crime, Desmond.

On June 26, a prisoner who was also on remand in Cloverhill Prison with Desmond, contacted the investigation team with some information. He claimed that a week earlier he had overheard the Guinea Pig boasting about the murdered men while in the exercise yard. The prisoner claimed that Desmond had laughed about the murders and "how their heads went when they were shot".

A second inmate also came forward. He had befriended Desmond after he arrived in the prison. He claimed that Desmond told him he believed Patrick Murray was a "tout" or informant. He claimed that Desmond said he had taken Murray and Carey to the Glen of the Downs in County Wicklow, where he then shot Murray. He told the other prisoner that he used a Churchill shotgun and that Carey had panicked and told him that Murray was his friend. He described how Murray's head went when he was shot. He described a "puff of smoke" coming out of his head. He then shot Carey because he claimed he didn't trust him any longer. Desmond said that he took Carey out of the car on the night of the murder and brought him into a field where he had "battered" him with the shotgun, damaging the weapon in the process. He then dumped the weapon in a ditch. A few days later he had returned to the field where the body was lying and dumped it into the canal. The prisoner gave the detectives information that could be corroborated with their findings so far. The armed robber said he had come forward because he was appalled by the double murders but he refused to make a formal statement.

Desmond was aware that the three drug addicts had alleged he raped them. While in custody he wrote a number of letters to the *Irish Star* newspaper pleading his innocence and claiming that he was being set up. He threatened that he was going to "pull the other bird's head off" for making the rape allegation against him. He said that the Gardaí would not "get away with it" and they would "know all about it" when he got out. He was also concerned that he may have said too much to other inmates. He circulated a document, which stated that he had never discussed or talked about any crimes with other prisoners. He then circulated another document which read: "I [sic] Mark Desmond, I have nothing to say about any crimes or how someone might have done them or why. I take cell mates names because I don't want anyone telling lies about me that I was saying things about crimes at any time in prison." The back of document read: "I agree to what's on other side of this page." The document was then signed by a number of prisoners. Investigating detectives believed that Desmond had circulated the documents to warn off other prisoners from sharing their conversations with the police.

In August 2000, he wrote a letter to the problem page of the *Irish Star*. He said he was writing to discuss the matter of women making false allegations of rape. He suggested that any woman making such allegations should be jailed for seven years and that the accused should be allowed to take a lie detector test.

In September 2000, the murder investigation team submitted a huge file on the case, which included several volumes of evidence and statements, to the Director of Public Prosecutions. The covering report alone stretched to almost 400 pages. Investigators had painstakingly analysed every single piece of information. In addition to the murder charges the investigation team asked for directions on whether to lay a further 12 criminal charges against Desmond including the rape of the three drug addicts; the shooting of Gordon Marsh and Noel Hanlon; four charges of possession of firearms with intent to endanger life and three charges pertaining to the importation, sale and supply of heroin. The report dealt in great detail with the level of violence and intimidation Desmond had inflicted during his reign of terror. The Gardaí considered him to be such a serious threat that they suggested that the trial be held in the non-jury Special Criminal Court, which had been used mostly for the prosecution of terrorist offences. It was also used for the trials of members of the John Gilligan gang.

* * * *

In April 2001, Noel 'Fat Boy' Foy was killed in a motorbike crash. Foy had spotted a detective unit squad car from Ballyfermot and tore off at speed on the 1,000cc machine, losing the cops in seconds. But he couldn't handle such a big bike and smashed into the back of a truck on the M50 motorway.

In the same month, Mark Desmond made another attempt to get bail. On a previous occasion he dropped his application at the last minute when he discovered the Gardaí had brought Thomas Healy to testify about the shooting incidents and intimidation he had personally suffered from Desmond. The Gardaí were extremely anxious that the Canal Butcher was not given bail. If he did get his freedom, Desmond would unleash mayhem and the case would fall apart.

During the two day High Court hearing, which began on April 23, Det Sgt Ashley O' Sullivan told Mr Justice Peter Kelly that he was "strenuously opposed" to the application by Desmond because of the seriousness of the charges and the nature and weight of the evidence against him. Gardaí gave evidence of four arrest warrants that had been issued for the Guinea Pig in the past on charges including robbery, assault and road traffic offences. He had failed to appear in court each time. Details were also given of Desmond's midnight run to Belfast, in his haste to get out of the country after the murders. Det Sgt

O'Gara also testified about the threat Desmond made against him in Tallaght Garda Station. The officer said he believed that Desmond had threatened to kill him. The officer told the court he believed that Desmond was capable of carrying out that threat.

In his application Desmond told a tissue of lies. He claimed that in 1996 he had not turned up in court because he had been the victim of a shooting the previous evening. He also claimed he was being "stitched up" by Gardaí and was pleading not guilty to the murders. Desmond said his trip to Belfast in January 2000 was to "deliver a pigeon". When questioned about his unusual route to London he said he was in fear of "spy agents" who he said were following him. He said that the London police had told him his life was in danger and had offered him protection.

The following morning Mr Justice Kelly turned down Desmond's application. As part of his deliberations he said that he had considered Desmond's history of failing to honour bail terms, resulting in warrants being issued for his arrest. The judge said he was satisfied that the gunshot injury had been "self-inflicted" and was indicative of the measures Desmond was willing to go to evade justice.

He also pointed out three more instances when warrants had been issued in the District Court in more recent times. None of the explanations put forward were convincing, nor did they excuse the non-appearance. The judge said that the applicant had a considerable history of non-observance of bail terms and it was the Court's opinion that the past was a good indication of the future. There were other aspects of Desmond's behaviour that satisfied the court that there was a reasonable probability of non-appearance if bail was granted. Desmond had left the country after the bodies were discovered in the Grand Canal. He went to London via Belfast and used a false name and took back roads through the night. The judge described the Guinea Pig's explanation that he was returning a pigeon as "suspicious and unbelievable". As well as using a fake driving licence, Desmond had used a false name in London. He had also given a false name to police following his arrest there. Mr Justice

Kelly refused to accept this story or the claim that Desmond was offered protection by the police officers who arrested him in London. The judge cited another example of Desmond trying to evade justice, when he had fled after being stopped at a Garda checkpoint in July 1999. He also noted that there was the likelihood of interference with witnesses as suggested by the DPP, and the likelihood of committing criminal offences.

While he was locked up, the DPP decided to charge Desmond with four counts of possession of firearms with intent to endanger life.

Desmond instructed his legal team to demand that depositions be taken in the case before the trial. During such a hearing, which is held in the District Court, the testimony of each witness in an upcoming trial is given under oath and recorded. It also gave Desmond an opportunity to confront his accusers in person. During the depositions hearing at Dublin District Court on September 6, 2001, Rachel Stephens retracted her evidence about the murders. She claimed that she was lying about Desmond's admission of committing the murders in her original statement. Stephens was due to return to the court the following week. After the hearing, a copy of the book of evidence, charge sheets and deposition statements were stolen from the court room and passed out through a toilet window. The documents were found a week later, with the help of a relation of Darren Carey, in a bin in Dunawley Avenue in Clondalkin.

On the advice of the DPP, Det Insp Kennedy met Stephens to establish why she had retracted her evidence and if she had been threatened. Stephens told him that she was terrified of Desmond. She said she had lied on September 6 when she withdrew her statement. She said that she received a visit from an associate of the Guinea Pig's, the night before the depositions hearing. She told the officer that she was terrified of Desmond. "Mark Desmond could have me killed the way he killed those young fellas," she told Kennedy. Stephens, who was placed in the Witness Protection Programme (WPP), then indicated that she was prepared to go back to the court. In the WPP she would be accompanied at all times by two armed officers and also taken to a secret location to live.

On September 14, she stood over her original statements, implicating Desmond in the murders. Desmond's trial in the Central Criminal Court was set for November 2002.

Four days before the trial, however, there was a major set back in the case. Rachel Stephens approached Gardaí from the Witness Protection Programme and told them that she again wished to retract her statement about the murders. Det Insp Kennedy and Det Sgt O'Sullivan met her on November 14, at Terenure Garda Station to establish why. Stephens told the detectives that she was terrified and indicated that she would not testify against Desmond in relation to the murder charges. Stephens again said that she feared Desmond would kill her. She said she was only prepared to testify about the firearms charges. She said she had received word warning her to "keep my mouth shut about the drugs or Amsterdam". Stephens was adamant that she would not change her mind this time around.

It was a major blow to the State's investigation. Kennedy relayed the information to the DDP who decided to drop the murder charges as a result. Stephens was the State's main witness in the murder case. Instead it was decided to proceed with the four firearms charges.

With just days to go before the commencement of his trial, Desmond sacked his legal team, which had been led by Scottish barrister Mr Niall Murray QC. It was a ploy which had often been used by John Gilligan, in a bid to delay his trial from going ahead for as long as possible.

On the morning of November 18, Desmond was arraigned on the firearms charges before the Central Criminal Court. The charges included the unlawful possession of three double-barrel shotguns and one long rifle, with intent to endanger life between October 1, 1999 and February 17, 2000 at Lally Road, Ballyfermot. He was further charged that on the same dates at Lally Road, Ballyfermot he was in unlawful possession of a 12 gauge shotgun cartridges with intent to endanger life.

When he was formally arraigned on the four counts before Mr Justice Paul Carney, Desmond replied: "Not guilty, stitched up by the police and State." Desmond then asked the judge for an adjournment in order to appoint a new legal team.

Mr Justice Carney, however, was having none of it and said it had all the "hallmarks of somebody who is playing ducks and drakes" with the court. "You have taken it upon yourself to sack your legal team one year after being returned for trial," he told the accused.

When Desmond then threatened to take his case to the High Court, the judge replied: "You are in the High Court at this moment." He directed that a jury be sworn in and the case forwarded to Mr Justice Liam McKechnie for trial. He also directed that his colleague be provided with transcripts of that morning's proceedings, "so that he [Mr Justice McKechnie] can have knowledge of the ducks and drakes being played by the accused".

Desmond had little choice but to defend himself. This could, however, prove to be an advantage for the Canal Butcher. He could personally question – and intimidate – the witnesses lined up against him and he could do so in the full view of the court. And there was nothing that anyone could do about it. His one disadvantage was that he was incapable of disguising his thuggish personality from the jury. In an ill-fitting suit and a tie, which stretched almost to his knees, he was a comical sight as he took his position on the bench normally reserved for defence barristers and solicitors. He had a basic grasp of the trial process and had been coached by a number of well-known criminals while awaiting his trial in prison. One of his mentors was Eugene Patrick Holland or 'Dutchy', the elderly hit man who shot journalist Veronica Guerin on behalf of John Gilligan.

The trial began before a jury in the Central Criminal Court the following morning, Tuesday, November 19, 2002. Before it opened, Mr Justice McKechnie imposed a reporting ban on any references to the murder charges. The judge did not want the jury to hear about this on the grounds that it could be prejudicial to Desmond's defence. There was heavy security for the biggest gangland trial since the Gilligan gang. Armed members of the Emergency Response Unit stood guard in the packed court room. Measures were put in place to protect jurors, in case there was an attempt to intimidate them. The trial would last three and a half weeks. The mothers and relatives of the murdered men attended the case every day.

Opening the State's case, prosecuting counsel, Patrick Gageby SC, told the jury that the accused had been in unlawful possession of the cache of guns found under a garden shed. Mr Gageby said the three firearms seized at Lally Road Ballyfermot on February 17, 2000 were linked to another shotgun discovered sticking out of a hedge at Nangor Road in Clondalkin by a passer by. He said forensic evidence would show a link between that weapon and two disused shotgun cartridges also discovered during a Garda raid at the Lally Road house on February 17. The court was told that the weapons were stolen in separate burglaries throughout the country. Mr Gageby said it was the State's case that while Desmond was not suspected of having stolen the weapons, he nevertheless had them in his possession for an unlawful purpose.

After a few days, it appeared that Desmond was actually beginning to enjoy masquerading as a lawyer. On one occasion he was making a point to the trial Judge when he was distracted. "And furthermore Me Lord"... the defendant/barrister was in mid-sentence when the sound of a mobile phone going off at the back of the court interrupted his flow. "Turn off that phone," he ordered, with a flourish of his arm worthy of any senior counsel.

"Who's running this court?" one of Patrick Murray's relatives muttered loudly.

Throughout the trial Desmond made a string of gaffes, which caused outbursts of laughter. At one stage Desmond admitted that he could not read "tached writing" so everything had to be typed for him. He was pulled up by the prosecution when he appeared to misread a witness statement by quoting the words "I thought" instead of "although" and asked to read it correctly.

"I am," he protested, "the word is 'I thought' – that's what it says."

"No, Mr. Desmond," said Patrick Gageby, "the word is 'although' –a-l-t-h-o-u-g-h."

He squinted at the copy he held in his hand. "But there's no D in it!" he exclaimed in surprise.

"No, Mr Desmond," agreed Gageby, "there is no D in it", as laughter rippled through the court.

"I was converted" – instead of conveyed from one prison to another and "It's overwhembling" for overwhelming were other examples of his habitual gaffes. When cross-examining a witness who he knew well, he would introduce himself as: "And the accused – Mark Desmond – that's me."

Despite Desmond's comedy antics, the presence of Derek 'Dee Dee' O'Driscoll in the court for much of the first week added to the atmosphere of tension that was palpable throughout the trial. O'Driscoll and a few associates stood at the back of the courtroom each day. During the cross-examination of a witness Desmond made a point of ensuring that everyone was aware of Dee Dee's presence. He announced that O'Driscoll, who had been prepared to give evidence in the trial, was "now in court overseeing the proceedings".

Desmond could not restrain his contempt for the various Garda officers called to give evidence. And he took full advantage of his role as his own advocate to hurl abuse and allegations at the detectives who had been on his case. "Your telling lies guard – I'm now going to caution you under the perjury act – do you know what perjury is?" was a frequent refrain from Desmond when cross-examining Garda witnesses during the first week. This was until Mr Justice McKechnie warned him he was well out of order.

The "hearsay rule" was another favourite of Desmond and he raised it over and over again. At one stage he even used it to object to an ordnance survey map of Ballyfermot. Hearsay evidence consists of testimony based on information that a witness has obtained from a third party and is usually ruled inadmissible in criminal trials. Det Sgt Michael Campbell, a Garda mapper, denied suggestions by the accused that the Ordnance Survey map was "not credible" because it was a photocopy.

"I am not satisfied in the leastest [sic] terms of the Garda's answers. Each time he's like Charlie McCreevy ducking and diving," Desmond exclaimed. He continued: "Garda, for the seventh time today, have you got an original map?"

The witness replied he had not. He had requisitioned a copy from the Ordnance Survey office.

"Well there you go," said Desmond.

The trial heard evidence of the theft of the shotguns and rifle. The owner of the house in Drumraney, Athlone told the court that on October 1, 1999, her home was burgled. She said a gun safe, containing two shotguns and a rifle, was stolen. One of these weapons was the Churchill shotgun which the Gardaí believed had been used in the murders. The jury were not told this.

Desmond objected to her evidence as hearsay. He asked if the Gardaí had ever informed her of any suspects that may have burgled her home.

"No," she replied.

He then asked if her husband had given permission for anyone to burgle their home.

When Mr Justice McKechnie intervened by asking the accused if he had any further "factual questions" for the witness, Desmond replied: "You are playing ducks and drakes with me, My Lord."

The owner of the house on Lally Road in Ballyfermot, where the guns were found, told the court that the house had been vacant since October 1999 when her elderly mother was hospitalised. She said she received a phone call from the Gardaí telling her they wanted to search the house in February 2000.

Desmond asked her if she was surprised that certain items were recovered.

She replied, "I was shocked."

The accused then asked if her late mother had given anyone permission to enter the back garden "and put stuff" in the garden.

"No," she replied, "She would never allow anything like that."

When Desmond suggested that she "could not be 100 per cent" certain, she responded: "I knew my mother... I could be 100 per cent."

On the third day of the trial, the judge lifted the gagging
order preventing the reporting of the murder charges after
Desmond, in whose interests the order had been issued,
informed the jury of their existence himself. The Guinea Pig
proceeded to give the jury extensive details of the murder
allegations against him, despite the explicit advice of Mr Justice
McKechnie not to. The trial judge repeatedly warned Desmond
to refrain from making frequent outbursts and to confine
himself to the proper cross-examination of witnesses. At one
stage the judge told Desmond that the trial was "almost out of
control" because he [Judge] had been "far too lenient and far
too indulgent" with him. Desmond raised the murder charges
during his cross-examination of Det Insp Padraig Kennedy.
Desmond declared that Rachael Stephens had falsely implicated
him in the murders. He said she had retracted her statement,
which he claimed contained a number of inaccuracies. One
inaccuracy he cited was that she alleged he had put the bodies
into his car to dump them. He said that the car was "off the
road" before the murders. He also claimed that Stephens was
pressurised into making the incriminating statements about
him in February 2000.

In response Det Insp Padraig Kennedy said he didn't know
why the murder charges had been dropped. The officer told the
court that Rachel Stephens had retracted her statement at the
depositions' hearing on September 6, over a year earlier, because
she said she was terrified of Desmond. Stephens retracted her
original statement because she feared Desmond would kill her,
the detective continued. He explained that on September 14,
2001, Stephens had then "retracted her retraction".

When Desmond cross-examined him, DI Kennedy said he
did not know when Stephens entered the Witness Protection
Programme. Desmond turned to the jury and declared that he
was being "stitched up' on 'trumped up' firearms charges and
had already spent two and a half years in custody.

Det Insp Kennedy told the court of Stephens' decision
four days before the trial in November to again withdraw the
murder allegations. When questioned about the differences in
her testimony, Det Insp Kennedy said: "My lord she appeared

very afraid on the 6th [September 2001] and she appeared very nervous on the 14th [November 2002] as well." He added that she was still willing to testify against Desmond on the firearms charges.

Desmond put it to DI Kennedy that Stephens was lying. "I have spent two and a half years in fucking prison because some junkie was telling lies," he declared. Desmond also claimed the Gardaí: "Wanted to seek a way out of the mess they got themselves into with Rachael Stephens by introducing trumped up firearms charges."

Desmond then put it to the Det Insp Kennedy that Tony Long, his former drug supplier and partner of Dee Dee O'Driscoll, had been arrested for the same firearms offences that he was charged with. Desmond claimed that Long would testify that while in custody, senior Gardaí allegedly told him they had serious reservations about his [Desmond's] guilt.

DI Kennedy replied that he was not aware that Long had even been arrested.

"Well I'm after telling you he was," Desmond challenged him.

The accused then told the jury that Long was prepared to testify to that effect if the murder trial had gone ahead. He said Dee Dee O'Driscoll was also prepared to give evidence. In an apparently veiled threat to certain people in the court Desmond remarked: "He is here overseeing the proceedings."

"Did you see Derek O'Driscoll?" the accused asked.

"I did see him, yes," the detective replied.

Desmond asked Kennedy if he remembered O'Driscoll from 1996 when he was convicted of bribery as part of the investigation into the Veronica Guerin murder. Long was never called by Desmond to give evidence. He just wanted people to know that the gangster was also backing him up.

When Jonathan Desmond entered the witness box as a witness for the prosecution, he was flanked by two ERU officers. He was living under the Witness Protection Programme. He told the court how he had travelled twice to Holland with Mark Desmond, in late 1999. On the second trip they met Patrick Murray and Gary Kelly. In his testimony he gave details of the drug deals and how they were organised. Murray and Kelly were to bring it back through Dublin Airport but he said: "Mark changed his mind at the last minute and they were told to go back through England." Jonathan said that he heard after that there had been a problem at the airport. "I took it to mean the drugs had been seized," he said. He described the meeting with Patrick Murray after he was released. He said the atmosphere was "a nervous, tense type". He added: "Patrick said he put his hands up for the drugs and that he brought them in for himself and not for Mark. He (Mark) asked me did I think Patrick was telling the truth. I said yes, I think he was. Mark wasn't so sure."

Jonathan also claimed Mark Desmond questioned Gary Kelly about what he had said to the police but told him that if "he kept his mouth shut everything would be ok". "Mark said if he [Gary Kelly] said anything he'd blow his head off. Darren was trying to calm him down," he continued.

Jonathan Desmond stated that his cousin had showed him three shotguns and a number of cartridges over the back wall of a house on Lally road.

During the subsequent cross-examination by his cousin, Jonathan admitted that he had handled drugs in Dublin on behalf of Mark Desmond and collected money from dealers at Fatima Mansions and Bulfin Road. He would then leave the cash at a flat in Meath Street.

Mark Desmond put it to his cousin that he had made no mention of that in his statement of January 2000.

"At that particular time I was in fear. Mark Desmond had just stabbed me and left me for dead," the witness replied, without returning his cousin's stare.

The Canal Butcher put it to Jonathan that he [Mark] had never been charged with the importation of drugs.

"I haven't brought drugs in My Lord, Mark Desmond has," Jonathan replied. The protected witness added that he had been "conned" into going to Amsterdam. "I didn't know there were any drugs involved until I got there," he said.

Jonathan Desmond told the court that he had surgery for the stab wounds inflicted on him by his cousin at the Christmas party in 1999. He was in a "poor condition" when he was released from hospital on December 30.

Mark Desmond put it to Jonathan that a number of witnesses had told Gardaí they heard three gunshots coming from the Alymer Bridge area at about 7.15pm on New Year's Eve. He suggested to his cousin that he fitted the description of a man seen acting suspiciously in the area at that time. "Did you let those shots off, Jonathan?" Desmond asked.

"My Lord, that's a despicable accusation," Jonathan replied. He said he was at his mother's house at the time and was still weak after the stabbing incident.

"Some person shot Darren Carey and Patrick Murray on the 31st," said Desmond.

"I could barely bloody walk my Lord," his cousin replied.

Desmond then put it to his relation that as he had never been charged with handling guns or drugs he [Jonathan] had everything to gain by telling lies.

"They were not my drugs and they were not my guns, My Lord," he replied. "I viewed those guns at 100 Lally Road. They were shown to me by Mark Desmond."

When he was finished with his evidence Desmond was taken away by his police minders.

Rachael Stephens was also flanked by bodyguards when it was her turn to testify. She described seeing Desmond with a gun in the home of his girlfriend, Jennifer Devine a short time before the Grand Canal victims disappeared. She said another girl had been smoking heroin upstairs and when Mark came in he thought that it was Jennifer that had been smoking it. "He put the gun to her head and said if he found her smoking heroin he'd kill her," she said.

When questioned by Patrick Gageby about the type of gun, Stephens said: "It was a long gun, with two holes at the end of it."

Gageby asked: "What did he do with the gun?"

Stephens' replied: "He put it to her neck."

When she was cross-examined by Desmond, Stephens admitted to "falsely implicating" him in the murders. However, observers noted that the accused man appeared to "tread very carefully" with Stephens. He didn't want to push the issue of the murders any further with her.

Jennifer Devine gave evidence that she had also seen Mark Desmond twice using a firearm. She denied that her account of the incidents conflicted with those of Rachael Stephens.

Desmond asked her if she knew anything about guns at 104 Lally Road.

She said she hadn't.

"Did I ever tell you I kept guns there?" Desmond asked.

"No" she replied.

The group of six criminals from Athlone, who had given detectives statements admitting that they sold Desmond the stolen guns in return for heroin, changed their stories when they were called to testify. They were declared hostile witnesses. With the exception of one of them, the gang claimed that they didn't even know him. They also claimed they knew nothing about any guns.

The first member of the midland gang to testify, Michael Horan, said he'd been on heroin since the age of 15. He admitted that he had a "long" criminal record and was currently serving a jail term for "robbing". Asked if he remembered doing anything in October 1999 of relevance to the case, he replied, "No". Asked if he recalled being interviewed by the Gardaí in Naas Garda Station in May 2000, he replied: "I've been interviewed by Gardaí half my life."

Mr Gageby then asked him: "With what was the heroin bought?"

"Money," Horan responded.

Under direct examination, he refused to name Desmond as the person "who did the deal" for the heroin. The stolen Churchill shotgun was then produced and the witness was asked if Gardaí had shown him this.

"They showed me nothing," he said.

The rifle was then produced in evidence and Horan was asked if it had been shown to him by the police.

"No," Horan replied.

Asked if he ever travelled outside Athlone for drugs, he said he went to Galway and to Dublin city centre and Inchicore. When asked if he ever went to Dublin "for a different reason," he replied: "No, not necessarily."

When cross-examined by Desmond, Horan said he had signed a statement that implicated the accused in the firearms stolen in Athlone. But, he claimed, the Gardaí "made it all up" and he "just signed" his name.

Desmond asked the criminal if he had told Gardaí during questioning that he did not know him.

"A hundred times," the witness replied. "I didn't care what statement I was signing. I just wanted to get out of the barracks."

Desmond then suggested to the witness that he "went along with everything just to get out".

"Yeah," Horan replied. He told the court he was on "gear" [heroin] and he needed to get out of the Garda station.

"You never gave any firearms to Mark Desmond?" Desmond asked.

"No".

"Did you give guns to somebody else and then put me in their position?"

"No," Horan replied, adding that he never had any guns. "Whatever they wanted to write down I signed it and that was it."

Another Athlone criminal, Jimmy Gaffey, also denied knowing Desmond. "I don't know Mark Desmond from Adam," he told prosecuting counsel. Gaffey said he did not know anything about the firearms in question either.

Cross-examined by the accused, he claimed he lied to the Gardaí "to get out of the barracks". Curiously, however, Gaffey twice addressed Desmond as 'Mark', even though he claimed he had never seen him before in his life.

Paul 'Grasshopper' Green admitted that he knew Desmond because the pair had been in the same prison together. But he also changed his story in relation to the guns. He admitted to being a convicted armed robber, with a lengthy criminal record. He claimed that he had lied to Gardaí about selling the stolen guns to Desmond and had been prepared to lie in court. Then he announced that he was "an honest man at heart". Green said he had been arrested in May 2000 on suspicion of bringing firearms from Athlone to Dublin. He claimed that he only implicated Desmond because the Gardaí had falsely alleged that Desmond was a paedophile. He told the jury that for the first 24 hours in custody he had denied knowing Desmond. During his detention he claimed that Gardaí told him Desmond had "molested a young fella". Implicating Desmond in firearms was the only way they could put him away. He claimed he told the Gardaí: "I'll go along with this." Grasshopper said it was his belief that paedophiles were not common criminals like himself. "They are beasts," he said.

In cross-examination Desmond asked Green: "And you don't seek to hide your criminal past, don't you not?"

"No," Green replied.

"And you have convictions for robbery an' guns an' assaultin' bouncers and robbin' a bank?"

"Yeah" the witness agreed.

"And you'll probably rob another bank when you get out of jail won't you?"

Green looked utterly puzzled by the accusation. While he was still wondering what to say, Mr. Justice McKechnie pointed his finger at him. "Don't even think of answering that question Mr Green," he warned. "You are finished your evidence now, thank you."

John 'John Boy' Horan from Athlone told the court that he swapped a shotgun for heroin in Ballyfermot. The shotgun, which was not one of the weapons referred to in the charges, belonged to the father of another witness, James Gaffey. Gaffey had admitted in court to taking the gun without permission. Horan said he used to "score" heroin in the park at Ballyfermot. Asked by Patrick Gageby what he got in exchange for the gun he replied: "An eight of heroin".

Cross-examined by Desmond, the witness claimed the Gardaí made a deal that if he made a statement they would let him go "and they'd press no charges".

"They conned you?" asked Desmond.

"They conned me into it, yeah," Mr Horan replied.

"And did you ever get charged with those guns?"

"No and I'm not expecting any either."

Horan claimed he implicated Desmond because his "nerves were gone" in the garda station. "Myself and the Gardaí made a deal that they would not charge me," he said.

At the close of trial, Desmond invoked a little used section of the Criminal Justice Act 1984. This allowed a defendant representing himself, to prevent the prosecution from making a closing speech to the jury. Desmond had picked this up from his criminal advisers back in prison. As a result, Patrick Gageby was precluded from summing up the State's case against Desmond for the benefit of the jury. This created a serious disadvantage for the prosecution. Gageby could not summarise the important elements of the State's case.

In his own closing speech, Desmond claimed that the testimony of his cousin Jonathan Desmond was "all lies". He said: "People will tell lies when it's a self-serving lie. The easiest thing to do is to blame someone else." Other witnesses – who previously made statements implicating him – were telling the truth when they retracted those statements in court. He said the "ring of truth" was that none of the witnesses had ever been charged, even though they had also implicated themselves: "That's because they made false statements. And that's why I got them put in the witness box because I knew they were telling lies."

In his address to the jury, Mr Justice McKechnie reminded them that the accused was not on trial for drugs or murder. The only charges they could consider were the firearms charges before the court. As a result of the accused defending himself, his role had been that of an advocate in the case. As such, Mr Justice McKechnie warned, any "remarks, comments, suggestions" or "I told you so" comments the accused made during the course of the trial should be disregarded.

On the afternoon of December 11, 2002, the jury returned to the court with their verdict. They had deliberated for two and a half hours. The tension in the court was palpable. The room was crowded with press, members of the public and relatives of both Desmond and the murdered men. Additional armed

Gardaí and prison officers had also been called in. There was a real fear that Desmond might try to escape. Intelligence had been received that someone might also try to shoot the Guinea Pig.

The jury unanimously found Desmond guilty on all the charges. As the verdict was read out, relatives of the victims clapped and cheered. There were shouts of "You murderer" and "I hope Darren comes back and haunts you". Others, including the mothers of the two murdered men, openly wept.

After the guilty verdict was read out, Desmond claimed he was innocent. He said he was: "going to fight this case until I'm dead and my family will as well."

Before sentencing, Det Insp Padraig Kennedy read out Desmond's previous convictions. Mr Justice McKechnie then sentenced the Canal Butcher to eight years. It was to be back-dated to June 2000, when Desmond was first charged and remanded in custody on the charges.

Relatives of Patrick Murray and Darren Carey hurled more angry abuse at Desmond, who turned to the family with a sneering smile. "You murdering pig, murdering pig," they shouted. Another shouted: "You're only brave with guns in your hand." A number had to be restrained in the crowded courtroom as they tried to get to Desmond, who was surrounded by prison officers and detectives. "He's an animal," one woman shouted. Darren Carey's grandmother Angela wept at the back of the court.

"Look at you laughing. Two children dead over your drug involvement" shouted another.

"Eight years – I'll do it on me back," Desmond said, sitting back in his seat. As prison officers placed him in handcuffs he continued to taunt the hecklers.

"You'll be doing it on your back – dead," one woman roared back.

As the Gardaí tried to clear the court, Desmond, holding up a sheaf of documents in his hand, shouted threats at the relatives: "Grasses – I have all your statements."

Still grinning, he then turned to Det Insp Kennedy and Det Sgt Ashley O'Sullivan. "You're going down," he snarled.

"You're going down, Kennedy."

As relatives waited in the corridor outside Court 15, prison officers bundled Desmond through a door normally reserved for jurors. One man lunged at him with his fists but Desmond managed to avoid the blow. He was rushed downstairs huddled in the middle of a crowd of prison officers and Gardaí.

There was a crush as the group of relatives then tried to burst through the double doors leading to the stair exit. They had to be forcibly held back by police. "What are you protecting him for?" screamed one woman.

As they waited for Desmond to appear in the yard of the court complex, the families spoke to reporters of their extreme disappointment at the sentence. "Eight years when he could have got life? I am absolutely disgusted. He should have got 15 to 20 years," said Marie McSharry, Patrick Murray's aunt.

Angela Carey, Darren's grandmother, also wept as she hugged Sinead Kelly. She told reporters: "His [Darren] face was shot off. Thinking of what he went through before he died, not really knowing what was going on. It's a terrible thing to have to live with."

Darren's mother Noeleen Carey said she had to leave the courtroom when she heard the sentence: "He's making a laugh of the whole justice system. We feel so let down. The jury brought in the verdict and then this. The detectives have been let down too. They did a fantastic job."

When a reporter asked how they felt when Desmond laughed and showed no remorse for his crime, Kathleen Murray said: "What would you expect from him – he's only an animal and animals don't show any remorse."

The following day the two grieving mothers gave an extensive interview to the *Sunday World* newspaper. In it they expressed the anguish of every mother whose son had fallen victim to the godfathers of death. "We did not get justice this week. He [Desmond] should have got a much tougher sentence and now he'll be out in a few years, even when he was convicted. Desmond showed his true colours and threatened us and the police involved," said Noreen Carey. She nursed Darren's little boy, who had just turned three. A picture on a sideboard showed the murder victim blowing out the candle on his first ever birthday cake. He looked identical to the little boy on his mother's lap. It illustrated the futility of it all.

"He [Darren] loved children and he was a good lad. He was very protective of me and despite what some people have written about him, he was led astray by that scumbag Desmond," she said. "He was a placid, gentle child who hated aggro of any kind. I hope that evil scum suffers in the same way we have suffered. This was such a waste of a good life. It always kept me going thinking that he would be going down but I will go to my grave knowing who murdered my son."

Kathleen Murray wore a picture of her son on a gold chain around her neck. "My boy was never in trouble with the law before he was arrested for smuggling drugs for Desmond. He was a great kid, a great character with a big heart," she said.

The most painful aspect to the tragedy for the two mothers was the circumstances in which their sons died. "I don't delve into it too much, I don't think about the way he [Patrick] died. I can't think about if he was crying for help before he died."

The news of Desmond's conviction was welcomed by many of his long-suffering neighbours and drug pushers. The two and a half years he had been on remand awaiting trial, had brought a sense of calm to the area, although there were plenty of others to fill the void.

Desmond served his sentence in Portlaoise Maximum Security prison, alongside some of the country's most feared criminal godfathers on E1 wing. But even there he continued to be involved in violence. In October 2004, he was moved to the basement of the prison after he stabbed the leader of one of the factions in a notorious gangland feud in Crumlin and Drimnagh, south-West Dublin. The feud has claimed ten lives since 2000. In the meantime Desmond was working on an appeal against his sentence.

In November 2004, this time with the aid of a legal team, he challenged his conviction in the Court of Criminal Appeal. Presenting Desmond's case, Paul Coffey SC said it could be argued that a lot of matters arose in the appeal because of the way Desmond conducted his own defence. If Desmond had been legally advised – those matters would not have "poisoned the well". Coffey said it was clear the trial "went off the rails to a very large extent". Desmond was at a disadvantage and issues that should not have been presented to the jury had been brought up, often by himself. This included mentions of drug dealing and a stabbing which he had elicited when questioning his cousin, Jonathan Desmond. He said Desmond, who was illiterate leaving school at 13, rectified this while in prison and his client's knowledge of the Irish Constitution was second to none. Desmond claimed he had been given inadequate time to defend himself in 2002. He had sacked his legal team at the opening of the trial and Mr Justice Paul Carney had refused an adjournment.

On December 3, 2004, the Court of Criminal Appeal overturned the conviction.

Mr Justice McCracken said the court was satisfied that the refusal of either of the judges who dealt with the case in November 2002 to consider Desmond's application for an adjournment had prevented him from obtaining a fair trial in accordance with the law and was contrary to the principles of natural and constitutional justice.

Mark Desmond was freed from prison in January 2005. It was a disappointing result for the families of the victims and the investigation team. But, at least, one of the most feared men in gangland had been taken out of circulation for almost five years. In the process the police had also managed to break up his drug racket.

* * * *

Desmond kept his head down after winning his freedom and moved between hotels in Kildare and Wicklow. Within a few months, Gardaí began picking up intelligence that the Guinea Pig was back in the drug business. But he was a marked man.

On May 14, 2005, Desmond's 22-year-old first cousin, Martin Kenny, was shot dead as he lay in bed in his girlfriend's home in Ballyfermot. Kenny was a small-time player in the drug trade and it was suspected he had been working with his cousin.

Armed detectives kept a discreet watch over the funeral, which was attended by the Guinea Pig and his other cousin Jonathan Desmond. The State witness had been living outside the country since testifying against the Canal Butcher.

Mark Desmond had been involved in a number of shooting incidents around the same time, although none of them had been officially reported to the police. There had also been a reported attempt to shoot him but he had escaped.

On the evening of Sunday, July 16, 2006, Mark Desmond was ambushed in Tallaght as he was being carried in a car driven by his dead cousin's brother, Kevin Kenny. The two relatives were waiting at traffic lights, at the junction of the Old Bawn Road and Seskin View Road. A motorbike carrying two men pulled up alongside and one of them opened fire on the passenger side of the car. Desmond was shot in the arm. The bullet went through the flesh and wounded Kenny in the buttock. Fortunately for Desmond the gunman's weapon jammed.

At the time of writing, Mark Desmond was still alive but keeping a low profile. He was rarely spotted around Ballyfermot.

The canal murders provided a shocking opening to the Millennium. But eight years later, however, the Irish public had grown accustomed to the spectre of double murders – and the Island of Saints and Scholars had gained a reputation for gangland violence. This was reflected in the media attention such outrages attracted, at the end of the first decade of the new Millennium. Gangland murders were only a one-day news item. There were also attempts to murder much larger groups of criminals at one time, with bombs and machine guns, but, so far, these have been thwarted by the police or the intended victims simply got lucky.

By 2008, the underworld's mass murderers had not yet achieved their objective. But observers agree, that may only be a matter of time. The most recent intelligence about Desmond suggested that he was running with a group of criminals from Finglas and one of the gangs involved in an ongoing gang war in Crumlin and Drimnagh in Dublin. He had joined forces with Finglas armed robber Paul 'Farmer' Martin who was the prime suspect in the murder of an associate called James 'Gonty' Dillon. Martin, who was an associate of Martin 'Marlo' Hyland, was behind a major criminal drug racket. In August 2008, Martin was gunned down as he sat in a Finglas pub on a Saturday afternoon.

Desmond continued to keep his head down and, at the time of writing, was moving between addresses around Dublin and the surrounding counties.

The world has not heard the last of the Canal Butcher.

THREE

JOEY THE LIP

"I want to tell you about all the shit that I'm mixed up in."

With these words the terrified young man began to spill the beans on a secret world of drugs, guns, violence and murder. It was a world where life was as cheap as a quarter gram of cocaine or heroin.

It was 2.35am on May 10, 2004, in a musty Garda interview room. The frail 19-year-old sat huddled and trembling in his chair. His mother sat beside him, listening in a state of disbelief to the gangland horror story spilling from her vulnerable boy. Across the table sat a senior detective who, an hour earlier, had been roused from his sleep by an urgent phone call from his colleagues. The teenager had just burst through the front door of Ballymun Garda Station in the company of his mother. At that moment in time he had two stark choices in his screwed-up life – talk to the police or be shot dead. He had a lot to tell. In the young man's vernacular, he *was* mixed up in a lot of shit – very dangerous shit.

Just over a year later, in the Central Criminal Court Mr Justice Michael Peart would describe the murder of drug dealer Jonathan O'Reilly "as the most cold, calculated and premeditated slaying of a young man that can be imagined." In the next breath he then sentenced O'Reilly's killers, Brian Kenny and Thomas Hinchon, to life imprisonment. Both men had been found guilty, thanks mainly to the testimony of Joseph O'Callaghan, alias Joey the Lip, the young man who had become embroiled in terrifying madness. This was one of the few gangland murder cases where the normally impenetrable wall of silence was broken and the hit men brought to justice. And the name Joey the Lip was added to the membership of an exclusive club no one wanted to join. He was one of the few who had broken the line and told what he knew. In the process Joey had done a major favour for society. To his criminal contemporaries, however, he would always be remembered as a tout, a rat, a supergrass – a dead man walking.

A nickname like Joey the Lip conjures up the image of a swaggering, menacing gangster. It suggests a mafia wiseguy, like Johnny 'The Bull' Gravano, the New York hit man who turned over his boss John Gotti. But the nearest Joseph O'Callaghan ever came to being a major league criminal was his moniker. He was not a drug dealer, a robber or a killer. He was as vulnerable and innocent as his baby-faced features suggested. Joey got the nickname simply because he had "big lips". By his nineteenth birthday he had discovered, the hard way, that there was nothing glamorous about life in gangland. When he ran to the police station that fateful night, Joseph O'Callaghan signed away his freedom. He later joined the Witness Protection Programme and was forced to leave the country.

The first time I saw Joseph O'Callaghan was when he gave evidence in the highly charged gangland murder trial in 2005. As he sat hunched in the witness box being verbally bombarded by defence counsel for the two killers, he was surrounded by armed detectives. When we met in the foyer of a hotel in a European city over two years later he had hardly changed. The 22-year-old still had the haunted, lost boy look about him. He appeared nervous and treated everyone with suspicion. Joey had emerged from hiding to tell his story.

"It is a long time since I got to talk about all this. But now is the right time to tell people my story and what all this gangland bullshit is really about. I can never see my family again and I will always be a marked man. That is the price I paid," he spoke almost in a whisper. "Every night in my nightmares I see Brian Kenny's face and he is beating me. I dream about meeting Thomas Hinchon and he is talking about what he is going to do to me but he doesn't know it's me. Then I wake up in a sweat."

This is the story of Joey the Lip.

* * * *

Joseph Noel O'Callaghan was born in Dublin on January 26, 1985. He was the youngest of five children and his parents were Mary and Noel O'Callaghan. From his earliest years, violence rather than happiness would be a constant feature of his life. His father was a chronic alcoholic who was brutal towards his wife. Shortly after he was born Joey's parents split up and his mother brought him and one of his sisters to live with her in England. Mary O'Callaghan began a relationship with another Irishman with whom she had a daughter. Some time after that, when Joey was still small, they returned to live in Dublin. Mary and her children suffered appalling violence at the hands of the new man in her life.

"He used to beat my ma, me and my sister all the time. As a result I grew up wanting to protect my Ma. I used to see him giving her terrible beatings. He would come home and take her money to go drinking," Joey recalled. "He used to bend her fingers back and she would scream in pain. I would shout at him to stop. When he finished with her, he would start on me. Once he smashed a lamp over my head when I was around seven or eight because I had the light on in my bedroom. Then one Christmas he went mad when I didn't like what I got from Santa. He threw me across the room and I landed on the Christmas Tree. I remember my mam and sister crying. On another occasion he was slapping and beating my mother and he was going so bad at her that my sister, who was only around 12 at the time, had to hold a knife to his neck to get him to stop. He was a real life monster and I still hate that man for what he did to us."

Eventually Joey's mother got rid of the brute when she could tolerate the abuse no more. "After he left, Ma changed the locks on the door. One night he came back and tried to put his hand through the letterbox and she smashed his fingers with a hammer. I never saw him again after that. Life was good then after he left. We were all much happier. We were all free at last."

Joey's mother decided to make another fresh start and moved her young family to live in a Local Authority house at Blakestown Road, Blanchardstown in West Dublin. Joey was around ten years of age. He attended the local primary school and later Blakestown Community School. He dropped out of Blakestown two years later at the age of 14. Joey had a tough time in school. He had learning difficulties and was regularly bullied. He was described as being a vulnerable "mammy's boy". Blakestown was in the heart of one of the toughest areas in Ireland. It produced a generation of young criminals, many of whom would go on to earn notoriety in gangland. The main kids on the block were members of the notorious Westies gang, Shane Coates and his sidekick Stephen Sugg, Sugg's brother Bernard and Mark and Andrew Glennon. To an impressionable kid these flash, brash thugs were heroes. Joey would mitch from school with other kids and hang around a spot they called 'The Wall' at the end of a local authority estate in the area. They reckoned they learned more there than they did in school. It was the equivalent of a youth centre for delinquents and aspiring delinquents.

"The Wall was a place where the kids from the area used to bring their robbed cars at night and rally them and then wreck them. We, the younger ones, used to listen to the older boys talking about robbing cars, drugs and how they fooled the judges in the Children's Court. They would take the piss out of the juvenile court because when you are under 16 you couldn't be locked up. There were always judges that they knew would just give them a slap on the wrist. The lads would be laughing at how the judge would let them off when he saw a small, defenceless looking kid standing before him all weepy-eyed. We looked up to them. My Ma was always giving out to me about hanging around with that lot. But at least I had the sense not to take drugs or get into the stolen cars."

When Joey was around 12, the Westies were beginning to make serious waves in gangland. "Shane Coates and his family used to live across the road from us and I fed a few horses he kept at the back of the Shanty Pub in Ladyswell. They were a very respectable family and Shane was the only one who went a bit mad. I was just a kid to him and I thought he was cool at the time. All the kids used to be talking about the shootings and beatings they were doing. It was like they were characters in a movie to them. To me Coatesy was very hard. He was always defensive, till he got to know you. If you said hello to him he would want to know why you did. He always thought people were taking the piss out of him. Everyone looked up to Coatesy as the main man. All the other young criminals wanted to turn out like him, to be feared and respected and have so much power. Sugg and Coates and the gang around them had an incredible name for violence. Even the police were afraid of them. That lot together was like a big bowling machine coming down the line at you, you couldn't stop it.

"At the time Blanchardstown and Ballymun were known as the junkie's paradise because there were so many smack addicts everywhere. Sugg and Coates were flooding the place with the stuff. Coatesy used to drive around the place in an FTO sports car and different jeeps and high-powered bikes. He was always dressed to the best with expensive jewellery. It wasn't just the likes of us kids who were impressed. All the older lads wanted to be like Coates as well. When Coates and Sugg weren't around the Glennons used to say that Coates didn't have a punch in him, that he couldn't beat his way out of a wet bag. But they, like everyone else, were terrified of the two boys because they used guns. Mark and Andrew Glennon used to take bets on who could rob the best car and not get caught by the cops in a chase. There was no fear of the police at all. They would be talking about crime and guns and drugs and the police. When me and my mates were around eleven or twelve we looked up to these guys. It all seemed so fucking glamorous at the time. It is no wonder that crime continues to thrive when people are turned on like that."

By Joey's twentieth birthday, the Westies gang, who had lived by gun had all died by the gun. The Glennon brothers and a number of other gang members decided to stage the gangland equivalent of a coup, in the Summer of 2003, when they shot Bernard 'Verb' Sugg dead in a Blanchardstown pub. After that they took over the drug dealing operation. Sugg and Coates had moved to live in Spain a month before Verb was whacked. Less than six months later, the most notorious duo in the Irish criminal underworld were murdered when they were ambushed in a row with other Irish hoods over drugs. Their bodies were eventually found in the Summer of 2006, buried under a warehouse floor in Alicante. In the meantime the Glennons had also fallen out with their partners in the Westies take over. The Glennons had carried out a brazen machine-gun attack on their two former pals outside Blanchardstown Garda Station. They fired at least thirty rounds at their targets who were injured but survived to fight another day. The following year the Glennons were murdered in two well-planned hits. Several others who hung around the Wall with Joey were killed, either violently in feuds or when they crashed stolen cars. Others died as a result of their drug habits.

Joey could count the names of at least ten of his contemporaries who had since been jailed for serious crimes, including drugs, possession of firearms, attempted murder and murder. When he went through the list of names it made the supergrass philosophical. "It tells its own story when you think that a lot of the guys we looked up to have all been shot and killed. It makes this whole gangland thing so completely stupid but none of those involved seem to notice how ridiculous it all is until it is too late."

Joseph O'Callaghan had only been living in Blakestown a short time when the local milkman knocked on the door. Brian Kenny was canvassing the nearby houses for business. Joey chanced his arm and asked him for a job.

A few weeks later Joey met Kenny who offered him work collecting the money on his round. The youngster was excited at the prospect of having a job and the chance to make some pocket money. Kenny made the vulnerable kid feel important. One of the difficulties in Joey's short life was that every male he looked up to either betrayed or abused his trust.

Meeting Kenny, in Joey's own words, was to be the

"beginning of the end of my life". And that was no exaggeration. He recalled: "He was a very charming, jack-the-lad type that all the kids – and the women in the area – liked. He was a bit of a pied piper. Kenny wore the best of clothes and was big into the women. He used to call in to women on his milk rounds and give them more than just a daily litre. After a while he gave me a job delivering the milk. I used to work from 3am to 8am and then I would go to school. We would have a laugh and he'd look after me. I used to bring him back stuff like key-rings from holidays. I looked up to Kenny and I suppose I saw him like a father figure. Old women on the round used to ask me if he was my Dad."

Behind Kenny's charming façade, however, lurked a monster who brutalised everyone he came into contact with. At the same time he was delivering a lot more than milk or love to the frustrated housewives on his rounds, Kenny was also a heroin dealer. Born on July 1, 1969 he grew up in Drogheda, County Louth with his parents, one brother and two sisters. In 1994 he bought a house, Mitchelstown Cottage, at Kilshane Cross. It was situated on a back road in the north County Dublin countryside, three miles from Finglas. For several years he had been involved in burglaries from factories and warehouses. In 1991 he was convicted on three counts of larceny and handling stolen property for which he was bound to the peace for two years.

In February 1998, Kenny and two other milkmen, Peter Kiernan and Peter Joyce, were arrested and charged with possessing £5,000 (€6,350) worth of heroin for sale or supply. Kenny's 50-year-old father, William, a carpenter by profession, was also arrested in the bust. The group had used their milk rounds as a cover for distributing drugs around north West Dublin. They took orders on a mobile phone and then made their deliveries. It was a relatively small operation. The drugs were supplied by a drug gang, based in Clondalkin, West Dublin. In July 1999, the four men each received a five year suspended jail sentence when they pleaded guilty to the charge. In the Dublin Circuit Criminal Court, Judge Elizabeth Dunne described them as "a very unusual group" to come before the courts on a drug supply charge.

Following his conviction, Premier Dairies sacked Kenny and Joey found himself without a source of pocket money. A few weeks later Kenny called to Joey's house with the offer of another job of sorts, collecting pallets in local industrial estates. Then Kenny got Joey to babysit for him and his partner Rita Harling. The couple had been living together since 1995 and they had a son two years later. Joey would stay over night and sleep on the floor. Then, gradually, he began to stay for a few nights at a time. That summer he also helped Kenny build a large shed at the back of the house. "He was always putting pressure on me to stay at his gaff, telling me to bring clothes with me. When I went home to change and wash he would come with me and bring me back to his place. I didn't realise it but he was gradually taking control of my life."

In December 2000, Joey's father died suddenly from a massive heart attack at the age of 54. The 15-year-old was heart-broken. Although he had never lived with his father, Joey had spent weekends with him throughout his life. And Brian Kenny was a shoulder to cry on. "On the night of the funeral he asked my Ma if it was ok for me to stay with him and his partner and child for a few days and she agreed. Then after a few weeks I decided to stay there full time and my Ma agreed. She thought that he might keep me out of trouble. I felt good that Brian cared about me when my Dad died. I often think that if my Da was alive today that I wouldn't be in hiding. I would never have ended up with the likes of Brian Kenny. My Da would have killed him."

After the death of his father, Joey's mother and the rest of his family then moved back to live in his house in Ballymun where they had originally lived.

Joey soon realised that Kenny was into a whole lot more than just collecting wooden pallets. Kenny was a full-time thief and ran with two notorious criminal brothers from Finglas who were classified by the Gardaí as career criminals. Kenny and the Finglas brothers were also associated with Martin 'Marlo' Hyland who later became one of the country's most wanted criminal godfathers. *(See Chapters Four and Five.)* On the night after his father died, Joey met the Finglas brothers for the first time.

"I was sitting in the front room and these two big fellas walked in the back door. I heard one of them asking: 'Where's Joey the Lip?' Then they came in a shook my hand and said they were sorry about me dad and to keep my head up. After that I got to know the brothers very well because they were up with Brian all the time. They were always stroking [robbing] together."

Martin Kenny and the two Finglas brothers were wholesale dealers in stolen goods. Kenny dealt with a large network of criminals including a number of well known members of Sinn Féin and the Provisional IRA, and members of the travelling community. Other well-known young thugs from Finglas such as Anthony 'Anto' Spratt, Declan Curran and John Daly *(See Chapter Six.)* were also involved. The mob robbed factories, storage depots, warehouses, farms, anywhere they could lay their hands on something that they could sell. The shed Joey had helped Kenny build at the back of Mitchelstown Cottage became a storage depot for hot property.

"They were robbing frozen foods, nappies, electrical goods, you name it. The shed at the back of the house was always busy with stolen gear being brought in and out. Different groups of lads were calling in and out collecting stuff and dropping other stuff off. There were cars being stripped down, robbed tools, stolen bikes, windows, computers and laptops. I saw container truck loads of drink, cigarettes and clothes. They even stole jet skis and a big boat once which they used for fishing trips off Clogher Head."

From the time Joey moved in to live full-time in Mitchelstown Cottage, Kenny brought his impressionable protégé with him on jobs. "I went out with him and the brothers when they were doing burglaries and I would keep sketch [look out] for them. If there was a small window on a place and they couldn't get through it, they put me in because I was so small. One time they pushed me through the toilet window at the back of a filling station in Finglas. As I was getting through it, I discovered that there was a man in the jacks and he began roaring. Kenny and yer man tore off in a car and left me and the other brother to run for it. I thought it was great craic at the time."

"I remember once me and Kenny were just driving out around Clonsilla [West Dublin] when he spotted a caravan parked in the garden of a house. He told me to jump out and lift the tow bar when he backed up to it. Then he drove off like nothing happened and brought the caravan to a knacker's camp [travellers] in Ladyswell and dropped it there. He was never afraid of anything and to me, as a stupid kid, he looked invincible and I admired him. He never looked bothered, like he was untouchable. Then after a while I realised why he didn't worry about the consequences."

The reason may have had something to do with the fact that Kenny was also a registered police informant. During his subsequent trial for the O'Reilly murder, this matter was not disclosed by either the defence or the prosecution. Kenny would often brag about his relationship with the policeman to Joey. But he also used the connection to convince Joey and his other victims that there was no point informing on him because he was already well in.

"I remember one time they stole a TNT truck full of booze and cigarettes and brought it back to the yard. But they didn't know there was a tracker on it. Some time later the place was surrounded by the cops and Kenny tore off in his truck and the Finglas brothers ran out through the back garden. Nothing ever happened after that. I think they were all touting to the police. Kenny and one of the Finglas brothers were often slagging each other over the two cops they were talking to. I often saw Kenny meeting with his cop handler and heard him talking to him on the phone. That was why, in my lowest times, I had never gone to the police because I thought he would find out straight away."

On one occasion, Joey recalled how Kenny put his car into a garage to be repaired. But the garage was taking too long to complete the work and Kenny became impatient. "He was going mad because he had someone lined up to buy the car. So one night [on January 8, 2001] he went to the garage and jumped the wall with a two litre container of petrol. I was waiting for him in the car and suddenly heard a big bump when the place went up in flames. The next day he went back to the garage owner and demanded to be paid compensation for his car, which he was."

Without noticing it, Joey had become Kenny's slave. He was completely under his control. It was then that he began to witness the dark side of his 'father figure'. Constant violence was a central feature of life under Kenny's roof. The gangster subjected his girlfriend, Rita Harling, to ferocious beatings. In the follow-up investigation prompted by Joey's sudden appearance in Ballymun Garda Station, detectives interviewed her about life with Kenny. She told them a horror story. After she gave birth to their son in 1997 Rita Harling became seriously ill. As a result of internal bleeding, she spent some time on a life support machine. She had to have a hysterectomy and, eight months later, had her gall bladder removed. On the day she returned home from hospital, Kenny locked her in a bedroom and then tried to choke her on the bed. During the attack he stood on her stomach. She was too terrified to tell anyone what had happened.

The following passage is Rita Harling's description to police about her life with the monster: "Through my time with Brian he was violent and abusive to me, he assaulted me on many occasions, he punched me in the head, he left me with bald patches on my head after pulling my hair out, he stood on my head, he's kicked me to bits. Driving out the North Road one day, I had the two kids in the car, he slammed my head into the dash of the car. There was one time I had to spend two days lying on a couch because he battered me so much. Brian would lock me in my bedroom, lock me out of the house, take my mobile phone and my car keys so I couldn't go out anywhere or speak to anyone. He (Kenny) is a control freak, he was capable of killing me ... I am still terrified of Brian Kenny. I am afraid of my life of him."

Kenny also began beating Joey the Lip. "He used to give Rita awful beatings. Whenever I tried to stop him he would lay into me. I remember once he was strangling her in the hallway and I was crying and shouting at him to stop. He turned around and punched me in the face sending me flying into the sitting room. He had huge hands – even the cops said that to me."

In December 2000, things came to a head for Joey when he refused to mind Kenny's son. "At Christmas Brian asked me to babysit. I told him I had already looked after the kid several nights and that I wanted to go over to me mates in Blanchardstown. Brian started to go ga ga. He had a knife in his hand. It was in the sitting room and he held me and held the knife into my throat. He was hurting my neck 'cause he had the knife in tight to my throat. He was angry, very angry that I wouldn't babysit for him. He then let me go and I had a red mark on my neck from the knife. I said to myself: 'I'm not taking that shite'. I rang me Ma to pick me up. She did and I left with her and that was it, I went back to live with her in Ballymun. After that I didn't see Kenny for about a year. I got work in a factory making chairs and did a bit of painting. Today I remember that year as one of the best in my life."

In the meantime, Joey began to have rows with his mother who objected to his behaviour. Joey would go out drinking with his mates and disappear for days. He was also having problems with his older brother. One day he bumped into Kenny in Finglas. "He came into this café I was in and said: 'I want you to come up to the house for dinner' and I just went with him. It suited me because of the trouble I was in at home.

And then I was back in that hell again. I still cannot explain why I returned. He was back in control of my life just like that. I had a tiny room in the attic that you couldn't stand up fully in because the ceiling was so low."

* * * *

By the time Joey returned to live with Brian Kenny, there had been some major changes. Kenny had swapped robbing for dealing in drugs. Soon he was turning over as much as IR£5,000 (€6,350) worth of cocaine and heroin every day. Kenny had also developed an addiction to both drugs, which made him more volatile and dangerous than before. Rita Harling had finally fled from her life of hell in Mitchelstown Cottage. She had also obtained a court order barring him from going near her or their child. In February 2003, Kenny married 29-year-old Amanda 'Mandy' Joyce from Finglas. It was her brother Peter who had been convicted of possession of heroin with Kenny in 1999. Mandy Joyce's husband had been murdered in London in 2001. She met Kenny when she returned to Ireland with her five-year-old son.

In the meantime, Kenny also had a bitter falling out with the Finglas brothers which resulted in an exchange of death threats. On the night of June 23, 2002, two masked men, armed with a shotgun, broke into Kenny's house. When he ran out the back garden they fired a number of shots, hitting him once in the back. He was hospitalised after the attack but refused to co-operate with the Gardaí. Kenny blamed the Finglas brothers for the attack and threatened to kill them.

Kenny bought his heroin and cocaine from members of a Clondalkin-based gang, led by two violent young brothers, Paul and Simon Doyle. The Doyle gang were typical of the new breed of gangsters who emerged to fill the void left after the 1996 push against organised crime. Paul Doyle, who was born in 1978, and his brother Simon, who was one year his junior, controlled a drug dealing operation in Ronanstown, Neilstown and Clondalkin. Like their contemporaries around the country, the gang achieved market share through violence and menace. Their father had been extremely violent towards the brothers when they were children. Paul Doyle's mother, Carmel, would later tell a court that her husband had beaten her son so badly as a child that he had often been hospitalised. His father had subsequently starved himself to death.

Jonathan O'Reilly was one of their most trusted lieutenants. O'Reilly, who was the same age as Paul Doyle, grew up around the corner from them in St Mark's Gardens in Clondalkin. Other key players in the gang were local thugs Richie McCormack, Robbie O'Hanlon and Les Rowan. They were all around the same age. The gang used violence on anyone who crossed them. In January 1997, the two Doyle brothers and O'Reilly were arrested after a vicious attack on a number of men they accused of owing them money. During the incident they had dropped a concrete block on a man's head. In another incident Paul Doyle attacked two men who he claimed owed him IR£20 (€25) with a machete. One of the men received 150 stitches while the other, who was almost decapitated, received 160 stitches. In January 1999, Paul Doyle was jailed for four years for the two attacks while Simon Doyle received two and a half years inside.

In 1998, the local Detective Inspector for the Garda district covered by Lucan and Ronanstown Stations, Todd O'Loughlin, set up a major operation to put the Doyle gang out of business. O'Loughlin was a hugely respected officer who had been pivotal in the Veronica Guerin murder investigation and breaking up the Gilligan gang. DI O'Loughlin knew all too well the dangers of allowing a gang to get too powerful, as was the case with Gilligan. Over the period of a year the operation, which was spearheaded by Det Sgt Martin Walsh and the Ronanstown drug squad, inflicted considerable damage on the business being run by the new bad boys on the block. During that time they busted 15 people in possession of almost IR£2 million (€2.54 million) worth of heroin, cocaine, ecstasy and hashish, which they were distributing for the gang. In all the cases, those arrested were prepared to go to jail rather than give evidence against the Doyles.

Les Rowan was one of the first to be caught in 1998. In August 1999, Jonathan O'Reilly was also nabbed with IR£30,000 (€38,100) worth of drugs. In 2000, O'Reilly was jailed for 18 months for his part in the assault with the Doyles. He was given a further five years on the drug charges and served both sentences concurrently.

The Doyles and O'Reilly continued to build their drug business from the comfort of their cells in Wheatfield Prison with the use of mobile phones. On the outside, McCormack, Rowan and O'Hanlon ensured the operation grew from strength to strength. Gardaí estimated that the gang was turning over in excess of IR£100,000 (€127,000) per week.

When Simon Doyle was released from prison in March 2001, he took control of the operation and the trade continued to flourish. The gang bought a number of automatic pistols and stolen shotguns. They were to be used in the growing number of confrontations they were having with rivals, attempting to cash in on their lucrative patch. The Doyle mob was making a lot of enemies. Then the inevitable happened. On the night of December 22, 2001, Simon Doyle was shot dead on the doorstep of the family home at St Mark's Avenue in Clondalkin. There were many criminals with a motive to kill the 22-year-old mobster. The murder signalled the beginning of a shift in the balance of power.

Paul Doyle, due for release in April 2002, vowed to avenge his brother's death. He told his associates that IR£150,000 (€190,000) Simon was hoarding had gone missing. In the meantime, the investigation of Doyle's murder gave Det Insp O'Loughlin and his team an opportunity to further their efforts of breaking up the gang. Over the following month all the known gang members were arrested and questioned. One of them was Richie McCormack. He was considered to be one of the most violent members of the mob. He was described as being a devious and cunning individual. McCormack decided to break his code of omerta or silence and began talking to the police. So too did Les Rowan. They told detectives that they were living in fear that Paul Doyle would force them into a bloody gangland feud. As a "goodwill" gesture they handed over four of the gang's weapons. However, Det Insp O'Loughlin suspected that the two hoods were helping the cops put Doyle away so that they could take over the operation for themselves.

Four months later, Paul Doyle was released from prison. In the same month 56-year-old Maurice 'Bo Bo' Ward was shot dead at his home in Ronanstown. It was a suspected revenge attack for the Simon Doyle murder. It was suspected that Bo Bo Ward, who had declared himself an anti-drugs activist and had a young family, had fingered Doyle [ordered his murder]. In his day, Ward also had a reputation as an extremely dangerous individual. His murder was chillingly symbolic of the new era in gangland – the young brutes, who had replaced Bo Bo and his like, had eradicated him. It was the underworld's interpretation of the law of the jungle. In any event detectives believed Ward had nothing to do with Simon Doyle's murder.

Paul Doyle immediately resumed his role in the drug trade,

alongside his henchmen. But the gang soon began to implode. In August 2002, Paul Doyle escaped serious injury when Les Rowan tried to kill him. Rowan, who owed IR£35,000 (€44,450) for drugs he had sold while Doyle was inside, fired six shots at his former boss. The ruthless young gangster suffered only superficial injuries. One bullet had grazed his skull while the other grazed his back. Rowan, who had been convicted of heroin dealing, went on the run to London.

A few weeks later, however, Doyle was not so lucky when the local Drug Squad swooped on his home. This time he was caught holding a bag of heroin worth over IR£250,000 (€317,500). The other gang members had decided that there was more than one way of getting rid of Doyle.

Paul Doyle was remanded in custody while awaiting his trial. He was refused bail, following strenuous objections by the local Gardaí.

In April 2003, there was surprise in court when Doyle pleaded guilty to the drug charges and received a relatively lenient five-year jail sentence, with the final year suspended. The judge in the Circuit Criminal Court had been impressed when he heard Doyle had become a listener for the Samaritans while on remand and had joined a steering committee. Det Insp O'Loughlin told the court that Doyle had been involved in a feud with other drug dealers when he was arrested and had received four years for two horrendous assaults.

When he received his sentence Doyle thanked the Judge who replied: "Don't thank me, you merited it."

No one, with the exception of the judge, believed Doyle's road to Damascus-style conversion.

In the meantime, control of the gang had shifted to Richie McCormack, Robbie O'Hanlon and Jonathan O'Reilly, who was released from prison during the same period. Brian Kenny had been dealing with the Doyle gang from the time he was running the milk round in West Dublin. He had been friendly with Paul Doyle and it was Doyle who had introduced Kenny to Thomas Hinchon, who was also from Clondalkin. Born in 1979, Hinchon had been in trouble with the law since childhood. By the time he was 20 years of age he had 40 convictions, most of them relating to car theft and joy riding. He had become a central player in the growing Doyle gang. Every few weeks, Kenny collected his supplies of heroin and cocaine from Hinchon. The pair became close friends. It was a friendship that would be marked by blood.

* * * *

Kenny now had more need for Joey the Lip than ever before. "The first few months were fine and Kenny was nice to me. Then one day he handed me this little bag and told me to run up the road to the nearby Roadstone plant. I handed this guy the bag and he gave me €120 that I brought back to Kenny. I only realised then that I had delivered my first deal of smack [heroin]."

Joey was soon working full-time, managing Kenny's burgeoning drug trade.

"I became an expert in heroin and cocaine. I used to cut it up, weight it and bag it. Then I hid it in a nearby field. I made about 20 drops every day. Kenny sat around the house smoking heroin and taking orders on a special mobile phone which he called his 'work' phone. He would take the order and then send me to deliver it. At first I used to run up and down the road to make the deliveries to the junkies. After a while he got me a small motorbike and I would travel around delivering stuff in Ballymun and Finglas. When I bagged the gear [drugs] I used to wrap it in a second bag and put it in my mouth. If the cops stopped me I could swallow it and then get it later when I went to the toilet. I'm glad I never had to do that because I know Kenny would have battered me senseless if I didn't. Kenny was buying around two kilos of smack and six ounces of coke every month from Thomas Hinchon and Paul Doyle. He was tripling his money. If he got a bad batch of smack he would keep it and then mix it with good stuff."

Like the Westies, and every other gang on the street, Kenny used violence to maintain control over his turf. Joey recalled: "He would say that he wanted to be better and bigger than the Westies. He wanted people to fear him. I saw him threatening to shoot junkies if they hadn't paid up. One junkie from Swords had to tell the welfare she was renting a room from him so that her cheques were sent directly to him to pay for her gear. He got me to get a letter from my Ma saying she had kicked me out so he could collect my social welfare accommodation allowance. Sometimes he used to have sex with some of the women in return for smack. He didn't care about anything. One night he said that he would give this junkie free smack if she had sex with me but I said that I wouldn't do that to the girl. It was sick."

Soon after his return to Mitchelstown Cottage, Joey the Lip again felt the brunt of the madman's anger. This time the beatings were more vicious than before. Joey still has a dent in his skull to prove it. "He was getting more and more out of control and began timing me when I went out anywhere. If I was a minute late he would beat me. I was even timed every morning when I left Mandy's son to school. When I came back he would interrogate me about who I met and did I talk to anyone and what did I say. It was totally crazy. That house was like a prison camp. He had the doors locked all the time and there were high walls around the house. With Brian you could not ask why or what or how. You could only ask 'Can I?' or 'Am I allowed?'."

"I remember counting up to €20,000 at a time and then delivering it to a house in Finglas. Like the other drug dealers in the area he was paying money to the IRA and a guy who was involved in Sinn Féin in Finglas. I collected money from the junkies and dealers who were working for Kenny. Some of them used to be dying sick and wouldn't have all the money they owed and I would take pity on them and let them off with the rest. I sometimes put my own money in to make up the shortfall so I wouldn't be battered. But the junkies always rat you out and then I would get a serious beating. He used to say to me: 'They [addicts] will think you are soft and then they'll walk all over you.'"

"He and Mandy spent all day smoking heroin, you could smell the stuff everywhere. I used to be off me head from the stuff in the air. It made him crazy and he would run around the house in his boxers, carrying a shotgun thinking there was

someone outside coming to get him. I used to wonder why I was
so important to him. One time Thomas Hinchon was staying
in the house because he was on the run from the police who
had warrants for his arrest. He asked me if I wanted to go and
work for him distributing his heroin in Clondalkin. I just said
no, that I was happy where I was because I didn't know if he
was playing one of Kenny's mind games. When he left the next
day, Kenny called me out to the shed. He starting shouting at
me over what Thomas had said. I told him that I didn't want
to leave. He told me I was lying and began beating me in the
head and legs."

Kenny imposed a tortuous regime on Joey and his wife's
little boy: "Me and the kid were only allowed to have one bath a
week and we had to use his bath water. Once I saw him forcing
the little lad to eat dog food because he wouldn't eat his dinner.
I didn't like the orange drink he gave me with my dinner one
day so he poured it over my food and made me eat it. He would
often beat me if I did something wrong and then make me stay
in my room for days on end. I had to call down the stairs to ask
could I go to the toilet. My food would be left on the bottom
step and I would have to eat it in my room. After a few days he
would call me down and tell me why he had to punish me."

In January 2004, Joey had just turned 19 when he became
a father when a girlfriend, with whom he had a brief fling, had
a daughter. At first Joey was not allowed to see his child. "My
former girlfriend eventually agreed to let me see my daughter
when she was three months old, in March 2004. When I asked
Kenny to let me go to see her he went mad and began boxing
me around the kitchen. I ran out of the house and down the
road but there was no where to run to because it is in the middle
of the country. He came after me in the car and ran me into a
ditch. He put me in the car and brought me back to the house.
Inside he pinned me down on the couch and punched me and
bit me in the head. After that I was made to stay in my room
for three days. I had clotted blood in my hair and eyes and
couldn't wash it off. The reason he went mad was because my
ex-girlfriend lived on the same road as the Finglas brothers.
In his paranoia he thought I would have been helping plot to

kill him. It was crazy. When Kenny beat me all those times I
thought I deserved it even though I had done nothing wrong.
When you are in a situation like that you always think that it
is your fault."

* * * *

By the beginning of 2004, unrest was brewing elsewhere.

Over in Clondalkin, Jonathan O'Reilly began moving out
on his own which led to tension between himself and Thomas
Hinchon. By then, Kenny and Joey were collecting over a kilo
of heroin from Hinchon every fortnight. In gangland terms it
was a good working relationship. Hinchon heard that O'Reilly
was telling his dealers that he planned to take over from him.
He asked Kenny to help him murder O'Reilly because he feared
O'Reilly would kill him first. In return Hinchon had agreed to
help Kenny murder one of the Finglas brothers. Some months
earlier Kenny, Hinchon and Joey had gone to his house to shoot
him. However the plan was aborted. Once O'Reilly was done
they planned to go back and finish one of the brothers off.

"Brian was out this evening with Hinchon and I was in the
house with Mandy and the kid. She told me that Thomas was
saying that this fella [O'Reilly] was going around calling him
a muppet over in Ronanstown and that he was going to blow
Hinchon's head off. She said that O'Reilly had been selling
heroin to Hinchon. But behind his back O'Reilly was ripping
him off and telling Hinchon's dealers that he was going to get
rid of Hinchon and kill him."

Robbie O'Hanlon was involved in the plot. He had secretly
agreed to set O'Reilly up to be murdered by Hinchon and Kenny.
They hatched a plan, whereby O'Hanlon would offer to bring
his unsuspecting friend in crime for a drive and then leave him
exposed to be shot. The gang decided to do the hit outside
Cloverhill Prison. Hinchon would ride the motorbike to be used
in the attack and Kenny would do the shooting.

Saturday, April 17, was a storm-lashed day, with torrential
downpours and gale force winds. It was to be Jonathan O'Reilly's
last day on earth. Earlier O'Reilly had watched a football match

on TV with his pal, David Murray. O'Hanlon had arranged to meet Murray and O'Reilly to go shopping in the Liffey Valley Shopping Centre. He phoned and arranged to pick them up in his car from Murray's house at Rowlagh Gardens in Clondalkin. O'Hanlon was accompanied by convicted drug dealer Gordon Kelly when they picked up the two friends. O'Hanlon and Kelly had earlier visited another associate, Gavin Thompson, who was serving a seven year stretch for drug trafficking in the Midland Prison at Portlaoise. On the way to Liffey Valley, O'Hanlon announced he had to drop clothes off to his brother, Jimmy O'Hanlon Junior, who was a prisoner in Cloverhill Prison.

Twenty-three year-old O'Hanlon ensured that O'Reilly was sitting in the front seat of his two-door BMW coupe. Even though he had "no visible means of income", O'Hanlon could afford to buy high performance cars. At Cloverhill he parked his car outside the prison gates shortly before 2.50pm. O'Hanlon purposely parked the car across the road from the prison entrance in such a way that the passenger door was nearest to the centre of the road. He told his passengers that he would only be a few minutes. He got out and ran through the downpour to the prison gates with his bag of clothes. Jonathan O'Reilly suspected nothing.

O'Reilly was turned around in his seat talking with Kelly and Murray. The three men were having a laugh about a pornographic DVD and video that Kelly found on the floor of the car.

Two minutes later a Kawasaki 400cc motorbike pulled up alongside. Jonathan O'Reilly heard the bike engine revving over the pounding rain and turned to look out his window. On the motorbike Brian Kenny pulled out a powerful .38 revolver and fired a shot through the window, smashing it. He then fired two more shots at O'Reilly, hitting him in the chest.

O'Reilly screamed 'Ahh', as the bullets struck. The force of the initial blast pushed him across the car to the driver's seat. Murray and Kelly cowered down in the back seat but Kenny showed no interest in them. Seconds later the gangland murderers sped off.

O'Reilly was rushed to Tallaght Hospital where medical staff tried to save his life. He was pronounced dead at 3.45pm.

Joey took up the story. "That morning Kenny told me to stay at home and not dare go out the door. Mandy warned me not to call him on his mobile in case it would pinpoint his mobile. She told me that Brian and Thomas did a deal that if Brian helped him kill O'Reilly then Thomas would help him kill one of the Finglas brothers. Later Kenny and Hinchon arrived back at the house. When they came in they began smoking heroin. Kenny called me down from my room and told me to read the teletext."

"It came up that a fella had been shot in Cloverhill. It said that he was seriously injured and in hospital. Kenny and Hinchon began to panic and that's when I realised that they had shot him. Brian was asking what would they do if he wasn't dead. A short time later it came up that the man was dead and they were relieved. They were saying: 'Fuck him...did you see the size of him [O'Reilly]. He was a big fella.' Brian said he hit him in the chest, he wasn't sure if he hit him in the head, he said O'Reilly went all white when he was at the car and the other fellas [Murray and Kelly] were jumping all over the place. Thomas was saying that the bike was a fuckin' weapon, it was no good. Then Kenny gave me the gun, which he had wrapped in a plastic bag, and told me get my wellies on and hide it up the fields."

Kenny then handed Joey a meat cleaver and ordered him to cut up the leather motorbike gear they had been wearing. He was also told to break up the helmets and burn the lot in a stove at the back of the garage.

"Then Kenny told me: 'Don't open your mouth about this to anyone or else I'll kill you and I won't be able to stop Thomas killing you.' Then Thomas came in and told me: 'Joey I'll kill you if you tell anybody about this.' After that they kept screaming and roaring at me that they would shoot me. Kenny said that he had done it once and he had no problem doing it again. I couldn't think of anything else, I was terrified. As well as threatening me, he said that he'd shoot my Ma, burn my sister's car out and that he would go down and shoot up my girlfriend's house where my kid lived so that I would never be allowed see the child again."

Over the next few weeks Joey O'Callaghan began to fear for his life. About ten days later Kenny sent Joey to pick up a pump-action shotgun. He wanted to buy it from a well-known criminal in the travelling community who lived in Ballymun. The night after he brought the weapon back to Kenny, Joey went with him to a field to test fire it. He fired off a number of shots before turning to Joey. "He fired a shot over my head and then pointed the shotgun at me and said: 'This is the gun I'm going to shoot you and the Finglas brothers with.'"

After the O'Reilly murder, Joey had begged Kenny to let him leave, promising him that he would never talk about what he knew. But every time he made the request the drug trafficker beat him. In Joey's mind it was only a matter of time before he too ended up like O'Reilly.

On the evening of Sunday, May 9, Joey made his frantic bid for freedom. He believed that he was only hours away from being murdered. Kenny and Hinchon had threatened to kill him and he had no reason to disbelieve them. "That evening Mandy Joyce told me that he and Hinchon planned to bring me up to the field at the back of the house and shoot me because they were afraid that I would talk about the murder of Jonathan O'Reilly. Brian had already stuck the barrel of a shotgun in my mouth and he had fired shots over my head in the field at the back of the house. He told me that he had done it once and doing it to me would be no problem for him. I couldn't handle it any more. So I ran as soon as I saw my chance."

"Kenny had been watching me all the time and there was no way I could get out of the house. I took my chance when he went into the bedroom to smoke heroin. I was shitting it as I packed me bag. I knew that if he caught me leaving I was dead and I knew that once I did leave I was also dead. Either way I was completely fucked. My sister came to collect me. I was terrified that he might come out with his pump action shotgun and kill me. Kenny started ringing me and threatening to burn my family out if I didn't come back. I went with my sister to meet my Ma and I told her what had happened and that I didn't trust the police."

At 1.15am the following morning, Joey's mother phoned Sergeant Stephen Daly, an officer she knew at Ballymun Station. Fifteen minutes later she met the officer in the station and told him her son was in fear that he was about to be murdered because he had information about the O'Reilly murder. Joey arrived at the station 20 minutes later. The officer would later reveal that Joey was "very agitated…he seemed to be quite nervous and afraid."

Sgt Daly phoned Det Insp O'Loughlin who arrived at the station within a half hour. At the same time the experienced detective filled in his colleagues Detective Superintendents Hubert Collins and John McDermott. Det Supt Collins, who was in charge of detectives in the Garda western division, had a good track record investigating gangland murders. He had been involved in solving two notorious murders of gangsters Mark Dwyer and Chester Beatty, in the inner-city. McDermott was attached to the National Bureau of Criminal Investigation (NBCI). He had been involved in serious crime investigation for most of his career and was one of the officers who had helped establish the Criminal Assets Bureau. It was decided that if the appearance of Joey the Lip proved to be a serious breakthrough in the case, then everyone involved in the investigation would need to be ready to move. Unwelcome phone calls were made to the homes of detectives all over Dublin.

Det Insp O'Loughlin met Joey the Lip in an interview room, with his mother. He reassured the terrified teenager that he was now safe and O'Callaghan began to relax a little. Then he told the officer: "I want to tell you about all the shit that I'm mixed up in."

Over the next number of hours Joey the Lip told the Inspector everything he knew. While the interview was going on he received a string of threatening text messages from Kenny which clearly showed that he was furious that Joey had fled. He demanded that he return immediately. He was looking for the heroin Joey hid, so that he could sell it on. Kenny had no idea that his slave was sitting in a police station.

In the meantime, a large force of Gardaí from Ronanstown and Lucan Stations, including the Emergency Response Unit and the NBCI, had been mobilised. The frantic text messages and calls from Kenny to Joey showed that he suspected that all was not well. They would have to move quickly before vital evidence or the killers disappeared. Det Supt McDermott hurriedly obtained search warrants to search Kenny's home. Arrest warrants were also obtained for Kenny, Hinchon and Joyce. Detective Sergeant Mick 'Shakey' Doyle from Ronanstown Station led the swoop on Mitchelstown Cottage. All officers were instructed to carry firearms and wear bullet-proof vests. They knew that Kenny was armed and potentially dangerous.

At 7.40am the search and arrest operation swung into action. Det Sgt Doyle and his squad, with guns drawn, quickly surrounded the house. At the kitchen window Doyle spotted Kenny inside, brandishing the pump action shotgun. The officer aimed his pistol at Kenny and shouted: "Armed Gardaí drop the gun...drop the gun." Kenny put down the weapon and opened the door as ERU officers rushed in and placed handcuffs on him. They recovered the weapon and disarmed it.

Det Sgt Doyle then arrested Kenny and Mandy Joyce under the Offences Against the State Act. They were immediately whisked away in squad cars to Ronanstown and Lucan Garda Stations.

Later when Kenny was questioned about the shooting, he said: "I'm fitted up, someone must have handed my name up. I can't believe it." When asked did he murder Jonathan O'Reilly he replied: "I don't even know the chap."

When asked about his association with Joseph O'Callaghan, Kenny remarked: "He [Joey] had a hard life. I took a shine to the young fella and took him in. He's a bit mixed up, hanging around with the wrong crowd."

That afternoon Kenny received a visit from Det Insp O'Loughlin. He sat across the table from Kenny and smiled. He knew that the drug dealer was a registered informant and wanted to dispel any illusions that he might have about getting special treatment. He wanted Kenny to know that the show was finally up. "You won't be pulling any strings to get off this one Brian... and that's a promise."

Joey the Lip was huddled in the back of a waiting police car, as detectives moved in on Kenny. "Todd O'Loughlin and Stephen Daly brought me out to a yard at the back of Ballymun Station and there was about 30 policemen getting into cars and vans. There were ERU men all tooled up, with machine guns and helmets and other detectives in bullet-proof vests. I was shepherded to a car and we drove off in this big convoy to Kilshane Cross. I could see the ERU surrounding Kenny's house and charging into it."

Joey the Lip then showed the officers where he had hidden the murder weapon and Kenny's drugs. He went home under armed guard, to sleep for a few hours. Later that morning he returned to the house with Det Insp Todd O'Loughlin. He pointed out the stove where he had tried to burn the clothes Hinchon and Kenny wore during the attack. He also pointed out the motorbike they had used. That afternoon he also showed them the home of Hinchon's sister at Liffey Lawns in Lucan. This was where the same bike had been hidden for a few days after the O'Reilly murder. At 3.30pm, 22-year-old Elena Hinchon was arrested by Gardaí, who also searched her home for evidence.

Four hours later, Thomas Hinchon was picked up and arrested by Det Sgt Doyle. It was then decided to bring Joey the Lip to a hotel near Lucan where, under armed guard, he could make further statements. Joey detailed everything he knew about Kenny's drug operation and other crimes. He also identified the weapons seized by Gardaí.

"The first few days I spent locked up in a hotel room, with two or three armed officers standing outside the door. I had no phone or any way of contacting the outside world. The police did not want anyone talking to me or trying to influence me. Everything seemed to be done by the book. Over the next few days, I made dozens of statements. We seemed to be going day and night. After that I was brought to a hotel in County Kildare where they [Gardaí] stayed with me."

Hinchon and Kenny were questioned for up to 72 hours after their arrests. The investigation had moved into top gear as evidence was collated and the case was built against the pair.

Detective Chief Superintendent Martin Donnellan of the NBCI had a meeting with the Director of Public Prosecutions. At 6pm on Wednesday, May 12, 2004, the DPP directed that Hinchon and Kenny both be charged with the murder of Jonathan O'Reilly. Det Sgt Doyle charged both men an hour later.

The following morning they were brought before Kilmainham District Court where they were remanded in custody until their trial. They were also charged with threatening to murder Joseph O'Callaghan. Kenny was further charged with illegal possession of the pump-action shotgun and ammunition at the time of his arrest.

"From then on I was in the company of police 24 hours a day. The detectives from Ronanstown and Lucan Stations minded me. They were good to me and I got to really like them. I spent around two months with them. The manager of the hotel, it was a little old place, used to say that she would pray for me. At night when I was on my own I felt very lonely and used to cry a lot. I missed my family. All the time I asked myself what had I gotten myself mixed up in. I hadn't a clue what was going to happen next and had never heard of the Witness Protection Programme [WPP]."

* * * *

The first real test of Joey's resolve to testify against the two killers came a few weeks later, when Kenny applied for bail in the High Court. One of the biggest obstacles Gardaí face in dealing with organised crime is the ease with which dangerous criminals facing serious charges are granted bail. This often happens, despite strenuous objections from investigating officers. Being back on the street gives the criminal an opportunity to intimidate witnesses and therefore scupper the case against him. The O'Reilly murder investigation team were not going to take any chances with Kenny's bail hearing. It was decided to get Joey the Lip to testify on their behalf.

"Todd O'Loughlin and Mick Doyle came to me and said that I would have to go to Cloverhill Court and give evidence against Brian Kenny because he was applying for bail. One of the detectives that I got very close to brought me to a place on this quiet country road in Kildare. The ERU were waiting in two big jeeps and two powerful cars. I got into the back seat of one of the cars, beside Todd O'Loughlin. I was very nervous but Todd smiled and told me that everything would be alright."

Joey was whisked off in a blaze of blue lights and sirens to Cloverhill Court, which is situated beside Cloverhill and Wheatfield prisons, the scene of the actual crime. The court was ideal for hearings involving criminals who were classified as highly dangerous. The courtroom was connected to the prison by means of a tunnel, which eliminated any risk of escape.

"It was all mad. Here I was, at the scene of the crime, helping to keep Brian Kenny in custody for it. Inside the court I was brought to this room to wait for the case to be called. I was crying because I was scared and I didn't want to get into the witness box. The guards were reassuring me, saying that I would be fine and that they would be beside me all the time."

Then it was time for Joey to go into the courtroom. "The courtroom was packed with people. Police surrounded me and I kept my head down and didn't want to make eye contact with anyone. I got into the box and I saw Kenny was sitting in another box just across from me. I was beside the judge. Kenny was only feet away from me. He suddenly stood up and was staring at me. I was terrified because I could feel his eyes burning into the side of me head. When he stood up, I started to move in my chair to get out of his way.

"Then someone ordered him to sit down. The State's lawyer began asking me questions about what had happened on the day of the murder. Then Kenny's defence solicitor got stuck into me and began accusing me of being a liar. I asked the lawyer was she there when the murder was committed. When she replied 'No' I said to her: 'Then you don't be telling me what happened if you weren't there. He [Kenny] murdered that fella because he told me he murdered him. He told me to hide the gun in the field. He also told me he would murder me if I told anyone.' All my fear seemed to go as soon as I was accused of being a liar. I just let it all out."

After hearing Joey's evidence, the court refused Kenny's

application for bail and he was put back in custody. After his appearance the new supergrass was brought to another room in the building where DI Todd O'Loughlin introduced him to two senior Gardaí attached to the Witness Protection Programme.

"They were big men in smart suits and they scared me a bit. They asked me questions about every aspect of my life. I didn't know then but they needed this information to erase my identity as Joseph O'Callaghan. Then they asked me was I willing to give evidence in the trial and would I be prepared to go into the Witness Protection Programme. I said yes but only as long as I wouldn't have to leave the country. I was told that would be no problem and I signed a piece of paper. They shook hands with me and then left. I spent the next few weeks with the Lucan and Ronanstown detectives. They were great to my family and me. Normally there was one particular officer with me most of the time and I got to trust and like him a lot. Whenever I was brought to meet members of my family there would be six or seven detectives around me."

Despite all his problems at the time, Joey the Lip had been studying for his Junior Cert. The Lucan detective who was acting as Joey's bodyguard helped him prepare for the exams. In June, Joey sat his Junior Cert exams, under armed guard in an interview room in Naas Garda Station.

"I think the local guards actually thought I was the son of one of the other supergrasses like Charlie Bowden who had given evidence against the Gilligan gang. I did the exam in this room with the detective sitting behind me and a supervisor in front of me. I did English, Maths, Geography, History and Irish. Some months later Todd O'Loughlin picked up my results for me and I had passed everything."

Then Joey the Lip's situation suddenly changed. He was contacted and told that he had been accepted into the Witness Protection Programme. "Todd O'Loughlin and the other detectives who had been with me said that they would have to leave me the following day and would not be able to have any further contact with me. I was very lonesome and there were tears in my eyes when Todd's people left me. I did not like being in the Witness Protection Programme. From that moment I had a new name. The police took away every picture that had been taken of me. I used to be left on my own a lot in an apartment. I could go out night-clubbing on my own as long as I didn't go anywhere near North Dublin."

But in January 2005, six months before the trial, Gardaí discovered a plot to murder Joey. The information was that he had been spotted by an associate of the gang and an order was given to murder him. A number of criminals were arrested and questioned about the plot. No one was charged but it had shown friends of the two killers that the cops were on to them. Joey was moved in the middle of the night to another location. After that he could only go out when two armed officers were with him.

"After the plot to kill me was discovered I was moved to another area in Dublin, a real posh part of Blackrock, but then I started getting harassed by the local police because they thought I was just a gouger down robbing in the area. The WPP officers had to go to them about it. After another two months I was moved again, this time to an apartment in Carlow."

* * * *

The trial of Brian Kenny and Thomas Hinchon, opened in the Central Criminal Court in Dublin on June 8, 2005 before Mr Justice Michael Peart. They both denied the charges of murdering O'Reilly and threatening to kill Joseph O'Callaghan. Kenny also pleaded not guilty to possession of a firearm and ammunition with intent to endanger life.

Addressing the jury on the opening day of the trial, prosecuting counsel, Shane Murphy SC, said: "The key question for you to decide is who were the people who shot Jonathon O'Reilly. This was a calculated, cool and calm killing." He said it was the prosecution's case that "it was the accused" who carried out the crime.

State pathologist, Dr Marie Cassidy, gave evidence that O'Reilly died from two gunshot wounds to his trunk which inflicted seven wounds to the body. She said the second gun shot wound was most likely inflicted when O'Reilly was slumped over in an attempt to protect himself from his assailant.

Detective Garda Thomas Carey from the Ballistics section at Garda Headquarters told the jury that he had attended the post-mortem of the deceased and took possession of the discharged bullet, removed from the chest cavity by Dr Cassidy. Detective Carey said the bullet taken from the deceased's body was of lead construction. He then produced the "tiny" bullet to show it to the jury. "It has six land grooves which show it has been discharged through the barrel of a gun," the detective explained. The type of weapon used to fire such a bullet, he said, would generally be a revolver.

Eileen McLoughlin, a visitor at Cloverhill at the time of the shooting, said there was "chaos" immediately afterwards. "There were people running saying someone had been shot". Ms McLoughlin said she heard two loud bangs before she heard what she thought was a car screech off. When she walked up to the roadway she said she saw a green car, with two paramedics working on a man lying on the road.

Jonathan O'Reilly's friend, David Murray, told Shane Murphy's second on the case, Sean Guerin BL, that he was in the back seat of the car when O'Reilly was fatally shot. On the day of the incident, Murray and the deceased watched the Manchester United and Portsmouth match in Murray's home. He told the jury that sometime after the match ended, Robbie O'Hanlon rang Jonathan O'Reilly's mobile phone and asked the pair if they wanted to go to Liffey Valley shopping centre. Murray said Gordon Kelly was sitting in the back of the car with him while O'Reilly was in the passenger seat. On the way to the shopping centre, Murray said that O'Hanlon announced he was going to drop clothes off to his brother in Cloverhill Prison.

"Two blokes came on a motorbike. The motorbike stopped at the passenger side, right up at the door. A gun was produced by the man on the back of the motorbike... three shots were fired," Murray told the jury. "Jonathan dived towards the driver side, he said 'ah', when he was shot. I ducked when the shots were fired."

Under cross-examination from Kenny's defence barrister, John Phelan SC, Murray said he had not thought of the "parking arrangements" since the fatal incident. Phelan asked the witness did he not think it was "odd that Robbie O'Hanlon went to the wrong side of the road to park his car", leaving the murdered man sitting in the passenger seat exposed on the side of the road.

The defence barrister went on to ask Murray did he know of the incident involving O'Reilly that had taken place at the "Glue Pot" pub in 1997, in which a concrete block was dropped onto the head of a Patrick Hegarty.

Murray said he "didn't know the chap".

Phelan asked Murray did he know that two of the assailants in that assault – O'Reilly and Simon Doyle – had since been shot dead. A third [Paul Doyle] was shot and wounded and a fourth was driven off the road by another vehicle. The suggestion was that the murders were in revenge for the brutal assault and was therefore attempting to cast doubt on the guilt of the defendants. The defence barrister put it to Murray that O'Reilly was also convicted of drugs possession and that he was "a serious player in the drugs scene in West Dublin".

Murray disagreed with this contention saying: "No, he wasn't."

Under cross-examination from defence barrister, Brendan Nix SC, who appeared for Hinchon, Murray said he thought it "could be" a coincidence that nearly all those involved with the alleged assault on Patrick Hegarty in 1997 had since been the victims of violent assaults.

The second back seat passenger, Gordon Kelly, told Sean Guerin BL for the prosecution that earlier on the day of the murder he and O'Hanlon had visited a friend in Portlaoise Prison. When they returned home, Kelly drove O'Hanlon's BMW car to O'Hanlon's house in Arthur Griffith Park. The pair then left for Cloverhill Prison. Kelly said he had been sitting in the front seat of the two-door car but that he let O'Reilly take his seat when they picked him up.

"Jonathan screamed when the shots were fired," said Kelly of the actual shooting. "I was in shock for a few seconds before I got out of the car."

In response to John Phelan, Kelly admitted that he had

used a false name when visiting his friend earlier that day in Portlaoise Prison. He also admitted that he had been convicted of possession of drugs worth IR£10,000 (€12,700) and agreed with the defence barrister when he suggested that he had "no regard for the law".

Kenny's counsel suggested that Kelly "couldn't care less" if he knocked someone down when he was driving O'Hanlon's car from his house to Lucan on the day of the murder.

Kelly replied: "That's correct."

The convicted drug dealer claimed it was "definitely wrong" when the defence barrister suggested that the reason the car was parked on the wrong side of the road was that "you were effectively setting up Jonathan O'Reilly". John Phelan went on to suggest that the reason why O'Reilly was in the front passenger seat and the car was parked in such a manner was to "aid the assassin". "All these crocodile tears were a load of old codswallop," the senior counsel chided Kelly, to which he responded: "Whatever you think."

Robbie O'Hanlon, who was then in custody awaiting trial for a brutal assault on his ex-girlfriend, became extremely aggressive when he was accused, under cross-examination, of setting up the murder. In his direct evidence he told the court that when he came out of Cloverhill Prison, after dropping off clothes to his brother, he heard "glass breaking". He said the gunman was about two to three feet from the car. When he ran down to the car, he saw Jonathan O'Reilly "slumped over onto the driver's seat with his hand on the horn". Robbie O'Hanlon admitted that he had no insurance on the BMW car O'Reilly was shot in.

Mr Phelan then suggested to O'Hanlon that the logical place to have parked his car was on the left-hand side of Cloverhill Road, instead of parking it on the right and leaving O'Reilly exposed on the road.

O'Hanlon shouted at the defence barrister: "You're talking shit, get your facts right."

The defence barrister asked O'Hanlon "why or how the assassin knew precisely which car and what time you would be at Cloverhill Prison" to which he replied that he had "no idea whatsoever".

"You were the one who deliberately drove him there," Mr Phelan suggested.

"Watch your mouth," O'Hanlon threatened the counsel. He turned to the judge: "This fella is making accusations against me. He's also putting my life in danger." Then he turned back to Phelan: "Your putting ideas in people's heads, you're bleeding brain dead."

Phelan went on to suggest to O'Hanlon that it was strange that he ran towards his car when he heard gun shots, alleging that this had been purely for "show".

"You watch your mouth, I'm standing out of this box," he said, before leaving the witness box.

O'Hanlon later returned to the stand, after the trial judge interceded and asked him to resume his seat. In response to Hinchon's counsel, Brendan Nix, he agreed that, "there was word going around" that revenge was being sought against the four men, including the Doyles and O'Reilly for the serious assault in 1997. O'Hanlon was asked by Nix why he had not told Gardaí after the fatal shooting that the motorbike did a U-turn at Wheatfield Prison before stopping at the BMW car and firing at the deceased.

O'Hanlon responded: "Go fuck yourself, don't be pointing your bleeding finger at me."

The young thug complained to Mr Justice Peart that he didn't like the barrister's attitude.

When asked by Nix how he could afford to buy a Volkswagon Golf for €13,000 cash and a BMW coupe for €6,250 cash when he didn't work, O'Hanlon told him it was none of his business and then warned him: "Don't fucking raise your voice at me, you fucking thick ya."

Mr Nix went on to ask O'Hanlon how much money did he make, if the source of his income came from greyhounds.

The accomplice said he didn't want to answer any questions that might incriminate him.

The following day, June 15, was Joseph O'Callaghan's turn to testify. He was ushered into court, huddled in the middle of a group of officers from the Witness Protection Programme.

He sat hunched in the witness box. His mother sat at the back of the court, flanked by armed officers, to hear her son. The sense of tension in the packed court was palpable. Friends and associates of the two men were there to purposely intimidate the witnesses, especially Joey. Mandy Joyce and Brian Kenny stared at the nervous supergrass in a bid to put him off his stride. Joyce was never charged in connection with any aspect of the O'Reilly murder.

Over the next three days, Joey was bombarded with a succession of accusations by the two capable defence barristers. The accusations were intended to discredit him and put a doubt in the mind of the jury as to the veracity of his testimony. In his direct evidence Joey recounted everything that had happened on the day that Jonathan O'Reilly was murdered. He recalled in detail being asked to read the teletext carrying news of the shooting and being ordered to hide the murder weapon and then cut up and burn the helmets and leather gear worn by Kenny and Hinchon. He also told how his life had been threatened by the two murderers: "Brian Kenny told me he shot yer man, that he'd done it once and he'd no problem doing it again. He said he'd kill me if I opened my mouth. I didn't know what to do, I was afraid."

Joey the Lip was asked by prosecuting counsel how did he feel about the whole incident and replied: "I wanted to go home to my Ma."

Defence counsel, John Phelan, suggested that Joey the Lip had agreed to give evidence against Kenny and Hinchon in return for getting off the relatively minor charge of possessing heroin valued at €160.

O'Callaghan admitted that he had been arrested a year earlier for the offence while making a delivery for Kenny.

The senior counsel put it to Joey that he had been given "complete immunity" from prosecution and that the decision of the DPP was "unconditional and irrevocable". "You're free as a bird from these drug charges," Mr Phelan SC suggested. "You were facing serious charges, now suddenly you are giving evidence, pointing the guilt at my client. You are as safe as a house, you will not be prosecuted now or in the future."

The defence counsel went on to suggest that O'Callaghan was "facilitating the Gardaí in this trial". He claimed that there was not a shred of evidence to suggest his client, Kenny, was responsible for the murder, except for Joey's evidence. Phelan challenged the star witness: "You presented yourself as the picture of innocence, I have to suggest to you that you are a criminal."

O'Callaghan replied: "Not anymore, I'm changed. I've changed for good."

A week later, Joseph O' Callaghan was recalled to the witness box at the request of Kenny's defence counsel, John Phelan. He put it to Joey that when he was arrested for possession of €160 worth of heroin he told Gardaí that he had supplied heroin on previous occasions.

Joey agreed that that was correct.

The defence barrister went on to say to O'Callaghan that when his car was seized by Gardaí for not having insurance or tax, that he took off over the wall of his mother's house. Was this not a strange thing to do, Mr Phelan SC suggested.

"Not where I come from, you see the guards and you run," he replied.

Mr Phelan then suggested that Joey told Mandy Joyce that Gardaí had brought him in for questioning, after stopping him for having no tax or insurance.

"I've been brought in a few times for drug searches," he answered.

The defence barrister suggested that O'Callaghan had been giving information to a Detective Garda Maurice Cullen from the drug squad at Ladyswell graveyard and as a result of this a number of his friends were raided.

O'Callaghan denied the allegation.

"Until your car was seized by Gardaí you received lots of phone calls from this Garda", Mr Phelan suggested.

"I can't remember," O'Callaghan replied.

"Why would Mandy say that?" Mr Phelan asked him.

"She's lying," said O'Callaghan.

Phelan suggested to the supergrass that he was a self-confessed criminal and that he wouldn't know the truth if it jumped up and bit him. "You knew Garda Cullen and you were giving him information. You made this nonsense up, you concocted it up to save your own skin," Mr Phelan accused the State's witness.

"You don't accuse people of murder because your car is been taken, this is 2005, get real," Joey told the barrister. "Just because I don't have tax and insurance, that I would accuse someone of murder? Get a life."

Under cross-examination by Brendan Nix, O'Callaghan said it was sometime around 5.30pm on the day of the fatal shooting when he read the teletext about the shooting.

Mr Nix said Gardaí had conducted inquiries with the breaking news website run by Thomas Crosbie Media (TCM). A representative of the company, Mr Gill O'Sullivan, had told Gardaí that the TV3 text carried the story regarding the shooting at 6.56pm. "So, you're not telling the court the truth, you said the news item came up on the text at around 5.30pm," Nix suggested.

"It was definitely on one of them," O'Callaghan replied.

"You are telling me lies," Nix suggested to which Joey replied: "Ok."

O'Callaghan agreed that he was relieved when he hadn't received a summons from Gardaí regarding the drugs offence. He said he had "expected to be summoned". O'Callaghan was asked why it took him a month before he went to the Gardaí to tell them about the murder.

"Brian has friends in the guards. He used to threaten me with them. He said he'd get my ma set up with heroin. I was afraid that they'd get my family," he replied.

When his testimony concluded Joey was whisked off by his minders from the WPP.

Detective Garda Christopher O'Connor, a crime scene investigator, said that no finger or palm prints had been found on the outside of the BMW car. He also examined the .38 colt revolver and found no finger-prints on the gun. When the black plastic bag, which contained the revolver, was examined, it revealed the finger-print of Joseph O'Callaghan's right fore-finger. Under cross-examination Detective O'Connor said that neither of the accused's finger-prints had been identified.

Forensic scientist Claire Greaney told prosecuting counsel that small pieces of black leather, recovered by Gardaí at Kenny's house, were consistent with remnants of leather found at a fire in a field near St Margaret's, in North County Dublin.

Evidence of analysis of a selection of mobile phone numbers and their connectivity on the day of the fatal shooting was presented. An engineer had estimated the approximate locations of the particular phones when they made various mobile calls. One of the phone numbers was that of Thomas Hinchon. Between 13.50pm and 14.46pm on the day of the murder, his phone had received or made 16 phone calls. These phone calls were consistent with the radio base stations of Ballyowen, Palmerstown, Liffey Valley, the West Link, Fonthill and the Lucan Bypass areas. All these areas were consistent with the escape route taken by the killers.

Detective Garda Jim O'Sullivan of the National Bureau of Criminal Investigation told the court that he interviewed Thomas Hinchon at Clondalkin Garda Station. Throughout the course of interviews he said Hinchon "at all times denied all involvement in the murder of Jonathan O'Reilly".

Detective Sergeant Michael O'Leary of the NBCI told the court that on May 10, 2004, he interviewed Brian Kenny at Ronanstown Garda Station. When Gardaí put it to him that he was being questioned in relation to the murder of O'Reilly. Kenny told them: "I don't even know the chap". Kenny at first claimed that he had been looking after his son at the time of the murder. This proved to be a lie.

Kenny's former partner Rita Harley testified that she had a son with the accused man and had previously lived with him at Kilshane Cross between 1997 and 2001. On April 17, the day of the murder, she said Kenny was due to collect their seven-year-old son from her mother's house, to spend the day with him. He hadn't turned up.

Dr Muiris de Voit told the Central Criminal Court that on May 10, 2004, Joseph O'Callaghan had "swelling to the left side of the face" and was "tender on the inside of the right biceps". Both his legs were also grazed. The evidence was

offered to corroborate Joey's claims that he had been regularly
beaten by Kenny.

After 20 days of evidence, counsel for both sides began their
summing up of the case. The jury of ten men and two women
would then be sent out to consider their verdicts. Neither Kenny
nor Hinchon had taken the stand during the trial.

For the prosecution Shane Murphy asked the jury to bear in
mind how O' Callaghan had given his evidence, his demeanour
and the way he had conducted himself in the witness box.
Murphy told the jury to ask themselves was what O'Callaghan
said true and, if it was true, did it satisfy them beyond reasonable
doubt that Hinchon and Kenny were responsible for murder.
The prosecutor said Joey the Lip "freely admitted his criminal
past and admitted difficulties in the past." He said O'Callaghan's
evidence was of central importance in the case: "I suggest to you
that there is a clear and compelling picture that those guilty of
the charges on the indictment are the accused.". "I invite you to
consider that the prosecution's case demonstrates proof beyond
reasonable doubt of the guilt of the accused."

In his summing up Kenny's counsel, John Phelan, asked
the jury why Joseph O'Callaghan had never received a
summons for being caught with €160 worth of heroin. "Why
in these circumstances was Mr O'Callaghan not prosecuted?"
Mr Phelan asked the jury. "We questioned Gardaí about this
and they said they couldn't question the DPP's decision."
Effectively, Mr Phelan told the jury, O'Callaghan was given
"total immunity" by the DPP. "Why would such a man be
given such a guarantee?" Phelan answered his own question.
"He became a snitch, a supergrass."

Phelan then read a legal article entitled 'The Emergence
of the supergrass' to the jury. It warned that the danger from a
man who is "caught out" is that '"he purchases immunity by
falsely accusing others"'. Phelan commented: "We know Mr
O'Callaghan was couriering drugs for other parties, we know he
got caught and we know he went to the police station." He said
it "concerned" him that a situation had arisen where immunity
was given with no reason. "It is our business and it's very, very
scary," he added. "Other than his word, there is not a shred

of evidence on my client. This is a very disturbing case. This gentleman [Kenny] was set up like a lamb to slaughter but it's the details that let Mr O'Callaghan down."

Like his colleague before him, Thomas Hinchon's defence barrister, Brendan Nix, also made much of O'Callaghan's arrest for heroin possession. He suggested to the jury that O'Callaghan was given immunity from prosecution for possession of drugs from the Director of Public Prosecutions (DPP). He asked the jury why Joey was not prosecuted when he had admitted he was a regular dealer.

"Heroin is the plague of our society and long it will continue when O'Callaghan, who is a self confessed dealer, goes un-prosecuted," he said to the jury. "Joseph O'Callaghan is a bought man, a bought and paid for man. And what consideration has he been given? His immunity from prosecution, a free pass; pass by jail and do not go in. He's an aider and abetter and he's a bought man.

My client repeatedly said he didn't do it," he said, adding that no motive had been offered for the murder. "Do you believe that it was a total coincidence that this car was parked with the passenger side by the road?" he asked. "There are more questions asked by this case than there are answered. I have to suggest to you that it would be perverse to convict the accused."

The counsel also reminded the jury of the scandal of police corruption in Donegal, in which attempts were made to frame members of the McBrearty family for a murder that was never commited. The analogy didn't impress the jury.

On July 5, after deliberating for three days, the jury found Kenny and Hinchon guilty of all charges. Mr Justice Peart sentenced the two hit men to life for the murder of Jonathan O'Reilly. Kenny was also sentenced to three years and Hinchon to eighteen months for threatening to kill Joey. Kenny was also sentenced to three years for possessing the shotgun and the ammunition. It was a major victory against the crime gangs.

Afterwards, as Kenny and Hinchon were led away in handcuffs to a prison van, Detective Inspector O'Loughlin told reporters: "The guilty verdicts send out a message to people who are involved in crime that they are not immune to prosecution and investigation, and ultimately their crimes will end up before the courts. We are extremely pleased, it was a very difficult investigation and we are pleased that it has come to a successful conclusion."

The successful conclusion to the trial was a vindication of sorts for Joseph O'Callaghan. But it had been a harrowing experience for which he had paid dearly. "During the trial I was in the witness box for two or three days and I was given a really hard time but I was fine. You cannot make a mistake when you are telling the truth. Hinchon and Kenny's people came into court and did their best to intimidate me. They had associates in court who were there to intimidate me and make me change my mind."

When I met Joey four years later he did not regret helping to bring the murderers of Jonathan O'Reilly to justice, even though he practically paid for it with his own life. During his lowest moments, when gripped by depression and remorse, a simple letter of thanks from the murdered man's family provided some solace.

"I am happy I gave the O'Reilly family some closure. The men who murdered their son are in prison for what they did. After the trial the O'Reilly family wrote me a lovely letter in which they thanked me for testifying. They said it meant a lot to them that Kenny and Hinchon had been convicted. They said they recognised how much I had sacrificed to go to court. They sent me a key-ring with a picture of Jonathan on it to remember him by and the letter was signed by all the family. It meant a lot to me and I kept them. When I start feeling down about my situation in life I take out the letter and read it. It reminds me that what I have done wasn't a total waste. The O'Reillys were good people. It wasn't their fault that Jonathan turned out the way he did."

For the remainder of the young drug gang the life, and death, struggle continued. Robbie O'Hanlon was shot dead as a result of another drug feud. It was almost three years to the day that he had helped set Jonathan O'Reilly up for murder. He had been playing a soccer match near Liffey Valley for his team

Landen United on the evening of March 15, 2007. O'Hanlon was changing on the sideline when a masked gunman emerged from hiding in nearby trees. He shot him three times in the head and chest. The young, violent drug dealer died at the scene. He was 25 years old. He became the third gangland murder victim in the Clondalkin area since the beginning of that year.

Garda intelligence sources believed that O'Hanlon was murdered by a criminal associate who owed him around €80,000 for drugs and was afraid he would be killed. He had decided to kill before he himself was killed. O'Hanlon's reputation for violence was possibly the reason for his own brutal end.

One of the suspects behind O'Hanlon's murder was Richie McCormack who, a few years earlier, had run with him in the Doyle gang. The 29-year-old was the fifth member of the original gang to perish. He was shot dead outside his brother's house in Ronanstown in March 2008. The killing fell a week before the first anniversary of O'Hanlon's death. It was the fifth gangland slaying in 2008. Forty-eight hours earlier another former gang associate, suspected hit man and drug dealer, 29-year-old John Berney, was shot dead in the bedroom of his home in Newcastle, County Dublin.

Paul Doyle served his sentence and was released from prison. The Doyle gang has long since been replaced with another mob of ruthless young men.

With the trial out of the way, Joseph O'Callaghan had to face the reality of the rest of his life as a marked man. He was not a happy man. He was particularly upset by his treatment in the Witness Protection Programme. During the actual trial he had been living in an apartment in Carlow town. At night, he claimed he had been left on his own by the WPP officers: "One night a detective told me that when he left to make sure and keep the door locked. He said I should put a wardrobe in front of the door just to be sure. I couldn't believe it."

What was to emerge was that Joey the Lip had found himself caught in the cross-fire of an ongoing factional feud between two groups of officers involved in the Witness Protection Programme. O'Callaghan was being manipulated by one side, who for unexplained reasons, tried to discredit and cause trouble for the other. In the meantime Joey's mental health began to suffer. "After the trial the pressure began to build up on me because of the situation I was in. I felt that people were messing with my head and my mental health was beginning to deteriorate. I felt I was being treated very badly. I could not believe what was going on and my Ma was also very upset. Then one night I decided I could not tolerate any more and I took an overdose of about 40 tablets. When I woke up there were four of the WPP guards standing around the hospital bed. One of them had saved my life."

The Gardaí and the Department of Justice paid to have Joey resettled abroad, where he was given a new identity. Despite his protests, O'Callaghan eventually agreed to leave the country. Since his departure, he had gone back to school and qualified for a job as a care assistant. Arrangements were made that he would return to Ireland for weekends to visit his family and baby daughter. While the trial was still pending, Joey and his Garda minders had attended the Family Courts where he was granted visiting rights to his child. Detectives testified that they would ensure there would be no risk to either Joey or his child during those visits and that they guaranteed his protection. However, Joey claimed he was left on his own with his daughter in a pokey flat during the weekend visits. He made a complaint about his treatment and made allegations against certain detectives.

A major investigation into the operation of the WPP and Joey's treatment was ordered by the then Garda Commissioner, Noel Conroy. It soon became clear that the young informant had been sucked into a bitter internal feud between officers attached to the Special Branch and the WPP. O'Callaghan also made serious allegations against a detective who he claimed had a corrupt relationship with Brian Kenny. An internal investigation later completely cleared the officer of any wrong-doing. The allegations were unfounded, all of his dealings with Kenny had been above board and recorded. Changes were also implemented in the way the WPP was operated.

At the same time, Joseph O'Callaghan indicated his wish to leave the programme and his legal team negotiated a substantial financial severance package with the Department of Justice. The money was intended to help O'Callaghan set up a new life for himself. In January 2007, he officially signed himself out. Joey kept his new identity and continues to live abroad to this day. He met a new partner and the couple had a child together. But Joey hates the lie he has been forced to live.

Even in sleep O'Callaghan is denied refuge from his living hell. The sleeping pills and anti-depressants do little to ward off the demons in his head. "My life was bad enough before the O'Reilly murder in 2004 but ever since then it has been a living hell. I got a life sentence for telling what I knew about that murder. Sometimes I think that I would probably have been better off if Kenny and Hinchon had murdered me.

"I live a lie everyday. I live with a new family and I cannot tell anyone apart from those closest to me about who I really am or what I was or what I have done. My family don't come to see me and because I have no protection I cannot go home to visit them any more. I will probably never see my little daughter again. Every day that I wake up I have to look out the door to see if the coast is clear. I have to lock the doors and check them at least three times every night before I go to bed. I always carry my passport in case I am recognised somewhere so that I can get out quick.

"I don't drink very much and never touch drugs because I have to be in control all the time and not let my guard down. People who read about the case probably thought that I was some kind of big-time criminal, who was living a life of luxury in the Witness Protection Programme.

"If only they knew the fucking truth."

Four

THE GODFATHER

Martin 'Marlo' Hyland was never destined to die peacefully in his sleep. Like the many godfathers who had perished before him, sudden death – of the violent type – was an inevitable occupational hazard. His every waking hour was spent trying to survive in the volatile and unpredictable gangland jungle where he was king. Marlo Hyland relied on his street cunning and instincts to avoid the most feared predators in his dangerous world – the hit man and the cop. But his reign as Ireland's Public Enemy Number One came to an end in the last place he would have expected – asleep in his bed.

The godfather heard nothing when one of his trusted lieutenants tip-toed quickly into his bedroom. As he lay on his stomach, Marlo would never know that his once close confidant had become his executioner. He wasn't awoken by the deafening explosion from his associate's powerful .45 semi automatic pistol. In that instant two slugs punched holes in the side of Marlo's head, behind his ear. Then he fired another four rounds into his boss's back to ensure he was dead. If Marlo's merciless executioner was working from an instruction manual, then this assassination was done by the book.

The murder of Marlo Hyland was as cold-blooded and callous as any professional hit could be. It was one of the most high-profile gangland slayings since the murder of Martin 'The General' Cahill twelve years earlier in 1994. When a major criminal figure is taken out it is always big news. At the beginning of the new century Marlo Hyland had emerged as the undisputed godfather of organised crime in Ireland. The Gardaí had acknowledged his status by officially classifying him, and his organisation, as their prime target. In the end, however, it was the hit man who ended Marlo's career.

The murder of a gang boss, although shocking, would not arouse much sympathy from a public growing increasingly weary of the ongoing bloodshed in the underworld. But it was what the killer did next that caused a palpable sense of anger, outrage and fear – and marked this crime as one of the worst in recent history.

A young trainee plumber called Anthony Campbell was fixing a leaking radiator when the killer and his accomplice arrived at the house where Hyland was staying. While the hit man went upstairs to kill Hyland, the terrified young football fan was held hostage, possibly at gun point, in the front room. No one will ever know the sense of dread Anthony Campbell must have felt when he heard the explosions of the gun in the bedroom above his head. When the hit man returned, he made a split second decision to protect his own identity. It later emerged that one of the killers was from the inner city where Anthony also lived and it is likely that the young plumber recognised him.

To the callous gunman, described by those who know him as "a creature devoid of all human feeling", the apprentice was simply in the wrong place at the wrong time. In his warped logic Anthony had to die. Examination of his body later revealed that the trainee plumber instinctively put his arm up to protect himself when the deadly handgun was pointed with murderous intent for a second time that fateful December morning. The single bullet ripped through Anthony's arm and hit him in the head. He slumped to the ground and died instantly. Marlo's ruthless lieutenants fled to a waiting getaway car and disappeared behind the wall Hyland had helped construct – the Wall of Silence.

* * * *

The story of the life and death of Martin Hyland could have come from the pages of a gangster movie script or even a Shakespearean tragedy. His story is a paradigm of the stereotypical godfather. A young hood starts off in life as a petty crook and makes it to the place where every aspiring criminal wants to be – at the top of the heap. He was the main man with the respect of his peers and it took him less than ten years to get there. In the modern underworld, however, staying there can be extremely precarious. Hyland's once powerful criminal empire imploded and for that he paid with his life.

During his reign Marlo had ushered in a new approach to organised crime. He forged contacts with several gangs around the country, including senior members of Sinn Féin/IRA and the INLA, in a bid to create one big nationwide crime corporation. It was a plan worthy of the Sicilian or American Mafia of old. In such a world there would be an "understanding" between the various mobs to pool resources – cash for drugs and hit men to deal with problems – for the profit of all. In Marlo's new gangland order everyone, as they say in Sicily, could "draw from the well". Territory would be agreed by mutual consent and negotiation. But Hyland just didn't have the same touch as the celluloid Godfather Don Corleone.

Martin Oliver Hyland was the fifth of seven children – four boys and three girls – born to William and Ellen Hyland who lived in Attracta Road in Cabra, West Dublin. On the day of his birth, September 1, 1969, organised crime was a world away – synonymous with the US Mafia and Hollywood films. In Ireland, criminal activity was limited to the odd burglary or safe cracking job. Armed robberies and other crimes of violence were practically non-existent. This was illustrated on the front page of the *Irish Times* of the same day which devoted space to a story about the burglary of £70 from the till of a city centre pub. The lead story covered the growing civil rights unrest in Northern Ireland which in a short time would explode into war. The net effect of the Troubles was that a tsunami of serious criminal activity hit the south and changed Ireland forever. The year of Marlo's birth was to be the last in an age of innocence. His birth coincided with the arrival of organised crime.

The Hylands were described by their neighbours as "good, decent people" although the young Marlo was considered "a bit wild". Cabra was one of the sprawling housing projects built in the 1950s to clear the inner-city slums. The Government policy, while well-intentioned, created sterile, dreary housing estates devoid of social life and a sense of community. Inevitably these working class areas – which had few support facilities and were crippled with high unemployment in the 1970s and 1980s – created their own social problems and became breeding grounds for crime. It is what criminologists refer to as "criminogenic environments". For kids like the young Marlo it was easy to be sucked into a life on the wrong side of the tracks.

In 1985, the Hyland family's happiness was shattered by the murder of one of their children. Marlo had just turned eighteen when his sister Julie was strangled to death by her husband in December. The barbaric murder devastated Marlo and his loved ones. It had a profound affect on the young criminal and was seen as a turning point in his life. Julie Hyland was married to builder's labourer Michael Brady and the couple had two daughters, Elaine aged five and Karen who was 18 months old. Born in Canada, Brady was abandoned by his mother as a child and left to be reared by his grandparents in Ringsend in Dublin. In his teens he had made contact with his mother but when they finally met she had spent just five minutes in his company. He was said to have been deeply hurt by the rejection. As a result he harboured a deep mistrust and anger against women. He took out his pent up emotions on his attractive young wife.

On the night of Julie Hyland's twenty-first birthday, when she was pregnant with their first child, Brady gave her a severe beating. He was described as physically very big and a strong man. The violence became a regular feature of her life, especially when Brady was drunk. As a result of the beatings Julie was forced to move back to her family in Cabra with her children for a period of four months. She returned to live with him at their home in Ronanstown, West Dublin after he promised never to drink again.

A few years later, on December 20, 1985, Brady went on a drinking binge with his work mates to celebrate the Christmas holidays. When he arrived home that night Julie was still polishing furniture and making preparations for Christmas, as their children slept upstairs. Brady gave his wife a savage beating and raped her in the sitting room downstairs. Then, in his mindless, drunken fury, he strangled his wife and went to bed. The next morning, five-year-old Elaine found her mother lying face down on a blood-spattered cushion in the front room. Her mother was naked from the waist down. The terrified tot went upstairs to wake her father.

Years earlier, Julie Hyland had told her mother that she intended growing her fingernails long so that if she was ever attacked, her assailant would be identified by the marks on his body. The first thing Gardaí noticed when they arrived in the house that morning was the deep scratches on Brady's neck and face. He claimed he got the marks when a concrete block had fallen on him at work. But it didn't take detectives long to work out the truth. Brady's blood and skin were found under his wife's fingernails. Her clothes had obviously been torn off her in the attack and there was evidence that she'd had sexual intercourse. The young mother, who was advised against having any other children due to an illness, was always careful to have protected sex. This too snared Brady. Julie Hyland's injuries were so severe – they included a broken bone protruding from her neck – that her heart-broken mother was unable to view her body in the morgue. Brady later admitted to his crime and was charged with murder. In July 1987, he pleaded guilty to the manslaughter of his wife and was jailed for ten years. The couple's two children were taken into the care of their grandparents who reared them as their own.

The Hylands were a close-knit family and they were distraught over the murder. Julie Hyland's daughters later disowned their father. In 1991, they visited him in prison for the last time and had no further contact with him after that. Marlo was particularly traumatised by the murder and vowed to avenge his sister's death, no matter how long it took. He developed a close bond with his two young nieces. They later described him as more of a cross between a protective big brother and a doting father, than an uncle. Marlo was also protective of his parents and siblings. Family members later revealed that he was the "man of the house". His oldest brother was ill and his father was an alcoholic. He was very close to his mother Ellie and he called to see her every day. Neighbours described how Hyland was "driven mad" by his sister's murder and fell in with the "wrong crowd". Another neighbour recalled him as: "A bit troublesome but a lovable rogue-type young fella." It was during this period of his life that he began getting in trouble with the law and he earned a reputation as a hard man in the area. To Gardaí and other locals, however, Marlo had always been more than just troublesome.

Officially his criminal career began in 1986, six months after his sister's murder, when three relatively minor offences, relating to being drunk and disorderly and receiving stolen goods, were recorded against him. In each case he received small fines and was given the Probation of Offenders Act. In the Irish criminal justice system, the probation act is intended as a reprimand – a chance for the first-time offender to see the error of his ways. Unfortunately it never worked that way for the likes of Martin Hyland. He steadily got involved in more serious crime and was soon involved in burglary, car theft and robbery.

While most of his family worked for a living, Marlo and his pals terrorised their neighbourhood. They snatched cash from insurance agents and rent collectors on their rounds in Cabra. They also robbed trains and trucks as they travelled through the area. Hyland was a so-called joy rider and was also considered a good handler of a motorbike. He used his "skill" during armed hold-ups in building societies and banks around the city. Although he never actually passed a driving test, Hyland was banned from driving several times. He ignored this and continued to drive. He was caught so many times that he was eventually banned for life.

A former friend described Marlo: "He was a great character as far as I was concerned, a real rebel who was up for anything. Martin was a good talker and very charming. He was always in control of things. I suppose he got that from when he was growing up. He was very mouthy sometimes and didn't know when to keep his trap shut."

In 1987, at 18 years old, Hyland received three jail sentences. They ranged from three months to two years, for conspiracy to commit robbery, burglary, malicious damage and dangerous driving. A year later he was again jailed for another eight months for larceny, malicious damage and car theft. He became a father for the first time while in prison when his partner, Sharon Maguire from Finglas, gave birth to a son. The couple, who later split, had two more children together – a daughter and another son.

On his release from prison in the early 1990s, Marlo began dabbling in the drug trade with a gang of local young hoods who regarded him as their leader. A number of these men remained steadfastly loyal to Hyland throughout his career and were prepared to do anything he asked. One local detective recalled: "Three or four of them adored Marlo. If he asked one of them to get up on a roof and watch a place for two days in the freezing weather they would do it for him. They were caught doing crimes for Marlo and were prepared to do time for him in prison. These guys were with him up to the end."

Initially Marlo bought his supplies of cannabis from 42-year-old Noel Mullen, a former associate of the General. Mullen was also a close associate of John 'The Coach' Traynor, John Gilligan's partner in their new drug venture. Mullen was a distributor for the Gilligan gang in the west and north-west of the capital. At first Marlo's mob dealt mainly in hashish but eventually moved on to heroin, ecstasy and cocaine. The money to buy the drugs came from armed robberies.

Hyland's relationship with the police was never exactly cordial – he despised most of them. He was regularly stopped and searched by Gardaí who recognised that he was becoming a dangerous criminal. He was often arrested for questioning about heists. As a result he embarked on a campaign of intimidation against them. In one incident in May 1995 the local authority impounded a number of horses. They were owned by Hyland and his friend Robert Hosey and were roaming wild on council property. Hyland and his pals shared a passion for horses which they entered in sulky races around the country. In Ireland the "sport" has been particularly popular among criminals and travellers for decades. The race meetings – usually held on public roads without any permission and posing a serious danger to motorists – double as a means for villains to network.

Noel Mullen convinced the young gangster that if he and his gang gave the Gardaí enough hassle then they would leave them and their horses alone. He advised Marlo to take the same action as the General – bring the fight to the cops and the authorities. He suggested slashing the tyres of cars parked in several middle-class estates in the area and outside a number of well-known pubs near the Phoenix Park, every time cops stopped or arrested a member of the mob. This was a tactic adopted by Cahill for a number of years leading up to his dramatic gangland exit and Mullen had co-ordinated many of the General's slashing offensives. Marlo also plotted to burn the truck used by the Local Authority to transport his horses as an act of revenge, but he later dropped the idea.

On the night of April 26, he sent a teenager to slash the tyres on all the cars parked at the Garda station. He managed to puncture the tyres on a squad car before he was spotted and forced to take flight. A week later Hyland and three associates were stopped by two local officers who had regularly crossed swords with the gangsters. Marlo became very aggressive and shouted at them: "You leave us alone and we'll leave you alone, you keep hassling us and we'll start hassling you."

Hyland liked the idea of intimidating individual police officers based at Cabra station. The following day, on Hyland's instructions, a female officer attached to Cabra was followed to her home by two young girls on bicycles. The following morning the officer spotted a member of the gang watching her apartment as she left for work. Two days later Hyland and another associate, Mark Dunne, parked outside the station watching officers changing shift and noting down the registrations of their cars. Other officers also noticed that they were being followed home and it caused a major security alert. The private car of one of the Gardaí targeted by Marlo was then burned outside his home.

On May 15, 1995 a large force of detectives and uniformed Gardaí raided the homes of Hyland and his associates. They also searched other properties the gang had access to. In the operation they seized a large quantity of hashish, a firearm and a stolen motorbike which was being held by Hyland.

Two weeks later, an officer Marlo blamed for the heat was followed to his home by a member of the gang. Once they had identified the Garda's house, Marlo planned to burn it down. An informant within the gang, who was giving information on the plot to the police, convinced the upcoming godfather not to go ahead with the attack. He said that it would attract too much attention from the police and Marlo dropped the idea. At the same time the Gardaí stepped up the pressure on Marlo and his pals to convince them that it would be wiser to back down. After a while the tense stand off calmed down. Hyland didn't have the stomach for such a fight. Despite his contempt for many officers, Marlo was always courteous to older, more experienced detectives in the area. He viewed these officers as "straight players" who should not be messed with. "He was nice to a few of the cops and always addressed them as 'Mister' when talking to them. Marlo reckoned that these lads were very clever and would be well able to do more damage to him than the younger ones," explained one former associate.

* * * *

Hyland's move into the big league can be traced back to his association with Finglas drug trafficker Peter Joseph 'the Psycho' Judge who he met through the drug trade. To the casual observer Judge was an unremarkable, average-looking man, with good taste in clothes. But behind the façade lurked a chilling, cold-blooded monster whose name was synonymous with terror. He controlled his large drug patch through fear and violence. Born in 1955, he had displayed a tendency to extreme violence from the age of ten. When he was 14 a group of kids from another estate convinced him to dye his hair. Afterwards his new hair colour caused other kids to make fun of him. He didn't like being mocked. In an act of revenge Judge broke into a gunsmiths and stole a shotgun and cartridges. He then used the gun to shoot up the home of one of the kids who had

convinced him to change his hair colour. For that he received
two years in an Industrial School for young offenders. When
he came out, Judge was even more dangerous and notched up
convictions for two armed robberies, including one where he
shot a postmaster and attempted to shoot an unarmed cop.

A retired detective who knew Judge for most of his life
gave a less than sanguine description of him: "I have known
practically every major criminal in Dublin for over 30 years
and I never met one like Judge. There was a behavioural kink
in the bastard. He was the worst, most evil fucker I ever came
across. When it came to violence he led the way for the likes of
the Westies and the others who came after him in the late 90's.
He loved inflicting pain on people and he certainly lived up to
his nickname. He was bisexual and he used to beat up both his
male and female lovers."

When Judge was released from prison in 1989, he got
involved in the drug trade. In 1993, he executed an associate,
Michael Godfrey, in a field near Finglas because of a drug
deal that had gone wrong. He also shot another drug rival and
tortured others. As a result he earned the sobriquet, the Psycho.
He was one of the biggest drug traffickers in the city by the time
Marlo Hyland became a business partner in his drug trade.
Judge began dating Marlo's sister Ellen Hyland. Despite the fact
he regularly beat his lovers, both male and female, there was no
evidence that he subjected Ellen to violence. Marlo learned a lot
from his sinister mentor and made many contacts who would
be valuable to him in the future. Judge was extremely security
conscious and was adept at counter-surveillance techniques.
He knew exactly how to give police the slip. He also remained
hands off in relation to the drug shipments he controlled and
used lackies to do the dirty work for him. As he built his own
criminal empire Hyland would use the same methods to protect
himself.

Although he had a reputation as a hard man, Hyland was
not a particularly violent criminal at the time. He believed in
buying the loyalty of his henchmen and ingratiating himself
with other big players. As recalled by one former associate:
"Marlo was all mouth and not prone to violence like some

of the other lunatics around the place. He looked after people well with money and did favours for them." In the early stages, his association with the Psycho was often enough to win him respect.

Gardaí first officially confirmed the links between Hyland and the Psycho in March 1996. On the afternoon of March 11, Judge's car was seen parked outside Hyland's home on St Attracta Road. Cars belonging to eight other suspected criminals and an individual associated with the Provisional IRA were also parked outside. To the police this was a significant development and one to be watched. It was obvious that a meeting was taking place. The reason for the conference was the gruesome murder 13 days earlier of a small-time villain and drug courier called William 'Jock' Corbally.

Corbally had grown up across the road from Judge in Finglas. The two men had once been friends and were involved in crime together. Jock was a charming, popular and handsome man. He was described by those who knew him as a lovable rogue, always on the look out for a handy buck. Judge's suppressed sense of inadequacy made him intensely jealous and resentful of his neighbour. The situation really deteriorated when Corbally gave the unhinged psychopath a beating for using Jock's two young sons to sell drugs. The Psycho had lost face and therefore Corbally had signed his own death warrant.

In January 1996, Judge got the opportunity he had been waiting for when Jock smuggled a kilo of heroin from Holland. It was on behalf of another drug dealer from Coolock called Declan 'Decie' Griffin. Judge had also invested in the shipment. When Corbally returned he decided to pull a stroke with the heroin. Jock had been a low level police informant for some time and he decided to let the Gardaí 'seize' the shipment – but only after he had taken a quarter of the kilo to sell for himself. But he never reckoned on the media reports about the police seizing three quarters of a kilo. The value of the kilo on the streets was around IR£1 million (€1.27 million). Judge and his cronies had lost a lot of cash. The reports of the seizure convinced the Psycho that Corbally had ripped them off.

On the night of February 28, Judge, Griffin and a number of

other gang members organised the abduction of Jock Corbally. He was brought to a field near Baldonnel where Judge took pleasure in torturing his old foe. Griffin would later tell his own Garda handlers-he was also an informant-that Judge went beserk and purposely smashed in Jock's pearly white teeth with an iron bar. For Judge this was a delightful bonus. Corbally's teeth were a symbol of his handsome looks. The Psycho began stabbing his victim until he no longer reacted to the appalling torture. Judge dumped Corbally's body in the boot of a car and drove off on his own. He buried his former neighbour in an unmarked grave that was never located. No one ever knew if Corbally was actually fully dead when he was dumped in a hole in the corner of a country field. Twelve years later criminals still talk about Jock's awful end.

Word of the drug courier's gruesome demise spread like wild fire on the streets of Finglas and his family began a heart-wrenching search for his body. Mark Dwyer, one of the men who witnessed the murder, had openly bragged about what they had done to the hapless small time villain. Gardaí soon got wind of what had happened to Jock. Decie Griffin and another gang member, Martin Dunne from Finglas, had already filled the police in on what they had witnessed that night. The Deputy Commissioner of the day, Noel Conroy, had extensive knowledge of both Jock Corbally and PJ Judge from his time as a detective based in Finglas. Conroy knew how dangerous Judge had become and he decided that the Psycho had to be stopped. A major investigation was put in place to target Judge and several of his associates, including Marlo Hyland. At the same time detectives investigating the murder of Michael Godfrey were also making some inroads in the case. Although Hyland had not participated in the Corbally murder, officers were aware that he had full knowledge of what had happened. According to intelligence sources interviewed for this book, Hyland secretly passed on information to a particular detective about the crime. He also "helped" with information about other criminal activities. This was the only time that Marlo acted as a double agent according to those sources.

Over the following months, the pressure was heaped on

Judge and his mob. Everywhere they went gang members were stopped and searched. By then Marlo had adopted a calmer attitude while being "hassled" by the police.

"We often stopped Marlo while in the car with Judge. Hyland would sit back and sneer at us but he didn't make threats like he used to. Judge had taught him that," explained a member of the Corbally investigation team. The pressure was stepped up somewhat in the beginning of May 1996 when the *Sunday World* ran a special four-page investigation on Judge and the murder. The newspaper revealed in detail how he organised and controlled his drug empire. This information had been compiled from interviews with sources close to the case, on both side of the law and order divide. When he read the newspaper Judge went beserk and called a meeting with his henchmen. It was held in Marlo's house. At that meeting the paranoid and extremely dangerous godfather began an internal witch hunt to find out who had been talking. Marlo, who was in the Psycho's inner circle, began making "enquiries" on his behalf. While the newspaper continued its campaign to solve Jock Corbally's murder, Judge plotted to have this writer abducted, tortured and murdered. It was later revealed that Marlo Hyland had agreed to assist in the logistics of that operation.

On June 26, 1996, the gang got a brief reprieve of sorts when journalist Veronica Guerin was shot dead on the orders of John Gilligan. The awful crime, coming a month after the Sinn Féin/IRA murder of Detective Garda Jerry McCabe in Limerick, initially soaked up considerable police resources. It was to spark the single biggest offensive ever seen against organised crime in almost three decades. During the murder investigation the team discovered a strong link between Hyland and veteran armed robber and hit man Patrick 'Dutchy' Holland who had shot the journalist. On the day of the murder there had been mobile telephone traffic between them. Hyland also helped Holland when he made a run for it to the UK. As a result of the public outrage over the murder new legislation was passed which established the Criminal Assets Bureau to target the ill gotten gains of organised crime. This was bad news for Judge, Hyland and every other drug dealer in the country. Over the following months, the CAB seized over IR£100,000 (€127,000) of the gang's cash from couriers. A few months earlier, Judge's associates could have had the money returned to them simply by applying to a District Court under an ancient law called a Police Property application. But all that had changed.

In the same month, Michael Brady, Marlo's murderous brother-in-law, was released from prison and went back to work as a labourer on building sites in Dublin. He had no contact with his children or his wife's family. According to Brady's friends and work mates he had emerged from prison a changed man. He was described as a "gentle giant" who worked hard and had given up alcohol for good. When Marlo learned of his brother in law's release he decided to finally avenge his sister's murder. He wanted Brady dead and now had the clout to organise a professional hit. PJ Judge was happy to help.

Over the next few weeks Marlo and his associates began monitoring Brady's movements. His brother-in-law was living in an apartment off Sarsfield Quay in the north inner city, beside the River Liffey. At night he parked his car in a secured underground car park at a nearby apartment block, Clifden Court.

On the evening of Thursday, September 5, Brady returned home after playing a soccer match in Ringsend. Around 9.30pm, he pulled up at the electronic gates to the car park. As he was waiting for them to open, a motorbike drew up alongside. The pillion passenger got off and ran over to the driver's door. The hit man fired four shots hitting Brady in the head and chest. He died instantly and became the thirteenth gangland murder victim in two years.

The following morning's newspapers carried front page pictures of Brady's lifeless body, still sitting behind the wheel of his car. His mouth was open and his head leaned back on the head rest. The powerful and shocking image became an icon of Ireland's growing problem with gun crime. The following day Ellie Hyland told the *Irish Independent* newspaper that her family, including his two daughters, were not sorry to see Brady dead. "I'm not going behind the door, I'm open. I'm not sorry he's dead. I'll never forget that day [Julie's murder] ...inside

Gardaí at the scene at the Grand Canal at Kearneystown, County Kildare, where the bodies of Patrick Murray and Darren Carey were discovered in January 2000.
© *Photocall Ireland*

Darren Carey, who was last seen alive on December 29, 1999.

Patrick Murray, who was last seen alive on December 28, 1999.

Mark Desmond, the criminal known as the Guinea Pig, being brought to court in Dublin, where he was originally charged with the Grand Canal murders.
© *Collins Photo Agency*

Detective Sergeant Gabriel O'Gara (now Superintendent), one of the principal officers involved in the Canal Butcher investigation whose life was threatened by Mark Desmond.
© *Collins Photo Agency*

Assistant Commissioner Tony Hickey, the officer with overall responsibility for the Canal Butcher case.
© *Liam O'Connor/Sunday World*

Noeleen Carey and Kathleen Murray pictured outside the Central Criminal Court in Dublin after the trial of Mark Desmond, in December 2002.
© Ronan Quinlan/*Collins Photo Agency*

Detective Inspector Padraig
Kennedy, who investigated
the Canal Butcher case.
© *Sunday World*

Members of the Garda team involved in the investigation of the
Jonathan O'Reilly murder. (*Left*) Det Sgt Michael 'Shakey' Doyle
and Det Sgt Ian McLoughlin. (*Right*) Det Supt Hubert Collins,
Det Sgt Colm Church and Det Insp (*Retd*) Todd O'Loughlin.
© *Padraig O'Reilly*

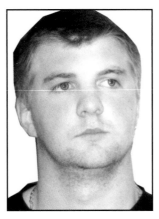

Murder victim Jonathan
O'Reilly, who was shot dead
outside Cloverhill Prison.
© *Sunday World*

Ballyfermot drug dealer,
Derek 'Dee Dee' O'Driscoll.

Amanda Joyce, the wife of
drug dealer Brian Kenny,
leaving the Central Criminal
Court during the Jonathan
O'Reilly murder trial.
© *Padraig O'Reilly*

Assistant Commissioner (*Retd*) Martin Donnellan, who had over-all responsibility for the Jonathan O'Reilly investigation and Detective Inspector Todd O'Loughlin who cracked the case.
© *Padraig O'Reilly*

Drug dealer Brian Kenny, who was convicted of the O'Reilly murder.
© *Padraig O'Reilly*

Drug dealer Thomas Hinchon, who
was convicted of the Jonathan
O'Reilly murder.
© *Padraig O'Reilly*

Murdered Doyle gang
member Richie McCormack.
© *Sunday World*

Clondalkin drug dealer Paul Doyle,
head of the notorious Doyle Gang.
© *Sunday World*

Gardaí at the scene of Jonathan O'Reilly's murder at Cloverhill
Prison, Dublin, on April 17, 2004.
© *Val Sheehan/Sunday World*

Simon Doyle, who was
murdered in December 2001.
© *Sunday World*

Joseph O'Callaghan, aka
Joey the Lip, the young man
whose evidence solved the
Jonathan O'Reilly murder.
© *Sunday World*

Murdered criminal Robbie O'Hanlon,
who helped set Jonathan O'Reilly up
to be murdered.
© *Charlie Collins/Collins Photo Library*

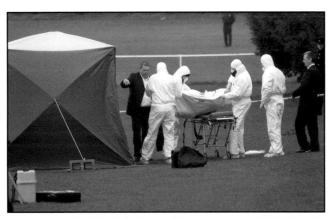

The scene of Robbie O'Hanlon's murder, near Liffey Valley
Shopping Centre, Dublin in March 2007.
© *Charlie Collins/Collins Photo Library*

The Godfather, Martin 'Marlo' Hyland, who was shot dead in Finglas in December 2006.
© *Sunday World*

Martin Hyland with one of his closest associates who was subsequently arrested and charged as part of Operation Oak.
© *Sunday World*

A country cottage at Kingsfort, Moynalty, Co Meath. The money used to purchase this house by Hyland was traced back to Sinn Féin/IRA activitist John Noonan.
© *Sunday World*

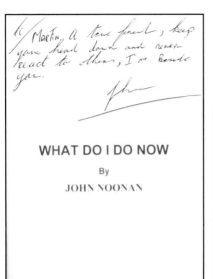

WHAT DO I DO NOW

By

JOHN NOONAN

John Noonan's hand-written dedication to his friend Martin 'Marlo' Hyland.

John Noonan
© *Hotpress*

Sinn Fein/IRA member and founder of the Concerned Parents Againt Drugs, John Noonan (*right*), 'protecting' Bono at a U2 function in Dublin.
© *Charlie Collins/Collins Photo Agency*

Andrew 'Chicore'
Dillon murdered
in August 2005.
© *Sunday World*

Det Sgt (now Inspector)
Ciaran McEneany, one of
the lead investigators into
the murder of Baiba Saulite.
© *Padraig O'Reilly*

Murdered godfather Martin 'Marlo' Hyland and his best friend
Mark Dunne (*left*) pictured together outside the Four Courts in
Dublin when he sued the *Sunday World* for calling him a drug
trafficker.
© *Padraig O'Reilly*

Innocent victim Anthony Campbell who was murdered by the killers of Martin 'Marlo' Hyland. This picture was taken when he was 11 years old.
© *Sunday World*

Anthony Campbell with his mother Christine. This happy family picture was taken two months before the apprentice plumber was shot dead simply because he was in the wrong place at the wrong time.
© *Sunday World*

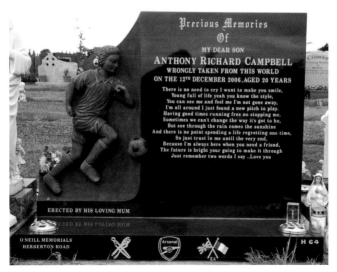

Anthony Campbell's grave.
© *Sunday World*

Det Insp (now Superinten-
dent) Walter O'Sullivan, the
officer in charge of the Baiba
Saulite murder case.
© *Collins Photo Agency*

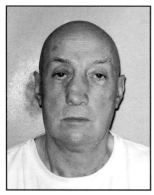

Patrick 'Dutchy' Holland.

INLA killer Dessie
O'Hare.
© *Conor McCaughley/
Sunday World*

The house on Scribblestown Lane in Finglas where 'Marlo' Hyland and plumber Anthony Campbell were both murdered in December 2006.
© *Padraig O'Reilly*

Michael Brady was shot dead in 1996 on the orders of Marlo Hyland, his former brother-in-law. Brady had been convicted of the 1985 murder of the drug lord's sister, Julie Hyland.
© *Padraig O'Reilly*

Underworld killer, Patrick Doyle (*right*) who was shot dead in Spain in 2008. With him is Gary Hutch, nephew of The Monk, Gerry Hutch.
© *Sunday World*

PJ Judge
© *Sunday World*

Underworld figure Troy Jordan, one of Hyland's associates, who was questioned in relation to Baiba Saulite's murder.
© *Sunday World*

I'm shaking but I'm happy," she said.

Marlo Hyland was also happy and celebrated over the following few days. He hadn't taken part in the actual murder. Two of his loyal henchmen were happy to do the honours. Marlo made no secret about the fact that he and his family had finally been avenged. The following week's edition of the *Sunday World* carried a story which pointed the finger of suspicion at the gangster. That afternoon he bought up all the newspapers in a local shop and gave them out to customers in his local pub where he was celebrating. An associate phoned this writer and told me: "Marlo wants you to know he was delighted with the coverage of the shooting."

The following day, he was spotted with Judge and one of his trusted lieutenants in the Royal Oak bar in Finglas. They were laughing and in a celebratory mood. Hyland and Judge were overheard congratulating the lieutenant on a "job well done". The henchman was overheard remarking that the bike used in the hit had been no good. "It wouldn't pull the socks of ya," he laughed.

Hyland, Judge and a number of other associates were subsequently arrested and questioned about the murder but there was no evidence to link them with the crime and it remained officially unsolved.

The Garda investigation of the Corbally murder increased the pressure on the gang which was already high after the Brady hit. Every gang in Dublin was also being turned over in the massive offensive launched by the Guerin murder hunt team. It was all completely disrupting the crime business. As an indirect result of the police operation, dozens of criminals were arrested and charged with other serious criminal offences. Huge amounts of drugs and guns were also seized. As part of the actual murder hunt, over 330 arrests were made and 1,500 individuals interviewed without arrest. The officer in charge of the offensive, Assistant Commissioner Tony Hickey, planned to divert the huge resources allocated to the Guerin murder hunt to focus on Judge and his gang as soon as they reached a successful conclusion.

The Gardaí also began making major drug seizures from

the mob. When detectives seized a large shipment of cannabis in a warehouse in Sandyford Industrial Estate, South Dublin, it caused a major headache for Marlo who had ordered it from his sister's boyfriend. As a result he owed Judge an estimated IR£130,000 (€165,100) and he didn't have the cash to pay him. The primary rule of the drug game is that the purchaser of a shipment must always pay up, even if it is intercepted. This development put Marlo in a difficult situation. He knew how dangerous and volatile Judge could be, even if he was owed money by his closest associates. Hyland knew he would have to work off his large debt.

The situation was exacerbated by the fact that the pressure over the Corbally murder was getting to the Psycho. The publicity wasn't helping either. The Psycho – although not yet fully identified – was becoming a household name. With so much public notice there was pressure on the police to get him. Judge became increasingly paranoid and suspicious of the gang members around him. He began asking his terrified lackies awkward questions which showed he suspected them of talking to the media and the cops. Decie Griffin once told this writer: "He [Judge] was the type of mad fucker who, if he even suspected you of talking about him, he was liable to have you taken up to Scribblestown [area of waste ground near Finglas] and put a bullet in your head. He was crazy and totally unpredictable." Everyone, including Marlo, was getting nervous.

At the same time, the Provisional IRA, who had a strong presence in Finglas and Cabra, also began making enquiries into the Corbally murder. There was intense disquiet in Finglas over the manner of Jock's death. The dead man and his family were well-liked and there was a lot of sympathy for Jock's heart-broken mother Maureen Corbally, a gentle, God-fearing woman. The Dublin Brigade of the IRA – most of whom were Sinn Féin activists and election workers – had effectively controlled the Concerned Parents Against Drugs (CPAD) from the time it was first formed in the early 1980s. Many of the people who took part in the CPAD, however, were genuinely concerned with the harm drugs were causing to their communities and families.

The most effective tactic used by the CPAD was to out known drug dealers in a particular area and march on their homes, forcing them to leave.

Marlo Hyland had first had a run in with the Republican movement in Cabra in 1994, following the murder of the General. A number of well known Provos from the area had questioned him about his drug dealing activities and if he was selling heroin. They were particularly interested in the kind of money Marlo was earning. After being forced to leave the area for a period in the mid-1990s, Marlo had developed a good working relationship with the IRA. He paid them and they'd left him alone. This would explain why, despite their booming drug trade at the time, Hyland and Judge were left untouched when a major campaign was launched by the Concerned Parents Against Drugs (CPAD) in Finglas and Cabra in 1996. In later years there was extensive evidence that some of the high-minded patriots of the Dublin Brigade were ultimately corrupted by the drug trade. Sinn Féin/IRA activists used their own gun power and the CPAD to secretly extract "donations" from drug dealers all over Dublin. Many criminals saw it as a protection tax in return for the Republicans' turning a blind eye and keeping the CPAD off their backs. A number of prominent Provos based in Finglas – including a member of the IRA Army Council – pocketed a large portion of the cash and put the rest in Sinn Féin's party coffers. They were nothing more than another layer of criminal bureaucracy. Local Gardaí who monitored the protests corroborated this association. They reported how the CPAD had left Hyland and Judge alone.

The Provos, however, were just as disturbed as the local criminals about the level of Garda attention Judge was attracting to the area. They were finding it difficult to operate their own rackets. Garda intelligence sources, who used well placed informants in the Sinn Féin/IRA camp and electronic surveillance, revealed that a number of prominent Republicans met with Marlo Hyland to discuss the situation. They suggested that he get rid of the Psycho and take over the operation himself. They were pushing an open door. Hyland and some of his most trusted associates were coming to the same conclusion. Peter

Joseph Judge's days as a feared crime lord were numbered.

On the evening of December 7, 1996, Judge went for drinks at the Royal Oak pub in Finglas with Ellen Hyland. Marlo and another associate also joined them. They were the only people who knew where the gangster was going to be that night. As Judge was preparing to leave the pub Marlo slipped away to make a call from the pub's coin box. He didn't use his mobile phone. Judge and Ellen Hyland got into his car at 12.30am. Just as he started his car a lone figure emerged from the shadows and fired two shots, at point blank range hitting the Psycho in the back of the head. He slumped over the driver's seat, dead. Marlo ran from the pub to check that his sister was safe. Although deeply shocked, she had escaped injury.

Very few mourned the death of PJ Judge and his murder attracted considerable attention. Marlo and many of his associates were conspicuous by their absence from their boss's funeral. Unlike the Brady murder, Marlo was careful not to be connected to this one. The execution had benefited everyone involved. The media put the murder down to the work of Hyland's friends in the Republican movement which suited them. It reinforced the false impression that they were taking action against the big drug dealers. Three days after the funeral Mark Dwyer, one of Judge's associates who had participated in the Corbally murder, was also the victim of a gruesome murder. Hyland circulated a rumour that Dwyer had taken out Judge. Marlo was arrested for questioning in relation to the Judge hit but nothing ever came of it. Whenever he was in custody, he refused to answer any questions and just stared at a spot on the wall.

When the dust had finally settled, Hyland began to emerge as the new godfather on the block. Unlike his murdered predecessor, Hyland used cash instead of fear to control his troops. He paid everyone well and relied a lot on his most trusted lieutenants. From Judge he had learned how to stay a safe distance from the drugs he bought and sold, to avoid a stint in prison. Within a few years he controlled a large gang whose membership came from Cabra, Finglas and Ballymun. He used a group of young dangerous thugs from Finglas to do his dirty work for him including Declan Curran, John Daly and Anthony Spratt. *(See Chapter Six.)* After a while, no criminal activity happened in Cabra or Finglas without the nod or involvement of Marlo. Hyland paraded around the area like a godfather and was driven everywhere by two of his closest associates.

In 1998, Hyland was dealing with the same Manchester-based criminals who had supplied the Psycho. He was also sourcing his drugs from two ex-patriot Irish criminals based in Amsterdam. One of them was a former IRA man from Cork and the other a former INLA man, Tommy 'The Zombie' Savage. Savage, from Swords, was one of the first criminals in Ireland to move into the drug trade in the 1980's. The Zombie was considered an extremely dangerous criminal who was suspected of involvement in a number of gangland murders including an INLA blood feud in 1987. He had been forced to flee Ireland after the 1991 murder of another former associate, Teasy Weasy McDonald, in Dublin.

Marlo ensured that neither of his two suppliers knew that the other was doing business with him. He used a number of truckers to smuggle shipments of drugs from Amsterdam to his UK associates and into Ireland. He also organised his drivers to transport drugs and stolen goods for other gangs. In the meantime, the Garda National Drugs Unit (GNDU) launched a number of operations to target Hyland's gang. In October 1997, Noel Mullen was caught with IR£400,000 (€508,000) worth of hash which he was delivering for Marlo's gang. Mullen was to be paid IR£5,000 (€6,350) for the delivery – instead he pleaded guilty and was jailed for five years in December 1998.

On April 5, 1998, the GNDU chalked up their first significant victory against Marlo when they seized IR£2 million (€2.54 million) worth of hashish as it was being transferred from a lorry into a van at a car park in Ashbourne, County Meath. Hyland's brother, Patrick, and two of his closest associates were arrested. One of them, a long time friend of Marlo, had been jailed two years earlier for what was described as one of the worst cases of animal cruelty to come before a court in 30 years. Starving greyhounds had been forced to eat another dog to stay alive. When the GNDU swooped, Marlo's pal shouted at one of his accomplices to keep his mouth shut and say nothing. He subsequently pleaded guilty to the drug charge and was jailed for six and a half years. He did not implicate anyone else in the seizure. We can not name him for legal reasons at the time of writing.

Patrick Hyland, who had a number of previous convictions, including one for robbery, was acquitted by the same court on the direction of the judge. The jury had heard that he pleaded with arresting Gardaí not to shoot him at the time of the swoop. He shouted out: "Jesus take it easy. Don't shoot. It's only a bit of hash for fuck's sake." Gardaí, however, agreed with Patrick Hyland's defence team that his fingerprints were not found on either the truck or the van used in the drug delivery. The Judge ruled that there was insufficient evidence before the court to sustain the charges.

Three weeks after the Ashbourne bust Marlo's social welfare payments were cut off following an investigation by the Criminal Assets Bureau. Hyland had been claiming unemployment assistance since 1993 from his home address at Attracta Road although he was really living with his partner and three children in Finglas. The probe was prompted by a *Sunday World* article in March 1997 which highlighted Hyland's emergence as the new Mr Big in the drug trade. He was not named at the time and his picture had been blurred out. But everyone knew who he was.

Hyland appealed against the decision and fought it every step of the way. The Circuit Civil Court eventually upheld the decision on the grounds that he had not furnished officials with a proper address or explained his financial situation. At the same time Hyland was also suing the *Sunday World* over the stories published about him. No one in the anti-drug movement or any of the political parties, who had been so vocal about the drug scourge, would agree to testify about Hyland's reputation as a drug dealer. In December 2000, the newspaper reached an out of court settlement with the gangster which in turn gave him a further opportunity to disguise his ill-gotten gains from the Criminal Assets Bureau. Hyland showed that he was just as prepared to use his lawyers to protect himself, as the more traditional gangland methods.

At the same time, he was using a city centre pet shop as a front for his large drug trafficking operation. While his lawyers were protecting his good name from an exposé in the *Sunday World*, he was importing up to several hundred kilos every few weeks, some of it hidden in pet foods. He was also bringing in weapons for his own group and for sale to other villains. Members of the group, which consisted of a hard core of 15 members, were involved in the systematic theft of high performance cars. They were then re-plated and parked up until needed for use in armed robberies and murders. Some of the vehicles were stolen to order and sold to a gang specialising in the sale of high spec cars. Marlo also supplied cars to other crime gangs.

In February 1999, gang members Anthony Spratt and Francis Fitzgerald, who were both from Finglas, stole two cars from a Fiat showroom on Richmond Road in Dublin. Fitzgerald had been one of the suspects for the murder of Michael Brady in 1996. On Hyland's instructions the cars were parked in the grounds of Dublin City University and he was given the keys. Hyland never told his associates what the cars were intended for unless they needed to know. One of the cars was used a month later in the shooting of a drug addict called Alan Byrne. Byrne was a state witness in a manslaughter case against 12 members of the CPAD in the south inner-city. His friend Josie Dwyer, who was also a drug addict, was beaten to death by a violent mob on May 14, 1996 in Basin Street flats. During the frenzied attack, the HIV-infected junkie was beaten with several weapons including a lump hammer. A number of those accused of involvement in the killing were well known members of Sinn Féin and the IRA in the inner-city. Byrne was shot three times in the back in what was a clear attempt to murder him. The addict survived the attack and later gave evidence in a string of court trials. A total of five men were subsequently convicted of violent disorder and one of manslaughter. The remaining six accused were either acquitted or the charges were dropped.

Another car stolen by Marlo's men, a VW Golf was used in the gangland murder of 34-year-old drug dealer Tom

O'Reilly on March 31, 1999. O'Reilly had just arrived at Premier Dairies in Rathfarnham, where he had worked as a forklift driver for 15 years, when his assassins struck. He was shot twice at point blank range as he tried to get out of his car. The car had been supplied by Hyland as a favour to a friendly gang. Around the same time Hyland, Spratt, Fitzgerald and a number of others, used one of the cars for a robbery at a bank in Ballyfermot. The gang cut through bars on a window at the rear of the building. They struck just as staff opened the safe, taking over IR£250,000 (€317,500) in cash with them. The job was a replica of a similar one at the same bank which had been organised by the Penguin, George Mitchell, ten years earlier. After the robbery the money was split between the gang, with Hyland taking the lion's share. Underworld sources claimed that Francis Fitzgerald and Spratt gave their cut – IR£40,000 (€50,800) each – back to Marlo to invest in a drug deal which stood to quadruple their investment. But the plan came unstuck when the GNDU swooped and seized the €2 million cannabis shipment their money had paid for. Fitzgerald demanded that Hyland refund his money and was still looking for the cash when he was shot dead in November 2000. The murder had nothing to do with Hyland. Two weeks earlier Fitzgerald had tried to murder his uncle, Gerard 'Concrete' Fitzgerald, as part of a family blood feud in Finglas. In November 2001, on the anniversary of Francis Fitzgerald's death, Concrete Fitzgerald was also executed.

Despite these few setbacks, Marlo Hyland continued to build his empire. He was an ambitious criminal with big plans for the future. In 2002, he and Anthony Spratt organised an elaborate €2 million construction industry VAT fraud with their friends in the Republican movement. At the height of the construction boom so-called C2 frauds, which exploited a loophole in the tax system, were a popular source of income for the Republicans for several years. Hyland, Mark Dunne and Spratt set up a number of bogus companies to carry out the scam. These companies then submitted claims for refunds of fictitious taxes to the Government. C2 fraud cost the Irish taxpayer countless millions. In one instance the paper trail showed how Hyland and

Spratt resigned as directors of one fraudulent company which had claimed huge amounts of VAT refunds and were replaced by two brothers from Cork who worked for the racketeering Republicans. In another case Hyland, Spratt and five other well-known Sinn Féin/IRA activists were registered together, as both directors and employees of a bogus security company.

The VAT scam was just one piece of the pie. The godfather worked hard to manoeuvre himself into a position of strength and power. He liked being in control of what was happening and brought other gangs together with a view to pooling resources and splitting up turf. It was a plan worthy of the Mafia. Hyland was good at networking and nurtured the aura of a strong man who could get things done. He established links with gangs throughout the country, including the notoriously violent McCarthy/Dundon gang in Limerick. They had emerged from a ferocious gang war which blew up in the city in the beginning of 2003 and claimed several lives. The feud was still going on at the time of writing. *(See Chapters Nine and Ten.)* Marlo also did business with two drug gangs based in Manchester and Liverpool, one of which was headed by an ex-British soldier who had served tours of duty in Northern Ireland.

Marlo was working closely with another major player in the criminal drug rackets, Troy Jordan, who was based near Allenwood in County Kildare. Originally from Tallaght, South Dublin, Jordan came to prominence as a result of the gangland upheaval of 1996. He had built up a huge drug trafficking operation. Jordan also had strong links to the Limerick gangs and the INLA. His brother Arthur Jordan, an INLA member, was facing firearms charges when he was killed in a motorbike crash in 2003. Like Hyland, Jordan was an avid fan of sulky racing. He had a string of convictions for appalling cruelty to animals as a result of his involvement in organising dog fighting events. Troy Jordan had been the target of several major Garda investigations which resulted in huge drug seizures. He had always maintained a hands-off approach to his business. At the time of writing he was still high up on the Gardaí's 'most wanted' list.

Hyland also used the prison system as a means to network

and acted as a benefactor to villains on the inside who he considered to be of worth to him. Since the new millennium Irish prisons had become glorified centres for organised criminal activity. Godfathers pulled the strings, organising drug deals and murders from the comfort of their cells with the use of smuggled mobile phones. Official prison records showed that Hyland visited Dutchy Holland at least 13 times, over a two year period. Marlo also built up a friendship with INLA killer Dessie O'Hare, who was serving a 40-year jail sentence for the kidnap of Dublin dentist John O'Grady. The contacts were made through Marlo's associations with INLA thugs on the outside.

On one occasion Hyland was stopped from visiting a member of the McCarthy/Dundon mob when a senior prison officer recognised him. Convicted criminals are not permitted to visit prison inmates. But on most other occasions it appeared that the godfather had little difficulty getting through the visitor's gates unrecognised. If he didn't go himself, he sent visitors to see the prisoners, with messages. He also lodged money into individual prisoner's accounts so that they could buy goods from the prison tuck shop – and drugs from other lags. He gave money to the wives and girlfriends of some associates who were doing time. Marlo also helped out with drug deals organised by other jailed mobsters. It was a way of ingratiating himself with big players and buying loyalty. He was the quintessential glad-handling Mr Fix it. A source who knew the gangster well explained his motivation: "Hyland always tried to surround himself with big players and ingratiated himself with people by giving them money and doing them favours. He reckoned it was a way of protecting himself by having a secure network of serious criminals around him. But that only works for a while."

By 2004, Marlo was firmly established as the central figure in the largest criminal network in the country. His inner circle had expanded to include about 20 hardened villains, most of them from Finglas and Cabra. On the periphery there were another 20 hoods, who were used as couriers and heavies. Hyland began organising huge shipments of cannabis, cocaine, ecstasy and heroin. The mob was also involved in car theft, armed robberies, protection rackets and the supply of firearms. Marlo acted as a consultant for other criminal groups in the planning of robberies and drug deals for which he charged a fee or a slice of the profits. He had become Mr Big.

Detective Inspector Brian Sherry was one of the leading detectives in the Garda Western Division until his retirement in 2007. The well respected and experienced investigator first encountered Hyland when he was involved in the investigation of the Jock Corbally murder. In 2002, Sherry was promoted from sergeant to the rank of detective inspector with overall responsibility for all detectives in the Garda districts of Blanchardstown and Cabra. Marlo Hyland was the top criminal on his beat.

"Marlo was a very interesting, but not a very pleasant, character to deal with. There is no doubt that he was the first criminal who tried to involve everyone in his enterprise. He was a facilitator who brought the different gangs under the one umbrella, in one network, a bit like the Mafia. Marlo had nurtured friendships with subversives in the IRA and the INLA. He was involved in everything that was happening," he recalled. "It was a very dangerous situation to have one man in such a powerful position. He was pulling all the strings. Before his death Marlo's name was coming up in investigations all over the place. At one stage it seemed like nothing happened in this town without some involvement from him. In the end he became too big for his boots."

Hyland never flaunted his ill-gotten gains but he still liked to party with his pals. Joseph O'Callaghan, Joey the Lip, recalled how Marlo would attend 'mad' parties hosted by two of his closest associates, two brothers from Finglas. Joey was brought to the parties with Brian Kenny *(See Chapter Three.)* The parties took place in a converted shed at the rear of the brothers' family home. "Marlo and (one of the brothers) would sit there snorting cocaine and listening to the music of Gilbert O'Sullivan. They loved his music and they liked the image of themselves sitting there like two big time godfathers. There would be loads of women there and some of them would be passed around like joints. All the talk would be about who they were fighting with, and robberies and coppers. Marlo was treated with respect, like he was the godfather," Joey would recall.

Between 2002 and 2004, Marlo Hyland's gang set up a spate of robberies. They targeted cash in transit security vans, delivering money to ATM machines in the Dublin area and surrounding counties. In the years prior to this there had been a dramatic drop in heists as criminals everywhere moved into the drug trade. Banks and other cash-holding businesses had also become almost impossible to rob as new security systems were introduced. In the 1990s four criminals had been shot dead and several arrested when cops swooped during heists. This had discouraged a lot of would-be bank robbers. But Marlo and his associates discovered a major weakness in the delivery of cash to ATMs. They carried out surveillance on vans and also recruited a number of corrupt employees in the security firms they planned to target. It was like taking candy from a baby.

In a ten month period alone, between October 2003 and July 2004, the aptly dubbed 'Hole in the Wall' gang got away with an estimated €3 million. The robbery gang was made up of a hard core of 15 hoods from Finglas and Cabra. Two of the main players in the conspiracy were the two brothers from Finglas. They were so successful that it led to a crisis in the security industry. There was a showdown between the companies involved and the Department of Justice and Gardaí. As a result the whole industry was forced to undertake a complete overhaul of their security systems. Brinks Allied, one of the main security companies in the country, was forced to introduce a new fleet of security vans fitted with state-of-the-art security equipment and procedures to foil raiders. A number of specialist Garda squads were put together to mount Operations Delivery and Baywatch to specifically target the mob.

All the criminal activity meant that Hyland and his associates were soaring to the top of the 'most wanted' list. By the beginning of 2005, the Gardaí were given a special additional budget of €20 million to fund an intensive offensive against organised crime gangs in Dublin. Under Operation Anvil extra personnel were deployed on the streets to carry

out armed checks. Known criminals in each division were
identified and whenever they were spotted they were stopped
and searched. Major search operations, sometimes involving
hundreds of officers, were conducted for the purpose of gleaning
valuable intelligence. Over time the operation led to the seizure
of a large amount of firearms, drugs and several arrests. Marlo
Hyland and his mob were top of the Operation Anvil list.
As Gardaí built up a picture of Hyland's activities they were
growing increasingly alarmed at the extent of his involvement
in criminal activity. But the security conscious gangster was an
illusive target.

Two years earlier, in 2003, every police station in the
country had been equipped with audio and visual equipment to
record interviews with suspects in custody. This was designed
to protect the rights of prisoners while in detention and to avoid
allegations that villains had been framed. A suspect had the right
to obtain the tapes of an interview through a solicitor. Marlo
was the first criminal to discover the value of the new system.
He conducted "classes" to educate his gangland associates on
how to behave and say nothing while being interrogated. Hyland
would arrange meetings where a gang member's interview tape
was played. He would pause the tape intermittently, to point out
a "mistake" or identify strategies detectives regularly used to
trick the suspect into telling them something they should have
otherwise kept to themselves. But not all the 'Fagan' school
lessons were designed to educate.

In one incident a number of gang members were arrested
as they were about to do a wages snatch in County Louth. The
team of detectives set up to investigate the robberies were lying
in wait for the gang with the Emergency Response Unit. The
men were questioned and then released from custody while
a file was prepared for the Director of Public Prosecutions.
After the hoods were released Marlo demanded copies of their
interview tapes. He wanted to know what they'd said. One of
them, a robber in his early twenties, broke the cardinal rule and
incriminated himself. He also let slip information about Marlo
and the rest of the gang. After viewing the tapes the godfather
organised a de-briefing session with the gang members in a

house in North Dublin.

Hyland took the terrified thief into a separate room and gave him a ferocious beating. Marlo warned his associate that he would be shot dead the next time he opened his mouth. Sometime later the same gang member was arrested after another attempted hold-up, this time in Finglas. Detectives had identified him as a potential informant following their previous encounter and wanted a friendly chat. This time however the hood was obviously in total fear of Hyland. He broke down in tears as he begged the officers not to say anything during the interview that might suggest he had been helpful. He said he was going to say nothing because if he did he would be dead as soon as he hit the street. When Hyland heard the robber's next tape he was satisfied that his underling had learned his lesson.

In February 2005, a major undercover operation was put in place to catch Hyland. Gardaí learned of a plan to spring an associate who was on trial in the Four Courts in Dublin. The cops watched as Hyland and five members of his gang – including the Finglas brothers – turned up in the vicinity of the courts that morning. But at the last minute Hyland's sixth sense caused him to abort the job. The prisoner, a convicted drug dealer, was too well guarded.

Inevitably the godfather began using more violence to maintain control of his organisation. Garda intelligence sources linked him to a number of shooting incidents, including the gruesome execution of Andrew 'Chicore' Dillon from Finglas. Dillon had been a member of the Westies gang before he moved over to Hyland. He had taken part in several cash in transit hold-ups organised by Marlo. In 2004, the 26-year-old villain was accused of stealing drugs belonging to veteran Finglas drug trafficker John McKeown, an associate of Hyland. Dillon had sold the drugs and put the money he made from the deal in the bank. When McKeon demanded the money the hapless thief couldn't get his hands on it – the Criminal Assets Bureau had frozen the account as the proceeds of crime. At the same time Dillon was wanted by Gardaí in connection with robbery and firearms offences. In August Chicore was forced to flee for his life to the UK after McKeon and another associate ambushed him. Hyland wanted to make an example of the errant gang member. He decided to lure him back to Dublin.

Dillon did not like being away from home and Marlo's intermediaries convinced him that it was safe to return. "Marlo sent him word that he could come back and that everything would be alright," recalled DI Brian Sherry. "We knew that everything would not be alright and tried to advise him to stay where he was. But he was really a harmless idiot who got in over his head. He wanted to believe everything was sorted because he couldn't survive on his own in England. It was a big mistake."

When Dillon returned to Dublin in May 2005, he intended going straight. He apologised to members of his family for what he had been involved in. At the same time he moved between addresses in case he was attacked. But circumstances soon forced him back to his old ways. Marlo gave him a few drug delivery jobs to convince him that he had nothing to worry about. Meanwhile the godfather had organised for some of his associates to set him up. On August 18, 2005, Dillon met with three members of Hyland's mob on the pretence of collecting a stolen car for another robbery. The group met for lunch in a pub near Dublin Airport and were picked up on the CCTV cameras.

Gardaí later discovered that 45 minutes after the group left the bar to pick up the fictitious car, Andrew Dillon was dead. At 4pm that afternoon two men spotted the body dumped in a muddy ditch on Green Lane in The Ward. It's an isolated area of countryside beside Finglas. He had been shot at least three times, under the chin, the temple and shoulder. As a result Gardaí initially had difficultly identifying the body. He was the third gangland murder victim in the country, in the space of just eight days. The criminals who had lured Chicore to his death were arrested but there was insufficient evidence with which to charge them.

* * * *

The godfather was now a source of grave concern at the highest levels of the Garda Síochána. Reams of intelligence reports from various squads were flooding into the National Criminal Intelligence Unit (NCIU) in Garda HQ. The NCIU collates and analyses all intelligence police reports from throughout the country. Marlo's name was in bold print on a pile of them. He was facilitating a veritable crime wave and becoming so big that he could soon be out of control. He was to the new Millennium what Martin Cahill was to the 1980s and John Gilligan the 1990s. Decisive action would have to be taken.

In September 2005 – a month after Chicore Dillon's murder – a secret conference was held in Garda HQ to discuss Marlo Hyland. It was chaired by Assistant Commissioner Nacie Rice who was in overall charge of the secretive Crime and Security Branch, based in the Phoenix Park in Dublin. C and S, as it is colloquially known, has primary responsibility for the security of the State and is unofficially referred to as the "spook branch". Crime and Security is the Garda equivalent of MI5 in Britain. It collates all intelligence on what is classified as crime ordinary and subversion activity.

At the conference it was agreed that while other investigations into Hyland by different Garda units had enjoyed some degree of success, it had not prevented the godfather's steady rise to power. It was decided to adopt a full on multi-agency tactical approach. Fachtna Murphy, the Deputy Commissioner with responsibility for all Garda operations, had pioneered the multi-agency approach to tackling crime when he was tasked with setting up the Criminal Assets Bureau in 1996. He was appointed Garda Commissioner in 2007. With skill and tact, Murphy broke down many of the old professional rivalries and barriers that had existed between the various agencies, such as the Customs and the Gardaí, and got everyone singing from the same hymn sheet. Murphy wanted everyone working together to put Marlo out of business. "It is vitally important to get everyone working in unison to achieve a common goal. When we set up the CAB, and brought all the agencies together, it worked very well. With all the stake holders and disciplines working in unison you can hit a target much more effectively from all sides. That's what we did here," Murphy later explained to this writer. The secret plan to catch Marlo was codenamed Operation Oak.

A secret Crime and Security memo was circulated to the chiefs of specialist units operating under the umbrella of the Garda National Support Services (GNSS) on September 9, 2005. It summarised the need for radical action. It read: 'Ongoing intelligence at this branch confirms that Martin Hyland continues to be heavily involved in serious crime. Hyland is recognised as the leading figure in a criminal gang based primarily in West Dublin. However, Hyland is linked to a substantial number of the crime gangs operating throughout the DMR (Dublin Metropolitan Region) and beyond. Hyland continually endeavours to establish links to the most violent criminals in this jurisdiction. His gang are involved in murder, armed robberies, procurement of firearms, drug distribution and major fraud. In recent times Hyland has become closely linked to both Dessie O'Hare and Patrick "Dutchy" Holland.'

The investigation included all the units in GNSS. It would be overseen by the National Bureau of Criminal Investigation (NBCI) and include the CAB, GNDU, Crime and Security Branch, the Garda Bureau of Fraud Investigation (GBFI) and the Special Detective Unit (SDU). In addition the investigators could call on the Emergency Response Unit (ERU) and the National Surveillance Unit (NSU) whenever necessary to intercept or watch gang members.

Detective Chief Superintendent Noel Whyte had control of the operation, while his second-in-command, Detective Superintendent Dominic Hayes, co-ordinated the investigation on the ground. Hayes' colleagues considered him to be something of a maverick who had earned the approval and admiration of many of his peers and superiors as a very capable investigator. Always sharply dressed in business suits, Hayes was not a popular figure in certain areas of the Gardaí. He had a reputation of being aloof, arrogant and prepared to walk over his colleagues to get where he wanted to be. He was often accused of breeching internal protocols by mounting drug swoops which should have been passed to his colleagues in the GNDU. Hayes was a secretive and controversial character. But he was at the centre of most of the country's serious crime investigations. He was considered to be an extremely enthusiastic, and successful thief-taker. Det Supt Hayes ensured that Marlo's life was changed forever.

The secret investigation adopted a classic gang busting approach. The first step was to compile all available intelligence on everyone associated with Marlo's organisation – no matter where they stood in the pecking order – using every agency at the State's disposal. The CAB and the money laundering unit attached to the GBFI examined the bank accounts, properties, tax affairs and social welfare status of everyone identified. SDU, or Special Branch, gathered intelligence on the associations between Hyland and Sinn Féin/IRA and the INLA. Connections between the Cabra godfather and gangs in Northern Ireland and the UK were also collated and shared with police forces there.

"It is a bit like peeling back the layers of an onion. You start at the outside and work your way inwards... it was the same methodology used in the Veronica Guerin enquiry," explained one senior officer.

The gang-busters also commenced covert surveillance on Hyland and his gang to get a picture of how they operated. "It was clear after a while that Hyland operated on a number of different levels. He only really trusted his own family and relatives. Then he had his inner circle of associates with whom he met every day to discuss business. Then there was an outer layer of people involved on the periphery. We then established his contacts in the other gangs including subversives like the IRA and the INLA," the same source revealed. The investigators soon discovered that Marlo would not be an easy prey. He was extremely cautious and careful in everything he did.

Marlo and his inner circle continuously changed their unregistered mobile phones to prevent them being tapped. If the phones were seized the cops would not have the opportunity of identifying the various contacts between the gang members. Detailed analysis of the activity on a mobile phone can give investigators a huge amount of information about a suspect. It can track the user's movements as he makes and receives calls.

Each number called can also then be traced and similar analysis done. This type of analysis is used in most criminal investigations and has provided vital corroboration in investigations. It has led to the conviction of several murderers and other criminals.

While Operation Oak was in its initial stages, Hyland's operation continued. On October 12, 2005, a Northern Ireland registered container truck unloaded a legitimate cargo near Dublin Airport. When that was done Marlo's men collected 600 kilos of cannabis which had been hidden under the other load. The shipment was brought to a warehouse on Richmond Road in Dublin 3 which the gang was using as a storage depot for drugs and firearms. Marlo was charging his associates €1,150 per kilo at wholesale level which gives an indication of how much he was turning over at the time. His take was €690,000. By the time the hash got to the streets in individual deals – and everyone along the chain took their own slice of the profit – the haul would have turned over an estimated €4 million. The godfather didn't keep all the profit for himself. Informants in the gang revealed that he kept €50 from every kilo sold for associates and friends in prison. This was Marlo's way of keeping everyone on his side.

While Hyland's mob was prospering, he was keeping a watching brief on another gang war which was raging on Dublin's Southside. In 2001, a lethal blood feud had broken out following a bitter split in a gang of young drug dealers from Crumlin and Drimnagh. Over the next seven years it had escalated into an all out war which had claimed the lives of ten gang members. It had resulted in the injury of several other criminals and innocent people who were caught up in the cross fire. There were scores of shooting incidents, arson attacks, and more disturbingly, the use of grenades and improvised bombs. At the time of writing, this war was still raging with little sign of a let up. In the first six months of 2008 there had been no less than 17 incidents in which improvised bombs and military grenades had been used as part of this feud. In 2007 the situation deteriorated dramatically with the arrival of the INLA on the scene. This was in the person of a psychotic thug called Declan 'Wacker' Duffy. Duffy, a close associate of Dessie O'Hare, had accepted a contract to wage war on 'Fat' Freddie Thompson, the 27-year-old leader of one of the gangs involved in the feud. At the time of writing, a number of criminals had offered Duffy €100,000 to whack Thompson. For legal reasons *Crime Wars* cannot yet tell the full inside story of this lethal feud.

One of the worst episodes in the Crumlin/Drimnagh gang war occurred during a 48 hour period which began on Sunday, November 13, 2005. Around 9.40pm, two members of Thompson's gang were ambushed by two gunmen at Carrickwood Estate in Firhouse, South Dublin. Twenty-five-year-old Darren Geoghegan and 30-year-old Gavin Byrne were lured into a trap to meet an associate. When they arrived they were blasted to death by two hit men using automatic pistols. They didn't even have a chance to get out of their car.

On the evening of the following Tuesday, November 15, Noel Roche, a member of the gang pitched against Thompson, was also ambushed and murdered. The 27-year-old was shot dead as he travelled in a car through leafy Clontarf, on Dublin's Northside. His younger brother John had also been shot dead eight months earlier as part of the same feud.

The three suspects involved in John Roche's murder were associates of Marlo Hyland. One of them was 25-year-old Paddy Doyle from the inner-city, who had a fearsome reputation as a hit man. His accomplices were both from Cabra and Finglas. Doyle was also aligned to the Thompson gang. He asked Marlo for urgent assistance when Roche, who had been in hiding, was spotted earlier in the night at a Phil Collins concert in Dublin. Intelligence later discovered that the car used in the Roche hit had also been provided by Hyland's henchmen. This was an example of the godfather's diplomacy.

Hyland assisted Doyle and Thompson because he wanted the Crumlin/Drimnagh bloodbath to continue. He reasoned that the murder spree would soak up police resources and keep specialist units busy on the south side – and far away from his patch on the other side of the River Liffey. As part of the same strategy, he tried to keep a lid on gangland feuds simmering on his own patch. He moved quickly to intervene when a row broke out between two rival gangs in Coolock. A former criminal

associate of PJ Judge tried to kill a rival who had ripped him off.
If the two sides went to war Hyland knew it had the potential
to be every bit as bloody as the Crumlin situation. Dublin's
equivalent of Don Corleone sat down with the hood and
"reasoned" with him. Marlo gave the gangster €10,000 in cash
and promised that he would get the rest of the money back on
the strict condition that the violence did not escalate any further.
He didn't want a feud attracting extra detective units into the
north side. It made for good criminal sense. Unfortunately for
him Operation Oak was already under way and was not going
to be distracted from its primary target.

The triple murders had again placed the gangland crisis at
the top of the political and policing agendas. The November
killing spree brought to 18 the number of underworld executions
in 2005. All of them, with the exception of four, had taken place
in the Dublin region. It was the highest number of underworld
murders ever recorded in a single year. As a result Garda
Commissioner Noel Conroy announced the establishment
of the Organised Crime Unit (OCU). It would provide much
needed extra personnel to specifically target serious criminal
gangs. Initially the OCU consisted of 50 young Garda officers
– many of them from uniformed sections – who had been
earmarked for dispersal through other specialist detective units.
It was not good news for Marlo. The OCU was mobilised to
spearhead Operation Oak. The young, enthusiastic cops were
ordered to get up close and very personal with Marlo and his
men.

In the meantime, other units in the Operation Oak
investigation had made significant inroads into Marlo's
organisation and compiled a huge amount of intelligence about
his activities and associates. They had built up a good knowledge
of the gang's operations and inner workings. The main source
of information was obtained through physical and technical
surveillance. A number of registered informants also provided
intelligence. The surveillance operation had also confirmed the
close links between the godfather and several senior figures in
Sinn Féin and the IRA. Operation Oak began to unravel their
political hypocrisy.

The first strike in the offensive was made eight days after the Noel Roche murder. Cocaine valued at almost €300,000 was seized in Limerick. Three people associated with the McCarthy/Dundon gang were arrested in Limerick train station after collecting the drugs from Marlo's people in Dublin. The cops wanted the mob to think the bust was the result of the local Gardaí.

A week later, Operation Oak notched up a much bigger success. This time they busted two of Marlo's associates while they were transporting a tonne of hashish, with a street value of €7 million, on the Swords Road on Dublin's Northside. The two suspects had been involved in running the Richmond Road warehouse.

That bust was quickly followed by a raid on one of Marlo's cocaine mixing factories in Skerries, in north county Dublin. Detectives seized €210,000 worth of cocaine and enough mixing agent to more than double the value of the material seized. Two associates were arrested and charged with the find. The following day in Stamullen, County Meath, over €200,000 in cash was seized from a 36-year-old gang member. Detectives later found a specially constructed hideaway under a garden shed which the bag man used to store cash. He was arrested under money-laundering legislation. The money also belonged to Marlo's gang.

The New Year's resolution of the Operation Oak undercover squad was to continue the pressure on their number one target. On January 5, 2006, Marlo's nephew, Karl Hyland was arrested for questioning about a Securicor van robbery. He was later charged with road traffic offences.

Friday, January 13, was not very lucky for gang member David 'Soss' Mulvey. The 22-year-old from Berryfield Drive in Finglas had planned to rob the post office on Faussagh Avenue in Cabra with two other men. Shortly after 10.30am Mulvey and one of his associates went to a yard at the rear of the building and slammed an iron girder into the post office door. Unfortunately for them the ERU and the OCU knew their plans and were lying in wait. Mulvey was arrested and later charged with attempted robbery.

Marlo had started 2006 with a brief financial respite. On New Year's Day he officially became "employed" by a company which specialised in the sale of quads, motorbikes and other sporting machines. Described as a security consultant, Hyland began receiving "wages" of €500 by credit transfer every few days from the company. The CAB and the GBFI later established that Hyland and a number of other associates had invested drug money in the company as part of a money-laundering scam. The owner of the company, who had an unfortunate cocaine habit, had fallen heavily into debt with the gang. The godfather saw the company as a convenient money-laundering vehicle and the owner had little choice but to do whatever he was told. Two days after the attempted post office robbery in Cabra, Hyland struck it lucky in the National Lottery. On January 18, his father William bought a Lotto Plus 2 ticket at the Tesco store at Clearwater in Finglas. The winning ticket was worth €200,000. On February 2, Marlo claimed the money at the offices of the National Lottery. However his luck didn't hold for very long.

Two days later, one of Marlo's most trusted loyal associates, arranged to collect a shipment of hashish worth over €340,000 from a van parked at Millmount Place in Drumcondra in Dublin. The 38-year-old, who was originally from the north inner-city but living in Blanchardstown, had been running with Hyland for years. Operation Oak had established that he was part of the godfather's inner circle, who managed a large part of the gang's drug distribution business. He had 21 previous convictions. An Operation Oak surveillance team watched as he collected a black hold-all bag from the back of a van and put it into the boot of the car he was driving. The cops moved in as he was about to drive off.

When he was arrested one of the detectives asked Marlo's friend what was in the bag. "Hash, what do you think? That's what happens when you owe people money." He said "the job" of collecting the drugs was worth €2,000 to him and was to be taken off a €9,000 debt he owed. He wouldn't share any further information with his captors. He and a second man arrested at the scene, were both later charged under the Misuse of Drugs

Act. We can not name Marlo's friend for legal reasons.

On February 7, the undercover cops struck again. This time they seized cocaine worth almost €500,000.

Ten days later, on February 17, the investigation team busted another cocaine processing factory. This time they seized €200,000 worth of cocaine. Three more gang members were arrested and charged under the Misuse of Drugs Act. One of them had already been charged in relation to the €7 million seizure the previous November. On the same day, €21,000 in cash was seized from another gang member.

Operation Oak continued to hit the gang hard throughout Spring 2006. On Thursday, April 6, four members of the gang set off in a convoy of two cars and a van from Dublin. They planned to rob a cash-in-transit van in Balbriggan in North County Dublin. Marlo and a number of others shadowed the gang to monitor the heist from a safe distance and to also keep a look out for the police. Unknown to them the National Surveillance Unit (NSU) had all of them under observation. The investigation team hoped to catch their number one target in the act. As the gang prepared to make their move on the security van which was carrying €80,000 in cash, an ERU team got the order to swoop. The four gang members were arrested while Marlo and his surveillance team peeled off and headed back to Dublin. There was no point arresting him because there was no evidence linking him with the job. Among those arrested was 'Soss' Mulvey who was already on bail for the attempted robbery in Cabra. A second gang member arrested was 23-year-old Derek Devoy, from Balbutcher Drive in Ballymun. They were later charged with possession of a loaded shotgun. The arrests were making life very difficult for Marlo.

The sudden surge in police swoops threw Marlo Hyland and his organisation into a spin. By the end of April, Operation Oak had seized drugs worth €9 million and ten gang members had been charged for drug offences and attempted robbery. Files on eight other mob members were being prepared for the Director of Public Prosecutions on charges relating to possession of drugs, money laundering and handling stolen goods. The ongoing operation was causing panic in the gang. On a daily basis, gang members were being stopped and searched by the Garda squads involved in Operation Oak. The Criminal Assets Bureau also began raiding their homes in search of their money and assets and the offices of solicitors and accountants working for the criminals.

With his empire under sustained attack, Hyland was growing more paranoid and volatile by the day. Drug shipments were still getting through the Garda net but the losses were soaking up profits. As the drug seizures mounted up, cash flow became a major problem. He still had to pay his suppliers in Spain and Holland. Declaring bankruptcy is not an option in gangland and the people he was dealing with were much more ruthless than him. Marlo knew that if he couldn't pay up he would find himself in the sights of an automatic weapon.

He had the equally pressing problem of finding out why the cops were suddenly being so successful. Marlo launched an investigation to find the Garda mole he believed was in the midst of his mob. He grew suspicious of some of his closest and most loyal lieutenants. Everyone who was arrested or stopped was debriefed by the godfather. The investigation was causing disharmony among the mob. In an effort to see where the leaks were coming from Hyland began a process of elimination, by compartmentalising different parts of his operation. He picked different gang members for separate crimes to see if they were detected by the cops. Despite his best efforts he couldn't find a spy. Hyland's state of mind was further exacerbated by his cocaine habit. He was gradually losing control of the situation.

The vulnerable godfather was desperate to surround himself with as many heavy-hitters as he could muster. Marlo reckoned that if he had enough formidable allies they would provide a comfort zone. He would be safe against potential underworld enemies. In April Patrick 'Dutchy' Holland and Dessie O'Hare were both released from prison. Holland had served nine years of a 12 year sentence for drug trafficking. O'Hare was freed on licence from his 40 year prison sentence as part of the *Good Friday Agreement*. The condition of his release was that he would be returned to serve the remainder of the 40 years if convicted

of any offence that carried a jail sentence. Hyland welcomed
the two men on the outside and provided money to set them
up. Holland stayed rent free in a house Marlo owned in Cabra.
O'Hare also stayed in another house owned by the godfather in
County Meath. Despite his years, Dutchy was still considered
a dangerous man. Hyland hoped that the two killers would
reinforce his position.

One man who had so far escaped the attentions of
Operation Oak was 42-year-old Paddy Harte. Originally from
the inner-city, the father-of-four had been a close friend and
business associate of Marlo for years. He was also a close friend
to some of Hyland's most loyal lieutenants. But in recent years
he had become a business competitor when he branched out
on his own to run a very lucrative drug distribution network.
Like Hyland, Harte carefully nurtured the image of a man
with little money. He never flashed his money, rented a house
and had a modest second hand car. But behind the façade he
had done very well for himself. The Criminal Assets Bureau
later discovered that he had accumulated a property portfolio
in Ireland and Spain worth an estimated €3 million. He was
also in the process of building a large house in Dunsoghly in
County Dublin. Harte also enjoyed close links with the same
members of the Dublin Brigade of the IRA. In the 1990s he
had provided them with logistical assistance such as cars and
guns for robberies and bombings. When they swapped war for
racketeering he continued to deal with them.

Harte incurred the wrath of his former friend when he began
selling drugs on Marlo's patches. What made matters worse was
that he flooded the area with so much product that he drove
down the prices and took a lot of Hyland's clients away from
him. The two men had a bitter falling out over the situation
and Marlo threatened to have him shot. He even suggested
that his friends in the IRA would sort out his competitor. Harte
laughed at this. He too had a lot of contacts in the corrupt
Republican brotherhood and knew where a lot of skeletons
had been buried.

In his paranoia, Hyland also suspected that Harte was
behind the string of Garda successes against him. He shared

this assertion with his equally paranoid lieutenants. It is also probable that Hyland simply used Harte as an excuse to cover his own back. He convinced two of his lieutenants, one of whom had been a friend of Harte, that the former associate was the root of their problems and would have to die. Marlo wanted to show his peers that he was not someone to be messed with. He offered his lieutenants €50,000 to murder Harte. In gangland a criminal's first loyalty is to money – a person can easily change from friend to foe, depending on who has the most cash.

At 9am on the morning of May 29, 2006, Paddy Harte dropped two of his children to school and returned to his home on Edenmore Avenue in Raheny. As he sat in his car, the pillion passenger on a motorbike, dressed in black and wearing a helmet, walked up and shot Harte three times in the head with a powerful .357 magnum handgun. The shooter jumped on the back of the motorbike and sped off. He left Hyland's competitor slumped dead at the scene. The godfather had made his point to anyone contemplating taking him on.

The murder, however, did not stop the inexorable Garda offensive as the drug seizures and arrests continued. In May, one of Marlo's lieutenants was arrested when detectives caught him processing €1 million worth of cocaine for distribution in a house in Swords, North County Dublin. The following month, three more gang members were arrested when detectives seized a cannabis shipment worth €2.5 million. A month later, on August 5, the undercover squad located another cocaine processing plant which was being used by Marlo's mob. This time detectives surrounded an outhouse at a property in Mooneystown near Athboy, Co Meath. When the officers looked through the window they saw three men busily using blenders to mix pure cocaine with a glucose bulking agent. They were packaging it for collection by gang members from Dublin. The three men were arrested and the officers seized €400,000 worth of the drug. A 40 foot container parked next to the garage was full of stolen generators and power tools, worth up to €50,000 each. As a result of the arrests, investigators later uncovered a cache of nine firearms and ammunition.

One of those arrested was 26-year-old Paul Reay, a father-of-three from Drogheda, County Louth. After the seizure Hyland's gang suspected that Reay had been turned by the police and had led them to the arsenal. Reay was not a career criminal but the lure of easy money had landed him in a dangerous situation. Reay and his co-accused were subsequently charged under the Misuse of Drugs Act and released on bail of €30,000 each. After his release Reay began wearing a bullet-proof vest and clearly feared for his life.

Ironically, the godfather giving rise to Reay's anxiety would soon find himself facing a similarly life-threatening predicament.

FIVE

MARLO'S DOWNFALL

Marlo Hyland had begun to resemble a character in a Shakespearean tragedy. His once powerful empire was crumbling around him and people, who had been among his closest confidants, were gradually distancing themselves from him. He saw spies and conspiracies around every corner and trusted only his own flesh and blood. His fatal flaws were greed and ambition – and attracting police attention. Operation Oak had all but destroyed his organisation. By the time the investigation came to a conclusion it had led to the seizure of over €20 million worth of heroin, cocaine and cannabis and an arsenal of 16 firearms and ammunition. The total haul of narcotics included: 30 kilos of heroin valued at €8 million; 35 kilos of cocaine, valued at €2.5 million; and 1,427 kilos of cannabis worth €10 million. A number of stolen vehicles and over €200,000 in cash, were also recovered from the mob. But it was the sheer number of his associates who had been nabbed, including his closest lieutenants, which would cast him adrift as a pariah, a Jonah who had brought bad luck on everyone around him. By Autumn 2006, a total of 41 people were arrested, 26 were facing serious criminal charges under the Misuse of Drugs Act, attempted robbery and possession of firearms. Operation Oak had prevented at least three gangland murders and thwarted another three attempted robberies. In policing terms it had been a spectacular success. For Hyland it was a disaster.

As the situation deteriorated Marlo became more isolated.

Members of the gang, who were facing serious charges, fell out with the godfather, blaming him for their predicament. There were murmurings of resentment over the Harte murder from those closest to Marlo. It was also rumoured that he had reneged on his contract with the two gangsters he'd sent to carry out the execution. Gang members were becoming as dangerously paranoid about a rat in the camp as their boss. And the finger of suspicion was moving in the direction of Marlo himself. After all he had organised the operations that had been busted but he was always a safe distance from the action.

At the same time the pressure was mounting for him to pay his suppliers for the intercepted shipments. The former joy-rider from Cabra was running out of scams to recoup the money. The success of Operation Oak meant few wanted to work with him. It had left gang members looking over their shoulders and too afraid to set up a job for fear of being caught in the act. Despite these huge pressures, Marlo was careful to ensure that he stayed on good terms with the Republican movement. He still made regular payments to a senior Sinn Féin and IRA figure living in Finglas. The Republican, who had been involved with Hyland since the mid-1990s, was also a Sinn Féin election worker. It was this man who had "advised" the godfather to get rid of PJ Judge. The relationship was no secret in the local neighbourhood. In Cabra some locals used to refer – albeit in hushed tones – to one Republican's lavishly refurbished house as "the house that Marlo built". Hyland was making "donations" until his death.

There was even evidence that Hyland had turned to God in a bid to halt his descent into hell. In October, local detectives searched the home of his former partner in Finglas. They had received a tip-off that Marlo was hiding guns there. A few years earlier, he'd left the mother of his three children and moved in with Lorna Daly. She was the 24-year-old sister of a dangerous armed robber called John Daly, with whom Marlo had another child. They lived together in a house at Cloonlara Park in Finglas, which had been purchased by Marlo's niece. In recent months Marlo had been a regular visitor to his former partner and his children. He would spend a few hours with them most evenings. To those who knew him, it appeared that he was anxious to rebuild his relationship with them and was trying to make amends for lost time. When the cops arrived at the house, the godfather was stretched out on the couch watching TV.

He was uncharacteristically courteous and appeared relaxed. When an officer searched the godfather's pockets he found a bundle of religious prayers, miraculous medals and a scapular-stuffed in the middle of a wad of €600 in cash in his pocket. The detectives found it strange and wondered if their old adversary had turned over a new leaf. Perhaps the godfather had become superstitious in his old age. Rumours of a gypsy's curse had swept Finglas and Cabra after several members of the same violent young gang had died. The "cursed" gang members, including Anthony Spratt and Declan Curran, had all been associates of Marlo's. *(See Chapter Six.)* The contents of his pockets symbolised his two beliefs in life. Perhaps he felt the holy pictures and prayers would protect him against a violent end. If that failed maybe cash could buy him some breathing room. But Marlo Hyland would soon prove that he was beyond redemption.

"Marlo had become a desperate man and was showing weakness to his other cronies. He tried to ingratiate himself with people by doing them favours but that doesn't buy you respect or loyalty in that world," was how one senior detective described Marlo's predicament. "In the end even the most loyal gouger [criminal] will pick the leader who is strongest. Loyalties change over night. There is no soul searching involved. The gouger will just ask himself where can he get the best deal and who is the strongest player around. There is no loyalty in the criminal world."

The godfather was indeed prepared to go to any lengths to curry favour. It would prove to be the worst mistake of his life.

* * * *

Baiba Saulite left her native Latvia in 1998 and moved to Ireland in search of a new life with her boyfriend. The beautiful, vivacious 20-year-old with dazzling blue eyes, grew up in Riga where both her parents were dentists. She had planned to study hotel management and improve her English. On arriving in Ireland she worked briefly as a manicurist in a Dublin beauty salon. She split from her boyfriend when he returned to Latvia and found herself vulnerable and alone. Around Christmas 2000 an Irish couple she had befriended invited her to a festive party. That night she met Hassan Hassan, a charming Lebanese national. Born of Syrian parents, he had immigrated to Ireland several years earlier and had become an Irish citizen.

Baiba was immediately attracted to Hassan, who was ten years older. She found him charming and roguish. He drove flash cars, wore designer clothes and never seemed short of cash. Hassan was smitten by his Latvian lover and showered her with expensive gifts, nice clothes and jewellery. Her friends later recalled how Baiba, probably in her innocence, turned a blind eye to the source of her future husband's wealth. Hassan Hassan had become involved in organised crime since arriving in Ireland and led a gang made up of hoods from the Middle East and Africa. Garda intelligence believed that he had extensive links with crime gangs in the Lebanon which specialised in the sale of illegal firearms.

Hassan had forged links with a number of Irish gangs, including Marlo Hyland and his associates in West Dublin. He controlled a sophisticated multi million euro car "ringing" racket in which high powered cars were stolen to order. They were fitted with the registration plates and chassis numbers of similar cars which had been written off in crashes. The cars were then shipped out of the country to the UK and Eastern Europe. Similarly, cars stolen in the UK were smuggled to Ireland as part of the scam. The gang also dealt in valuable parts stripped from robbed cars. Marlo's associates were among his suppliers. Hassan would 'order' specific makes and colours to be stolen. As already revealed here Hyland had members of his gang out stealing high-powered cars on an almost constant basis. The thieves' modus operandi was to target houses and apartments with high spec cars parked outside. When the occupants were asleep they broke in, stole the keys and drove off.

The couple moved in to live together a short time after meeting and subsequently married. Shortly after they wed there were signs that this was not going to be a marriage made in heaven. When the Lebanese criminal married Baiba he'd told her he was a Christian of Greek origin. Then, after the birth of their first son, Ali Aleksandra, in 2001, Hassan admitted he was really a Muslim. Two years later they had a second son, Mohammed Rami. The couple moved to live in a house in Kinsealy in north County Dublin. At first they had a good relationship but then Hassan began to abuse his wife. In 2003, he was arrested with a number of his associates when detectives from West Dublin – who had uncovered his link with car thieves in Finglas and Cabra – raided his operating base at a car repair garage near Clane in north Kildare. The investigation was led by Det Insp Brian Sherry. In the swoop the detectives found two dozen high-powered cars, which had undergone skilful modifications, ready for export. Some of the cars were already in containers for transportation to Dublin Port. At the time investigators estimated that the gang had shipped out €3 million worth of cars from the garage. Hassan was subsequently charged and released on bail.

In the meantime, Baiba could tolerate no more abuse and she left him. She was later granted full custody of their two boys. They maintained a cordial relationship and Hassan had regular visits with his children. On December 6, 2004, he collected the boys for a day out. But he never returned. He had abducted the children and sent them to live with his mother in Syria. As the two children were Irish citizens, Gardaí began a criminal investigation into the kidnapping.

Solicitor John Hennessy had just opened his new legal practise in Swords, in October 2004, when Baiba Saulite walked through the door. She was one of his first clients. Hennessy, who had grown up in London, was an idealistic young lawyer who believed in the power of the law to protect people. But this was not going to be a straight-forward family law case.

Hennessy was deeply moved by the plight of his client. She was distraught over her missing sons and terrified of her husband. The young lawyer immediately initiated legal proceedings against Hassan Hassan and sought a court order compelling him to return Ali and Mohammed to their mother. Baiba had also obtained a barring order against her estranged husband.

Over the next year, Hennessy worked extremely hard to reunite his client with her sons. He kept up the pressure on the Gardaí to take action against the Lebanese car thief. In the process, Hassan developed a deep hatred for the crusading solicitor. Hennessy's first case would almost cost him his life.

On foot of the proceedings Hassan was ordered to appear before Swords District Court to explain where the two young children were being held. The judge ordered Hassan Hassan to return them to Ireland. When he failed to meet the court's deadline, Christmas Eve 2004, Hassan was jailed for three weeks for contempt of court. In the meantime Baiba Saulite was inconsolable over her missing children. In January 2005, she appeared on Joe Duffy's Liveline programme on RTÉ radio to appeal for help from the public. She believed that her boys might still be in Ireland. She won the hearts of the listening public as she described her plight, during a 35 minute interview with Duffy.

The tearful young mum spoke of her life with Hassan Hassan. "He told us [Baiba and her sons] what we could eat, what we couldn't eat, what I have to wear, what I have to do. He wouldn't let me go out to see my friends, nothing," she said.

"These children have always been with me, every day, every minute; these children must be very upset. The little baby [Rami], he's a baby, it's probably more easy on him (sic). But Ali he's really a mammy's boy and he must be very upset about the situation because he doesn't know anybody. I never heard from them since the day I let them go. All that I want is just my babies back home safe with Mummy. Just think how would you feel if that happened to your kids? I am the mummy and any kid needs a mother."

In August 2005, Hassan Hassan was formally charged with two counts of kidnapping and was remanded in custody. He was already on bail for the car theft racket. When he applied for bail in the High Court on the abduction charges it was granted on the condition that he returned the children to Ireland. Hassan took up the court's offer and Baiba Saulite was reunited with her boys after ten agonising months. She was overjoyed and began rebuilding her life. Baiba told friends she planned on opening her own beauty salon. But her problems were far from over.

In the meantime Hassan Hassan was convicted of running the car theft racket. At the end of his trial he lied to the court. Hassan claimed that he was the sole custodian of his sons. He argued that his children would be placed in care if he had to do time in prison. There was a strong case for the court to suspend a custodial sentence. However the Gardaí prosecuting the case contacted John Hennessy who was more than happy to give the court the true picture. By doing his job the young solicitor had become a marked man.

Around 1am on the morning of February 27, 2006, the fire alarm woke Hennessy and his girlfriend. The house was full of smoke. Petrol had been poured through the front letterbox and set alight. The hallway was engulfed in flames. The solicitor had woken in the nick of time and managed to get his partner and himself to safety. Gardaí believed it was a murder attempt. Despite the attack, Hennessy travelled to the Circuit Criminal Court in Naas a short time later and testified that his client had been granted full custody of the two boys and not the defendant. Hassan was jailed for four years and the dangerous gangster swore vengeance.

On October 11, 2006, detectives from Swords Garda Station called to see John Hennessy. They had just received detailed intelligence, through the Crime and Security branch, that a Moroccan asylum seeker had been hired by Hassan Hassan to murder him. The car thief was sharing a prison cell with John Dundon, a member of the bloodthirsty McCarthy/Dundon gang from Limerick. Dundon was serving a four year stretch for threatening to murder another Limerick criminal called Owen Treacy. *(See Chapters Nine and Ten.)*

Dundon had helped source a murder weapon and a silencer to kill the lawyer. The hit was foiled when the asylum seeker was arrested on a separate matter by officers from the Garda National Immigration Bureau (GNIB).

Hennessy was kept under observation by armed and uniformed Garda units for two weeks until the Crime and Security Branch were satisfied the plot had been thwarted. At the same time Baiba was still being threatened and intimidated by her former husband. She told her friends how she was living in fear of Hassan Hassan. She talked of leaving Ireland for good with her children and returning to Latvia.

In October, her car was petrol bombed outside her home in Kinsealy. As a result Baiba had been forced to move to a two-bedroom terrace house in Holywell Square in Swords. Unknown to anyone at the time, Hassan Hassan had set up two further attempts to have both Baiba and her solicitor murdered. Detectives would later discover that two men had located Baiba's new home and had her under surveillance. The non-nationals decided that they couldn't go ahead with the crime when they saw her with her little boys. It was also learned that another man had refused to take the murder contract because the money he was offered was too little – €10,000. Hassan Hassan again turned to his ruthless cell mate, John Dundon, for help with his problem. Dundon took out his mobile telephone and called his old friend Martin 'Marlo' Hyland. If anyone could organise it, the Cabra godfather could.

The request from Dundon came at a time when Marlo needed friends – particularly powerful friends in the drugs and murder business. Marlo was anxious to ingratiate himself with as many heavy-hitters as possible, as he found himself slipping further into a perilous situation with his own associates. The ruthless McCarthy/Dundons were valuable allies. It was later learned that Dundon had also been in touch with Paddy Doyle, who had been lying low in Spain since the Noel Roche murder. Between Hyland and Doyle, they organised one of the most shocking murders in gangland's bloody history.

Doyle contacted his two accomplices who had also taken part in the Roche hit. Both aged 22 and from Cabra and Finglas, the pair had no qualms about who they murdered – just as long as the price was right. On November 7, two other young gang members, one of whom was a relative of Marlo, stole a powerful BMW 520D from a house in South Dublin. The car was to be used in the murder. Both Baiba and her lawyer were placed under surveillance by associates of Hassan Hassan. On Tuesday, November 14, a Garda patrol spotted Marlo Hyland and Dessie O'Hare meeting over coffee in a local hotel in Swords. It was never established if this meeting was connected to the gang's murder plot.

Around the same time, one of the hit men collected a package on the Naas Road in Dublin. It contained a photograph of Baiba Saulite and a map of the Holywell Estate. There was also a piece of paper with directions on how to get to the house from the M 1 motorway which bypasses Swords. The house was marked on the map. On Friday the same thug received a phone call from his accomplice to arrange the collection of the stolen BMW. The killer was overheard remarking that he had "a date with a BMW". On the same afternoon Dundon is understood to have called Marlo from his prison cell to arrange collection of a firearm. According to sensitive security sources, Hyland is supposed to have asked the Limerick hood where the "piece of graft" – the shooting – was to take place. Dundon said it was in Limerick.

Garda intelligence sources would later learn that Hyland had asked Troy Jordan in County Kildare to supply him with a "clean" Magnum revolver. The weapon was part of a cache Jordan was holding for Hyland. On Friday evening he called Jordan and arranged to pick up "the silver thing". The following day Hyland arranged for one of his associates to collect the powerful handgun from Jordan in Allenwood. The gang member in turn recruited a 'courier' to bring the gun back to Cabra. Marlo's associate and the courier travelled to Kildare in separate cars. Around 9pm that night Jordan handed it over. A subsequent Garda investigation revealed that Jordan had no idea what the gun was to be used for. The courier returned to Dublin with the weapon, shadowed by Hyland's henchman in the second car. This was the modus operandi used by the gang when moving guns and drugs. The courier would be expendable if intercepted by the cops. Hyland's secret watchers had no idea about the unfolding plot.

On the evening of Sunday, November 19, 2006, a pizza

delivery arrived at Baiba's door. She hadn't ordered one. At the same time Hassan Hassan received a phone call in prison informing him that the victim was at home. Dundon then called the hit team in Cabra to give them the go ahead. The killers headed for Swords around 8.30pm in the stolen BMW. At least two other gang members were involved as lookouts and getaway drivers. One of them agreed to take part in the crime to satisfy a €10,000 debt he owed for cocaine.

Shortly before 9.45pm Baiba appeared at the front door of her new home to share a cigarette with a friend. She didn't like smoking in the house in case it affected her two little boys who she had just put to bed.

As she stood at the door a man, wearing a scarf and baseball hat, suddenly ran up to her. He pulled the handgun from his jacket and shot the young mother, four times at close range. Baiba was hit twice in the chest and once in the shoulder. The impact of the bullets pushed her backwards into the hallway of her new home. She collapsed on her back, gasping for breath as blood flowed in a torrent around her body. The bullets had caused devastating injuries to Baiba's lungs. The defenceless young woman choked to death on her own blood. The callous murderer ran to the stolen BMW and made his escape. A short distance away they abandoned the car and set it alight.

Within minutes of the shooting, Gardaí began to arrive at the scene. Among the officers to respond to gangland's latest atrocity were detectives who had been investigating the plot to murder John Hennessy. Detective Sergeant Ciaran McEneany was in charge of the enquiry and had already dealt with the victim. He and his colleagues were sickened by what they found. Det Sgt McEneany and another detective stepped across Baiba's body to find her two children. The boys had been awoken by the shots, the screams and then the sirens. The two cops soothed the bewildered tots. They wrapped them in blankets and bundled them into their arms. The officers covered the children's heads to protect their innocent eyes from the horrific sight of their lifeless mother on the ground. The children were immediately taken into care. When the gunman opened fire that evening he had also destroyed their innocent lives.

As Garda units began to flood the area, Det Sgt McEneany sent armed officers to find John Hennessy who had been working late in his office. He was told to pack a bag and was then taken under armed guard, with his partner, to a hotel outside Dublin. At the time of writing John Hennessy was still living under full-time armed police protection. Later that night detectives from Swords visited Hassan Hassan in prison and searched his cell. He was subsequently arrested and taken from prison for questioning about the murder.

Not since the murder of Veronica Guerin had a killing so enraged and shocked the entire nation. Baiba's murder struck a cord with the public. It was proof that gangland crime was getting utterly out of control. Now completely innocent people were being deliberately gunned down. In 2002, a Limerick bouncer called Brian Fitzgerald had been executed on the orders of the McCarthy/Dundon gang and in March 2006, another young mother, Donna Cleary, had also been shot dead. *(See Chapters Six and Nine.)* Baiba's murder brought to 20 the number of gun murders in Ireland in 2006 – 17 of which were classified as gangland attacks. The level of public revulsion and anger could be gauged through Joe Duffy's *Liveline* phone-in show. Over the following days, thousands of callers flooded the show's phone lines trying to express their anger, shock and revulsion. Hundreds of people later attended a memorial service for Baiba which was held in a local church in Swords.

The Taoiseach of the day and the country's most senior politicians felt compelled to add their voices to the chorus of condemnation. A number of emergency conferences were held in the Department of Justice, with senior garda management and officials, to review the situation. There were also meetings between the Law Society and the Gardaí to discuss the threat to murder an officer of the court, as the plot to kill Hennessy was also revealed. It was seen as a step too far by the underworld. The crisis bore all the hallmarks of the Guerin murder a decade earlier. For those of us who had witnessed it before it was like déjà vu. The criminals had crossed the line again and showed they were afraid of no one.

At a press conference three days later, the outspoken officer in charge of the investigation, Detective Inspector Walter O'Sullivan, reflected the mood of his investigation team when he made an impassioned plea for help in tracking down the killers. Rarely had a senior cop been so passionate and forthright in his comments. "This was a truly horrific crime. A young woman gunned down in the prime of her life, the mother of two children. I would appeal to all persons who enjoy life, who love life, and all that life has to offer, to come forward. There are no words left to describe this crime," he said.

On the following Friday, Hassan Hassan made an application to the Dublin Circuit Criminal Court for temporary release to attend Baiba's funeral and to see his sons. There was heavy security for the hearing. Five armed detectives, wearing bullet-proof vests, escorted Hassan to the court. The Director of Public Prosecutions opposed the application on the grounds that John Hennessy had been subjected to months of intimidation. Sgt Liam Hughes from Swords station described the arson attack on Hennessy's home and the concerns that his life was in serious danger.

The court was also told that it was the strong belief of the Gardaí that the car thief would flee the jurisdiction if allowed out of prison. Hassan's counsel put it to the officer that her client had an "amicable relationship" with Baiba Saulite and that she had taken her sons to visit their father in prison twice a week.

"Any visits she made to prison she made under duress," replied Sgt Hughes.

Hassan Hassan jumped to his feet shouting: "Most of the evidence he has given is not the truth. He is lying. He is giving evidence that is not true."

The prisoner was told to sit down.

Then Det Insp O'Sullivan dispelled any lingering doubts the court might have had about allowing Hassan Hassan out of prison. "I am extremely concerned for his [Hennessy's] life and the persons associated with his office," he said. "I fear, from privileged information in my possession, that if Hassan Hassan is released on bail that he will commit more serious offences that, according to the information I have, include murder, assault, intimidation and interference with witnesses," the officer declared.

Det Insp O'Sullivan refused to answer a number of questions put to him by Hassan's counsel on the grounds of privilege. "My real fear is with regard to the information I have Judge, and I do not say that lightly," he added. The court refused Hassan's application and he was returned to prison in a convoy of police cars.

A month later, on December 18, the Circuit Criminal Court jailed Hassan Hassan for a further two years for abducting his children. He had pleaded guilty to the offence a month before the murder. In his own defence he told the court that he had felt compelled to take his sons away. He claimed Baiba had threatened to take the children to Latvia and never let him see them again. He said he regretted the kidnapping and was sorry.

Judge Michael White said the fact that Hassan pleaded guilty at an early stage and there was no issue of cruelty or neglect to the children all counted in his favour. But he added the abduction had been pre-meditated and well-planned. He also told Hassan there was no evidence his murdered wife had intended taking the children out of the jurisdiction. The court heard that Hassan had made clear efforts to intimidate his estranged wife into dropping her complaints over the children's abduction. The judge said they were serious offences and a custodial sentence had to be imposed.

* * * *

The Saulite murder caused consternation in Marlo Hyland's gang. Within days the police knew that he had been involved with the plot. The Operation Oak team soon connected him with the crime after analysing their latest intelligence reports. Hyland was deeply concerned about being connected with the outrageous crime. There were still some criminals around who would disapprove of such a murder. Killing other hoods was one thing – murdering a defenceless woman was completely different.

A sense of nervousness hit gangland as villains everywhere

braced themselves for a backlash similar to the one which had followed the Guerin murder. It hadn't taken Troy Jordan long to work out what the brand new gun he handed over had been used for. He was extremely angry at his business associate. He told Hyland he would not have handed over the gun if he had known its true purpose. Hyland claimed that he had no idea either and that Dundon had told him it was to be used in Limerick. This was a crime no gangster would want his name attached to. The Saulite murder added to the mounting pressure on the godfather. No amount of religious relics could save his soul.

Before the week had ended, Marlo's name was being connected to even more bloodshed. Four days after Baiba's murder, on November 19, Paul Reay was due to appear in Kells District Court. He was due to be further remanded on the cocaine factory seizure in Athboy in August. Reay decided not to wear his bullet-proof vest to the court. He didn't want the judge to get the wrong impression. Just after 9am, he got into a car driven by his sister Emmajean at his home at Tredagh View, Marley's Lane, in Drogheda. A gunman, dressed in a high-visibility jacket, got out of a car parked nearby and approached at speed. He fired at least five shots from a handgun into his target, hitting him four times in the upper body. Emmajean Reay was also hit in the shoulder and seriously injured in the callous attack.

Paul Reay died a short time later in hospital. The getaway car, a stolen Mazda 323 with false registration plates, was found burned out two miles from the murder scene. It had been stolen in Clondalkin two weeks earlier. (Reay's murder was the latest tragedy to hit his family. Six years earlier his father, Ned, a respected civil servant, had been beaten to death by drunken youths close to the family home.)

Marlo's gang was beginning to implode as Baiba and Reay's murders escalated the paranoia and suspicion which were turning friends into foes. More gang members and associates began to put a safe distance between themselves and the man they once called the boss. A rift developed between Hyland and two of his closest lieutenants, who had been with him for over a decade. They were the men suspected of taking part in the

Paddy Harte murder. The two gangsters were also facing serious gun and drugs charges as a result of their work for Hyland. One of them, the man suspected of actually pulling the trigger, had been a close friend of Harte.

Originally from the north inner-city he had been staunchly loyal to Hyland. A detective who knew this gangster for many years described him in rather blunt terms: "He is a character devoid of human feeling. He is an evil, cold hearted bastard. You would know that as soon as you met him."

When Marlo's murderous sidekick was arrested for questioning about the Harte murder he denied any involvement. During a break in his detention, when he was away from the cameras and microphones in the interview room, he broke down and sobbed about the murder of his friend Harte. "Marlo should never have killed Paddy... it wasn't right," he remarked. Then he muttered what most of his pals were thinking. "Marlo has got us all into a world of shite...fuck him."

If Marlo had ever watched the brilliant Oliver Stone scripted movie *Scarface* he probably saw similarities between himself and the central character, Tony Montana. Played by Hollywood legend Al Pacino, Montana was a Cuban petty crook who built a powerful drug empire in Miami after butchering his way to what he described as the "top of the world". But then he lost it all – and his life – when he fell foul of his Colombian business partners. Marlo was rapidly becoming the real life Irish equivalent of Tony Montana. "He was doing a lot of coke and popping pills and making threats all over the place. He had ballooned in size and had stopped training in the gym like he always did. "He was a fucking mess," was how one former associate described him. On the streets of Dublin, Marlo was a dead man walking.

Life was beginning to take its toll on the godfather. He split up with Lorna Daly around the end of the summer and had moved in to live at 8 Scribblestown Park. One of his relations later told Gardaí how he had become "very paranoid" and seemed to be reluctant to answer the door or even one of his many mobile phones. Hyland also became very cautious about his movements. He was trying to stay one step ahead of a hit man while he bought himself some time. Marlo found himself facing down the barrel of the same dilemma as many gangsters before him. He knew that his former pals were well capable of murdering him. So he contemplated drawing first blood and moving against some of his own inner circle – it was a matter of killing one of them before they got to him first.

The beginning of the end came when Marlo had a serious falling out with a former member of his organisation, a convicted heroin dealer who was classified by Gardaí as a major player in drug trafficking. The 33-year-old had been running with Marlo and members of John Gilligan's gang since his release from prison. In 1998, he had been jailed for a total of 13 years for selling heroin in Dublin's north inner-city. When he came out of prison, in 2004, the 33-year-old went straight into the big league. Around October 2006, the two former associates fell out in a row over money which Marlo owed him for drugs. Threats were exchanged and Hyland plotted to have his new enemy shot.

The convicted drug dealer became suspicious when he spotted a 26-year-old member of Marlo's mob keeping him under surveillance. In November, an attempt was made to shoot the drug dealer in Whitehall in North Dublin but he escaped uninjured. He knew Hyland had been behind the attempt on his life and plotted revenge. He didn't have any trouble finding allies. Marlo was running out of friends faster than he was money and drugs.

The drug dealer joined forces with another Finglas criminal who was beginning to make a name for himself in the underworld. The 30-year-old, who had also been involved with Marlo, was a very dangerous, and ambitious, hood who had no difficulty killing anyone who got in his way. He too had come to the conclusion that his former boss was a liability.

On December 8, the 26-year-old gang member who had been spotted keeping tabs on the convicted drug dealer was lured into a trap in Cabra. He was then shot three times by a lone gunman. Despite suffering serious injuries, the gangster never reported the attack to the police.

At the same time, Marlo's two loyal lieutenants who

had murdered their friend Paddy Harte, were also seriously aggrieved with the godfather. He had reneged on a deal to pay them €50,000 for the hit. The two men were also facing serious drug charges before the courts. They had been caught while moving Hyland's drugs and it greatly added to their sense of betrayal. They were easily recruited into the new alliance which was building against the godfather. Marlo had become a liability. He was out of control and dangerous but also weakened. It was time for the younger lions to get rid of the older king, who no longer dominated the pride.

As a result of the botched murder attempt in Whitehall in November, the Operation Oak team picked up intelligence that Hyland was also now a target. Local detectives were told to warn the godfather that a serious threat had been made against him. They left a message with his niece asking Marlo to contact Detective Sergeant Andy O'Rourke at Finglas Garda Station. Det Sgt O'Rourke had been a detective in the district for most of a long and distinguished career. Despite putting many of the local villains behind bars, they had a grudging respect for him as a fair cop. Det Sgt O'Rourke had been involved in more than his fair share of gangland murder investigations down through the years. He had quite literally seen them come and go.

When Hyland called to the station, he was remarkably friendly and very thankful for the warning. Det Sgt O'Rourke told him to watch his back. He was also obliged to offer security advice to the man he had been trying to catch for years. Hyland politely declined the offer, with a smile, and went on his way.

Marlo remained visible around north-West Dublin where he was driven around by one of his remaining associates. He was a creature of habit and most days he held meetings with his gang members in the house. He still had plenty of young hoods to fill the space of the lieutenants who had deserted him. For the first time in his life he didn't mind the constant attention from the police. When a patrol from the OCU stopped him with his driver, he told them he was glad to see them around. "It makes me feel safe seeing that youse lot are around," he laughed at them. And for the first time he probably wasn't joking either. His niece Elaine also noticed that he was being slowly isolated by other gang members. When she broached the subject that there were fewer members of the gang coming to see him, he replied that it was just part of their individual bail conditions.

On December 7, 2006, Gardaí visited him a second time with a new warning about his safety. Despite the threats, they noted how Hyland had become sloppy about his security arrangements. "We had no problem locating him whenever we were looking for him – neither did anyone else," remarked one detective.

On the evening of December 11, Hyland was visiting the home of a family member in Fairlawn Park, Finglas when the two henchmen responsible for the Harte murder called by to see him. One of them met Hyland in the house and they had a loud argument before the killer left. Shortly afterward the godfather was dropped to the home of his ex-partner and his three children which he still visited on a regular basis. He stayed until around 9.30pm, when he was collected and went off to buy a Burger King meal for his son. After that, his associate dropped him back to the house at Scribblestown Park. Festive lights and Santas festooned the front wall of the corner house.

Marlo sat up talking to his niece. He drank a few cans of Guinness and smoked some joints before going to bed. The following morning Elaine Hyland got her eldest child ready for school, while her partner went off to work. Marlo had woken up earlier with a headache and Elaine brought him some pain killers. She told him that there would be workmen downstairs and that they might have to go into his bedroom, which was the box room at the front of the house, to bleed the radiator. Marlo went back to sleep.

At 8.45am a plumber and his 20-year-old trainee assistant, Anthony Campbell, arrived to begin work on the heating system and repair a number of radiators in the house.

Anthony Campbell, was a well liked young man, who had been reared in London with his mother Christine. He lived there until he was 17 when they both returned to Dublin. The fanatical Arsenal soccer club fan had then moved in to live with his father, Noel Fitzgerald, in St Michin's House flats in the inner-city. He had recently completed a course, as a trainee plumber with FAS, but had been unemployed for some time. His father had approached a local plumber and asked him if he had any work for his son. Anthony started work for the tradesman on November 30. He was delighted to have the opportunity of doing a 'nixer' to earn some extra cash for Christmas. Elaine Hyland let the workmen in when they arrived and they began fixing the radiator in the downstairs sitting room. She left a few minutes later with her two little girls, to drop the eldest one in school. A short time later the plumber left to go to a local hardware store to pick up some parts, leaving Anthony working alone.

The killers had been monitoring activity at the house and when they spotted Elaine and the plumber leaving they made their move. They had visited the house on several occasions to meet Marlo and knew the lay out of the house. They also knew the room where their former boss would be sleeping. It is unclear whether they knocked at the front door of the house or had a key to get in. Police investigators subsequently pieced together what happened next.

One of the killers held Anthony downstairs while his accomplice, who was armed with a .45 semi-automatic pistol, crept upstairs. The lieutenant walked into the bedroom where his victim was lying face down, asleep. He pointed the weapon at the side of Marlo's head and fired two shots at close range into the left side of his head and behind his left ear. The godfather would have felt nothing, as the powerful rounds punched through his brain. Another four rounds were fired into Marlo's back.

In the end nothing could save Marlo Hyland. He had lived by the culture of the gun and he died by it – dispatched by a man who had once been a close friend. The lump of religious prayers and medals or the cash in his pocket were of no use to him. He didn't even get the opportunity to make one last stand with the machete that stood close to his bed. Martin Hyland died in the last place he probably ever expected. Crime Scene Investigators subsequently noticed how he hadn't moved when the gunman opened fire. It was proof that he'd heard and felt nothing, even though neighbours later reported hearing at least

three very loud bangs, in quick succession. If the godfather
had heard any sudden noise, he would surely have tried to put
up a fight. If the hit man had been contracted by Marlo to do
a similar job, the godfather would have been impressed with
the result.

When the murderer returned to the front room, where
Anthony Campbell was still being held, he made a split second
decision about what to do with the innocent tradesman. The
six loud shots could have been heard outside and neither he
nor his accomplice were going to hang round. He raised his
gun and took aim. The terrified apprentice raised his arms,
as if to shield himself. The hit man fired a single shot which
passed through Anthony's arm and hit him in the side of the
head. He fell to the ground beside the radiator he had come to
repair. He died instantly.

Investigators would later establish that the double homicide
had happened within a six minute time span between 9.19am
and 9.25am.

The two killers jumped into a black Volkswagon Passat,
which had been stolen in County Kildare ten days earlier. They
drove from Scribblestown Estate and headed in the direction of
Tolka Road. As they did so, they were followed in a second car,
an imported Vauxhall Vectra owned by one of the killers, which
was driven by the gangsters' new boss. The cars were spotted
by a number of eye-witnesses, driving at speed in convoy in the
direction of Finglas Road.

The convoy was also spotted by an undercover surveillance
officer who was part of the an NSU team assigned to covertly
watch the godfather that day. The modus operandi of the secret
spying operation was to pick up Marlo's tail and shadow him
after he was collected by his associate. The significance of the
sighting was not realised until after the alarm was raised. By then
it was too late. The stolen car was found burning on Glasilawn
Lane in East Finglas just as the Gardaí and Fire Brigade were
being alerted to the gruesome double murder.

The killers had left the scene no more than three to four
minutes before the plumber returned to the house. The door was
closed and when he rang the door bell he got no answer. He

couldn't see into the house and repeatedly phoned Anthony's mobile. Then he rang the doorbell several more times. Just as he was giving up, Elaine Hyland returned with her youngest daughter.

As she walked into the house with her little girl, she saw Anthony Campbell lying face down on the sitting room floor and she noticed that his hand had gone blue. She panicked and ran out of the house with her child to tell the plumber. At that same moment, Marlo's driver had arrived and was walking through the door. Each morning he delivered the newspapers and an energy drink to his boss. At first, they thought that the latest victim of mindless gang violence had suffered some kind of accident. Marlo's driver turned Anthony over and discovered he was covered in blood. He told the plumber his assistant was dead.

The driver then ran up to Marlo's bedroom and found his boss lying in the bed. He called out his name but got no response. Then he noticed the gunshot wounds in his back and smelt the thick acrid scent of cordite. He ran from the bedroom screaming: "He is dead in the bed. Martin. They've shot Martin." He began hitting the walls with his fists.

When the driver went out and told Elaine Hyland, she collapsed. For the second time in her life she had discovered the murder of a loved one. In a cruel twist of fate it was a week before the twentieth anniversary of Julie Hyland's awful murder. Elaine Hyland was hysterical and inconsolable, as police and an ambulance crew arrived. The young mother and her husband had been nervous about the threats against Marlo. A lot of people had suffered as a result of Marlo's ambition to be the country's most successful godfather.

It was later confirmed that one of the suspects had indeed known Anthony Campbell from the inner-city neighbourhood where he lived. Detectives believed that Anthony was sacrificed because the killer and his accomplice feared he would identify them. When the killer was subsequently arrested for questioning about the murders, he admitted that he knew the innocent plumber. Through crocodile tears, he denounced the murders and denied any involvement.

The murder of Anthony Campbell sparked fresh public outrage and revulsion. The fact that it came so soon after Baiba Saulite had been gunned down added to the gravity of the situation. It appeared that there was no let up in the spiralling level of violence. A few hours after the double murder, another innocent victim, shop owner Alan Cunniffe, was buried in County Kilkenny. He was shot dead when he tackled an armed robber who had held up his family shop. The Irish public was getting tired of hearing about outrageous and repulsive crimes. The murders in Finglas brought to 89 the number of gangland-associated killings since the start of the new Millennium. The blood-letting didn't stop there. Another three men were gunned down in the last two remaining weeks of 2006. It was the bloodiest year on criminal record.

Following the double execution, politicians argued and pointed fingers at each other as recriminations flew. The Justice Minister of the day, Michael McDowell had a row with the judiciary over the number of criminals being granted bail. The two main suspects for the double murder had been caught as part of Operation Oak and were out on bail for a number of serious offences. The vast majority of criminals were still being granted bail despite Garda objections and the fact that a referendum of the Irish public had led to the introduction of tighter bail legislation. The rows and the expressions of outrage were inevitable after such an atrocity. But equally inevitable was the fact that the event soon faded from the public consciousness – until the next time.

On Tuesday, December 18, the hearse containing the body of the murdered gangster carried him the few hundred metres from Massey's funeral home to the Christ the King Catholic Church in Cabra. His parents and family led the sombre procession which included dozens of his criminal associates. They clutched a framed picture of Ireland's Public Enemy Number One. Big floral tributes with 'Dad', 'Granddad' and 'The Budgie' adorned the hearse.

During the funeral service the following morning, parish priest Fr Gregory O'Brien had a special message for the killers in the congregation, which included Dutchy Holland. He told mourners that violent criminals "die twice, once on the inside, before eventually dying a physical death". He asked the congregation to pray for everybody who was already "dead on the inside". He described violence as being a "grave offence to God" as it contains the weight of the world's sin. "Once a person has killed another human being, he loses all respect for people. This violence destroys the love in the soul and that person dies inside," he said.

The exhortation from the altar meant little to the assembled underworld hard men. They had come to pay their respects, to be seen – and to see who else turned up. After the ceremony the gangsters and hangers on threatened and intimidated reporters and cameramen who turned up to cover the biggest gangland story of the year. A procession of stretched limos then followed the hearse on Marlo's last journey to Glasnevin Cemetery. The following day was the anniversary of his sister's death.

That following evening, while Marlo's mob drowned their sorrows, there were harrowing scenes of grief as thousands of mourners turned up for the removal of Anthony Campbell. Many of the mourners were there in solidarity with the family of a young man they hadn't known. Traffic came to a standstill, as a lone piper led the huge procession through the streets to John's Lane Church.

The next day he was buried in Newlands Cross Cemetery. For his grieving family, the pain was crippling. His courageous mother Christine later became a voice for the victims of organised crime. Anthony's family were as bitter against Marlo Hyland as they were against his killers. On his descent into disaster he brought two innocent people with him – Baiba Saulite and Anthony Campbell.

"I will never see my son grow up. I will never be a grandmother. These evil men have taken my only child, they have taken my life. The animals who did this deserve the same kind of death and I hope they get it," Christine Campbell told me.

The gang members had more on their minds than grief or the wrath of God – they wanted to know where Marlo's loot was hidden. They began hovering like vultures around members of their former godfather's family. At first, there were a few vague questions and then sinister threats and demands. Gardaí warned one of Marlo's brothers that a death threat had been made against him.

In January one of the killers approached one of Hyland's relatives in a pub in Finglas Village. He appeared drunk and had white traces under his nose, suggesting he had been snorting cocaine. He told the woman that Marlo had owed him €80,000 when he was murdered. Then forgetting himself the stoned murderer blurted out: "I didn't kill him, [name of other suspect] did." Then he realised what he was saying and changed tact: "But that might just be paper talk. I'll be seeing you again."

Marlo's associates all wanted to know where the money was. But Ireland's version of the law-enforcing Untouchables was well ahead of them.

The CAB dimension to Operation Oak had started in earnest in May 2006 and was still going on when Marlo was shot dead. Over the following months, Bureau officers, Detective Gardaí Tony Brady and Martin Harrington, trawled through a huge amount of material as they unravelled Hyland's labyrinthine financial affairs. They initially examined a total of 81 properties which had been linked in some way with Hyland. As the financial forensic investigation continued, they discovered that the godfather had used intermediaries to buy a number of properties in Dublin and Bulgaria. They found a bank account through which he had lodged over €800,000. Marlo had used it as a float for day-to-day expenses.

But one of the most remarkable discoveries they made was a direct link with a number of prominent members of Sinn Féin and the IRA. Bogus companies set up by Anthony Spratt and Hyland were traced to a group of Republicans, one of whom was Hyland's long-term gangland mentor from Cabra. Through the paper trail, connections were made between other major drug traffickers and card carrying members of Sinn Féin. The scale of the interaction between the mob and the Republican movement in Dublin was astonishing. In turn it led to other investigations of individuals who thought they were safely under the radar.

Sinn Féin/IRA man John Noonan had joined the Republican movement when he was a teenager growing up in Finglas. He was in the IRA a short time when he was caught with arms and explosives in Newry in 1973 and he was jailed for five years. After his release he settled with his wife and six children in Tallaght. Noonan was one of Sinn Féin's most active members in Dublin and claimed credit for organising the Republican movement's electoral base in the working-class suburbs. A close friend of party leader Gerry Adams, he had been a candidate in both the European Union and local elections. He failed in both attempts. But his main claim to fame was as one of the founders of the Concerned Parents Against Drugs (CPAD) in the early 1980s. Noonan's involvement in the anti-drug movement led him into a deadly conflict with the General, Martin Cahill, and his gang in 1984. The IRA used the CPAD to exert pressure on the General for a share of the loot from the IR£2 million (€2.54 million) O'Connor's Jewellers robbery a year earlier. At the height of the tense stand-off, which almost erupted into a shooting war, a Provo active service unit was caught by police after they kidnapped Martin 'the Viper' Foley.

Noonan was one of the most senior members of the Dublin Brigade of the IRA throughout the 1980s and into the mid-1990s. He was not a supporter of the Peace Process but did not join any of the dissident groups who popped up as a result. Noonan was particularly proud of his work in the CPAD. In 2005, the 52-year-old published his memoir, ironically entitled *What do I do now?* In it, he proudly boasted about his fight against the Brits and the Dublin drug dealers. The blurb informed readers: 'This honest and forthright account of one man's fight against wrong is not to be missed.' In a chapter called 'Drug Thugs Threat' Noonan modestly revealed how he took on what he described as 'scumbag drug dealers'. He wrote: 'As the CPAD grew and grew, I was mostly the one to tackle the big drug dealers, to meet them and advise them to change their way or face the consequences.'

At some stage along the way Noonan developed a different sort of relationship with a major drug trafficker called Marlo

Hyland. He didn't choose to share this association with his readers. Garda intelligence first noticed the association between the unlikely pair in 2002. It was believed that he had been introduced by his Republican "comrades" in Cabra and Finglas, who had been in cahoots with Marlo for years.

Noonan made a fortune when he got involved in the private security industry. Sceptics might have seen it as a glorified protection racket. He effectively took control of providing security on film sets when the movie industry was booming in Ireland from the mid 90's. With Noonan and his Republicans on the scene, no other security company dared to compete. As a result of his good fortune, he bought properties and holiday homes in Wexford, Spain and Bulgaria. He and his business partner, who was another Republican, owned a company called Gold Card Security Agency and Gold Card Security Services. They both found themselves under investigation when the CAB discovered a direct link between the company and the purchase of a house in County Meath in 2003 as a result of Operation Oak.

The house at Moynalty, near Kells, was bought by Marlo's niece, Karen Brady, in 2003. The investigators found that three large cash payments had been lodged by Noonan's and Kelly's company to Brady's bank account. The money was then used to pay the deposit on the country cottage. Three months after the murder, the CAB launched a series of searches in pusuit of the money trail. In February 2007, the homes of the Republican partners were raided. In both houses the CAB found documentary evidence linking them and their company with Hyland. In Noonan's house they found documentation in the name of Marlo's brother, relating to the purchase of an apartment in Bulgaria. Kelly and Noonan had also invested in the project. In addition there was telephone evidence that both men had been in regular contact with the murdered godfather.

The CAB also raided the offices of the security company at the North Strand in Dublin. The ground floor of the building was being used as the election HQ for Sinn Féin candidate Mary Lou McDonald. She was contesting a seat in Dublin's

North Central constituency the following May. During the search of the company's offices upstairs, they found a vehicle registration certificate for a jeep registered in the name of one of Marlo's gang members. When Noonan was interviewed by CAB officers, he claimed his only connection with Hyland was when he had interviewed him for a "thriller" he was planning to write. Kelly also denied knowing the hoodlum, even though he had Marlo's mobile phone number listed in his own phone. One of the officers asked Noonan: "With your background in the anti-drugs movement why would Martin Hyland, who was believed to be one of the major drug dealers in the country, meet with you?" The anti-drug campaigner replied: "He probably seen an opportunity to ingratiate himself and if the truth was known, from my point of view, he was involved in hash and put out of Cabra by the anti-drugs people. As far as I was aware from then on he hadn't been involved in drugs and the anti-drugs people [in Cabra] would have had the same view." However, he later admitted to buying cars from Hyland for his children and a jeep for his security business.

In a subsequent interview with *Hot Press* magazine the Provo dismissed reports that he was under investigation by the CAB as "just paper talk". Effectively he said he didn't know Marlo Hyland and had nothing to hide. When the *Sunday World* revealed the connections between Noonan and Hyland in May 2007, it was dismissed as another "smear" against the Republican movement. Behind the scenes, Sinn Féin sent members to Dublin to "investigate" the outrageous allegations. It wasn't the first time that the anti-drug activist was asked awkward questions from his own organisation. In 2002, Noonan and a number of other Republicans – all of whom were involved with Hyland and other drug traffickers – were quizzed over the "misappropriation" of funds. In other words the Dublin Brigade had been siphoning money, from various frauds and protection rackets, for themselves. On that occasion Noonan's pal, Kevin O'Neill, a Sinn Féin election agent, was shot in the leg as punishment for his "crime". This time Noonan convinced his comrades that the articles were all lies and he was taking legal action about it. They returned to

Belfast satisfied with his story.

Then in July this writer received a copy of Noonan's book from an underworld source close to Hyland. It was further proof that Noonan had been telling lies. The book was a personally signed copy which Noonan had presented to his underworld pal. In the dedication he wrote: 'To Martin, a true friend, keep your head down and never react to others, I'm beside you. John"

Hyland cherished the book – it was the only one he possessed which had been signed by the author concerned.

Noonan's decision to stand by Marlo ultimately cost him dearly. When he discovered that the investigation was in an advanced stage, Noonan claimed that the money he used Marlo to hide belonged to the "cause" – the coffers of Sinn Féin and the IRA. When the CAB then served him with a tax bill for €2 million, Noonan appealed it to the Appeals Commissioner in Dublin.

At a subsequent secret hearing, he again claimed that the money concerned did not belong to him. It belonged to "others" he claimed in the apparent hope that the Appeal Commissioner would accept that. However his bluff was called when the Commissioner then suggested that he should call the "others" to testify in the appeal. After that Noonan agreed to settle his affairs with the CAB. At the time of writing it is understood that he was in the process of paying up.

While the investigation of Hyland's assets got results and clawed back some of his ill-gotten gains, the same could not be said of the murder enquiry. A huge effort was put into catching the gang responsible for the heinous crime and, at the time of writing, it is still a live case. Local detective units under the command of Det Supt Hubert Collins were backed up by the NBCI and the Det Supt Hayes' Operation Oak team. Over the months following the double murders, over 1,000 people were interviewed and 600 statements were taken. There were 42 searches and 14 suspects were arrested and questioned. Detectives had soon compiled a detailed picture of the crime and who was involved. A total of between four and six gang members – including the two prime suspects – had been involved in organising the plot. Analysis of the mobile telephones owned by the gangsters showed that they had been in the general location of Scribblestown at the time of the murders. One person told detectives that Marlo's killer had confessed to her that he had done the shooting. She was too terrified to testify and her information could be taken no further. A number of other suspects also gave information but none of them were prepared to enter the Witness Protection Programme.

Early in the investigation detectives were tipped off that the stolen car used in the murders had been parked at an apartment block at Santry Cross in Ballymun, North Dublin. The car had been left there from the end of November until December 12, the day of the homicides. As a result, the investigation team began a detailed examination of all the cars parked at the apartment block. It proved a worthwhile endeavour.

They located two stolen cars, both fitted with false plates, which had been stolen in North Dublin in the month before the execution of Marlo and Anthony Campbell. A van that had been registered to a fictitious company was also discovered. The vehicle had been specially adapted to carry large quantities of drugs. The search also opened a direct link with the ongoing investigation into Baiba Saulite's murder. One of the recovered cars had been stolen from the same address – and at the same time – as the one used by Baiba's killers. A discarded registration plate, found in the same place, belonged to a stolen car which had been found in Swords in November 2006. When the car was searched, a loaded Israeli assault rifle was found in the boot. This weapon was thought to have been intended for use in a murder attempt on crime boss Christy Griffin. *(See Chapter Eight.)*

When detectives looked closer they discovered that the car park had been a secret depot for Hyland's gang. It was well known that the mob always had a fleet of stolen cars parked up and ready for use in various crimes. It was established that the apartment block was being protected by a security company owned by the Finglas-based criminal who had hired Marlo's killers. A finger print uplifted from one of the stolen cars, also matched one of Marlo's former associates. This man was also facing drug charges, with one of the killers.

When an employee of the phoney security company was arrested he refused to tell the truth about the people he worked for. "I'm not telling youse anything. I'm not telling youse answers to questions on camera and then when I go out of here my ass is grass," he said.

Marlo had trained his henchmen well. An investigation of the security company revealed an elaborate money-laundering operation. Gang members were paid large weekly wages as employees of the company. Gardaí were later granted court orders freezing the company's bank account.

After a year of painstaking work there was still no firm evidence that could be used in court to secure a conviction beyond all reasonable doubt. The gangsters were safe on their side of an impenetrable wall of silence. The investigation team know the identities of the cold-blooded killers who by now are in the premier league of dangerous men. Several of them have featured in a number of major criminal investigations and a number are before the courts facing serious charges. The only other fear for these gangsters is that they will ultimately get what Marlo and Anthony Campbell got – a bullet in the head.

In the months following Marlo's demise, his once loyal legion of henchmen had filled the vacuum he left. The people who remained staunchly faithful to the end were pushed aside or given no option but to co-operate with the new regime. At the time of writing, the many members of Marlo's organisation who were caught during Operation Oak were still being processed through the slow-moving criminal justice system. Some of them have already been dealt with by the courts.

In March 2007, luckless armed robber David 'Soss' Mulvey pleaded guilty to the attempted post office robbery in Cabra and to possession of a loaded sawn-off shotgun in Balbriggan. He was given a total of ten years in consecutive prison sentences for the two offences. Derek Devoy from Ballymun was also jailed for seven years for his role in the Balbriggan incident.

In May 2008, one of Hyland's closest associates pleaded guilty to a major drug charge and possessing a loaded firearm when he was arrested in August 2007. We cannot name this man for legal reasons. He claimed he was carrying the gun for his own protection after he was told by police that he was a marked man. He was sentenced to a total of 14 years – ten years for the drugs and four years for the firearm. Judge Katherine Delahunt said, however, that the "special and exceptional circumstances" surrounding the gun possession – that the criminal had the gun for his own protection – meant it didn't warrant the mandatory term. She suspended the four year sentence in full.

Gangsters now talk of the life and death of the godfather with a sense of pathos.

"He was a great bloke, very good to people loyal to him but he just got too big and brought down too much heat on everyone else and that's not on. The lads who took his place are cuter and they are a lot more ruthless," one former friend remarked.

Marlo Hyland was living proof that crime simply doesn't pay.

Six

THE FINGLAS MOB AND THE GYPSY'S CURSE

"If you thought we were bad …just wait 'til you see… what's coming next." This chilling prophecy, barked from the door of a prison van over a quarter of a century ago, has become the catch phrase for organised crime ever since. It was shouted by the head of the once notorious Dunne drug family in 1982, as he was being led away to begin a long stretch behind bars. Larry Dunne was going down for selling heroin – the drug he and his siblings first introduced, with devastating consequences, on the streets of Dublin. It was probably the only truthful statement he ever made. His prophetic quote has gone down as one of the most profound in the annals of gangland history. It has been used many times over to summarise the following generations of Irish criminals. If the underworld fraternity ever designed a coat of arms, then Dunne's dark prediction would be its motto.

Not even the insightful godfather could have foreseen the type of gangster who would follow in his footsteps 20 years later. By modern standards, the likes of the Dunnes and the Cahills, who ushered in the new era of violent crime in 1980s Ireland, look almost harmless in comparison with their descendants. In 1982, the gangsters who would form the nucleus of one of the most bloodthirsty gangs ever witnessed in this country were still in nappies and learning to walk. By the new Millennium, this hard core of dangerous criminals had learned the dark arts of robbery and murder. Three of them, Declan Curran, John Daly and Anthony 'Anto' Spratt had become synonymous with violence and terror in the Dublin suburb of Finglas.

The terrible trio were the central players in a loose collection of around 20 ruthless young men from the same neighbourhood. They became known as the "Filthy Fifty". In a few short years, this particular crew caused unparalleled amounts of chaos and fear. From a very young age, Curran, Daly and Spratt were classified by police as being among the most dangerous armed criminals in the country. They had a penchant for violence that challenged even the notorious Westies who were operating at the same time, in nearby Blanchardstown. The Curran/Daly/Spratt criminal gang was closely aligned to Marlo Hyland and two brothers from Finglas who cannot be named for legal reasons. Hyland used the Filthy Fifty in armed robberies, drug dealing and as extra muscle. The lethal mob also forged an unholy alliance with the Keanes, one of the warring crime families in Limerick.

But there was another reason why this collection of cut-throats stood out from the rest of the gangland rabble. Superstitious villains believe that in 2003 the Filthy Fifty fell under the spell of an old gypsy woman's curse. The story goes that that the mother of a young man who had been killed by the gang asked an elderly traveller woman to put the hex on the mob. It was said that if the curse worked, a dozen of them would be dead within three years. Others would say that the infamous "curse" was the figment of the collective imagination of a few mischievous local detectives. It was designed to rattle the paranoid, cocaine-addled minds of the young desperados. If this was the case, it worked because the gang began to believe the yarn. And as they bought into the idea that a curse existed, more bad luck seemed to come their way. People who believe in the existence of a spirit world would claim that by believing that a hex was upon them, the gangsters made it a reality. Others, who prefer to stay in the real world, would say that the criminals' deaths had more to do with their chaotic violent lives.

Whether the story is true or not there is no doubt that the Filthy Fifty were the recipients of a disproportionate share of bad luck. They had good reason to be superstitious. More than any other criminal gang, they were beset by a string of unexplained calamities. As the so-called curse predicted, in the space of three years, 12 gang members had died. Four of them were shot dead in gangland attacks – an occupational hazard. But the others expired as a result of accidents, suicide and sudden death. The gang members even believed that Marlo Hyland had fallen victim to the Gypsy spell.

* * * *

Declan Curran from Cardiffsbridge Avenue and John Daly from Cloonlara Park in Finglas were born in 1980, within a few months of each other. Spratt, who was seven years older, came from Ratoath Drive, also in Finglas. They displayed an apparently natural predisposition to violent crime that could be traced to their early teens. Together they were a lethal combination who caused mayhem wherever they went. They were the embodiment of a crime wave of drug dealing, armed robberies, intimidation, shooting, stabbing and murder. The three young gangsters also symbolised the complex nature of organised crime where individual hoods "work" with different criminal outfits whenever it suits them. As a detective inspector in the most crime-affected region of the country – the Garda Western Division of the Dublin Metropolitan Region (DMR) – Brian Sherry had good reason to acquaint himself with Curran, Daly and Spratt.

"The three of them were the main players in a tight group of very violent young men who came from an area of Finglas that we dubbed the murder triangle. They were very loyal to each other and protected their little group by murdering anyone they considered to be a threat to them. They had no respect for human life. The members of this gang were interconnected with Marlo Hyland and the likes of the Westies. They were pumped up on steroids which made them even more aggressive. There was a certain chemistry between them that when they were together – especially Curran and Daly – they were liable to do anything," DI Sherry explained.

The so-called murder triangle included a geographical area that stretched from Cappagh Cross and Ratoath Road to the Griffith Avenue Extension and back to Cardiffsbridge Road in the heart of Dublin 11. It became the epicentre of the worst crime wave in Irish history. Between 2003 and 2007, the Garda districts of Blanchardstown, Finglas and Cabra recorded 19 murders, most of which were categorised as gang related. Apart from Limerick, it became the first area of Dublin to be openly patrolled by the Emergency Response Unit. They wore paramilitary attire and toted machine-guns and rifles, in a bid to quell the violence.

"We were swamped with murders, attempted murders and shootings and this bunch were at the heart of the action," Det Insp Brian Sherry revealed.

The Filthy Fifty were no different from every other mob in the country – they started off life as car thieves, burglars and joy-riders. Their first encounters with the police usually occurred when they rammed squad cars during high speed chases. By the time they reached their late teens, they had moved into the bigger league, graduating to armed robbery, drugs and protection rackets. Inevitably they began attracting a lot of attention from the police. They were described as utterly ruthless and completely out of control. Spratt had a head start on his younger cronies, as he was a blagger [robber] from the mid-1990's. He was one of the key players in the Hyland gang that specialised in holding up cash deliveries to ATM machines. This earned them the nickname the 'Hole in the Wall' gang.

Spratt was a prolific thief. He was known to have organised and taken part in at least 20 major jobs in the four years between 1999 and 2003. He was clever enough to avoid being caught, however, and this was reflected in a relatively short criminal record most of which related to road traffic offences. Spratt was a carpenter and joiner by trade but his only period of employment had been for the six years up to 1995. He had then claimed unemployment assistance for a short while. By 1999, with so many armed robberies to be done, he no longer needed hand-outs from the State. He was also involved in a number of VAT fraud scams which he organised with Marlo and members of Sinn Féin and the IRA. In 2001, he was a registered "employee" of a bogus security company which had one of Sinn Féin/IRA's most important back-room operators as a director. The company only lasted for six months.

Declan Curran was the most violent and feared of the bunch. "He was a truly frightening character who burst onto the scene and was a one-man crime wave. Everyone was scared of him because he was capable of doing anything or anyone. He was pure evil," was how a community activist in the area described him.

Curran's first recorded conviction was for car theft and criminal damage when he was 17 years old. Like the rest of his mob, he was also a regular drug user. Fun for Curran, Spratt, Daly and the rest of their group was getting stoned and ramming squad cars. His brother Ciaran had been killed in a stolen car crash in the mid 1990's.

Curran took his first life when he was 18 years old.

In the early hours of Wednesday, March 10, 1999, Curran and another gang member, 21-year-old Anthony Ledwidge, broke into a secure underground car park at the Law Library near the Four Courts in Central Dublin. The car park was used by members of the judiciary and barristers attached to the Law Library. Cars were often left there at night. Around 4am, 51-year-old security guard Pat O'Donnell spotted the two thugs breaking into a black VW Golf. He called the police for assistance.

Two officers from the nearby Bridewell Station were there within minutes. O'Donnell stayed outside on the footpath while the two cops walked down the ramp to investigate. Curran spotted the officers ,as he and Ledwidge were driving out with their latest acquisition. Curran stopped the car and reversed a short distance. He then revved the engine and drove at the officers with speed. The car glanced off Garda Chris McGraw, breaking his arm in the process. Curran then rammed the car through the 12-foot high reinforced steel gates at the entrance. The force of the impact knocked one of the gates off its hinges. As the car careered out onto the road and the two young hoods made their escape, the heavy gate landed on the security guard.

Pat O'Donnell was pinned to the ground and fatally injured. He died in hospital a few hours later. Curran and Ledwidge abandoned the car in nearby Arbour Hill. They were both later arrested and questioned about the killing but there was not enough evidence to sustain charges.

Curran and the gang were embroiled in a number of petty feuds in the Finglas area. At the time, Gardaí investigated several incidents in which shots were fired and petrol bombs were thrown at targeted houses. The Filthy Fifty were terrorising the place. On June 8, 1999, one of the men Curran was trying to kill decided to be proactive. Curran was shot twice in the lower back by two men outside Anthony Ledwidge's house on Ratoath Drive. As a result, he suffered spinal injuries and lost a kidney. Curran was forced to wear a colostomy bag and was left with a limp. Despite his near death experience, the out-of-control gangster refused to make an official complaint about the attack to the police. And it didn't dissuade him from his life of crime.

As soon as he was physically able, Curran was back stealing cars and causing trouble with his pals. His experience had left him even more violent and unpredictable. One former associate confided that Curran could no longer "perform" sexually. "He used to have to lie on his back and let the woman do the work when he was getting laid because of the injuries. That used to make him even more fucking mad than he already was," the sidekick later explained.

Curran decided to put his colostomy bag to use in his encounters with the police. Whenever he was arrested for questioning, it was not unusual for the young sociopath to disconnect the bag and pour the contents over his head to distract his interrogators. On another occasion when he was taken to a Garda station after an arrest, he took off the colostomy bag and sprayed its contents around the front office.

He took part in several armed robberies with Daly and Spratt. In July 2000, he was arrested following an armed robbery and a high speed car chase in which he rammed several squad cars. In January 2001, he was jailed for three years and disqualified from driving for ten.

By that stage John Daly had also run into trouble with the law. At 8.45pm on January 24, 1999, Daly walked into the Esso Service Station at Violet Hill in Finglas wearing a motorbike helmet and carrying a sawn-off shotgun. He stuck the gun into the hatch and began shouting at the attendant inside. "Gimme all the money... put all the money in the hatch, now," he screamed. Then he fired a shot into the hatch, missing the terrified shop attendant, who began putting cash from the till in the hatch. "Put all the fuckin' money in the hatch or I'll kill ya," the thug continued. He left with just IR£300 (€381) in cash.

A week later Daly decided to hit the same place again. This time he arrived at 4.30pm on the back of a motorbike. He ran into the shop, brandishing his shotgun but the staff ran into a back office and locked the door. Daly began kicking the door and making threats. "Open the fuckin' door or I'll kill ya," he shouted. When the staff stayed put Daly decided to abort his mission and ran out. On the way he took a poor box from the counter which was full of coins for a much more deserving cause. He left and went home.

Unfortunately for Daly, Detective Garda Kevin Stratford was involved in the investigation of a spate of armed robberies in the area. Attached to Mountjoy Garda Station, the young officer was one of the most talented and respected detectives in Dublin. He came from a family of police officers – his mother and father had been Gardaí and so were his two brothers. Catching criminals was in his blood.

Det Gda Stratford had identified the Filthy Fifty as a group that were heading into the big league of serious crime and he was determined to do something about it. Within a few hours of the second robbery attempt, an informant tipped him off that Daly had brought his shotgun home with him after the raid. Stratford and a team of detectives raided Daly's home at Cloonlara Drive and found the weapon and a shotgun cartridge in his bedroom. He was arrested and brought in for questioning. Daly knew he was in a tight spot and that the cops had enough evidence to charge him. So he decided to come clean. He made statements admitting both robberies and possession of the firearm.

He told Stratford and his colleagues that on the day of the

first robbery he had been drinking with his mates. When they ran out of drink and money he decided to do a robbery. He claimed that the gun went off accidentally. He gave the same reason for the next hold up, saying he again needed money for drink. He described in a matter-of-fact manner what happened when he ran into the Esso Station.

"I went in the door and the little cunt behind the counter seen me coming in. He ran into a room. That was it. No one could get near the money. I tried kicking in the door a few times but couldn't get in," Daly casually recalled. When he refused to say who gave him the gun Daly was asked was he afraid to name the person.

"I'm afraid of nothing," he replied.

"Nothing scares you at all?"

"Just big dogs and police with loads of statements," Daly grinned.

"What do you mean?"

"Police with statements against me from some rat."

The 18-year-old was charged with two counts of robbery and one of possession of an illegal firearm. He was subsequently granted bail.

Over the following months, while out on bail, Daly was involved in another spate of robberies. In June he was arrested and charged with another hold-up. This time it was an off-licence in Finglas. By the time Daly was arrested again in June, he had twice failed to appear in court for a remand hearing relating to the robbery charges. Bench warrants were issued for his arrest. Between June and November he failed to appear on three more occasions. In November 1999 Kevin Stratford succeeded in having Daly brought before the court and remanded in custody.

On July 25, 2000, Daly pleaded guilty to a total of four charges, two counts of robbery and one each of receiving and possession of a firearm. Judge Elizabeth Dunne jailed him for a total of nine years.

A review of the sentence was set by the court for July 25, 2002, when Daly could then apply to have the remainder suspended. But Detective Garda Stratford intended to object to the robber getting out. He knew, more than most, that Daly was a dangerous criminal.

In a bid to scupper Det Gda Stratford's subsequent objection, Daly's family made a number of false and vexatious allegations about the detective to the Garda Complaints Board. One of the complaints claimed that the detective had spoken in "disparaging terms" about the young thug. The complaint was found to be without foundation and thrown out.

Despite the objections from the Gardaí, Daly was released in July 2002. The conditions of the release were that he entered a bond to keep the peace for three years, remain under the supervision of the probation services for a year and sign on every week at his local Garda station. Daly had told the court that he was a reformed character and had a roofing job to go to when he got out. By the time he hit the street, Curran was still behind bars and Spratt was becoming one of the city's most prolific armed robbers. For Daly it was soon back to business.

On the night of March 17, 2003, Daly and Anto Spratt were arrested for a public order offence by Gardaí in Finglas. The two thugs were drunk and abusive. On the way to the station Daly and Spratt attacked the two arresting officers in the back of the paddy wagon. Daly kicked one of the officers in the ribs and broke his nose with a head butt. Spratt then told the other Garda that he was going to "find your house and crucify your fucking family." Then Daly made more threats. "I'm going to check your fucking car reg and destroy your house, then I'm goin' to rape your fucking wife you dirty pig bastard." And for good measure he added: "I'll tell you something [he called out the officer's shoulder number] I'm goin' to put a .38 to the back of your fucking head and blow if fucking well off."

The two hoods were charged with public order offences and Daly was also charged with assault. He was remanded in custody to Cloverhill Remand Prison and Spratt was freed on bail. In the days following Daly's court appearance, during which the injured Garda had given evidence about the assault and threats, the Garda noticed Spratt and one of his associates following him. The two hoods were spotted again a week later. This time they were watching Mountjoy Garda Station where the officer was about to finish his shift. Around the same time, Detective Garda Stratford also made the disturbing discovery that the dangerous mob had a contact in the Motor Taxation Office who could provide the names and addresses of car owners. An investigation into the dodgy civil servant, who also came from West Dublin, was launched by the NBCI. He was arrested and questioned about his connections with the mob but refused to make any admissions. Gardaí were unable to prove what specific information he had passed over to the gang, although investigators had strong intelligence that he'd had dealings with them. As a result, the civil servant was moved to another area where he would no longer have direct access to such information.

While Daly was remanded in custody on the assault charges, Det Gda Stratford contacted the office of the DPP to have Daly's armed robbery sentence reactivated. This was on the grounds that he was clearly in breech of the conditions of his release. On April 28, after a long wait, the DPP formally applied to the Circuit Criminal Court to have the gangster put back in prison, to serve the remainder of the nine year sentence he'd received in 2000.

Daly made several attempts to obtain bail but was refused after objections by Kevin Stratford and his colleagues. They told the High Court that Daly had made serious death threats to an arresting officer. He had also displayed scant regard for the bail system. The young criminal had failed to appear in court to answer charges on eight occasions and had been twice convicted for related offences. He was, however, granted bail on August 21, 2003.

By the time Daly got out the bloodbath had already started.

* * * *

The Garda 'K' district covers the working-class suburbs of Finglas, Blanchardstown and Cabra. In the summer of 2003 it had become a powder keg, a veritable war zone with shootings taking place on a daily basis. The 'K' district was without doubt gangland's hottest conflict zone, after Limerick. It was home to three of the most dangerous and prolific crime gangs in the country. The Westies in Blanchardstown, the Curran/Daly/Spratt mob in Finglas and the godfather himself, Martin 'Marlo' Hyland, in Cabra. The officers with overall control of serious crime investigation in the area were Detective Superintendent Hubert Collins and Detective Inspector Brian Sherry. As the Detective Superintendent of the Western Division of the DMR, Collins also had responsibility for the other trouble spots of Ronanstown, Clondalkin and Ballyfermot. Between them the two men had a vast knowledge of the underworld. They knew that the situation was getting out of control.

Declan Curran had been freed from prison in Spring 2003 and immediately got stuck back into committing crimes with Anto Spratt. The dangerous gangster had ensured that he always had a gun nearby, in case he ran into problems. One evening, shortly after his release, Curran was drunk and hanging around near his home on Cardiffsbridge Avenue. When he was drunk Curran's limp was more pronounced and he fell over. His jacket opened and the other youths he had been talking to spotted two handguns stuffed down the front of his trousers. Curran didn't care who saw them.

A feud had been simmering between the family of 33-year-old Willie O'Regan and associates of Curran and Spratt. O'Regan was a recovering heroin addict from Virginia Drive in Finglas. He was also considered a hard man and had a criminal record to match. The origins of the feud lay in an incident in November 2002 when Anthony Ledwidge and another associate had stabbed the boyfriend of O'Regan's cousin. The men had a row over a car they claimed he sold to them. O'Regan's mother was also pushed to the ground during the incident.

The feud flared up again around 5am on the morning of May 24, 2003, when Willie O'Regan and his brothers had a showdown with Curran and Spratt on Berryfield Drive. A ferocious running battle ensued, with both sides using sticks, knives and machetes. Other associates of Curran also joined in the melee which continued down the road, leaving a trail of blood behind. During the hour long pitched battle, O'Regan

stabbed Curran and got the better of him. He also smashed
the nose of another gang member. O'Regan was described as
"delirious" by witnesses, as he brandished two knives. The
crowd dispersed when they heard approaching sirens. Declan
Curran and Willie and Anthony O'Regan were taken to hospital
where they were treated for serious stab wounds. None of them
wanted to make a complaint when Gardaí arrived to interview
them.

Over a week later Curran's friends attacked another
brother of O'Regan's. He was hospitalised and treated for head
injuries.

On June 7, 30-year-old Christine Mahon from Berryfield
Drive in Finglas spent the night drinking and snorting cocaine
with Declan Curran and two of his associates. Mahon was a
heroin addict who had known both O'Regan and Curran all
her life. Curran had gone to school with her brother, David
'Soss' Mulvey, an armed robber who had also run with Marlo
Hyland's mob. Mahon had two children who were being reared
by a relative and she commuted between Finglas and the house
she shared with her boyfriend in Drogheda. Later that night the
group went back to Curran's house.

When the gangster was changing his top, Mahon noticed the
large bandage on the stab wound inflicted by O'Regan. She told
him it looked sore. "It's nothing compared to what's going to
happen to O'Regan. It was over for him when we were fighting,"
Curran replied. Then he produced six bullets for a handgun and
placed them on a chest of drawers. "There's someone's name
on them," he smirked.

O'Regan had made Curran lose face during the street fight
and for that he was going to pay with his life. The following
night Mahon slept with Curran for the first time. He couldn't
have sex because of his various injuries and he flew into a
rage. Willie O'Regan had become the root of all his problems,
including the sexual ones.

"It's nothing compared to what's going to happen to Willie.
That's it, I'll finish him. I'm goin' to kill him. He will be six
feet under when I'm finished with him. It's going to happen on
Tuesday, I'm not leaving it any longer, I want it over and done

with," he ranted.

Mahon later described to Gardaí how her would-be lover lay on his back, with his hands behind his head, staring at the ceiling as he considered O'Regan's fate.

It was after 10pm on Tuesday, June 10, when builder Patrick O'Driscoll returned to the block of flats where he lived on New Cabra Road. He locked his van up for the night and was walking up the steps towards the main door when a voice behind him said: "This is a hold-up."

O'Driscoll spun around and spotted the two men in balaclavas running towards him. One of them had a pistol and the other a sawn-off shotgun. They ordered him to open the door. Once inside they asked where apartment 10 was and if he knew who lived there. He didn't and they told him to lie down on the ground and not move. Number 10 was at the top of the stairs and was the home of Willie O'Regan and his partner Linda Ellis. The couple had been together for almost seven years.

Curran and his accomplice found the door they were looking for. O'Regan and Ellis had spent the night watching videos. They were sitting on the couch in front of the TV in line with the door which the two killers suddenly kicked in. O'Regan sprang up from his seat but he was too late. The gunmen stood in the doorway and began blasting their victim. O'Regan was hit six times in the salvo of bullets and buckshot. He was hit twice by the shotgun and four times by the revolver. He collapsed on the ground, moaning. He had been hit in the left side of the head and arm. The power of the blast had almost severed his left arm and hand.

Curran and his henchman escaped into a waiting car, which had been stolen a month earlier in County Kildare, and made their escape. It was later found burnt out. O'Regan was rushed to hospital but there was little surgeons could do to save him.

Two days later he died from his injuries.

The Gardaí subsequently identified six people who had taken part in the murder. Curran and a 26-year-old associate did the shooting. Anto Spratt and two others had organised the getaway car and the firearm. The detective unit based in

Mountjoy Garda Station carried out the investigation. They already had a major interest in the suspects.

Almost a month later, on July 8, Curran and another gang member, Victor Murphy, collected two firearms for another shooting. This time the target was a member of the travelling community who was living in a halting site on the edge of Finglas. Thirty-year-old Murphy, from Deanstown Green, was a member of the gang but was not considered to be dangerous. A detective who knew him described him as harmless. "He wasn't like the other lot. He was just into horses and drinking and fooling around. You could say he was an ordinary decent criminal."

Murphy sat in the passenger seat of the stolen Mitsubishi Lancer driven by Curran. He rested a sawn-off shotgun in his lap, with the business end aiming upwards. As Curran drove at speed across speed bumps through the Avilla Park camp, Murphy's gun suddenly went off. His head took the full brunt of the blast. Curran immediately turned the car around and sped out of the area.

A short distance away, in nearby Dunsink Lane, he dumped his pal's body at the side of the road. Then he abandoned the car on Berryfield Road and took the weapon with him. The next morning Murphy's body was discovered by a passer-by. When Gardaí found the car, the dead man's blood was on the front passenger seat and brain tissue was spattered on the rear window. It didn't seem to have bothered Curran very much. He probably put it down to the gangland equivalent of "an industrial accident". Other hoods put the accident down to a lot more than bad luck. The more superstitious amongst them were beginning to believe the rumours of a gypsy's curse.

A month later, on the evening of July 27, Curran was drinking with two men, Patrick "Podge" Sheridan and Terence 'Becker' Mulhall, on open ground at the rear of the Church of the Annunciation on Cardiffsbridge Road. Curran was always looking for trouble. A fight broke out between the three men and 'Becker' Mulhall gave Curran a serious hammering. The dangerous criminal told Becker he was going to shoot him. He went away and returned shortly afterwards, brandishing a handgun. He ran after Mulhall, who was trying to get back to the safety of his nearby home. Fifty yards from the front door Curran shot him a number of times in the upper body. Although seriously injured in the attack, Mulhall survived. He refused to make a statement to the Gardaí about the shooting. In the absence of a complaint or a witness there was nothing the cops could do about it.

By the time John Daly was released on bail that August, Finglas was like a powder keg. Curran, Spratt and company were threatening and intimidating anyone who got in their way. Gardaí monitoring the situation knew that with the deadly trio together again, there could only be an escalation in trouble. With Daly back in circulation the situation was about to get a lot worse. The Filthy Fifty enjoyed the patronage of the local godfather Marlo Hyland, who was also living with Daly's sister Lorna. With his backing, they considered themselves untouchable.

A few days after his release, on Saturday, September 13, Daly and Curran were thrown out of a pub in Cabra. The bouncers knew that the pair were trouble and had already thrown their henchmen out for selling drugs on the premises. As they were bundled out onto the street around 10.30pm, The hoods told the doormen that they would be back. They went away and returned 15 minutes later in a white Opel Vectra which was driven by Daly. They jumped out of the car, wearing balaclavas and armed with a pump-action shotgun. They walked up to the front door of the pub and had another scuffle with the doormen, one of whom managed to take the gun from them. The bouncers later claimed that the mobsters then produced a second sawn-off shotgun. One of the gunmen fired two shots at the bouncers who returned fire with the confiscated weapon. Daly and Curran jumped in the car and sped off.

They drove down Ratoath Road, heading in the direction of Scribblestown and Dunsink Lane where they intended to dump the car. As they went over a hump back railway bridge, they met a Garda squad car coming in the opposite direction. While the squad car was turning to go back after them, Daly and Curran drove the car up an embankment and abandoned it. They ran in opposite directions, leaving the engine running and the doors open.

As Daly was making his escape with the shotgun, he met 27-year-old Liam McAllister from Belfast. McAllister was a nephew of Sinn Féin leader Gerry Adams. He had moved south two years earlier after being run out of his home town. The son of Adams' sister was a petty crook. McAllister had served time in prison on both sides of the Border, for offences including burglary and car theft. McAllister and Daly had met when they were both on remand in prison the previous July. Adams' nephew asked Daly was he alright and did he need any help. Daly told him what had happened but said he didn't need any assistance.

Meanwhile the abandoned car was taken away for technical examination to Finglas Garda Station, where it was parked outside the front door. Daly and Curran regrouped later and were watching developments from the shadows. They were worried that the car could provide cops with enough forensic evidence to put them back where they belonged – in prison. And they had no intention of allowing anyone put a stop to their terrifying rampage.

Around 4 am the two hoods arrived at the Garda station on a motorbike. One of them smashed the front passenger window of the car, threw a container of petrol inside and set it alight. Gardaí ran from the station and quickly extinguished the fire, as Daly and Curran sped off.

Later that day Daly's getaway car was loaded onto a tow wagon and moved for safe-keeping to a yard at Mellows Road in Finglas. At 8pm the car was set alight as it sat on the back of the tow truck. This time it was completely destroyed.

About half an hour earlier, that same evening in September, John Daly had another "job" to deal with. He kicked in the front door of 30-year-old Anthony 'Anto' Carmody's home on Berryfield Drive, armed with a handgun. Carmody had been a close friend of Willie O'Regan and was with him on the night of the street battle with Curran's mob. In the twisted minds of this psychotic gang, that made Carmody a marked man. Carmody was resting at home as he was recovering from a previous gun attack. On August 13, while Daly was fighting to obtain High Court bail, Declan Curran and Anto Spratt had made their first attempt to shoot Carmody. They'd pulled up outside his home on a motorbike and shot him in the leg. However he wasn't seriously injured in the attack.

This time Daly was determined to do a better job. He shot Carmody four times, hitting him in the hip and stomach. Then he turned the gun on Carmody's partner, Joanne Dempsey. He shot her once in the foot, before running out to a waiting motorbike. The couple, whose two young children were in the house at the time, were rushed to hospital. They knew who had shot them but were too terrified to make any statement or complaint to the Gardaí. They had first-hand experience of the chilling consequences of crossing swords with these blood thirsty mad men. The couple recovered from their injuries and joined the growing ranks of people who were too terrified to talk.

Daly, Curran and Spratt had shown they were prepared to go to any lengths to protect themselves. Once the car used in the Cabra pub shooting had been properly burned, Daly's thoughts turned to Liam McAllister. He was the only person who could positively connect Daly with the incident. He didn't know McAllister very well and didn't trust him. He was also suspicious of what he referred to as "Nordie bastards".

On September 17, Daly phoned McAllister shortly after 1pm and arranged to meet him on the pretext of a "job". He told McAllister that he wanted to threaten a few people and his Northern accent would help get the message across. He said he first wanted to test fire a weapon he was going to use on the job. McAllister was more than willing to help his new associate because he wanted to get in with the big boys.

Daly collected McAllister on a scrambler motorbike around 2.30pm. They set off for an area called 'The Trench' in Scribblestown, on the edge of Finglas. Scribblestown was a large expanse of overgrown, undulating waste ground. It was popular among locals for horse riding, motorbike scrambling and drink and drug parties. The isolation also meant it was popular among criminals across West Dublin for hiding guns, drugs and money. They also used it as a place to bring errant villains for a beating – because no one would hear the screams of pain. And it was their killing field. Two criminals, Mark Dwyer and Michael Godfrey had been executed there. Declan Curran had also dumped Victor Murphy's body in the nearby lane.

Daly stopped in a dip under a small hill and they both got off the bike. The killer dug a sawn-off shotgun out of a rucksack on his back and fired a shot into the brush to see it was working. Daly told McAllister to go down to hedgerow below them and retrieve spare cartridges he had hidden. As the Northerner walked down to investigate, Daly calmly reloaded the weapon took aim and shot him in the back to disable him. The blast gouged out a large hole in McAllister's lower back which was the size of a human fist. He collapsed onto the ground screaming in agony.

At first the Northerner thought he had been shot by accident. Then Daly used his boot to turn McAllister over onto his back. "Did you shoot me?" he cried.

"Sorry I had to do that…you know too much," Daly smirked, as he reloaded the weapon. Standing above his victim he took aim at his head and squeezed the trigger for a second time. McAllister instinctively put his hands up to protect his face as the shotgun exploded. His right hand took the brunt of the blast which blew off three fingers and splattered blood and tissue over his face.

The amount of gore on McAllister's face convinced Daly that he was dead. He put the gun in his rucksack and looked around to see if anyone was watching. Satisfied the coast was clear, he got back on his motorbike and drove off.

Miraculously the wounded man survived the callous execution attempt. He never actually lost consciousness, even though he was critically injured and in immense pain. He dialled '999' on his mobile phone and called for an ambulance. He told the dispatcher that he had been shot and was lying in a field in Scribblestown. Garda units from Cabra, Finglas and Blanchardstown rushed to the scene and began searching for the caller. A short time later he was found lying on his back in a hedge row. He was rushed to hospital where he underwent a number of emergency operations. When Detective Inspector Brian Sherry arrived at James Connolly Memorial Hospital (JCMH) in Blanchardstown a doctor told him Gerry Adam's nephew "has not got a hope" of surviving. The tough Northerner proved him wrong and was placed under armed guard in case the mob came back to finish the job. The doctors in JCMH were very experienced in dealing with gunshot wounds.

"McAllister was very seriously injured and was left with extensive damage to his hand and internal organs. It was a miracle that he actually survived and the doctors saved his life. Daly had showed that he was as cold and calculating a killer as we had ever seen. The first shot was intended to knock his victim down and the second to finish him off. It was a classic example of a so-called professional hit," DI Sherry later recalled. "It showed that this gang was prepared to go to any lengths, including murder, to clean up loose ends and prevent any chance of being caught. They were extremely devious individuals who had no respect for human life. They really were out of control."

McAllister spent several weeks in intensive care and suffered excruciating pain. Despite this, on September 26, he gave Detective Sergeant Peter Noonan a full statement in which he named Daly as his would-be assassin. He said he was prepared to testify in court and go all the way. McAllister remained in Blanchardstown Hospital, under armed guard, for over a month. When he was well enough, he was transferred by ambulance, under police escort back to a hospital in Belfast. The Gardaí in Finglas were quietly confident that they were finally going to put away one of the worst thugs on their patch. They began putting together a case to have Daly charged with attempted murder.

The word was also put out that Daly and his cronies were in "serious bother" with the Republican movement because of McAllister's family connection to Adams. Sources have claimed that Daly later offered "compensation" through Republican intermediaries. It was also claimed that Daly organised to pay €100,000 to the injured man although this could not be confirmed. Despite the impending problems, Daly, Curran and

Spratt planned to do some more cleaning-up.

Over in Blanchardstown, another potentially lethal gang war had broken out after Bernard 'Verb' Sugg was shot dead in the Brookwood Inn on August 17. The cold-blooded execution of one of the Westie's front men signalled the beginning of an internal power struggle. Sugg was the brother of Stephen Sugg, who led the Westies, along with Shane Coates. As Gardaí braced themselves for a backlash, Detective Superintendent Collins and Detective Inspector Sherry asked Garda HQ for more resources. They wanted to try to keep a lid on the volatile situation. Operations West and Crossover were established, in co-operation with Assistant Commissioner Tony Hickey of the Garda National Support Services. As officers began investigating the various shootings and murders in the K district, the idea was that the operations would compliment each other.

Part of the strategy was to do everything possible to smash the deadly Finglas gang. The investigating team wanted to press charges against Curran for the attempted murder of Terence 'Becker' Mulhall who was still being treated for the injuries he'd suffered that July. They also had information that 27-year-old Patrick 'Podge' Sheridan had witnessed Curran shooting Mulhall. 'Podge' Sheridan was a drug addict from Ratoath Avenue in Finglas. The hapless father of two young children was a potential witness and they tried to bring him on board. Detectives were also trying to encourage Mulhall to join the Witness Protection Programme but he was refusing to co-operate. Sheridan also refused to co-operate.

But Gardaí knew that he had a lot more information to offer and they weren't willing to give up that easily. A detective phoned him on a number of occasions and left a message asking Sheridan to call to the station for another chat. In a cruel twist of fate Sheridan had given the sim card for the number to another drug addict who received the messages from the police instead. The drug addict reported back to Curran who decided that 'Podge' had become an informant.

Podge Sheridan's fate was sealed.

On Monday, October 6, Sheridan got a call from John Daly. He offered Podge the chance to earn €1,000 to "look at a job" with him, Curran and Anto Spratt, later that evening. Sheridan arranged to meet them on Cardiffsbridge Road around 5pm.

That afternoon Podge was seen to stagger as he walked up the road. He had been drinking earlier in the day and was intoxicated. On his way there he phoned Christine Mahon, who was a good friend. She later recounted their last conversation to detectives.

"Podge told me that he was going off to look at a job. He said there was a thousand pounds in it for him. He said he was going off with John Daly and Decie Curran and nothing could go wrong. I said just think what your doing. I begged Podge not to go with them. He never had money and a thousand pounds was a lot of money to him. I felt it was a scam, I told him not to trust Curran or Daly," she said.

That evening Podge went with Curran, Daly and Spratt to 'The Trench' – the same spot McAllister had been lured to. This time the cold-hearted mobsters ensured that there were no mistakes. They shot him twice in the head, at point blank range with a .38 revolver. His body was dumped into bushes in a copse of trees.

The following day, after he failed to come home, Sheridan's family reported him as a missing person. The day after that, Thursday 9, Detective Inspector Brian Sherry was contacted by the Crime and Security Branch at Garda HQ. They had received intelligence that Sheridan had been murdered and his body was left somewhere in the Scribblestown area. Det Supt Collins called out the Divisional Search Team, who began combing the area. They eventually found the body and another gangland murder investigation was underway.

The senseless killing caused revulsion in Finglas. The feeling of the community was summed up by their outspoken Parish Priest, Seamus Ahern. He could barely hide his frustration and upset at the way the ruthless gang were terrorising his congregation. In an interview on RTÉ he put it to the authorities to do something about the thugs. He queried why bin-tax protesters were being jailed while bona fide criminals were walking the streets.

"We don't seem to be able to get rid of the thugs who

destroy our lovely community. I can't bear a few people holding us to ransom. I can't bear people being obsessed with the fear of something happening. I can't bear the fact that some of our good people [bin tax protestors] are stuck in Mountjoy. I find the law cruel," Fr. Ahern declared angrily. He then said what everyone believed should be happening: "I think those who harass the community have to be harassed by the law. Their homes must be visited by the police."

At the same time, two investigation teams were doing everything they could to do just what the local priest had suggested. Two days after Podge Sheridan's body was found, Det Sgt Peter Noonan from Finglas arrested Daly for questioning about the attempted murder of Liam McAllister. Christine Mahon's brother, David 'Soss' Mulvey was also arrested. He was suspected of supplying the motorbike used by Daly. He was later released without charge.

Two days later Daly was charged with possession of firearms with intent to endanger life and assault causing serious harm. He was remanded in custody and was subsequently charged with attempted murder.

On October 16, detectives from Mountjoy and Fitzgibbon Street Garda Stations arrested Declan Curran, Anthony Spratt and four other associates for questioning about the O'Regan murder. One of the men arrested was Darren Gilligan, the drug-dealing son of John Gilligan. During their two day detention they refused to answer any questions.

While the interviews were continuing, Christine Mahon met with Detective Sergeant Gerry McDonnell and Detective Garda Terry McHugh. She had decided to tell them everything she knew about the murder. The cold-blooded manner of her friend Podge Sheridan's death was the catalyst for her decision to come forward. Sheridan was well liked and considered harmless by everyone who knew him. Mahon told the officers that she had met the younger brother of a close associate of Curran, Daly and Spratt the day before. He told her he had been instructed to collect a handgun the day before Podge Sheridan's appointment with death.

"He was crying and very upset. He kept calling them

[Daly/Curran/Spratt] scum, even his brother who told him to get the gun," she recalled.

Then, with tears in her eyes, the struggling drug addict explained why she was coming clean. "The word is that Podge was shot dead because he was an informer, a rat. Podge wasn't a rat, he wasn't an informer. I am not a rat either, I'm not an informer but Podge was the last straw. If everyone just sits there and keeps their mouths shut the police won't find out nothing. I want to see an end to it, to the killings, innocent people getting killed for nothing. I am sick of all this, innocent people getting killed, as I said, Podge was the last straw."

Over the next two days, Christine Mahon gave detectives four lengthy statements, outlining everything she knew about the O'Regan murder. She revealed how Curran had repeatedly told her he was going to murder O'Regan on Tuesday, June 10. She also told how a few days after the hit Curran was waiting for her outside the drug rehabilitation clinic in Finglas.

"He warned me to keep my mouth shut. He said that if I said anything, the same would happen to me. I took this to mean that he would kill me," she said.

Christine Mahon said she was prepared to testify against Curran.

On October 18, Curran and his accomplices were released without charge. Mahon's statements had to be further investigated before charges could be brought against him. At the same time, two armed officers from the O'Regan investigation team were assigned to protect Christine Mahon at her home in Drogheda. The protection was lifted six days later on the orders of Garda HQ. Mahon was distraught because she knew that she was exposed. Investigating Gardaí produced a detailed document for their superiors, recommending that Mahon be accepted into the Witness Protection Programme (WPP). They explained that if Mahon did not receive adequate protection, she would be murdered by Curran's associates.

In the interim the investigators found protection of another kind for their witness. They executed a number of outstanding penal warrants which were in existence against Mahon for non-payment of fines. She was detained in the women's prison, the

Dochas Centre, at Mountjoy, until November 24.

Shortly afterwards, her father Denis returned from England after being contacted by his son David. 'Soss' Mulvey wanted his father to convince Christine to retract her evidence. However she refused to change her mind and travelled to London with her father on her release from Mountjoy Prison.

In the meantime, Gardaí presented a file on the case to the Director of Public Prosecutions who gave the go ahead to charge the dangerous thug.

On November 12, armed detectives from Mountjoy arrested Curran. When they burst into his house at Cardiffsbridge Road, they found Curran lying in bed fully-clothed, wearing a bullet-proof vest.

Curran was formally charged with murder later that day and remanded in custody where he joined John Daly. Curran later applied for bail in the High Court but was refused when detectives argued that it was likely he would do a runner. A follow-up investigation had uncovered a disturbing link between the gang and the Keane mob in Limerick. The bullet-proof vest was one of five purchased in the UK by a man who was related by marriage to the Keane family.

With Curran and Daly behind bars, their associates did everything in their power to have the charges dropped. Marlo Hyland and Anto Spratt had been making exhaustive enquiries to find out where Christine Mahon was living in London. Unknown to the hoods, she had been offered full-time police protection back in Ireland but had refused to take up the offer. Andrew 'Chicore' Dillon, who was part of the gang, was going out with one of Mahon's relatives. He found out where Mahon was living in London and passed it on to his pals. Since Christmas the State's witness had been living in a small house in Hounslow in Middlesex. She was living on the dole and attending a heroin addiction clinic.

On April 6, 2004, two armed and masked men broke into her house while she was upstairs. She peeped down the stairs and saw the shadows of two men, with hand guns creeping towards her. Mahon made a few frantic calls to the police and her father. As she slammed her bedroom door, to keep the hit men out, she heard one of them speaking in a Dublin accent: "I could see her from here. I can get her I have a great shot, just shoot her."

Mahon went to the window of the first floor room to jump out. As she did so, her father arrived just in time and caught her. Armed police also surrounded the house. When they broke in the two hit men had left.

Mahon was extremely distraught and shaken by the experience. She phoned Det Sgt Gerry McDonnell in Fitzgibbon Street and told him what had happened. She said she wanted to come home. Mahon travelled to Heathrow Airport with just Stg£10 in her pocket. She was met by the police when she got there. They stayed with her while the Gardaí booked her on the next available flight to Dublin. A few hours later she was under full-time armed guard in Ireland.

Declan Curran's trial for the murder of Willie O'Regan opened in the Central Criminal Court in Dublin on July 26, 2004. In the meantime, despite being under constant guard, Mahon had a change of heart. It was suspected that Curran, Daly and Spratt had all made personal contact with her by phone and issued threats she could not ignore. Counsel for the prosecution, Paul O'Higgins SC, outlined the State's case against Curran and the circumstances of O'Regan's murder. When Christine Mahon entered the witness box, she was obviously nervous and uneasy. It was soon apparent that the intimidation of Curran and his pals had paid off. Mahon was declared a hostile witness when she retracted her statements. She agreed with Paul O'Higgins that she had given signed statements to detectives implicating Declan Curran in the killing. Bt she claimed she "made them up" because she was annoyed with him.

O'Higgins suggested that what she told the Gardaí was true but that she was now retracting out of fear. He read out the four statements she had made on October 17, 2003.

Mahon claimed her statements were "all lies". She said she was annoyed at the accused because she said, "Deckie was using me" so she made it up. Mahon claimed she only signed the statements to get out of the Garda station. She told counsel she was on heroin and the heroin substitute methadone.

Paul O'Higgins SC, then read a portion of her original statement in which she said: "I knew Deckie was going to shoot Willie O'Regan but I didn't think he was going to kill him."

"Did you say that?" counsel asked.

"No," Mahon replied.

Counsel then put it to her that, as she left the court during a short adjournment, a detective heard her ask her brother David 'Soss' Mulvey: "I'm doing it right, aren't I?"

She denied this and said she and her brother just went outside for a cigarette.

"The reason you're giving your evidence the way that you are is you've been told you'd better not swear up to what you told the Gardaí truthfully," O'Higgins accused her.

"That's not true," she replied.

"Haven't you had a bad time since you told the Gardaí. You've been terrified ever since by the fact you said it," O'Higgins continued.

Counsel further suggested that Curran had threatened her that if she opened her mouth "the same would happen to her".

On the second day of the trial, Paul O' Higgins put it to Mahon that she made her statements on October 17 and 18 after her friend 'Podge' Sheridan disappeared and his body was found in Scribblestown on October 6. He suggested that she was sickened by the killing. "Too many people were being killed and you came clean about the William O'Regan killing," he suggested. "You were in fear of what may happen to you."

He further suggested that after Podge Sheridan was found dead she had told Gardaí "I'm afraid for my life but I'll give evidence in court if I have to."

"No." Mahon replied, "I made it up...I lied."

She told the court that she was under Garda protection but denied suggestions that she had requested it. O'Higgins then put it to her that she had retracted her statements because she was "scared witless".

"Didn't two men come into the house in England with guns?"

"I was on crack cocaine so… that's what I thought I saw," Mahon replied, adding that she may have been hallucinating.

O'Higgins reminded her that she rang 999 immediately after the incident. "You were scared out of your wits, I suggest to you."

"I got a fright that night. I don't know whether or not I was hallucinating or not but I got a fright."

With Christine Mahon refusing to stand over her statements about Curran, the DPP was left with no choice but to withdraw the charges against him on the third day of the trial. He sat smiling in the dock.

Acceding to the prosecution's application to formally withdraw the murder charge, Mr Justice Paul Butler noted that Christine Mahon appeared to him to be under "severe pressure". Discharging the jury, the judge reminded the court that this case involved a brutal slaying and he extended his sympathy to the deceased's family.

Curran's defence counsel, Brendan Grehan SC, opposed the application and said he was seeking a verdict of "not guilty" by direction. He said Curran was entitled to an acquittal as there was no evidence before the jury upon which they could properly convict him. He said the prosecution, having put forward no evidence, could not enter a nolle prosequi "in the hope of re-activating this particular prosecution in the future." To do so would offend against the principle of double jeopardy.

Grehan added that Justice Butler had the opportunity of assessing the witness's demeanour in the witness box where "she came across as a very relaxed person".

The judge interrupted Curran's counsel saying that on the contrary Mahon gave every indication "of someone under severe pressure".

Mahon left the court under escort by two detectives. Curran was returned to prison to serve the remainder of a separate sentence for theft and malicious damage. He was due for release a few months later.

Mahon left the WPP shortly afterwards.

Daly, meanwhile, received unwelcome news. Thanks to the tenacity of Detective Garda Kevin Stratford, Daly's nine year sentence for the armed robberies in 2000 was finally reactivated in July 2004. Daly had another three years to serve of his nine year stretch. He developed a deep hatred of the hard-working cop as a result. Stratford's colleagues and friends believe that Daly would have tried to murder the officer when he was released. (Tragically, Kevin Stratford died after a long illness in June 2006. On the night of his funeral Daly phoned his lackies and instructed them to daub graffiti celebrating his death on walls around Finglas. The sick slogans were signed 'JD'.)

The previous January, Daly had received three months for a breach of the peace for the St Patrick's Day incident in which he attacked and injured a Garda. Both he and Spratt were acquitted of the assault charge on a legal technicality. In the summer, Spratt received a 12 month prison sentence for a number of road traffic offences.

With the three hoodlums out of circulation the people of Finglas got some peace.

Daly was transferred to E1 in Portlaoise Maximum security prison where the country's toughest and most dangerous criminals are housed. It was an acknowledgement that Daly had indeed made it into the premier league of Ireland's low life. He built up a close association with Limerick godfather, Christy Keane, the head of the notorious Keane crime family, who was doing ten years for possession of drugs. Daly was also close to John Gilligan. The young gangster continued to dominate events back in Finglas from his cell, with the use of a mobile phone. He organised drug deals and shootings. As a result of the unholy alliance in Portlaoise Prison, the Limerick and Finglas gangs began working together in the drug business. They organised the movement of guns and drugs between the two cities and also provided hit men.

An example of the closeness of the relationship was an incident which Daly organised that Autumn. Christy Keane's gang in Limerick were involved in a ferocious blood feud with the opposing McCarthy/Dundon and Ryan gangs. It had blown up in January 2003 when Keane's brother, Kieran, was ambushed and shot dead in a double cross by the McCarthy/Dundons. The feud had attracted unprecedented Garda activity in Limerick in a bid to stop the killing. *(See Chapters Nine and Ten.)* As a result the constant patrols and searches had completely disrupted the drug business. Keane's sidekick, Brian Collopy, had taken the pragmatic decision to organise an unofficial truce in the hostilities so they could all make money. Christy Keane was furious with the suggestion of a peace deal. He reckoned that not enough blood had been spilt to avenge his brother's murder. He turned to his dangerous pal from Finglas for some assistance.

Through Daly, a drug deal was organised with Collopy. But when the Limerick thugs turned up to collect the shipment and pay for the drugs, they were surrounded. A number of shots were fired and their money was taken off them. They were then told to "fuck off" back to Limerick, before they got hurt. The incident caused a rift in the Keane/Collopy camp and it was followed by an attempt by the Collopys to shoot up Keane's home.

Declan Curran was freed from prison and back on the streets when the Collopy scam was carried out. He and the Filthy Fifty gang continued doing robberies and selling drugs. With Curran back in the neighbourhood, the number of shootings inevitably escalated.

But his luck was about to run out.

On the afternoon of Thursday, November 11, 2004, Curran and another gang member, 23-year-old Paul Cunningham, set out to rob the Sutton branch of the Permanent TSB in North Dublin. From Mulhuddart, Cunningham had also been an associate of the Westies but had joined with the Finglas gang in selling drugs, doing armed robberies and terrorising people. At the time he was facing charges for possession of a firearm and receiving stolen motorbikes. He had 20 previous convictions.

The two friends parked a stolen car near the branch at Sutton Cross and ran inside armed with a shotgun and a pistol. At the same time, 27-year-old probationer Garda Ann Roche was on the beat nearby and was alerted to the raid. When she looked through the door, she saw the two hoods holding up staff and she called for back-up. The plucky cop confronted Curran and Cunningham, as they made their escape with a bag of cash. Garda Roche hit Cunningham on the head and back, as he ran for the getaway car. She tried to open the car door and began smashing the windscreen, in a bid to stop him, but he drove off. At the same time, Curran had made a run for it, in the opposite direction, but was caught by a detective unit 500 yards away. His gun was also recovered.

Curran was arrested and brought to Howth Garda Station for questioning. The man who had been the target of so many operations had been caught as a result of pure good luck and a very brave trainee cop. (Garda Roche later received a Scott Medal for her bravery.)

On Saturday evening Curran was brought before the Dublin District Court where he was formally charged with armed robbery. He was remanded in custody to Cloverhill Prison in Clondalkin where he shared a cell with two relatives.

The following morning, his cell mates went to the chapel for Sunday Mass. Curran appeared to be still asleep. When they returned to the cell they couldn't wake him up – the 23-year-old gangster had died in his sleep. It was later discovered that Curran had a cocktail of prescribed and illegal drugs in his system which had caused heart failure. Suddenly the rumours of a curse no longer seemed so fantastic to the doped-up gangsters.

Daly heard the news almost immediately and was upset for his best pal. Then a girlfriend rang him to say that families who had been terrorised by Curran were celebrating his unexpected demise. Daly went berserk and contacted Paul Cunningham, screaming for revenge. Over the following 24 hours, on his mobile phone from the comfort of his prison cell, he orchestrated mayhem on the streets of Finglas o.

In the first incident the gang shot and seriously injured Francis Griffin when he answered the door to his home on Ratoath Drive in Finglas West, at 8.15pm that evening. A relation of Griffin had been involved in a row with Curran some years earlier. Two hours later the mob fired shots through the door of the home of Willie O'Regan's mother on Virginia Drive. They had first tried to get in and shoot the occupants. Acting on Daly's instructions, the gang returned again at 3am the following morning and tried to petrol bomb the house.

The bomb hit the front window and smashed onto the ground, failing to ignite.

Scores of extra police, including the Emergency Response Unit, were mobilized in an attempt to stop the ongoing madness. Gardaí were even drafted in to guard Curran's coffin when it was brought to his local funeral home the following week. A group of individuals close to traveller Victor Murphy plotted to "rob" Curran in his coffin and dump it on a laneway. It was intended as a symbolic gesture to ridicule the once notorious gangster. In death, Curran could thank the cops for protecting his mortal remains.

On the morning of Sunday, November 21, Paul Cunningham was asleep with his partner Jennifer Kieran at his mother's house in Dromheath Avenue in Mulhuddart. His 18-month-old son was also sleeping in the room. Around 3am two men broke into the house, through a back door and crept up stairs. They burst into Cunningham's room and shot him twice in the chest with a sawn-off shotgun, before he had a chance to wake up. His partner and child had a lucky escape.

Cunningham's funeral was worthy of a London East End villain. His remains were brought to the local cemetery in a horse-drawn carriage, followed by a fleet of limos and what seemed like every drug dealer and robber in West Dublin. Several members of the Keane gang travelled form Limerick to pay their respects.

It was later speculated that Cunningham had been shot in retaliation for the crime spree his gang had unleashed a week earlier. While researching *Crime Wars*, however, reliable intelligence sources revealed a theory that Cunningham had actually been murdered on the orders of John Daly. The sources confirmed that Daly blamed Cunningham for "running away" when he and Curran were confronted by the Garda in Sutton Cross. Daly maintained that his partner-in-crime would have lived if he hadn't been arrested. The intelligence came to light as part of another criminal investigation.

A month later, Liam McAllister's case came to trial. He refused to turn up in court to testify in Daly's trial for attempting to murder him. At first McAllister had refused to take any calls from the Gardaí who investigated his case. When he did make contact, he said he didn't want to go back to Dublin because he was afraid. Gardaí then offered him the opportunity to testify via video-link from Belfast which he also declined. By the time it came to the date for the trial, the police couldn't locate McAllister. When Mr Justice Michael White heard that the injured man had failed to answer questions about his decision or accept phone calls from Gardaí, he issued a warrant for his arrest.

Just four months later, the 'gypsy's curse' struck again. On March 5, Anto Spratt hung himself in his cell in Mountjoy Prison. The 31-year-old's body was found by the sons of William 'Jock' Corbally. Their father was the victim of one of the worst gangland murders in the past twenty years. There was considerable surprise at Anto Spratt's suicide. He was within two weeks of being released from his 12 month sentence and he was returning to a thriving drug business. His family later claimed that he had been a suicide risk but the prison authorities had no record that he had ever tried to take his own life before. The family claimed at his subsequent inquest that he had been "upset and disappointed" that he hadn't been granted temporary release to attend his son's Confirmation ceremony a week earlier. Associates of the once feared gangster and armed robber later confided that Spratt had been consumed with guilt over his involvement in the Willie O'Regan murder. It was claimed that he had regularly cried over the crime and regretted his involvement. The more superstitious criminals believed his depression was caused by the Gypsy's curse. The Criminal Assets Bureau subsequently obtained a High Court order freezing the gangster's bank accounts, which contained over €100,000.

Meanwhile the gang's inexplicable bad fortune continued unabated. Gang members Stephen Bradshaw and another close relative also took their own lives. Anto Ledwidge, Curran's accomplice in the the Four Courts incident in which the security guard was killed, suddenly dropped dead on a building site at the age of 30. Three months later his brother Kevin, who was also an associate of the gang, was shot dead at his front door, after a row broke out at a cocaine party. Andrew 'Chicore' Dillon who ran with Marlo Hyland and the Curran gangs was shot dead on the godfather's orders in August 2005. Convicted armed robber and murder suspect, Paul Boyd, was killed when he crashed his motorbike into a pole while being chased by police. Another victim of the curse was 22-year-old Dwayne 'Bilzer' Foster.

* * * *

Despite his tiny stature and a chronic drug addiction problem, Dwayne Foster had a big reputation as a hard man and a violent thug. He had been causing mayhem with Curran and Daly from when they were young teenagers growing up in Finglas. By the time he was in his late teens, he was also involved in armed robberies and shootings. Even by the standards of the gang leaders, he was considered to be utterly reckless. His temperament became more volatile when he was diagnosed with throat cancer at the age of 20. He had also fathered two children during his short chaotic existence.

On March 5, 2006, Foster went on a drink and drugs-fuelled binge with three other gang members, convicted drug dealer Jeffrey Finnegan, and armed robbers Wayne Harte and David Geraghty. The four thugs gate-crashed the 40th birthday party for Edel Murtagh at the Inisfail GAA club in Coolock. The hoodlums were well-known to the party-goers and were seen as trouble. They sat around a table, drinking and snorting cocaine which they scooped out of a bag with coins. At one stage they were seen injecting heroin in the toilets. They abused the people at the party and threatened to hit one man with a bottle. Later on the party adjourned to the home of Edel's sister, Rhoda Flanagan.

When Foster, Geraghty and Finnegan tried to get into the house they were refused by Rhoda Flanagan. When she shut the door, they smashed in the windows in the door and the porch. Finnegan was seen making threatening gun gestures with his hands. He was shouting: "Do you know who you are dealing with? We'll be back."

The drunken mobsters drove off in a car to a nearby house Foster was renting. He picked up a 9mm Glock automatic pistol and checked that it was loaded and cocked. They changed cars and returned to Rhoda Flanagan's house.

Twenty-three year-old catering assistant Donna Cleary was one of the guests at the party. The attractive young woman had a three-year-old son whom she doted on. Her son's father, Jason Larkin, had been sentenced to life in prison four years earlier. He had stabbed a man to death outside a city pub. Donna had made a comfortable life for herself and her son. When Rhoda's porch windows were smashed in, the young mother had volunteered to help sweep up the glass before the other guests arrived. She went back into the house and was standing with a drink in the kitchen when Foster and his gang pulled up outside for a second time.

Foster got out of the driver's side of the car and carefully aimed the firearm at the house and the people who were still cleaning up at the front. He fired five indiscriminate shots in rapid succession. Then he got into the car and drove off at speed.

The gunshots caused confusion inside the house. No one realized Donna Cleary had been hit by one of the bullets until she walked into a reveller, staggered into another room and slumped to the ground. The bullet had hit the young mum in the side of the chest and gone through her lungs and heart. As she lay injured on the floor, she cried out for her son Clayton. She said she wanted to see her baby. Donna Cleary died a short time later in hospital.

As Gardaí began a major murder investigation, there was widespread revulsion and shock at the murder of an innocent mother. Larry Dunne's infamous warning, 24 years earlier, had just been proved beyond all doubt. Immediately after the attack, Foster and his cronies sped out of town. They went to hide in a friend's house in the Curragh, in County Kildare.

Later that day detectives used mobile phone technology to track Foster down. Within hours they were arrested and taken in for questioning. Twenty-four hours later Foster was found unconscious in his cell at Coolock Garda Station. He was rushed to the Accident and Emergency unit at Beaumont – the same A&E Donna had been brought to a day before – where he was pronounced dead a short time later. A post-mortem later found that he died of natural causes, linked with his drug addiction and cancer. He was the third member of the notorious mob to die suddenly from natural causes.

* * * *

In the few years that Daly had spent finishing off his armed robbery sentence, the gangland he knew and loved had changed irrevocably. By the time Marlo Hyland was shot in 2006, Daly had lost a dozen of his closest associates. But he still had plenty of friends. As far back as 2004, the *Sunday World* wrote an extensive story about how Daly in particular was co-ordinating a crime wave from his prison cell, using a mobile phone. The story revealed how the volatile gangster was organising shootings and attacks on his enemies over the phone. But Daly, with just three months left to serve of his sentence, then used his phone to become a household name overnight.

In April 2007, this writer was invited onto Joe Duffy's *Liveline* programme on RTÉ radio. It was to debate the issue of the connections between organized crime gangs in Dublin and Sinn Féin and the IRA with Sinn Féin councilor Christy Burke. The debate stemmed from an earlier exposé in the *Sunday World* linking a party election worker and an IRA commander with a paedophile, drug trafficker called Christy Griffin. *(See Chapter Eight.)*

As a result of that confrontation, (a caller who cannot be named for legal reasons), another criminal figure from Finglas, got on the phone to abuse this reporter and accuse him of writing "all lies" about gangsters like him. At one point, John Daly famously phoned the programme to challenge me about a story I had written about him issuing death threats to other criminals back in Finglas. Daly was extremely agitated and highly strung. For the first time a radio audience got to actually hear two major criminals talking live on the airwaves. It made for extraordinary listening. The following is a summary of the conversation between this author, John Daly and the other caller who is referred to as Mr X for legal reasons.

Joe Duffy: John Daly's on the line. John, good afternoon to you.

John: How's it going? Alright?

Joe: You're in Portlaoise Prison at the moment?

John: I'm in Portlaoise right now, yeah, there's only one place I can be. Paul Williams knows that very well.

Joe: Take your time now, John.

John: I will do. How's it going Mr X, alright?

Mr X: Not too bad. Yourself?

John: Yeah. Thanks for the postcard while you were away. Now, Mr Williams. How many thousands of people would you say read your newspaper every Sunday?

Paul: Almost a million.

John: About a million? Do you know how much [sic] lies you tell every week?

Do you know I sent a registered posted letter today with an article from that newspaper that you just wrote saying that I carried out armed robbery when I got out on my review. I did not get arrested for any armed robberies.

Paul: You're in prison serving how many years?

John: It doesn't matter how many years I'm serving.

Paul: Actually, where did you get the mobile phone to ring out?

John: (Getting agitated). Who told you I had a spat against Mr X who was a friend of mine who I grew up with? I have a complaint in against you because if I didn't know Mr X and Mr X did not know me, you are kicking off a fucking gangland war.

Joe: John, the language, the language.

John: OK, but that's what his intention is, to kick off war.

Joe: John, you're in prison at the moment for armed robbery at an Esso station. Isn't that correct?

John: Yeah, back in 1999. I was 18 years of age.

Joe: And how many years are you serving in Portlaoise?

John: Nine years. Finishing off nine years.

Paul: You were let out of prison; then it was re-activated.

John: I'm going on holiday with Mr X when I get out.

Joe: So you're denying you threatened to kill Mr X ?

John: Denied? The date, it was all in the 'Herald' a week before Williams over in the 'Sunday World'. You check that date in that 'Herald' and you check this prison of when Mr X sent me a postcard that very same day.

Mr X: (chuckling) And that's someone I left the country over.

Joe: John Daly, are you still on the phone there?

John: I can't stay long. I can't stay long. I'm in a cell. Paul Williams, you are a liar. You make up lies to start war.

If I didn't know Mr X and Mr X did not know me, you would have kicked off a war there. People would be wanting to get one person before the other person got the other. Now I'm going. Get off the phone, you f***ing liar.

John Daly could never have dreamt of the storm of controversy and abuse he was gong to raise as he punched in the numbers on his prized phone, to talk to Joe. The call caused an overwhelming response. With just a month before a general election, Daly had indirectly sealed the political fate of Progressive Democrats leader Michael McDowell. The PD leader was the most controversial and highly strung Minister for Justice in the history of the Irish State. He had stormed around Ireland, making new laws on what seemed like almost a daily basis, as he gave the impression that he would personally change the world. McDowell had been accused of seriously interfering in the day-to-day work of the Gardaí. It was more than bizarre that a dangerous and highly strung criminal calling from the phone in his jail cell could put the final nail in McDowell's political career.

After the 2007 General Election, McDowell and his party were obliterated and were about to be finally wound up in October 2008. And John Daly didn't come out of the phone call debacle too well either. He was immediately moved to Cork Prison after the call as a punishment. Bad luck continued to stalk him.

Daly's phone call to *Liveline* was intensely embarrassing for the Department of Justice and particularly for the prison service.

Behind-the-scenes, McDowell was threatening to have people sacked. Within days there was a major clampdown in prisons across the country which produced even more remarkable revelations. The first prisoners hit by the specially organised searches were Daly's neighbours on E1. Flat screen TVs, DVD players, large quantities of booze, drugs and even budgies were seized from the gangsters' cells, along with hundreds of mobile phones. Daly's call had stoked up a hornets nest and he suddenly found himself becoming a figure of hate amongst former criminal friends like Gilligan and Keane. They had lost their privileges because of his stupidity.

When Daly's phone was seized, it was taken away for analysis by Gardaí. They soon found out that he hadn't just been calling radio stations. In the period of just one week before the seizure Daly had made 3,500 phone calls alone.

For his remaining four months behind bars Daly was shunned by many of his fella inmates because his big mouth had gotten everyone in trouble. At one stage, Gardaí received intelligence that some of his former friends on E1 had offered the Republican renegades €60,000 to whack Daly. But it appears that his gaffe was eventually forgotten.

As his release date approached, Daly began making plans for his freedom. He had already been in touch with a number of Marlo Hyland's associates, looking for money that he said the godfather had promised him upon his release. Daly had been ranting and raving at his former cronies and making death threats. Gangsters across West Dublin braced themselves for his return.

On August 14, 2007, John Daly was released from prison. The first people he ran into were the police. Only this time they wanted to help him.

"We had received a load of intelligence that there were threats all over the place to kill Daly and these were from wholly reliable sources," explained the former Detective Inspector Brian Sherry, who had been on Daly's case many times. "We had information that he wouldn't get up the road from Portlaoise. There was a hole dug with his name on it. There was a queue of people to kill him," Brian Sherry added. Daly showed his gratitude in typical fashion by telling the cops to "fuck off".

Daly lost no time making noise and throwing his weight around in Finglas. At one time he could do what he liked there but not any more. The whole bMr Xce of the underworld had completely changed. Most of his staunchest allies were dead, including his protector, Marlo Hyland. Daly didn't seem to care and began putting the squeeze on a number of hoods, including the man who had replaced the godfather and ordered the hit. In the end it was only a matter of who got to him first.

On October 12, Gardaí from Finglas were instructed to inform Daly of another serious threat against his life. Daly wasn't at his family home on Cloonlara Drive when they called, so they left a message with his mother.

Later that day Daly arrived at the Garda station in a rage. He hurled abuse at the detectives who were telling him to watch his back. He told them to "fuck off" and warned them never to go near his home again, unless they had a warrant.

But ten days later the same officers would be going back to his home and Daly would have nothing to say about it. It was about 1.45am on the morning of October 22, 2007, when the taxi carrying Daly and his friends arrived at his mother's home for a party. Daly was sitting in the front seat putting the fare together to pay the driver. At that moment a stolen land cruiser pulled up and a lone figure stepped out. He walked quickly up to the front passenger's door of the taxi and fired five shots into the feared mobster with his automatic handgun. Daly slumped forward and fell onto the terrified taxi driver. The gangster was rushed to hospital but was pronounced dead on arrival.

The attack had left another innocent victim. The taxi driver, who had a very young family including a new-born baby, was suddenly left without a means to earn an income. He was also severely traumatised by his near death experience and couldn't face the prospect of getting behind the wheel of a cab again. His taxi, in which Daly's blood had been spattered everywhere, had to be sold.

No one is every likely to be charged with the murder of John Daly. His murder was well planned and organised by a criminal godfather who is, to paraphrase the Dunne prediction, more cold-blooded and dangerous than anyone who came before him. The decision to murder Daly was based on common business sense. He was out of control and unpredictable and would have caused chaos. The criminals didn't want that and the rest is history. During the murder investigation forensic analysis discovered a direct link between the murder weapon and three other gangland hits. The weapon was supplied by the McCarthy/Dundons from Limerick. If the story of the Gypsy's curse is true then he was the last member of the gang to succumb to its spell.

Superstitious locals had claimed that the gypsy's curse would be fulfilled after 13 gang members had died. Most observers agree that Daly was the thirteenth member of the group to die. However, in the year since his death, at least two more former associates have also been shot dead.

Fact or superstition? No one will ever know.

SEVEN

THE SYNDICATE

Friday, August 30, 2002

The small Flemish town of Kortrijk, close to the border between Belgium and France, basked in the golden sunshine of an Indian summer. The driver of the Irish registered container truck had made good time since joining the E17 motorway, the main arterial route linking Brussels and Paris. He was en route from Holland to Cherbourg with a valuable load. He planned to take the ferry for Rosslare, County Wexford when he reached the French port. But panic set in when he spotted a police checkpoint in the distance. The 26-year-old trucker from County Louth made a split second decision. He chose to make a run for it, rather than risk a possible ten-year stretch in a Belgian prison. He pulled the truck off the motorway and parked at a services station. He locked the truck, left the keys under the front wheel and walked briskly away. He hitched a lift with another trucker and headed south.

Two days later, Belgian police made an astonishing discovery when they searched the abandoned truck. Hidden under the floor of the trailer, in specially constructed compartments, was an estimated €30 million worth of practically every type of illegal drug on the market. The haul included heroin, cocaine, ecstasy, amphetamine, a heroin substitute called Tamazepan and cannabis. It was the largest single drug seizure in the history of Belgian law enforcement and the first time that a so-called polyload of narcotics was intercepted in Europe. However, the success enjoyed by the Belgian cops was unfortunate for their Irish counterparts who had been secretly monitoring the sophisticated smuggling operation. They had planned to catch the big players behind the huge shipment – an interesting syndicate made up of the bad and very bad from the world of organised crime and terrorism.

The Garda investigation, appropriately codenamed Operation Syndicate, uncovered a complex and highly sophisticated international drug trafficking conspiracy. In a nine-month period alone, the group transported an estimated €100 million worth of polydrug-loads around Europe, in specially converted container trailers. The innovative syndicate had spotted a major business opportunity if they specialised in the transport of several types of drugs, at the one time. It was much more economical and efficient to have one major source of supply and a central distribution point for onward delivery.

The gangland cartel included an extraordinary collection of major league criminals from Ireland, England, Scotland, Holland and Spain. Also involved were members of murderous paramilitary gangs who were supposedly sworn enemies – the Loyalist Ulster Volunteer Force (UVF), the Loyalist Volunteer Force (LVF) and the Irish National Liberation Army (INLA). This was a criminal racket of truly epic international proportions. And it had its base in the small town of Ardee, County Louth near the Border with Northern Ireland – a region where smuggling is a way of life.

****

During the last three decades of the 20th Century, a section of the Border between the North and the Irish Republic became the epicentre of a vast underworld economy. Smuggling had always been a major source of income in the area straddling the Border between South Armagh and Counties Monaghan and Louth. Smuggling is largely accepted and not considered a "real" crime. In the impoverished 1950s, smuggling butter and livestock across the invisible meandering line between North and South was the only income for many households along the border. When the Troubles broke out in Northern Ireland in the late 1960s, the IRA relied on smugglers to keep the "war effort" afloat. Bombs and bullets replaced the butter that was stored in secret compartments, under trucks traversing the frontier. By the 1970s, they had established routes across Europe to transport arms and explosives. Smuggled oil, livestock, alcohol and tobacco all helped fill the war chest. The Troubles created a new boom industry in the region.

The Provisional IRA and their political wing Sinn Féin, largely funded their terrorist and political activities by controlling the industry, under the direction of Republican godfather Thomas Slab Murphy. Murphy, who was an influential member of the IRA Army Council, effectively ruled South Armagh, which was dubbed Bandit Country as a result. It was a no go area for the security forces and criminal rackets thrived there. In 2002, a confidential report compiled by Her Majesty's Customs and Excise estimated that the British Exchequer was losing up to €29 million a month alone, as a result of the racket controlled by Slab and his Border bandits.

Irish gangsters became major players in the international drug trade from the early 1990s. At the same time, there was a dramatic increase in the demand for illegal drugs in Ireland. Soon the number of shipments of narcotics coming into the country was reflecting the Irish fondness for getting stoned. In Holland and Spain, orders for various drugs steadily grew from tens to thousands of kilos at a time. Transportation was vital for this new boom industry. The difficulties of policing the Border meant that it was a perfect environment for bringing in drugs. The methods and routes were also already well established. The drug trade presented very lucrative opportunities for the border smugglers and bogus transport companies sprung up throughout the region.

Paddy Farrell from Newry was probably the best-known smuggler, turned criminal godfather, in the region. Despite being one of the largest drug importers in the country, he enjoyed the implicit support and approval of Sinn Féin and the IRA. Farrell – who began his career smuggling butter – used a network of dodgy transport companies and drivers. He dealt with criminals and terrorists from all sides, smuggling tobacco, drugs and guns. One of his closest business partners was the Gilligan gang. When they went into hiding, after the murder of Veronica Guerin in 1996 Farrell stepped in to help with the running of their lucrative operation. A year later, however, his activities came to an abrupt end when he was shot dead by his mistress. She blasted him with a borrowed shotgun as he lay in her bed after making love. She then turned the gun on herself. Farrell's death left a vacuum but there were plenty of associates ready to take his place.

The significance of the border area as a hub for international drug trafficking was exposed, quite by accident, a year after Farrell's ignominious demise. In December 1998, a truck delivered a load of pitta bread, imported from Holland, to a cold storage facility near Castleblayney, County Monaghan. While the load was being unloaded for transfer to another truck, one of the pallets burst open, revealing several kilos of cannabis resin concealed inside. Staff at the facility tipped off the local Gardaí. They decided to reseal the pitta bread and lie in wait for whoever turned up to claim it. A truck owned by Kieran Smyth from Dundalk, County Louth, collected it sometime later. Smyth, who had been an associate of Paddy Farrell, was one of the biggest smugglers in the business.

Subsequent investigations revealed how Smyth's company, Westlodge Freight, facilitated the trafficking of every kind of contraband including oil, drugs, guns and cigarettes for Republicans and drug dealers alike. Customs in Belgium, the UK and Ireland had seized large consignments of tobacco and cash from Westlodge trucks over the previous few years. The day before the pitta bread arrived in Monaghan, Belgian police had arrested Smyth while he was loading 21 million cigarettes onto one of his trucks. Smyth was beginning to attract a lot of unwelcome attention. When his truck was later stopped in Castleblayney, detectives found that the full pitta bread load contained 780 kilos of cannabis with a street value of IR£8 million (€10.16 million). Concealed beside the dope was something much more sinister.

Carefully wrapped and hidden in the middle of the bread,

were 15 lethal Intratec, 'Tec 9', machine pistols, capable of firing hundreds of rounds per minute. Each weapon was individually equipped with a silencer and spare magazines. The cache also contained ten automatic pistols and ammunition for the entire arsenal. At the time it was the largest arms find ever discovered with a shipment of drugs and it sent shock waves through the security services. Intelligence sources, on both sides of the Border, suspected that the weaponry was intended for dissident Republicans opposed to the Peace Process and for Irish criminal gangs. The discovery sparked off a major international investigation. Kieran Smyth and the truck driver were subsequently arrested and questioned about the seizure.

The mastermind behind the Castleblayney shipment was identified as convicted armed robber and kidnapper, John Cunningham. Originally from Ballyfermot in Dublin, Cunningham had once been a close associate of the General, Martin Cahill. In criminal circles he was nicknamed The Colonel. In 1986, the Colonel and two other men, his brother Michael and Tony Kelly, were convicted for the kidnap of Mrs Jennifer Guinness, the wife of a millionaire banker. Cunningham told cops that he had planned to extract a huge ransom from the Guinness family so he could retire to a life of luxury in the sun. Instead of a large ransom, he received a large 17-year jail sentence.

Cunningham had fled from an open prison in County Wicklow in 1996, where he was serving the final part of his time. With the help of his old pal John Gilligan, he established a major drug smuggling operation in Holland. In a three-year period, using Smyth and the Border connection, Cunningham's syndicate had smuggled drugs with an estimated street value of €120 million and an unknown quantity of arms and ammunition. A year after the Castleblayney seizure and, as a result of the ongoing investigation, French police seized IR£1.5 (€1.9) million worth of amphetamine on a Westlodge Freight truck at the port of Calais. Cunningham had organised the shipment. A few months later, Dutch police busted him as a direct result of the Monaghan investigation. In the swoop, drugs worth over €11.4 million and an arsenal of 23 high-powered weapons was seized. Cunningham was subsequently sentenced to seven years by a Dutch court.

As a result of the Castleblayney drug and gun seizure, the Criminal Assets Bureau began making enquiries. They discovered that Kieran Smyth had personally laundered in excess of €15 million, over a period of 18 months, up to October 1999. He was a customer of an illegal underground bank, masquerading as a Bureau de Change, on the Border at Dromad, County Louth. The 'bank', owned by local man Kieran Byrne, was, next door to a Garda station. It handled mind-boggling quantities of cash for both criminal drug gangs and Republican smugglers.

Between 1996 and 1999, Byrne had put €81 million through his company's legitimate bank account. However, the CAB discovered that the Bureau de Change had processed as much as €250 million, most of which had been transferred to bank accounts throughout the world. The gangland bank had also come to the attention of the Garda National Drug Unit (GNDU) when they caught a bagman for a Ballyfermot-based heroin gang depositing huge sums of cash with Byrne. When the Criminal Assets Bureau raided Dromad in October 1999, a lot of major criminals and terrorists feared that Kieran Smyth might blow the whistle on them. They had similar fears about Kieran Byrne. But Smyth caused them the greatest concern because he was also under investigation for the huge drug and gun seizure and the Belgian police had issued an international arrest warrant for him. If the Gardaí convinced him to talk then he could expose the embarrassing connections between organised crime and the Republican movement. In addition the faceless godfathers stood to lose millions.

On February 5, 2001, Smyth was abducted from his home and vanished. Four days later his body was found, dumped near Ashbourne, County Meath. He had been bound, gagged and blindfolded. There was evidence that he had been severely beaten and tortured before he was then blasted twice in the back of the head, at close range with a shotgun. Police believed Smyth's execution was the work of the Republican movement. The closure of the Border bank, the arrest of Cunningham, followed by Smyth's murder, caused considerable disruption to the massive underground business. With so much at stake, the gangsters and patriots had to regroup as quickly as possible. There was a serious market demand to be satisfied. Other illegal banks quickly opened and a number of criminals stepped in to replace Cunningham and Smyth on the drugs side.

Smyth's execution succeeded in achieving what the perpetrators had hoped for – silence. Kieran Byrne certainly got the message. In February 2002, he was jailed for four years after he pleaded guilty to charges of money laundering and operating an unauthorised Bureau de Change. Byrne refused to divulge the identities of his dangerous customers. He later paid the CAB over €3.1 million. At the same time that the mob's banker was being escorted to jail, a number of his and Kieran Smyth's former clients had already filled the gap.

* * * *

The lure of easy money had attracted a greedy young businessman called Benny Ward into the shady world of drug trafficking. Born in 1974 and from Ardee he had never intended following a career in organised crime – it happened by degrees. He was a perfect candidate. Ward had never come to the attention of the police and had no criminal convictions. A welder by trade, he ran a plant hire business in the town and dabbled in the haulage business. While Kieran Smyth was running into difficulties and out of time, Ward was being seduced by the underworld. After the Castleblayney/Cunningham investigations Smyth had been given the cold shoulder by his associates. They didn't want to join him in the police spotlight. This meant there were urgent vacancies for anonymous gofers such as Benny Ward.

By the start of 2002, Ward was the manager of a complex logistics operation for a syndicate of drug traffickers based in Ireland, the UK, Holland and Spain. He organised the collection and delivery of drug shipments between the Continent, the UK and Ireland. He hired drivers, sourced trucks and rented warehouses, where narcotics were stored before distribution to different gangs.

Ward's boss was a major player in the smuggling world. The wily 52-year-old Dublin-based mobster, who acted as a gangland power broker, had enticed Ward into the business. Originally from County Tipperary, he had been involved in organised crime and smuggling for decades. To those who knew him he was an extremely shrewd and cunning villain, with a flair for logistics and organisation. He was charming, devious and ruthless in equal amounts. To his neighbours in the cul-de-sac where he lived in Palmerstown, West Dublin, he was a happy family man. He ran a successful nationwide plant and tool hire firm as a front for his real business.

The Dubliner certainly did not display the appearance of a glad-handling gangster whose business associates read like a 'who's who' of organised crime. Pot-bellied and with wild bushy hair on either side of his balding head, he looked more like a cross between *The Simpsons* TV character, Krusty the Clown and Larry from the *Three Stooges*. But this man was anything but a clown.

While he might have been Mr Nobody to the rest of the world, he was something of a celebrity to a small circle, in both the law enforcement and underworld communities. He was known as a major player to police and customs in Ireland, the UK, Europe and the Drug Enforcement Authority (DEA) in the US. The Americans suspected him of involvement in the supply of huge quantities of ecstasy to the US where, like the late Paddy Farrell, he owned a number of properties in Florida. However, apart from a few relatively minor convictions for theft dating back to the 1960s and 1970s, Krusty had managed to avoid handcuffs. He was too careful and shrewd to be caught 'hands-on' with the product.

Reliable sources interviewed for this book claimed that he also kept himself relatively safe by acting as a police informant. Krusty passed on intelligence about his criminal competitors, which ultimately distracted the police from his own activities. Playing both sides is an important survival technique for many gangsters.

A detective who had personal dealings with Krusty described the relationship: "He talked to two people in Garda

HQ and gave them a few seizures. Being a registered informant gave him a degree of protection. He was playing a game with them. If you ask me he was so cute that he probably weeded out more information from his handlers than he gave in return."

Krusty, who had lived in the UK for a time, had major criminal contacts everywhere. He had connections across the Republic, Northern Ireland, the UK, Holland and Spain. Krusty also had strong links with the Provisional IRA. He was a close associate of the likes of George 'The Penguin' Mitchell, John Cunningham, Paddy Farrell and John Gilligan. The Penguin, who also started his career as a truck driver, fled Ireland to live in Amsterdam after the Guerin murder in 1996. From there, he became one of the biggest drug traffickers in Europe. Mitchell's brother Paddy, who took care of the Dublin end of the business, was also a close confidant and friend of Krusty. In 2000, the Garda Crime and Security section received intelligence that Krusty had been involved in the importation of heroin on behalf of Mitchell.

The facilitator recruited Benny Ward after the sudden demise of Kieran Smyth. The chubby businessman was a perfect candidate for Krusty's operation – he was greedy and easily manipulated. Krusty purposely targeted characters like Ward who appeared to be clean but had ample capacity for corruption. Krusty used his own plant hire business for the purpose of identifying and then recruiting people for his various illegal endeavours. He had hired out machinery to Ward at much lower rates than a legitimate company would offer. But then, when Ward's business ran into financial difficulties, Krusty put the squeeze on and sucked him in.

The same detective revealed: "[Krusty] was very manipulative, a total con man. He began by leasing equipment to Ward at cut price and loaned him money. Then he gradually put pressure on Ward about paying back the money. When the time was right, he gave Ward the opportunity to earn real money. In no time at all he had been sucked into [Krusty] web and there was no going back. At first [Krusty] used to pay his lackies and drivers loads of cash. This was to get them hooked on the easy money. Then, after a while, when they had bought the high-powered car or got used to the high life, he would make them work harder – and take more risks – to earn the money. In a way the relationship is a bit like that between a junkie and his drug dealer. You would be surprised at how easy it can be done. There are a lot of fools who have done time because of sharks like him."

By all accounts, Benny Ward had not taken much persuasion and even Krusty was surprised by his enthusiasm.

Michael James Howard had fallen in with Krusty in much the same way as Benny Ward. The 33-year-old father of two young children from Elton in County Limerick was self-employed. He'd worked as a grounds contractor for seven years when things started to go wrong. In December 2001, Howard found himself barely able to pay his workers' wages. Like Ward, he was an ideal candidate for Krusty. He had no criminal connections and was financially vulnerable. In January 2002, a friend introduced him to the gangland businessman to arrange the hire of a machine. The wily crook organised a sweetheart deal for the troubled contractor. Krusty arranged finance for the lease hire of the machine and told Howard to pay what he could afford. He sent Howard to a contact in a mainstream bank, who approved the loan within ten minutes. Howard was hugely impressed by his new benefactor, but the deal would cost him a lot more than just money.

A few days later Howard met Ward for the first time when he delivered the machine to Howard in Limerick. Krusty told Howard that Ward was a serious player in the plant hire business.

In turn, Howard introduced his friend to Ward and Krusty. Morgan McGrath was a 30-year-old truck driver from Emly, County Tipperary. Morgan was instantly impressed by Krusty and he asked him for help in financing the purchase of a container lorry for continental runs. Krusty said he would see what he could do.

After a few more meetings, he introduced the two men to his real business – smuggling. In the beginning, he pretended that he was solely involved in the importation of tobacco but then told them the truth when he saw how enthusiastic they were.

He described the type of money that was on offer – ten times more than anything they would earn in the legitimate world. It was an offer they could not refuse. Howard and McGrath had joined the drug trade.

Transportation is one of the most important aspects of the trade. A drug smuggling operation is at its greatest risk while the drugs are in transit through different jurisdictions. Law enforcement agencies prefer intercepting a shipment before it is broken down into smaller quantities at its final destination and dispersed in several directions. Some international drug traffickers now offer transport as part of a package deal. The costs are added to the price of each kilo purchased. In the business this is what is referred to as an "on the floor delivery".

Krusty arranged a meeting with Ward, Howard and Morgan. They met in the West County Hotel on the outskirts of Dublin, to set up the logistics operation for the new syndicate. Krusty put Ward in charge of the day-to-day operation. Howard and McGrath worked directly for Ward and Krusty. They were the gofers and dealt with people lower down the pecking order of the organisation. Like most international traffickers, Krusty used them as a safe buffer between him and the drugs. Working on Ward's instructions, Howard and McGrath arranged the collection and delivery of drugs coming in from the continent to Ireland. They looked after warehouses, transport and falsified freight documents. In a very short period, Howard and McGrath were part of an elaborate smuggling operation that included drug dealers throughout the 32 counties.

Around the same time, Krusty invited McGrath to a meeting in a hotel in Dublin where he introduced him to a man called Liam Judge. Judge asked Morgan how much he made for delivering a legitimate cargo to the continent with his truck. Morgan said €500. Judge pulled out €5000 in cash handed it to him and told him to go buy a truck. Cost was not a problem.

Morgan was delighted with himself. He went back to Howard and told him: "We're sound, there's no problem about money; we're in business."

The two friends bought a truck – a tractor unit for pulling

containers – for €50,000. Tracy Gilligan, John Gilligan's daughter, delivered part of the payment, €30,000 in cash, to Howard and McGrath in a hotel in Leixlip. The godfather's daughter, who lived with Liam Judge, brought the cash in from Spain. The two gofers recognised her from her picture in the newspapers. It was confirmation that they were playing with a premier league gangland team.

Liam Judge was one of the most important members of the syndicate and had been involved in international drug trafficking for several years. He and Krusty had been partners for a long time. Born in 1959 in Allenwood, County Kildare Judge had been one of the most significant, and colourful players in the Irish drug trade for 15 years. The Penguin had introduced him to the drug trade when Judge worked as a long distance truck driver, for a company based in the Midlands. Judge had an excellent knowledge of the transport business and the main routes across continental Europe. He also had plenty of contacts. He was described as a charming character who lived life on the edge. One former friend recalled that in the beginning the trucker had no idea about drugs. "He was a gent really; a real character and a serial womaniser. Judgey knew fuck all about gear [drugs] in the beginning. I remember once that there was a bag of speed [amphetamine] sitting on the table and he put a spoon of it in his tea thinking it was sugar. He was out of his head for days."

Judge soon learned everything there was to know about 'gear' and became the transport manager for the Penguin's growing criminal operation. The drugs were transported in container trucks from Europe to warehouses rented by Judge on behalf of his boss around Dublin and in the Midlands. In one elaborate scam, which lasted for several months, Judge and Mitchell imported huge quantities of ecstasy – popular on the 'Rave' dance scene from the early 1990s – inside secondhand car tyres that were delivered to Judge's yard in Allenwood. The instinctively suspicious godfather considered Judge reliable and trustworthy which was quite an achievement for the wayward trucker. Very few people ever got close to Mitchell. As a member of the Penguin's inner circle, other criminals treated Judge with respect.

There was another side to Judge that to only a few people knew about. Following his arrest for a road traffic offence in 1993, he had been recruited as an informant by one of the Gardaí's most resourceful and unconventional undercover investigators, Detective Sergeant Pat Walsh. Known as 'Feshty' to his colleagues, his reputation as a maverick who got amazing results, was legendary among the ranks of Ireland's thief-takers. Over a period of almost 20 years his work as a 'spook' led to the seizure of hundreds of millions of Euro worth of drugs and the conviction of dozens of major underworld players.

Judge lived a precarious existence as a double agent. Nevertheless, it also suited him in the long term when he did not want the law's eye coming down on his own activities. For an 18 month period in the mid – '90s Judge operated a chuck wagon for truckers on the Johnstown Road in County Kildare. It became popular as a meeting place for drivers seeking work of the less than legal variety and for drug traffickers who needed transport. What no one knew was that the chuck wagon had really been paid for – and equipped with bugging equipment – by Feshty and his colleagues. Intelligence gleaned from the talkative truckers and traffickers led to several arrests and no one ever suspected where the information was coming from.

In 1994, the Penguin rented a yard and large lock-up building in Mount Brown in Kilmainham, West Dublin. It became a depot for serious crime where the Penguin's gang – a dozen of the most ruthless and dangerous criminals in the country – regularly met to organise drug deals and armed robberies. With the help of Judge, Feshty and his team secretly bugged the yard. Judge's assistance had spectacular results. Gang members were caught red-handed delivering drugs and doing armed robberies. Feshty's squad also seized two separate caches of sophisticated weapons that had been smuggled into the country by Mitchell, as a present for the Provisional IRA. The same Garda squad also shut down a crude ecstasy factory set up by the Penguin – the day after it went into production. The plant would have had the capacity to churn out almost €50,000 worth of the drug every hour.

The unprecedented Garda successes forced the gang to break up and reorganise. During that process, Mitchell and Judge moved apart. It is not clear if the Penguin suspected him of 'touting'. If he had then Judge would certainly have been whacked.

The informant/drug trafficker's involvement with the Gilligan gang began in 1998 when Judge left his wife for Tracy Gilligan. The relationship also had the blessing of his Garda handlers who desperately wanted a spy in the Gilligan camp. Gilligan had been in custody since 1996 in Belmarsh Prison in London and was fighting extradition back to Ireland, to face charges for murdering journalist Veronica Guerin, as well as gun and drug trafficking offences. Judge helped to reorganise the crime lord's drug trade when he moved to live with Tracy Gilligan and her mother Geraldine, in Torrevieja, in Alicante on Spain's Costa Blanca.

Judge set about laundering Gilligan's hidden loot, which the CAB had been unable to find. He set up a number of businesses, including a plant hire company, a swimming pool construction firm and a bar appropriately called 'The Judge's Chambers'. Geraldine and Tracy took care of the running of the premises. Over the next few years Judge also invested Gilligan's loot in several properties including apartments and warehouses throughout the region. Together with Krusty, Judge used the plant hire business to sell heavy plant machinery and vehicles, stolen by their contacts in Ireland and the UK. They also organised the shipment of narcotics.

It was sometime in 2001, that Judge and Krusty combined their resources in a more calculated manner. They brought together a powerful syndicate of international drug traffickers and smugglers. The syndicate included drug gangs in Limerick, Dublin, Cork, Belfast, Glasgow, Liverpool, Birmingham and London. Despite being locked up, John Gilligan, who was represented by Judge, was a major investor in the project. One of the other main movers was 49-year-old Glasgow gangster Jimmy Rankin. He had strong links with Loyalist terror gangs, the UVF and LVF in Belfast. His partner-in-crime was drug dealer Gary Marno, who had been a member of both the LVF

and UDA. He lived next door to Liam Judge and Tracy Gilligan
in Alicante, where he was officially on the run from police in
the UK and Ireland.

Through their various connections, Rankin, Marno,
Krusty and Judge pulled in drug gangs in Glasgow, Liverpool
and Birmingham. The conspiracy also included the notorious
Adams family in London. The Adams were among the most
feared criminal mobs operating in the UK and had been involved
in several gang wars in the capital. As a result, they dominated
a large part of the drug trade in the south of England.

INLA hit man Kevin McAlorum Junior, from Belfast, had
no ethical difficulty about joining with Gary Marno and some
of his hated enemies from the Loyalist side. For him it was not
personal – just business. Members of various terror groups in
Northern Ireland began taking control of the burgeoning drug
rackets in the North from the early 1990s. The INLA, LVF
and UVF turned to organised crime with great enthusiasm. In
Dublin, the INLA had also become heavily involved in drugs
and had acted as John Gilligan's enforcers.

McAlorum was described as a "dead man walking" by
former comrades, after he murdered his former 'commander'
Gino Gallagher during a bitter blood feud in 1996. The INLA's
sorry history is soaked in the blood of many internecine wars.
The organisation has succeeded in killing off each other a lot
more than their actual enemies – the British Army and the
RUC. Two months after the Gallagher murder, the INLA raked
McAlorum's family home with machine-gun fire in retaliation
for Gallagher's death. The hit man's innocent nine-year-old
sister Barbara died in the hail of bullets meant for her older
sibling. The murder shocked the world. A year later McAlorum
was jailed for 16 years for possession of the weapon used to
murder Gallagher. He had been released after 12 months, under
the terms of the *Good Friday Agreement*.

Another comrade released as part of the same peace process
– who wasted no time getting involved in the drug trade – was
kidnapper and murderer Fergal Toal from Armagh. Toal was
a member of the notorious INLA murder gang led by Dessie
O'Hare. In 1987, O'Hare, Toal and three other accomplices

were jailed for the kidnap of Dublin dentist John O'Grady. Toal, who had also been sentenced to life for stabbing another man to death, got 20 years. While serving his sentence in Portlaoise maximum-security prison, Toal became a close friend and confidant of John Gilligan. The godfather had been jailed for four years in 1990 for a number of robberies. It was in Portlaoise that Gilligan had decided to move into the drug trade and the nucleus of his gang was formed. In the prison's E1 wing, where the country's toughest villains were housed, there were even rumours among the inmates that the relationship between Gilligan and Toal had gone beyond mere pals. When Gilligan was later jailed in the UK for drug trafficking, Toal worked with Liam Judge and Krusty, looking after his pal's interests on the outside.

McAlorum, Rankin, Toal, Marno and a number of other INLA/UVF/LVF members rented houses near the Border to be close to Benny Ward's operating base. At one stage, McAlorum rented a house near Slane in County Meath. Two members of the UVF lived there for a period in 2002. For the Loyalists it was like being in Mecca. It was near the site on the River Boyne where Protestant King William of Orange won a historic victory over Catholic King James in 1690. On the 12th of July, they even hung a UVF flag from the chimney of the modest bungalow to mark the big day.

* * * *

With everything in place the syndicate's drug smuggling operation began in early 2002. Judge, Krusty and Rankin took charge of the logistics of the operation. The syndicate pooled their resources to bulk buy various types of drugs, at the same time, from the main suppliers on the continent. Drug producers in Morocco, Colombia and Turkey prefer to sell their wares in multiple tonnes rather than a few hundred kilos – the bigger the order the bigger the discount on offer per kilo. The plan was to smuggle the various drugs back to Ireland for storage in warehouses close to the Border. Drugs destined for the UK market could be shipped from there. Routing narcotics into the

UK from Ireland, through the back door, was the safest option. Customs there tended to pay more attention to ports dealing directly with continental traffic.

In Holland, large shipments of ecstasy, heroin, amphetamine and Tamazepan – a powerful anti-depressant used as a heroin substitute by Scottish drug addicts – were organised through two other members of the syndicate. An associate of Rankin, known as "Small Scottish Jimmy" who was living in Breeda, in Belgium, and a Dutch national called William who lived between Holland and Spain. In Spain Judge and his manager there, an English villain from Wolverhampton, organised consignments of cocaine and hashish.

The operation involved several truck drivers from the border counties, who were experienced smugglers. A Scottish haulier was also involved. Within weeks, the operation was at full tilt and the gangsters found themselves working flat out to keep up with demand. Trucks were travelling between Holland, Spain, the UK and Ireland, collecting and delivering various types of drugs. Officers working on Operation Syndicate subsequently estimated that the cartel had moved €100 million worth of drugs, over a nine-month period. However, that was only the quantities the cops could actually trace.

One detective described the scale of the trafficking: "It was a huge operation and we managed to trace an estimated €100 million but the amount of drugs they moved around Europe is probably unquantifiable. It could easily be worth three or four times that much."

Howard and McGrath received their instructions on the various deliveries arriving in Ireland from Krusty, Judge and Ward. McGrath was in charge of organising all the details relating to the shipping and transportation of the loads. Howard was responsible for collecting and delivering individual shipments. He later admitted to detectives that he received between €4,000 and €7,000 for handling individual loads coming into the country. Once a month he was paid €1,000 for delivering hashish to a criminal in Limerick. The gofers also travelled to England to drop off and collect trailers that were sent over from Holland and Spain. McGrath regularly drove to Holland and Spain with trailers. Ward used a warehouse near the Border, where McAlorum, Toal and their Loyalist associates collect their shipments for the Northern and the Border market. Other trucks travelled between Holland and a warehouse in Liverpool.

Despite the careful planning, the transport operation also required a degree of luck. The smugglers had a few nerve jangling encounters with the law enforcement community. On one occasion, the driver, one of the syndicate's regular drivers, was dispatched to Alicante by Benny Ward to pick up a load from Liam Judge. It included a few tonnes of cannabis that were to be delivered to Ireland, via the port of Calais in France. On his way to the busy port, the driver stopped to relieve himself. When he was out of sight a group of Bosnian refugees, jumped into the back of the trailer. They had been hiding in nearby bushes, in the hope of being smuggled to Ireland or the UK where they could then claim refugee status.

As the driver entered the port, he heard noises coming from the trailer and stopped to investigate. When he opened up the trailer, he discovered his unwelcome guests and chased them out. Immediately Customs officers surrounded the driver and his stowaways. The trucker began to sweat – he thought his days as a free man were numbered. The Bosnians were arrested and taken away by the French. The Customs officers then sealed up the trailer – and the hash – to ensure no one else hitched an illegal ride. The relieved driver decided to ship the truck and its cargo home to Rosslare and he flew back to Ireland. He was rattled by his close shave. The French handed out some of the toughest jail sentences for drug trafficking in continental Europe. When it arrived in Rosslare, Mike Howard sent another driver – who had no idea what the real cargo was – to collect it and bring it back to Morgan's property at Roundhill in Tipperary. Later the two gofers unloaded the load into a van driven by two Dublin criminals, with links to the INLA.

As business improved, Krusty told Howard to treat himself and buy a new jeep to deliver the drugs. He also organised the leasing finance on a Mitsubishi L200 crew cab for Howard. With the money rolling in, the contractor was in optimistic mood and planned to finish work on his new home.

McGrath too was having a ball. He travelled regularly to Spain and he hoped to buy a villa there, with its own swimming pool.

One day Howard and McGrath set out from Tipperary with a load they had collected earlier. It was from a truck that had arrived from Judge in Spain and was to be delivered to Ward and the INLA in Monaghan. The back of the vehicle was filled to the brim with bales of hash. They were chatting and laughing about their plans for the new found wealth. Then they ran into a joint Customs and Garda checkpoint on the Portlaoise by-pass and their short lives as drug dealers flashed before their eyes. Panic set in and they did not know whether to run or bluff it out.

The officers were checking the tanks of diesel-powered vehicles for 'green' agricultural diesel. It is illegal for use in road transport vehicles which must use 'white' diesel. Howard decided to bluff it. He jumped out to greet – and distract – the Customs officer. Howard made small talk, as the officer dipped the tank to check its contents. The officer didn't notice the much more interesting illegal load stuffed to the ceiling in the back of the jeep. When the Customs' check was finished the drug traffickers were free to go on their way. Neither of them was able to speak for the rest of the journey.

On another trip, Howard had to deliver 500 bars of hash – worth around €400,000 – to the home of an associate of McAlorum. He was a Belfast INLA member who lived in the fashionable College Gate estate in Castleknock, West Dublin. Howard and Morgan made regular deliveries to the 25-year-old terrorist they nicknamed 'Topper'. In turn, Topper made smaller deliveries to dealers in Monasterevin, Finglas, Blanchardstown and Maynooth. Howard had packed the hash bars loosely in black plastic bags and dumped them in the back. When he opened the jeep outside the INLA man's home, the bags fell out onto the ground and bars of hashish spilled all over the road. The two syndicate members hurriedly whisked them up and put them in the terrorist's van. Their luck held and they had not been spotted.

In the early summer, Ward sent McGrath and Howard to Holland. They were told to rent a suitable warehouse for the Dutch side of the operation. They later located a warehouse in the village of Meijel in southern Holland, about an hour's drive from Amsterdam. It was an ideal location – quiet and out of the way. Small Scottish Jimmy and the Dutch criminal, William, organised to have drug shipments delivered to the warehouse. From there, trucks would collect the narcotics and bring them to Ireland, the UK and Spain. A Dutch national, later identified as Robert Dermur, was hired as a caretaker to watch over the depot.

Around the same time, Benny Ward rented a large yard and sheds at Mullenstown in Ardee, Co Louth.

The gang had decided that this would be the new depot for the international conspiracy. Ward announced a plan to convert container trailers. He intended to move up a gear by building hidden compartments under the floors to stash drugs. It was a novel idea. The syndicate had decided to begin smuggling all the main drugs – at the same time.

One large polyload of drugs could replace up to 12 individual runs to and from the continent. It cut down on costs and the risk of detection. It made sound commercial sense. Ward also planned to wrap the false trailer floors in lead to prevent x-ray machines picking up the secret loads in the ports. The ambitious plan was to have up to seven articulated trucks equipped with specially converted trailers operating at the same time. Ward even planned to build an underground chamber – disguised as a septic tank – to store the drugs before they were distributed onwards to the UK and around Ireland. It would make the smuggling operation one of the biggest ever seen in Europe, with a capacity to shift drugs worth hundreds of millions of Euro. It was drug trafficking on an awesome scale. So far, the syndicate had enjoyed a good run of luck. The operation, however, was about to hit a temporary glitch.

Thirty-three-year-old trucker Kevin Keogh from Pallasgreen in County Limerick had no idea what he was getting himself involved in when he accepted a job offer from Morgan McGrath. The syndicate used a number of drivers who were fully aware of what they were transporting. But the gang also regularly hired completely innocent drivers, such as Keogh, to collect drug loads. This way they avoided any extra attention from border customs' officers. The drivers were also dispensable if they were caught. Without knowing it, Keogh had already done a number of trips for the syndicate. He would later explain how he had been suspicious of the people he was working for. "But I loaded the trucks myself and checked the cargoes so I decided that there wasn't anything wrong," he would later say.

On Sunday, July 7, 2002, Keogh flew to Holland to pick up a tractor unit and drive it to Spain where he was to collect a trailer. McGrath met him in Schipol International Airport and brought him back to Meijel, where Small Scottish Jimmy had set up a transport company.

On the following Friday, Keogh took delivery of McGrath's truck and headed to Judge's plant hire company in Alicante. When he got to Spain, he was instructed to take the waiting trailer back to Ardee. He was to collect ceramic tiles from a number of factories on the way, for delivery in Ireland.

The trailer had been driven to Liam Judge's base on July 6 by his long-time associate and veteran drug smuggler, Dennis 'Dinny' Meredith from Monasterevin in County Kildare. Like Judge, Meredith, got involved in the drug trade as a result of his job as a long distance trucker. Originally from Ballyfermot, he had been a close associate of John Gilligan since the 1980s. Meredith brought in the Gilligan gang's first drug shipments in 1994 and he had delivered millions of pounds for the mob to their main supplier in Amsterdam before the Guerin murder.

Keogh made his ceramic tile collections and crossed the French border at Perpignan on July 18, where he was stopped at a police checkpoint. The French appeared to know exactly what they were looking for, as they started to search the trailer. They took out angle grinders and began cutting up the floor of the truck where the drugs were hidden a number of compartments. Officers found over a tonne of cannabis resin, expertly concealed in two hidden compartments under the flooring of the trailer. Even though he'd had no knowledge of his true cargo, Keogh spent the following 18 months in a

French jail. He was finally released in November 2003. They gave him papers confirming that they had established that he was a completely innocent man.

Although it has never been officially confirmed, it is believed that Liam Judge tipped off his Garda handlers about the drug shipment to keep everyone happy. It would also distract from the much more valuable shipments of polyloads which were being planned.

The syndicate had little concern about Kevin Keogh. As long as he did not bring the heat down on them, they could not care less. In any event Keogh was not in a position to nominate the main players behind the shipment because he had only dealt with McGrath. It would have been almost impossible to prove that McGrath actually knew the trailer had been loaded with drugs. The only thing that upsets a drug trafficker – apart from a stint behind bars or a hit man – is losing money. The French seizure had cost them an investment worth well over a million Euro but their new plans would more than make up for the loss.

In the beginning of August, Ward, Howard and McGrath began converting the first trailer that would be able to move the polyloads. They hired and bought a large amount of equipment from a number of plant and tool hire companies in Ardee for use in the conversion operation. Timber and sheets of flat steel were supplied by Krusty who supervised the work. After a number of days they had it finished. Rankin and McAlorum also visited the yard to view the finished job. Everyone was delighted. Howard and McGrath were rewarded with €5,000 each for their efforts.

A few days later, Howard and Ward travelled to Meijel to load up the converted trailer. It had been driven to Holland by a 28-year-old driver from Ardee. The driver, whose father and brother were also long distance truckers, had been recruited by Benny Ward. Howard was to be paid €20,000 and Ward €50,000 for their part in the job and the shipment was destined for Liverpool.

Two of Rankin's men and a representative of the Liverpool gang joined them in the Dutch warehouse. It took a number of hours to fill the hidden compartments. Based on subsequent admissions by Howard and the size of the Belgian seizure, police estimated the load to be worth up to €20 million.

The next day the driver set off and collected a load of Kinder chocolate eggs in Arlon in Belgium. They were to be delivered to Wolverhampton in the UK. When the truck left, Ward and Howard flew to meet it in Liverpool. When the truck arrived in England, it took the gang a day and a half to get the drugs to their destination because of engine trouble. A member of the Liverpool end of the syndicate eventually met them at a service station on the motorway at Lymms, outside the city. He guided the truck and its precious cargo to a warehouse in an industrial estate on the outskirts of the city. The gang unloaded the cannabis and ecstasy without a hitch. Everything was well organised. The packages of ecstasy for example, were colour-coded so that different clients turning up at the warehouse knew which ones to collect.

When they returned to Ardee, Howard and Ward were paid with cash delivered by one of the financiers of the illegal project, a man from Newry in Northern Ireland. The floor in the original trailer had to be repaired as it had been damaged by a forklift during the unloading in Liverpool. There was major pressure from the leaders of the syndicate to get the special trailer back on the road. Another big shipment was awaiting collection in the warehouse in Meijel. This time the bulk of the cargo was destined for Ardee. Part of the load would be dropped off to the Liverpool mob, as the truck drove through the UK. In the meantime, work began on a second trailer that Ward had purchased in the UK. A new truck was also purchased, to take the repaired trailer to collect the second polyload in Holland.

On August 27, 2002, the converted trailer left the yard in Ardee being pulled by a truck driven by Ward. Krusty followed it in his own car with Howard and McGrath as passengers. As they set off, an undercover team of detectives from Carrickmacross Garda Station, who had been secretly monitoring the activity in Ward's yard, followed them from a safe distance. The small convoy drove to Dublin where the trailer was then shipped to Holyhead, Wales. The driver from Ardee had taken the new truck on a separate sailing and planned to collect the container in Holyhead, before heading on to Holland.

In Holyhead docks, the truck's brakes seized. When the driver went to repair it, a brake pad exploded. It caused him serious injuries, including a fractured face, broken nose and deep facial cuts. He was brought to hospital and treated for concussion and shock. The driver phoned Ward and told him what had happened. That night Ward flew to the UK to get the smuggling operation back on schedule. Frantic and angry phone calls were being made, demanding that the delivery deadline be kept. Ward got the truck repaired and then drove to the hospital where the driver was being treated.

The driver subsequently claimed to cops that Ward then forced him, with threats, to leave the hospital. He claimed Ward asked him to sit into the cab of the lorry to talk and then drove off, even though the driver had a drip hanging out of his arm. He had to use the truck's first aid kit to change the dressings on his wounds. The job was more important to the syndicate than the driver's health and recuperation.

The driver subsequently told detectives: "He [Ward] started to intimidate me by telling me that people were watching my family and made the sign of the IRA on the dash or the truck with his finger. I was in a lot of pain, very confused and vulnerable. Benny said I had no choice. He explained that I had already done illegal things and that I was in and there was no way of getting out. Somewhere between there and the boat in Dover I got rid of the drip."

It was hard to know whether the story was true or if it was just a yarn spun by the driver to get himself off the hook. Mike Howard would later tell police a rather different story. He said the driver's only problem – apart from his injuries – was how much money he was being paid.

The following night Ward and the driver met Howard and Rankin's men when they arrived in Holland. Ward was in high spirits and decided that they should go to a local brothel for some light relief. The following morning, August 30, Ward, Howard and the driver drove to the warehouse in Meijel. Two Scots and a Liverpudlian accompanied them. Robert Dermur, the gang's caretaker, opened the large shuttered doors. The truck and a van were driven inside. The doors were closed again and two of the criminals produced hand-guns for their protection, in case the police disturbed them. Then the crew began loading the cargo.

The container was floodlit to help them see what they were doing. Howard and Ward removed the steel floor panels. Everyone put on paper overalls and gloves and went to work. Pallets of heroin, Tamazepan, cannabis, cocaine, ecstasy and amphetamine were loaded onto the truck with the help of a forklift. It took several hours for the seven men, working flat out, to get the job done. The parcels and slabs of drugs were carefully packed into each compartment to ensure that the trailer was filled to capacity. Bags of tablets that burst while loading were quickly re-bagged and vacuum-packed. A large quantity of drugs were left over because there was no room in the 40-foot long container.

The remainder of the load was to be picked up, when an additional shipment, already on its way, arrived at the Meijel depot. As soon as the polyload was delivered to Ardee, the container truck was to return to Holland. The truck was due to pick up the third load which was then to be dropped in Liverpool. By that stage, the syndicate planned to have the second converted trailer in operation. Both trucks would do runs, collecting narcotics in Holland and Spain and then delivering them to Ardee and Liverpool.

By the time the loading operation was complete, the converted trailer contained 48 kilos of heroin, 600,000 ecstasy tablets, 600,000 Tamazepan tablets, 48 kilos of hashish and 132 kilos of amphetamine. The entire load had cost the syndicate an estimated €4 million. This covered the purchase and expenses. They stood to make at least four times profit on their initial investment. When the drugs had gone through the system, they would have turned over between €25 and €30 million.

Morgan McGrath phoned to remind them to get a legitimate "back load" on the return journey, to avoid suspicion. It was important to have the documentation and cargo to prove to Customs that the truck had been on legitimate haulage business. The driver told Ward that he had organised a back load through a former employer of his. In a statement he later gave to detectives, the driver claimed he asked Ward what would happen if he was caught with the illegal load. "Benny just threw his hands in the air and said with a grin on his face: 'I don't know.'"

After a meal with the rest of the gang, the driver hit the road with his valuable cargo. He was still suffering from the injuries sustained in his earlier accident. Like before, Howard and Ward would fly to Liverpool and meet the truck there.

A few hours later, however, as they were waiting to get on the 4pm flight from Schipol Airport, panic set in. Ward, Howard, McGrath and Krusty, had all been phoning the driver but could get no answer. Ward and Howard hired a taxi and began a desperate search along the route the truck should have taken between Meijel and Cherbourg. They also visited the ports of Calais and Dunkirk checking if the truck had been booked on to a different ferry. They visited every service station along the route and eventually ended up in Brussels.

The driver and his cargo had vanished off the face of the earth.

The two syndicate' members gave up their search at 2am the next morning – the taxi fare had cost them €1,000. It would not be too long before they discovered what had happened.

The following morning Belgium's biggest ever drug seizure was headline news.

* * * *

When the driver of the huge drug shipment spotted the Belgian checkpoint, he really didn't need to panic. The police would not have discovered his illegal goods – they were only checking for documentation. In another way, the driver had probably been fortunate. For a number of months the drug dealing gang had been under secret Garda surveillance.

Operation Syndicate was set up when officers based in Carrickmacross received intelligence that a major drug smuggling conspiracy was afoot. The investigation included officers from the Northern Region drug squad, with back up from the GNDU, the CAB and the National Bureau of Criminal Investigation (NBCI). The man in over all charge had been on the case of Judge and Krusty for many years. Assistant Commissioner Kevin Carty, the Regional Commander in the border area, was a man with a reputation as a very capable serious crime investigator. Det Sgt Pat Walsh was a member of his team when he first turned Judge. Together they had chalked up the string of successes against George Mitchell's gang.

Assistant Commissioner Carty, who had spent much of his earlier career in the Special Branch fighting terrorism, was an astute strategist who believed in taking a proactive approach to investigating crime. He broke with the prevailing convention of investigating crimes after they had happened. He believed in the long game, watching and waiting for the right time to pounce on his target. Assistant Commissioner was a quintessential thief-taker. When he was appointed as Regional Commander to the Border area, he began investigating the smuggling rackets. At the same time, dissident Republican groups had begun to smuggle arms and explosives, in a bid to rekindle the war quenched by the Peace Process. Using good intelligence and informants in the Republican camps, the security services in a number of countries had foiled attempts to get arms and explosives back into Ireland. The Continuity and Real IRA were using the same smuggling methods and routes as they did when they were in the Provos. The leader of the CIRA, Liam Campbell, had been a prominent Provo until the peace process. He was also a wealthy smuggler.

The officer in charge of Operation Syndicate on the ground was Det Supt Tadgh Foley. He was in charge of all detective units along the Border. One of the lead investigators on his team was Detective Sergeant Fergus Treanor who was based in Carrickmacross. Det Sgt Treanor had worked with Carty on a specialist investigation team based in Garda HQ, in the early and mid-1990s. Det Sgt Treanor, who was a native of Monaghan, had also been centrally involved in the investigation of the Veronica Guerin murder. Foley and Treanor had won considerable praise for their work on Carty's investigation team that had uncovered a web of Garda corruption in County Donegal.

Operation Syndicate had gleaned a degree of good intelligence from a number of informants that a major drug trafficking operation was being operated from Ardee. By the beginning of August 2002, the cops knew that the international mob was involved in something big. They had made the connection between Morgan McGrath, Ward, Judge, Krusty and Dinny Meredith, as a result of intelligence they received following the arrest of Kevin Keogh in France less than a month earlier.

Det Sgt Treanor and his officers had placed Ward's yard under discreet surveillance for the following weeks. On the morning of August 27, when the small convoy left the yard in Ardee, they prepared to make their move. Assistant Commissioner Carty's plan was straightforward. They would monitor the drug shipment when it arrived back in Ireland and follow its progress. Then they would carefully pick off each gang involved in the plot, as they took delivery of their drugs. Across the Irish Sea, police forces and customs in England and Scotland were also gearing up for the same approach. However, they hadn't reckoned on the injured, and much aggrieved, truck driver from Ardee losing his bottle, as soon as he spotted the Belgian checkpoint.

Within hours of the driver's phone going dead, Assistant Commissioner Carty's people were aware that something was amiss. Using telephone intercepts and an informant, they soon learned that the truck had been abandoned. They alerted their Belgian colleagues who located the dope-laden truck and kept it under surveillance for 72 hours in the hope that someone would turn up to collect it. On September 1, when no one had shown up, they moved in and made their seizure.

There was intense disappointment back at Carrickmacross Station that the drug delivery had not gone through. They had been so close to snaring the big players in the plot. They knew the syndicate members would now all go to ground until the dust settled. Then, like all international cartels, they would simply set up another drug smuggling method. At the same time,

Baiba Saulite the young Latvian mother shot dead by associates of Martin 'Marlo' Hyland.

Lebanese-born criminal Hassan Hassan, the estranged husband of Baiba Saulite, who was suspected of ordering her murder.
© Sunday World

John Hennessy, Baiba Saulite's courageous solicitor, who was placed under armed police guard after a contract was ordered on his life, being interviewed by the author.
© Padraig O'Reilly

Finglas criminal Declan Curran, who died of natural causes in a prison cell.
© Sunday World

Anthony 'Anto' Spratt, a member of the Finglas gang who committed suicide in prison.
© Sunday World

Christine Mahon, who withdrew her evidence implicating Declan Curran in the murder of William O'Regan in June 2003.
© Garrett White/
Collins Photo Library

Gardaí and ambulance workers, removing the remains of Patrick 'Podge' Sheridan from waste ground off Scribblestown Lane in Finglas, October 2003.
© Colin Keegan/Collins Photo Agency.

Patrick 'Podge' Sheridan, who was lured to his death by John Daly, Anto Spratt and Declan Curran.

Retired Detective Inspector Brian Sherry, who investigated many of the murders and serious crimes committed by the Finglas gang.
© *Ronan Quinlan/ Collins Photo Agency*

Finglas gang member Dwayne Foster, who died in custody before he could be charged with the indiscriminate murder of mother-of-one, Donna Cleary, in March 2006.
© *Sunday World*

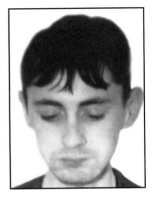

Finglas gang member Victor Murphy, who was killed when the sawn-off shotgun he was carrying accidentally went off.
© *Sunday World*

Gardaí removing the taxi cab Finglas gang member, John Daly, was sitting in when he was shot dead in October 2007.
© *Collins Photo Agency*

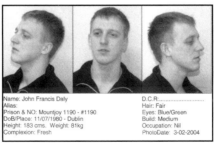

Name: John Francis Daly
Alias:
Prison & NO: Mountjoy 1190 - #1190
DoB/Place: 11/07/1980 - Dublin
Height: 183 cms. Weight: 81kg
Complexion: Fresh

D.C.R:............................
Hair: Fair
Eyes: Blue/Green
Build: Medium
Occupation: Nil
PhotoDate: 3-02-2004

John Daly's prison mug shots.

John Daly caught on a security camera, as he was holding up a petrol station in Finglas.

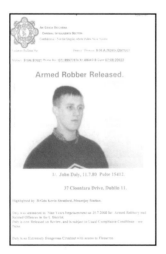

An internal Garda bulletin warning of the imminent release of John Daly, in 2002, who it described as a highly dangerous armed robber.

Detective Garda Kevin Stratford, the officer who single-handedly pursued Daly and his lethal gang. The courageous young Detective died on June 8, 2006, aged 34.
© Padraig O'Reilly

Wanted: Anto Spratt and friend Keith Groves pose in a mock wanted poster.
© *Sunday World*

Detective Sergeant Fergus Treanor, *(left)* one of the officers in charge of Operation Syndicate,arresting Brian Meehan the man serving life for the murder of Veronica Guerin.
© *Padraig O'Reilly*

The warehouse the Syndicate used in Meijel, southern Holland, where the multi-million euro polyloads of drugs were prepared for transportation.

Ardee businessman Benny Ward, who is wanted in connection with Operation Syndicate.
© *Sunday World*

One of the specially converted truck units which was seized by Gardaí in County Louth as it was about to be sent to Holland to collect a drug load for the Syndicate.

A portion of the €30 million polyload of heroin/hash/ecstasy/cocaine/amphetamine which was seized by Belgian police as a result of the Operation Syndicate investigation in 2002.

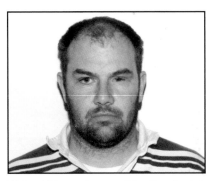

Michael Howard, one of the Syndicate's gofers convicted for conspiracy to import drugs.
© *Sunday World*

Morgan McGrath who was convicted for conspiracy as a result of Operation Syndicate.
© *Sunday World*

'Krusty the Clown', the mastermind behind one of the biggest drug trafficking operations in Europe.
© *Padraig O'Reilly*

Fergal Toal.
© *Sunday World*

Kevin McAlorum.
© *Sunday World*

Liam Judge.
© *Sunday World*

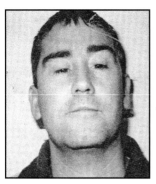

Christy Griffin aka, Tony Soprano.
© *Sunday World*

Colm 'Collie' Griffin.

Christy Griffin as a young armed robber.
© *Sunday World*

Danny O'Reilly, Griffin's nephew.
© *Sunday World*

Gerard 'Batt' Byrne, who was murdered as part of the Griffin feud in December 2006.
© *Sunday World*

Stephen Leddan, of Upper Oriel Street, who was shot dead as part of the Griffin feud in December 2006.
© *Ronan Quinlan/ Collins Photo Agency*

The scene of Gerard Byrne's murder in Dublin's IFSC.

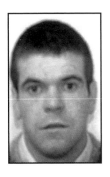

Eric Hopkins, who was shot dead by the ERU, along with Collie Griffin, during an armed robbery in Lusk in 2005.
© *Sunday World*

The Village Store in Lusk, County Dublin, where Griffin and Hopkins were killed.
© *Collins Photo Agency*

Brian Fitzgerald the night-club security manager from Limerick, who was murdered because he stood up to the McCarthy/Dundon gang.
© *James Horan/Press 22*

Hired killer, James Martin Cahill, who murdered Brian Fitzgerald for the Limerick mob.
© *Collins Photo Agency*

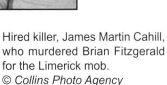

Jailed Limerick crime
boss Christy Keane.

Kieran Keane, who was
murdered in the McCarthy/
Dundon attempted
takeover.

Eddie Ryan whose murder
sparked the Limerick feuds.

Eddie Ryan's sons, Eddie &
Kieran, re-united with their
mother Mary in January
2003, after their mysterious
'abduction'.
© *Press 22*

Wayne Dundon.
© Padraig O'Reilly

John Dundon.
© Padraig O'Reilly

Dessie Dundon.
© Collins Photo Agency

Christopher 'Smokey'
Costello, who was convicted
with three others of the
murder of Kieran Keane.
© Collins Photo Agency

Underworld figure, Anthony Kelly, from County Clare who was acquitted of the murder of Brian Fitzgerald.
© *Collins Photo Agency*

Retired Assistant Commissioner, Gerry Kelly, who was the officer in charge of the Brian Fitzgerald and Kieran Keane murder investigations.
© *Padraig O'Reilly*

Detective Inspector (now Det Supt) Jim Brown and Superintendent (now Chief Supt) Willie Keane, who investigated many of Limerick's worst gangland murders.
© *Sunday World*

the operation had resulted in a huge seizure of drugs that hurt several criminal gangs. The cops were not yet beaten.

Operation Syndicate became the centre of a much larger international investigation, involving police and customs in Holland, Belgium, France, Spain, Britain and Northern Ireland. Operation Syndicate also involved the DEA and Europol. The incident room at its centre was based at Carrickmacross, a small country police station in the heart of smuggling country. From this room, information and intelligence was collated and shared between the various agencies.

* * * *

The Belgian seizure sent the syndicate members into a state of panic. Jimmy Rankin immediately instructed Ward to bring Howard with him to Spain, to get off-side. Everyone in the syndicate went to ground. Howard, who was afraid of the inevitable enquiry by his nasty employers, opted to go back to Ireland instead. Ward flew to Alicante to meet with Judge, Gary Marno and Kevin McAlorum. He went into hiding and did not return to Ireland again.

Krusty and McGrath picked up Howard from the airport and the three stayed in a Dublin hotel for the night. Krusty reassured his employees that they could not be charged in connection with the seizure because it had happened in a different jurisdiction. He also reiterated that they would be safe and untouchable as long as they remained within the syndicate. "He said if we ever left it we were fucked. We were always told never talk if arrested, he (Krusty) always gave the impression that he wouldn't be touched by the law and had contacts in the police," Howard later told detectives.

A few days later, Krusty organised a meeting in a hotel in Portlaoise. It was attended by Jimmy Rankin, two of the INLA members, Krusty, Howard and McGrath. Rankin claimed that the truck driver had 'stolen' part of the drug shipment before it had been seized and promised he would be "sorted". Despite the setback, the syndicate were determined to immediately regroup and get back to business.

A few days later Howard and McGrath were sent to Wolverhampton. Rankin told McGrath that the syndicate had three trucks and trailers, which had not yet been modified, waiting for collection in Belgium. When they arrived, Howard was given Stg£15,000 by a member of the Liverpool mob to cover the purchase of another trailer and the equipment to convert it. Two tonnes of hashish was waiting to be collected from Liam Judge and Ward in Alicante. The plan was to collect drugs in the new trailer and drop the load back to the warehouse in Liverpool. Rankin told them to hire a driver for Stg£40,000 to do the run. They rented a yard and went to work. Howard, McGrath and another gang member made a mess of the job. The trailer almost fell apart and was unusable. The syndicate abandoned the idea and decided to bring the stuff in under a load of potatoes. But the new operation didn't get off the ground.

On September 11, the Operation Syndicate team searched Ward's yard. They seized the partially converted trailer and two trucks. In the cab of one of the trucks officers found a piece of paper with directions to the warehouse in Meijel. They also searched Ward's family home at Arthurstown where they found invoices and dockets for the equipment used to covert the Belgian trailer. They also found phone numbers for Howard and McGrath.

The following day, Det Sgt Treanor and his team detained Krusty while he was making his way to a funeral on the Border. They brought him to Monaghan Garda Station for the purpose of a drug search. They wanted to get up close to him and see what he had to say for himself. In a conversation with the detectives, he made no secret of the fact that he had detailed knowledge of the Belgian drug seizure and named some of the people involved. He admitted to knowing Benny Ward and told the officers his pal was now hiding in Spain. The plausible gangster even offered to arrange for Ward to return to Ireland so that the Gardaí could arrest him. He promised to come back to them with the full inside story. Before he left the station, the detectives seized Krusty's mobile phone and diary.

There was another dramatic twist in the case four days later when Liam Judge's estranged wife, Helen, was abducted from the family home in the early hours of Monday, September 16. Her kidnappers were thought to be disgruntled members of the drug syndicate. It was reported that a ransom of €200,000 had been demanded for the safe return of the 41-year-old, who suffered from a heart complaint. She had no connection with her husband's activities.

In the early hours of the following Wednesday morning, an anonymous caller to Kildare Garda Station directed officers to Jenkinstown Wood, near Omeath on the Louth border within bandit country. The terrified woman was located a few hours later, freezing and disorientated. She was still wearing her nightdress.

It remains a mystery whether or not Judge ever paid the ransom, although underworld sources and police believe he did. The syndicate wanted part-payment of the cost of the drugs they had lost in Belgium and they blamed Judge. John Gilligan, in an interview conducted on his mobile phone with a journalist, vowed that the kidnapping would be avenged. Shortly after the incident, Judge phoned Morgan McGrath in England and blamed the gang for the abduction. Judge threatened McGrath, saying that he was going to be shot. The furious double agent told the trucker: "The rest of your gang is going to get it as well. You have caused nothing but grief; you've destroyed my family by kidnapping the wife."

When McGrath and Howard relayed the threats to Krusty he laughed and replied: "Don't worry about him [Judge] he has no back up except for Gilligan and he can't do anything."

The day after Helen Judge was found in the woods, a team of officers from the Criminal Assets Bureau arrested the Penguin's brother, Paddy Mitchell, in a house in Palmerstown. For the previous two years, they had been investigating Mitchell's ownership of up to 50 properties in Dublin that were used to launder the proceeds of crime. The CAB had directions to arrest and charge the Penguin's sibling for non-payment of taxes and issue him with a demand for over €1 million. (Mitchell was subsequently convicted and jailed for two years on those charges. Several houses were seized and sold to satisfy his tax liabilities.)

During the search, the officers found the tools, steel-plating and timbers used to convert the trailer in Ardee, dumped in the garden at the back of the house. Paddy Mitchell had helped Krusty clear the evidence out of Ward's yard. At first, the detectives thought the equipment had been stolen as it carried the names of the Ardee hire companies. When they told their colleagues in Carrickmacross about the find, an immediate connection was made. The tools were quickly traced back to the hire companies and, from there, directly connected to Ward. Forensic examination would later establish that the steel-plates were identical to those used in the Belgian trailer and on the partially converted trailer seized in Ward's yard. The investigating team could also connect Krusty to the purchase of the steel.

In the meantime, Gardaí also carried out detailed analysis of the phone records, which clearly established regular contact between the main players in the conspiracy. Krusty's diary, which contained day-to-day notes of his activities, also provided valuable corroboration of the information gathered. He had recorded details of payments made to Ward, Howard and McGrath and also various meetings. As the investigation progressed there were several conferences held in Dublin and Monaghan, which were attended by representatives of all the police forces involved.

The driver of the truck had been missing since he abandoned the multi-million Euro drug load. He feared the cartel of dangerous cut-throats he was working for would blame him for the loss of the drug shipment. After all, there were enough experienced killers among the various gangs involved to start a small war. After dumping the truck on August 30, the driver had hitched a lift to Paris with an English trucker. From there he took a train to Barcelona and went into hiding, living mainly in hostels. He also spent some time in Rome. The driver eventually decided to return home a few months later. He arranged to meet the investigating Gardaí, to tell them his "side of the story".

In a voluntary statement he made to detectives in

Carrickmacross on October 23, the driver claimed Benny Ward had forced him to participate in the Belgian smuggling plot. He said his family had received death threats since his disappearance and he was in fear for himself and his loved ones.

"I had no intention of getting involved in this and got out at my first opportunity," he claimed. "I've had time to think why Benny Ward did this to me. I hadn't the flexibility to work anywhere else. I came home of my own free will to clear my name. I need to get on with my life."

Two days later, the investigation carried out a second search of Krusty's property in Dublin but no hard evidence was found to link him with the drug seizure.

By early November, the Operation Syndicate team were ready to begin making arrests. On November 4 and 5, they arrested Krusty, Howard, McGrath and Topper under the Misuse of Drugs Act. Ward's girlfriend was also detained. Under the act, a suspect can be held for questioning for up to seven days. Krusty was held for four days, during which the gangland veteran refused to answer any questions. The crafty gangster was released without charge.

His accomplices also played tough – for a while at least. After several hours of questions, both Howard and McGrath admitted their roles. They were not hardened villains and they wept like babies.

When he finally came clean, Mike Howard told Det Sgt Treanor everything about the operation and who had been involved. He summed up his reason for getting involved: "The whole reason I got involved in this whole mess was debts and easy money. I wanted to get a few pounds together to get the house finished for the family. I got caught up in it as it went along. We ended up being told what to do, it was like we had no choice, we ended up in over our heads."

McGrath had a similar story to tell. "I am very sorry and I feel stupid for getting involved in drugs. I got involved in bringing drugs into the country and I ended up involved over my head. I was in way too deep. Once I was in there was no turning back. Everything I did was on the instructions of [Krusty]," he said.

The INLA man, Topper from Castleknock, also admitted that he had been involved in the drug trafficking operation and had helped distribute up to €5 million worth of drugs for the syndicate.

In the meantime, the investigation team had located the warehouse in Meijel. On November 18, Dutch police raided the depot where they found 25 kilos of amphetamine. A shipment of one tonne of hashish had left the warehouse a few days earlier. They were too late to catch it.

Mike Howard and Morgan McGrath were subsequently charged with conspiracy to import the drug shipment seized in Belgium. Files were also sent to the DPP recommending that Krusty be charged with the same conspiracy and Topper with the sale and supply of drugs. However, the Director of Public Prosecutions did not proceed with the charges against either man. The DPP decided not to charge Topper because, despite his admission, he had not been caught with the actual drugs he distributed! No reason was given for the decision not to proceed against Krusty. Howard and McGrath were reluctant, for fear of retribution against their families, to testify against him in court. The CAB commenced a major investigation into Krusty's tax affairs, however, and he was forced to pay a massive six-figure sum in unpaid taxes. He was also convicted for failure to make tax returns and received a two year suspended jail sentence.

Other members of the syndicate were not so lucky. At first, Liam Judge did not appear to suffer unduly as a result of the police crackdown. For a short time, he continued to organise drug shipments on behalf of associates of the Gilligan gang. Fifteen months after the Belgian seizure Judge died suddenly from a massive heart attack in December 2003. The pressure of life as a double agent, combined with years of heavy drinking and cocaine abuse, more than likely contributed to his untimely demise.

At the time of his death, he had been under intense pressure from Gilligan who treated him like a slave. In one phone call the diminutive mobster threatened to have him killed after he failed to do what he wanted. "Remember, I fucking own Spain and don't forget it," Gilligan snarled down the line, from the comfort of his prison cell in Portlaoise. Judge had always lived on the edge and there was no way he would have died in his sleep at a ripe old age. In the end his heart did the hit man's dirty work.

Fergal Toal also remained in the drug trade. A year later he was caught and subsequently convicted of, cocaine trafficking in Northern Ireland. In June that same year, 2004, Kevin McAlorum was ambushed and shot dead as he left a child to school in North Belfast. Two hit men dispatched the drug dealer in a hail of well-aimed bullets. It appeared his former comrades had finally caught up with him for the murder of Gino Gallagher. The day before McAlorum's murder, Gallagher's father had been buried in Dublin. Police later discovered that McAlorum's killer was a member of the INLA and the murder was over drugs and not vengeance.

In 2006, Jimmy Rankin and a number of associates were arrested as part of a major joint Belgian and Irish operation. The new cartel had been involved in an attempt to smuggle over €20 million worth of heroin to Ireland, on a private jet.

At the time of writing Benny Ward is still believed to be living in Spain, where he continues to be involved in drug trafficking. In the event that he ever turns up in Ireland, he will also be charged in connection with the conspiracy.

On Thursday, October 7, 2004, Mike Howard and Morgan McGrath pleaded guilty to conspiring to import the Belgian drug seizure into Ireland. Immediately after they made their pleas, Monaghan Circuit Criminal Court was adjourned for 15 minutes. Following this, there were legal arguments between the Defence and Prosecution in front of the presiding Judge Matthew Deery. As a result it was agreed that Garda evidence in the case would be subject to restrictions. The state had argued that this was necessary to prevent the murder of informants and protect the integrity of ongoing police investigations in Ireland and parts of mainland Europe.

Det Sgt Fergus Treanor told the court that the two men had effectively been small cogs in a much bigger criminal conspiracy. Howard and McGrath were each sentenced to 12 years in prison. Judge Deering complimented the Gardaí on a job well done.

A year later, the Court of Criminal Appeal reduced the sentences to eight years each. The court noted that there had been extenuating and mitigating factors. There had been many testimonials on behalf of the two men, they had no previous convictions and it was accepted they were in the lower ranks of the drugs gang and in difficult financial circumstances. Those who know Howard and McGrath say that it is highly unlikely that either man will ever get involved in serious crime again.

The Operation Syndicate investigation succeeded in closing down a drug trafficking operation, capable of moving vast amounts of narcotics. The probe also identified over 20 major players in the criminal drug rackets in England, Scotland, Holland and Spain. Vital intelligence was passed on to the relevant authorities in each country, which led to a number of multi-million Euro drug seizures on the continent and in the UK.

The investigation also illustrated, however, how difficult it is to put an international crime gang out of business. There are always plenty more vulnerable fools for Krusty and his cronies to exploit.

Eight

TONY SOPRANO

Christy Griffin's favourite TV programme was the American cult crime drama, 'The Sopranos'. He never missed an episode of the series which ran for six seasons. Griffin bought the entire DVD boxset which he watched over and over, delighting in the lifestyles and crimes of the fictional mob. Griffin idolised the drama's powerful central character, New Jersey mob boss Tony Soprano, and would often quote him to his minions. He modelled himself on the complex Mafioso and indulged in the fantasy that he was the real life manifestation of his celluloid hero.

In reality, there actually were a number of similarities between the Dublin gangster and his alter ego. They both headed family-based criminal gangs that controlled the tough neighbourhoods where they grew up. The real life and fictional mobs specialised in drug trafficking, protection rackets and large scale robbery scams. Griffin and Soprano were men to be feared – men who had "respect" – and protected their family interests through the enforcement of a strict code of omerta. If anyone stepped out of line they were dealt with using extreme violence. No one dared cross either man. In the underworld Griffin's gang was nicknamed 'The Sopranos' and he was known as 'Tony Soprano'.

Like the TV anti–hero, Griffin also used a waste disposal business as a front for laundering his drug money. His sister, her husband and two nephews were registered as the directors.

He used a large criminal network, including family members, to distribute cocaine and rob cargos of goods from Dublin docks. He had the guns, money, muscle and influence to ensure that he was an untouchable godfather.

But there the similarities between fictional gangster and real life hoodlum ended. If there had been a character like the real life Christy Griffin in 'The Sopranos' then Tony would surely have had him whacked. For behind the façade of a powerful underworld hard man lurked a dark, sordid secret. It was a scandal Griffin tried to suppress by unleashing a war on the streets of his inner-city neighbourhood which left a trail of fear, misery and death in its wake. Knives, guns and bombs were used as a consequence of his attempts to conceal his predilection. Christy Griffin was a paedophile and a rapist. In the flimsy moral handbook of the average gangster, the paedophile is the lowest form of life. There is only one other type of loathsome deviant in gangland – the informer.

* * * *

Christy Griffin grew up in Canon Lillis Avenue in the heart of Dublin's dockland on the north side of the River Liffey. Born on August 7, 1969, he was the fourth of eight children. The Corporation flats and estates of the north inner-city ghettoes had long been considered a breeding ground for criminal activity. The area had been blighted by poverty and deprivation for years. Its origins could be traced back to the awful tenement squalor that grew up beside Dublin's dockland during the 19th Century. Most of its inhabitants had worked as poorly paid labourers, unloading cargo ships. The unlikely combination of progress and economic depression, conspired to bring about the death of the dock yards. The vast acres of the port area, which once bustled with commerce, lay derelict and empty. The lines of cranes that once scooped cargos from ships, stood silent and rusting. The main source of income for many hundreds of impoverished families was gone forever.

Successive governments had ignored the plight of the population, most of who lived in appalling conditions. They suffered high unemployment for decades, until a massive docklands re-generation programme began in the 1990s. Proof of the despair that pervaded Dublin 1 was the startling speed with which heroin became a serious problem there in the 1980s. It is well documented that the drug took hold in the space of a few weeks. The growing prevalence of drug addiction added to the level of crime and sense of hopelessness. It became a human wasteland. Traditionally there had always been antipathy and suspicion towards the police, the arm of the State that they had the most encounters with. It was from this criminogenic environment that a new generation of dangerous armed criminals like Christy Griffin emerged.

Tony Soprano's biggest fan began his criminal career as a member of a group of tough, young teenage tearaways called the Bugsy Malones. They were named after a famous 1970s children's spoof gangster movie in which the bad guys were armed with machine-guns that fired cream cakes. One of the central figures in the Bugsy gang was a teenager who would become one of the country's most notorious armed robbery masterminds – Gerry 'The Monk' Hutch.

When they discovered guns and armed robbery a few years later, the angry young men, from Dublin's inner-city, unleashed mayhem. They were known as reckless and highly dangerous youngsters. Griffin's record was typical of the teenage hoods for whom crime was to be a way of life. He notched up his first criminal conviction for car theft at the age of 11. By the time he was 16, he had been convicted another eight times, for car theft, larceny and receiving stolen goods by the Metropolitan Children's Court. Griffin served five periods of imprisonment in institutions for young offenders. On his release, he was about to earn a reputation as a very dangerous armed criminal.

In gangland history the 1980s will be remembered as the decade of the blagger, or armed robber. All across Dublin, well-established gangs were pulling jobs in all areas of the country. They were hitting banks, building societies, post offices and pay rolls. It was the heyday of The General, Martin Cahill, and his Southside band of thieves. He was seen as a role model for the up and coming generation of robbers.

Christy Griffin and his peers soon had an awesome reputation as some of the most prolific young blaggers in the country. He was just 16 when he teamed up with three older associates. The gang targeted the suburbs of south County Dublin, in a string of armed robberies. Around 9.45am on the morning of October 16, 1985, the four thieves drove up to the Employment Exchange at Cumberland Street in Dun Laoghaire, in a stolen car. Dole offices were popular targets for hold-ups. At a time of crippling unemployment, across the country huge numbers were forced to queue to collect their paltry cash dole payments every week. It was a sign of the times that dole offices sometimes carried more cash than some banks. In the days before the Criminal Assets Bureau it was not unusual for criminals to collect their unemployment assistance at the local dole office and then return later to rob it.

Griffin had just been released from a four month sentence in St Patrick's Institution for young offenders. He and two other raiders ran into the crowded building, while the driver remained behind the wheel outside. They were armed with two sawn-off shotguns. As they burst through the doors, one gang member fired a shot in the air and ordered customers and staff to get on the floor. He covered them while the other two gangsters vaulted the partition which divided the public area from the payment hatches. It took the agile thieves around 30 seconds to scoop over IR£49,000 (€62,230) from three of the booths into canvas bags . They ran to the waiting getaway car and sped off. A few minutes later they changed vehicles in a car park in Monkstown. The gang drove off in a stolen Fiat Ritmo which they had acquired the previous night in Ballsbridge. They then tore off at speed back to the Northside of the River Liffey and home. The quickest route was to travel through the suburbs of Ballsbridge and Irishtown and cross the River Liffey at the East Link toll bridge. Once they were over the bridge, the robbers could easily disappear into the maze of inner-city streets that were their natural habitat.

As soon as the alarm was raised about the raid, armed detectives in two unmarked patrol cars were dispatched to the toll bridge to block off a possible escape route. At the time, special anti-robbery patrols were well used to blocking off main routes in a bid to stop the many blagg teams traversing the city. And they were well-practised – on most week days there was an average of four or more armed hold-ups in Dublin alone. The gangs from the north inner-city were involved in many of them.

At 10am the officers spotted the Ritmo driving towards them. They parked one of the squad cars across the bridge, to block Griffin's team. But the getaway car rammed it out of the way. The gang continued on in the direction of the flat complexes, beyond the derelict dockyards as squad cars descended on the area for the chase. At Saint Brigid's Gardens, a short distance from Griffin's home, they abandoned their getaway car and ran into the Corporation flat complex to hide.

Pursuing squad cars swamped the area. Armed detectives surrounded the flats and began searching for them. A short time later, they arrested Griffin with his two cousins, Gerard Duffy and Keith Hyland, after they emerged from two different flats. Twenty-two-year-old Duffy, from St Brigid's Gardens, already had convictions for assault and robbery. Hyland, who was a year older and from nearby St Laurence's Mansions, was even better known to the cops. He had almost 30 convictions for robbery and possession of firearms. Detectives recovered one of the weapons used in the raid. It had been stolen from a house in Drumcondra a year earlier. Hyland was subsequently charged with possession of a firearm and robbery. There was insufficient evidence with which to charge either Duffy or their young protégé Griffin, although investigators were satisfied they had done the job.

The close shave did nothing to dampen Griffin's enthusiasm for serious crime. With his brother, Colm 'Collie' Griffin, who was two years younger, he went out robbing on an almost daily basis. In appearance, the two desperados certainly did not look like dangerous villains. They each had a crooked eye and wore wide-rimmed glasses that made them look more like nerds than villains. As a result Collie Griffin was given the name 'Clarence' by local wags. 'Clarence' was the name of a cross-eyed lion in the popular 1970s children's TV program, 'Daktari'. Christy was simply called "the eye".

"Every Thursday when you were working you waited to hear where the robbery was after happening. And you could be sure that it was the two Griffin's and their mates who had done it. Despite their age they were known as very reckless and dangerous. They had no problem opening up [shooting] if they were in a tight spot," recalled one experienced city centre detective who had many dealings with the Sopranos.

On April 26, 1986, Griffin and another associate Paul Nolan stole a car for use in an armed robbery in the Cornelscourt area of South Dublin. Griffin had just been released a few days, earlier, after serving part of another seven months sentence he had been given in Saint Pat's a month after the employment exchange heist. At 5.35pm that evening, uniformed Gardaí Padraig Lyons and Joe Kelly spotted the two desperados on the Old Bray Road in Cornelscourt. They recognised Nolan as the driver, while Griffin was seated in the back. When the officers tried to pull them over a high speed chase ensued and the robbers took off in the direction of the city centre. As they sped down Stillorgan Road, the officers saw Griffin point a pump-action shotgun at them. The pursuit took the cops and the robbers into the inner-city and dockland areas. At Commons Street, behind Connolly Railway Station, the stolen car slowed down and Griffin again pointed his weapon at the pursuing cops through the open rear window to threaten them but didn't fire. The Griffins had intended dumping their getaway car in the area and slipping away, but this time they couldn't shake off the police.

The chase continued on into North County Dublin. At Baskin Lane, near Kinsealy, the stolen car stopped. Griffin got out and again took aim at the police car that had doggedly remained behind them. The officers, who were unarmed, swerved onto a side road to avoid being shot. The two robbers then took off again and the car was found abandoned a few miles away.

Two days later Nolan, who was also 16, was arrested and on April 30, detectives caught up with Griffin at his home on Cannon Lillis Avenue. The two teenagers were later brought before the Children's Court, where they were charged with car theft and firearms offences. Griffin and his pal were freed on bail.

In other incidents after robberies, the young 'Tony Soprano', his brother and their pals, were lucky not to have been shot by the police. The reckless thieves often opened fire on pursuing Gardaí as if they wanted an armed confrontation. In the 1980s two associates of Griffin and the Monk were shot dead during armed confrontations with Gardaí after heists. Another altercation happened shortly after an All-Ireland hurling final when Collie Griffin and another associate, Robbie Harrison held up the Red Parrot Pub on Dorset Street.

As two detectives, Enda Moore and Paddy Hannigan, arrived at the scene of heist, Griffin and Harrison ran from the pub and jumped into a stolen post office van. While the cops chased the robbers through the inner city streets Collie Griffin fired shots from the back of the van. One of the pursuing officers, who were being rammed by the van, fired up to six shots at the hoods. The thieves then rammed the stolen van into bollards and it was set alight. They ran into Philip Shanahan House flats, as Garda reinforcements descended on the area. Even though it was 11am on a Monday morning, the Griffins orchestrated a full scale riot which lasted for most of the day. As a result two squad cars were destroyed and the police were forced to retreat. Collie Griffin and Harrison were later arrested and charged with firearms and robbery offences. Two weeks later, while on bail, they were arrested again after another pub robbery. As a result they were each jailed for six years.

On Saturday, July 5, 1986 – just two months after his arrest for the Cornelscourt chase – Griffin was back at work again. At 5pm that Saturday – the busiest shopping day of the week – a Securicor van arrived at the Quinnsworth Store on Vevay Road in Bray to collect the takings for the day. It was staffed by security men John Scanlan and Charles O'Connell both of whom were aged in their mid-50's. O'Connell first went into the store and collected a bag containing cheques which he brought out to the van. Then he returned to the store and collected a second bag, containing IR£11,000 (€13,970) in cash. Griffin and his two accomplices, who had been watching the store and the movements of cash for a number of days, knew that the second bag contained the cash.

The gang struck as O'Connell was about to put the money bag into the back of the security van. Griffin and another hood ran at the security man ordering him to "hand it over". He did so but as they were about to run off, Griffin took aim, for no apparent reason, at John Scanlan who was standing a short distance away from his colleague. An eye-witness later recalled hearing the gun click as it misfired. Griffin fiddled with the mechanism and pointed the gun for a second time. He blasted Scanlan from a distance of just four feet and seriously injured the security officer. Scanlan was lucky to survive the attack. The gang jumped into a getaway car and escaped before Gardaí arrived. Their modus operandi was to abandon the car a short distance away and get into a second stolen car which they had parked earlier. On the way from a hold-up the robbers would put the cash, masks and guns into a bag. At a pre-arranged location they would throw the bag to a waiting gang member. It meant that if the robbers were then intercepted – in the second stolen car – they could only be charged with the unauthorised taking of the vehicle. There were would be no evidence of the robbery.

Unfortunately for the young armed robber this time, he was identified at the scene by a number of eye-witnesses. Over two weeks later Griffin, who had been lying low, was arrested at Canon Lillis Avenue. Detectives also found Griffin's fingerprints on a number of souvenirs which had been left in the boot by the owner of one of the stolen cars used in the robbery. He was again brought before the courts and charged with serious offences, including robbery and possession of firearms. Despite already being on bail for at least four other robbery and firearms charges, as well as shooting a security guard, Griffin was again released on bail. But his days as a blagger were coming to an end.

On October 6, 1986, he was jailed for four months for an outstanding aggravated burglary charge in which a weapon had been used. A month later, he received another 12 month sentence for driving without insurance. Then in December he was jailed for six years for another charge of possession of firearms and ammunition. This time he was sent to serve his time in Mountjoy Prison. He had just turned 17 and had already graduated from young offender to serious criminal. On March 30, 1987, he was given three years for threatening to shoot Gardaí during the Cornelscourt chase. The following May he was sentenced to a further nine years for armed robbery and shooting John Scanlan. All the sentences ran concurrently which meant that he had received a maximum of nine years – with a quarter of that knocked off for remission.

Griffin was 23 years old when he was released from prison in 1992. During his extended absence gangland had undergone a massive transformation. When he returned to the inner-city, Griffin found that there were a lot of lucrative opportunities for a reckless young hood like himself. The age of the blagger was being replaced by that of the drug dealer. The early 1990s saw criminals everywhere, who had originally shunned the trade, switch from armed hold-ups to narcotics, as they discovered the prodigious profits available. Ireland was changing. In addition to heroin, demands for other drugs such as cannabis and ecstasy had increased dramatically. Drugs were creating a multi-million pound industry for organised crime. By the latter half of the '90s cocaine would also emerge as the drug of choice for the Celtic Tiger generation.

Like his many contemporaries, Griffin had learned a lot from his foolhardy and utterly reckless escapades in the 1980s. He had had enough of prison life. The motto of the new brat pack of up-and-coming godfathers was 'get rich quick – and don't get caught'. Many of his closest associates had become major players and they introduced him to the nefarious trade. Despite growing up and witnessing firsthand the misery and devastation drugs had caused for their relations and neighbours, the young drug dealers had no moral qualms about getting their hands dirty. Among his old pals who had moved into drug trafficking were two local sporting icons; Thomas 'The Boxer' Mullen and Derek 'Maradona' Dunne.

By his mid-teens Mullen, who was from Dominick Street flats, had been representing Ireland as a light middle-weight champion at international tournaments. Boxing was one of

the few sports that kept young people off the streets and away
from drugs in the inner-city. Mullen was the quintessential hero
to the local kids and their parents. He was a symbol of hope
in an otherwise depressed, ghettoised world. By the time 'The
Boxer' was 19, he was coaching youngsters in a boxing club
on Buckingham Street. But Mullen committed the ultimate act
of treachery when he made a conscious decision to move into
the drugs trade – selling heroin in his own neighbourhood. His
customers included some of the kids he had been entrusted to
coach in the boxing ring.

Derek Dunne had arrived at the same decision. Dunne
earned the nickname Maradona, after the famous soccer player
as a result of his skill on the football field. The semi-professional
player with St Patrick's Athletic, was another north inner-city
sporting hero who had won the adulation of his community.
But off the field, Griffin's pal was making much bigger scores
as one of the largest suppliers of heroin in Dublin. He was also
well connected. Dunne was living with Rachel Mitchell, the
daughter of the Penguin, George Mitchell, who he subsequently
married. The relationship opened doors for Dunne and his many
associates, including Griffin. It put them in contact with major
suppliers in the UK and Holland. Another close associate of the
would-be Tony Soprano, Peter Mitchell, was also a member of
the inner-city drug dealing fraternity. By the time Griffin was
released, Mitchell, who was nicknamed 'Fatso', had a successful
drug distribution operation in the inner-city, specialising in the
sale of hashish and ecstasy. Fatso was the man credited with
convincing a then little known godfather called John Gilligan
that the future in gangland was the drug trade. Together with
Mitchell's best friend, Brian Meehan, the dangerous hoods
became Gilligan's most trusted associates.

Mitchell, Meehan and Griffin had a mutual friend in
another major drug dealer from the inner-city called Robbie
Harrison. As a teenager Harrison and a relation had taken part
in several robberies with the Griffins.

With so many well established contacts Christy Griffin's
return to freedom happened at the right time. He had soon set
up a well-organised drug trafficking network, selling heroin,

hashish and ecstasy and later became a wholesale supplier of cocaine. Griffin employed family members and associates to run his business, and he was careful to remain hands off-from the actual product.

Garda intelligence sources revealed that Griffin took part in a number of armed robberies to raise investment cash for his new business. In January 1995, he was nominated as one of the suspects who had taken part in the robbery of €3.6 million from the Brinks Allied security company's cash holding depot in North Dublin. The job, one of the largest cash robberies in the history of the State, was organised by Griffin's old friend, The Monk. Gerry Hutch and his group had already made a name for themselves in January 1987 when they robbed €1.7 million in cash from a security van at Marino Mart in North Dublin. Griffin was close to most of the gang members. In fact all of the armed robbers and drug dealers from the inner-city were connected and associated with each other in some way. The loyalties of self-styled 'ordinary decent criminals' like Hutch, who claimed the high moral ground by shunning the drug trade, were often blurred when it came to his old pals, even though they had swapped hold-ups for heroin. Members of the Monk's close-knit gang of robbers were suspected of also investing their ill-gotten gains in the drug trade.

The drug dealing brat pack that emerged in the early 1990s soon began making their mark on the streets. With the likes of Griffin, Mullen, Dunne and others getting involved in the wholesale distribution of heroin and other narcotics drug addiction in the inner-city communities soared to levels not seen since the early 1980s. Anger began to ferment among the ordinary decent citizens who were trying to give their children a chance in life. The situation was further exacerbated in June 1996 when John Gilligan's gang murdered journalist Veronica Guerin. The unprecedented public outcry which followed the murder led to a powerful backlash against organised crime and to the establishment of the Criminal Assets Bureau. In the north inner-city the remnants of the Republican-controlled Concerned Parents Against Drugs (CPAD) – which had been dormant since the late 1980s – began mobilising against the drug pushers again. They formed a new organisation called ICON – Inner City Organisations Network. The Boxer and Maradona were two of the men they targeted.

In April 1996, local independent TD and anti-drugs protester Tony Gregory took the momentous step of naming Mullen as a heroin dealer under Dáil privilege. On December 12, over 1,000 angry people marched on Mullen's luxury home in Artane, North Dublin, which he had bought with cash. The drug dealer and several of his associates, including Dunne, had been forced to leave the country as a result of the police pressure on their operations. The protestors left a white coffin on the front doorstep to symbolise the scale of the human devastation his business had brought to their lives. The newly invigorated grass roots mobilisation against the dealers – although short-lived – was a disturbing development for the drug dealing brat packs across the city. Curiously, however, Christy Griffin, who was well known as one of the major drug dealers in the inner-city, remained untouched. It later emerged that neither Griffin nor anyone else associated with his network, had been targeted by the protests although everyone knew what they were doing. It turned out that Griffin had powerful friends.

The Republican movement, in the form of the Dublin Brigade of the IRA, had long secretly controlled the CPAD in the working-class estates across the capital. It was part of their strategy to build a power base for Sinn Féin in the Republic. Using the menacing IRA killing machine as a type of vigilante force against drug dealers, was seen as a way of gaining public support for the movement. The organisation fed off the sense of despair and disillusionment that pervaded the worst affected estates. Many of the key figures in the Dublin Brigade were also senior figures in Sinn Féin and worked as election agents for the party. There is now considerable evidence, however, that in the mid-1990s, the IRA became as corrupt and morally bankrupt as some of the worst drug traffickers they claimed to be fighting. One example of this conspiracy of corruption is the relationship Martin 'Marlo' Hyland enjoyed with the Republican movement in Cabra/Finglas and with John Noonan, the Sinn Féin/IRA founder of the CPAD. *(See Chapters Four and Five.)* Christy

Griffin enjoyed a similar dodgy "friendship".

Dublin's version of Tony Soprano had developed a close working relationship with the so-called 'Officer Commanding' (OC) of the IRA's Dublin Brigade, who was also from the north inner-city. In fact so close was the relationship between Sinn Féin/IRA members and organised crime, that in 2005 it was dubbed the "Rafia". The top Provo, who also worked as a campaign worker for Sinn Féin in several elections, had impressive Republican credentials. In December 1980, he was arrested while in charge of an IRA training camp and was jailed for eight years by the Special Criminal Court. His wife was also very closely connected to the highest echelons of the party and the Provos in Belfast.

Three weeks before the murder of Veronica Guerin, an IRA robbery gang shot dead Detective Garda Jerry McCabe, as he was escorting a post office truck in Adare, County Limerick. The gang also shot and seriously injured McCabe's partner, Ben O'Sullivan. The leader of the killer mob, Kevin Walsh from Patrickswell in County Limerick, had opened fire on the two officers. He shot them at point blank range, showing no mercy. At first, Sinn Féin leader Gerry Adams had misrepresented the involvement of the IRA in the appalling crime but he was later forced to tell some of the truth. Intelligence gleaned from high placed informants in the Republican movement had revealed that the robbery had been sanctioned from the top. As a direct result of the embarrassment caused by the murder, Dickie O'Neill, the then OC of the Dublin Brigade with overall responsibility for organising the attempted robbery, was "stood down" from his position and replaced by Griffin's pal. O'Neill, who is still wanted in connection with the Adare robbery, has lived in Spain since 1996. He invested the Provos' money in property.

Operating from bases in Finglas, Cabra, Tallaght and the inner-city Sinn Féin/IRA established "special" relationships with major criminal figures such as Hyland and Griffin. Another major drug trafficker who was heavily involved with the Republican patriots was a man called Sean Dunne, from Donaghmede in North Dublin. Dunne organised multi-million

Euro C2 VAT frauds in the construction industry on behalf of the organisation. At the same time he also controlled a multi-million Euro cocaine and heroin empire. Based on the evidence available, it is fair to state that the IRA in Dublin morphed into an organised crime gang. This metamorphis would ultimately stall Sinn Féin's hopes of electoral gain in the Republic in the 2007 General Election.

Griffin, his brother Collie, and a number of associates became very important to the funding of the Republican movement. The Sopranos organised the systematic theft of containers of products being transported through Dublin docks on their behalf. Griffin had plenty of contacts operating in the docks and experienced little difficulty getting away with the loads. The gang stole millions of Euro worth of cargos including alcohol, cigarettes, confectionary and any other mass-produced goods that could be easily re-sold over the counter. The gang simply drove into the docks in stolen trucks, and with the help of inside informants, hooked them up to containers, which they then took away. The stolen merchandise was distributed through a well established Republican smuggling operation, to hundreds of shops on both sides of the Border and sold off the shelves. Legitimate businesses often had no choice but to "buy" their goods from the Provos' front men.

The proceeds from these hugely lucrative heists were used to fund the organisation – and line certain individual's pockets in the process. Griffin, who received a commission from each heist, was a "deniable" asset for the Provos. The organisation could use the gangster to stay a safe distance from the crimes. As a result, Sinn Féin/IRA could continue to deny claims that they were involved in criminality as "smears", while still enjoying a steady stream of "funding" from the rackets. In return, Griffin was never hassled and the angry citizens of the inner-city were convinced to ignore one of the biggest drug dealers in their midst.

The extent of the relationship between Griffin and the Sinn Féin/IRA godfather first emerged in 2000 after the murder of Griffin's friend, Thomas 'Tommo' Byrne. Byrne was a neighbour of Griffin and a career criminal. Born in 1959, he had a long criminal record with over 25 convictions for robbery and drugs. Married with one child, Byrne had a reputation as a hard man and a bully who acted as an enforcer in his old neighbourhood. He was a heavy drinker who became particularly violent and aggressive while drunk. Byrne and Griffin were close pals and organised drug deals together. In March 1996, Griffin, Byrne and a number of friends attended the Wayne McCullough and Jose Luis Bueno fight in the Point Depot in dockland. After the fight, Byrne had a verbal spat with the senior IRA man, the Dublin OC, while they were all drinking in a Northside pub with Griffin. The Provo, who portrayed himself as a senior anti-drug activist, accused Byrne of being a "drug dealing scumbag". The verbals were followed with a boxing match between Byrne and the Provo on the street outside. Byrne signed his own death warrant when he won the fist-fight – and gave the Provo godfather a severe beating in the process. The IRA man's wife was also assaulted in the melee and both of them required treatment for their injuries in hospital.

A few days later, Byrne and his family went to Spain on a pre-arranged holiday. While there, he received a message from the Provo that he should stay where he was and not return to Dublin – if he wanted to remain above ground! Byrne, realising that he was out of his depth, decided to stay where he was. He leased a pub in Torremolinos in the Costa del Sol, which was a popular hang out for his old pals and associates in the criminal fraternity. At the same time he began organising the large scale importation of drugs from Spain into Dublin with Griffin. He made a number of efforts, through intermediaries, to pay "compensation" to the Provo boss and his wife for the injuries he had caused. Sums of up to IR£60,000 (€76,200) were offered but were turned down by the Republican. The beating had greatly undermined the street credibility of both the IRA boss and the organisation in the inner-city. Like any other criminal, the Provo had to show that no one could cross him or his organisation and get away with it.

In May 1999, Byrne decided that he had been in exile long enough and returned to Dublin, much to the irritation of the OC of the Dublin Brigade. Byrne ensured that everyone knew he was back in the old neighbourhood. He went drinking and was soon causing trouble in various pubs in the city centre. He was barred from most pubs in the area as a result. The CPAD also issued a "list of undesirables" to all local pubs, with Byrne's name at the top. Byrne's friends, including Griffin, later claimed that he calmed down after a while and participated in an adult education programme with a view to completing his Leaving Certificate exam. Tommo had also involved himself in a constructive way in the local community and helped coach a local kid's' soccer team. In a rare display of co-operation with the Gardaí, Christy Griffin later told detectives that his pal's involvement in the community greatly upset the OC, especially the Provo's wife who wanted an example made of Byrne. He revealed that around March 2000 the Provos had again ordered Byrne to leave the area. Griffin claimed that his pal had decided to go back to Spain but he wanted time to sort out his affairs. Byrne's procrastination would cost him dearly.

On Sunday, April 30, 2000, Tommo Byrne was sitting with other drinkers, outside O'Neill's pub on Summerhill Parade. It was a hot Bank Holiday weekend and the punters were taking the sun. At 7pm a lone gun man walked up to Byrne and calmly fired a single shot into his head at point blank range with a .357 magnum revolver. The bullet hit Byrne behind the left ear and particles of his skull were spattered across the ground. The shot was so powerful that it travelled through the brain, exited his cranium and lodged in the arm of another man who was sitting close by. Byrne died instantly and his professional executioner walked away.

An intensive Garda investigation later identified a Finglas-based IRA man as the prime suspect for the murder. He was identified buying a bottle of petrol which was later used in an attempt to burn a getaway car used after the killing. The DPP, however decided not to proceed with charges against him. Detectives believed that Byrne's death had been sanctioned by the highest levels of the Republican movement as the only means of re-establishing the organisation's credibility in the area. The British and Irish Governments were in sensitive negotiations with Sinn Féin at the time and, in that atmosphere, such information was suppressed to keep them on side.

It was during Tommo's murder investigation that Griffin became uncharacteristically helpful to the police. He admitted that he was with Byrne on the night that the Provo godfather was beaten. Griffin claimed that the Dublin OC circulated a rumour that Byrne had used six men to ambush him because he didn't want it known that Byrne had beaten him in a straight fight. Griffin told the cops that he believed the PIRA had murdered Byrne and that nothing would ever happen to the shooter. He reminded the officers interviewing him that "they" [killers] had already killed one of "yours" [Det Gda Jerry McCabe] and would get out of prison in a few short years because of the Peace Process. Griffin was telling them there was nothing they could do about the murder. He revealed that he had met the Provo OC shortly after the 1996 assault and was reassured that he [Griffin] had no worries about retribution. He claimed he was told this in June 1996 when he met the Provo to discuss "another criminal matter". Although he didn't elaborate, the matter was believed to be the ongoing robbery rackets in the docks. Some detectives suspected that Griffin had "more than likely" assisted the Provo in setting up Byrne for the murder, as a show of his loyalty to his partners-in-crime.

The relationship reinforced the belief among locals in the inner-city that Griffin was untouchable. It meant that other criminals would not attempt to oust the patriotic crime boss. The protective blanket also ensured that Griffin's darkest secrets – that he was a paedophile and a rapist – were kept under wraps.

When he got out of prison, Griffin had rekindled an old relationship with a former girlfriend he had known before he was sent down in the 1980s. The woman was from a tough, but respected, local family. Griffin moved in to live with his partner who had two children – a boy and a girl – from two previous relationships. The couple also had two daughters, who were born in the mid-1990s. Shortly after the couple got together Griffin began molesting his partner's daughter who was eight years of age. The abuse continued on a regular basis, becoming steadily more serious. It culminated with Griffin raping the child when she was 16. The abuse was to last until 2002 when she was 17. It would also later emerge that the feared godfather had been sexually abusing his partner's younger sister who had been living with them. She was eight years older than her niece.

The following is the testimony of the sister of Griffin's partner, which she related in an interview with this writer in 2007. For the purpose of clarity this woman will be called Mary. "Griffin did untold damage to our family. We were a quiet family who minded our business. When he came into [sister's] life he fucked it all up. He thought he could do whatever and who ever he liked, Griffin had the power and money to do what he wanted. I was a child when he was abusing me whenever he got my sister's back turned. As a result of the abuse I became a heroin addict when I was around fourteen. Then he would offer me free heroin in return for sex. He was a sick animal. I had no power to do anything about the abuse. I felt no one would believe me and I kept it to myself. He used to bring me out with him in the car when he was collecting drug money. He got me to actually handle the money and hold it in case the police stopped us so his fingerprints weren't on it. Even on those runs he would try to molest me. In his house me and my sister [Griffin's partner] would help count the money.

"Eventually I got away from him and got off the heroin with the help of my family. Then one night my niece broke down and told me that he was also abusing her. I was sick. She wanted to go to the police and have him charged but I was afraid of what he could do to all of us. I didn't want it to get out. I thought I was protecting my family. That's why we kept it a secret for a good few years."

Mary also claimed that there were allegations that Christy Griffin and his brother Collie had been responsible for a number of sexual assaults in the area which the victims hadn't reported for the same reasons – a sense of fear and being powerless.

In one case, it was alleged that the brothers had abducted and then raped a local prostitute. The existence of this allegation was confirmed through experienced detectives in the area and by a number of residents who only broke their silence when Griffin was finally caught. In the inner-city communities reporting crime to the police was not considered a realistic option. Informing was almost as serious an offence as child abuse. In such cases people traditionally "dealt with" the problem locally. In any event Griffin's formidable reputation rendered him untouchable – for a while at least.

* * * *

While Griffin's sexual depravity might have remained under wraps for a few more years, there was no secret about his emergence as a major drug trafficker. From 1999, he was classified by Garda intelligence as one of the largest suppliers of cocaine in Dublin. Griffin organised the importation of the drug from UK and Dutch-based contacts. At the same time, it was known that the gang was involved in armed robberies and were still plundering the docks. The anti-terrorist Special Detective Unit also had a bulky intelligence file on his associations with the IRA. But his organisation proved hard to penetrate. Griffin and his closest associates maintained a safe distance from the actual business on the ground. The distribution operation was controlled by members of his own family including a sister and a nephew, making it harder for the police to establish a "tout" or informant in the camp. The family business had been the subject of several undercover investigations by the North Central Divisional Drug Unit at Store Street Station and the GNDU. While there had been several major seizures connected directly to the Sopranos, the main players had all evaded capture. Underlings who were arrested were too scared to open their mouths and testify against the boss. Taking the rap was the only option.

In March 2002, Operation In-Law was set up to specifically penetrate Griffin's protective shield and catch the big players. It was a joint investigation between the Criminal Assets Bureau and the North Central Drug Unit. Over time, the investigation team built a picture of how the operation was organised and identified the network of people involved from the top down. The inquiry team, based at Store Street Garda Station, received intelligence that Griffin's older sister, Jackie was using her home at Crinan Strand to cut up cocaine for onward street sale. Also involved in that end of the operation was his 26-year-old nephew, Gary O'Reilly, a son of Griffin's sister Sandra. O'Reilly had been heavily involved in the drug trade with his family for at least four years. In turn, the CAB discovered that Sandra, her husband Francis O'Reilly and sons Gary and Daniel were directors of a waste disposal company which had an address at Canon Lillis Avenue, the Griffin family home. Christy Griffin had set up the company to launder the proceeds of crime.

Sandra O'Reilly later admitted to the CAB that, over several years, she had channelled the proceeds of crime through many of the 70-plus accounts discovered by the Bureau, on behalf of the extended Griffin/O'Reilly family. The family had also purchased a number of properties around the city. Griffin and his family members were, like many other criminals in Dublin, big time pigeon fanciers. The Sopranos had birds valued in excess of €100,000.

In the midst of the property boom, Griffin had moved his partner and the four children to a detached four bedroom house at Ridgewood Green in Swords which he bought for €300,000 in 2002. The gangster had also bought a house on Emmet Street, for the extraordinarily low price of just €10,000 from a tragic young man called James 'Hoppy' Hayes. When he was nine years old Hayes was electrocuted and almost died when he broke into an ESB sub-station. As a result, his two legs had been amputated. He was later awarded IR£100,000 (€127,000) in compensation which was held in trust until his 18th birthday. Apart from buying the house on Emmet Street, James had soon squandered the money on alcohol, gambling and hand-outs to "mates". When he was at his lowest ebb, he agreed to sell his only asset to Griffin. However James Hayes died in 1998 before the deal had gone through and the money was paid. Griffin's partner and sister later ensured that Haye's heart-broken mother completed the deal and signed over her son's house.

Meanwhile, the operational side of 'In-Law' turned the spotlight on Jackie Griffin's home at Crinan Strand. The North Central Drug Unit had raided the homes of various gang and family members in the past but had not been able to find any

drugs or guns. This was because the gang used young local kids
and drug abusers to keep watch on the road outside. The early
warning system, which had been used in the area for many
years by other criminals, had proved quite effective. By the time
the cops got through the door, the narcotics were usually gone.
In January 2003, after nine months of work, Det Gda Johnny
Brady received reliable intelligence that Jackie Griffin and her
nephew were due to take delivery of at least a kilo of uncut
cocaine, worth €100,000, from one of Christy's contacts. They
were then to dilute the haul, using a mixing agent and repackage
it for street delivery. The gang would more than treble the profits
in the process. This procedure was carried out, on average, once
every two weeks. The problem the police faced was knowing
when to pounce. The success of the operation would depend
on timing and the element of total surprise.

On January 3, Det Gda Brady applied for a search warrant
for the home of 36-year-old Jackie Griffin and a number of
other addresses. It was believed the gang's drugs and guns were
hidden at these premises and it would be part of a follow-up
investigation. For two weeks, officers took turns watching the
house from a carefully hidden observation post in the area.
On the same day that the Operation In-Law team obtained
their warrants to hit the Sopranos, there was another totally
unexpected development which would have much more
devastating consequences for the crime boss.

Christy Griffin's partner arrived at Store Street Garda
Station in the company of her daughter and her sister [Mary]
and asked to speak with a senior detective. The visit was about
to set in train the beginning of the end of Griffin's reign. The
two women wanted to make formal complaints of sexual abuse
and rape against the main target of Operation In-Law. The
officers who met them were stunned by the story the women
told. Detective Sergeant Walter O'Connell had spent most of
his service as a police officer in the tough inner-city beat covered
by Store Street station. He had an in-depth knowledge of the
local underworld and the huge step the women had taken by
deciding to come to the law for help. Det Sgt O'Connell, who
would be the officer in charge of the sex abuse investigation, was

aware of the enormous implications of the claims the women were making. It they were true, he was being provided with an opportunity to catch a major league criminal.

Only on one previous occasion had a major gangland figure been caught as a result of child sex abuse allegations. It happened when one of the General's closest associates, a widower, raped his daughter in 1992. In the months leading up to the decision to go to the police Griffin's step-daughter – for purposes of clarity we will call her 'Joan' – had returned to live with her mother's parents, who were from the same city centre neighbourhood as Griffin. The gangster was away in the UK at the time. Joan, who was 17 at this stage, had been deeply traumatised by the years of sexual abuse and rape. One night it all came out and she told her relations what had happened to her.

As a result Mary also decided to break her silence to her family. She recalled later: "The family went crazy when they heard this and they told my sister (Griffin's partner). She called him and asked him about it and he admitted it. Then she told him she didn't want him back."

In her statement to the police Griffin's partner gave detectives details of what he said when she confronted him with the horrifying allegations. "When I asked him he said: 'I am an animal, I'm a beast, I'm sorry'. I asked him why and he said: 'I was abused myself as a child. Tell (Joan) I'll do whatever she wants me to do'." She also claimed that he said he would "never touch his own children" and that he had been sexually abused by a member of his own family.

The two young women spent several hours dictating their damning statements to detectives. Other members of the family were also interviewed and statements were taken which corroborated the allegations being made. On the surface it appeared that Griffin had a strong case to answer. The only problem Gardaí saw was the likelihood that his victims would retract their statements.

Within hours word of the allegations spread like wild fire through the inner-city neighbourhood controlled by the Sopranos. Almost immediately the battle lines were drawn between Griffin, his family and associates on one side and his in-laws and their supporters on the other. Griffin would do everything in his power to stop the case going any further. Both the family of the two victims and the Gardaí expected trouble. Everyone waited nervously for what would happen next.

They didn't have to wait long.

Two nights later, on Sunday, January 5, Griffin's nephew, Gary O'Reilly walked into a pub on Sheriff Street. Tony Soprano's two victims were drinking there with their immediate family, mulling over the scandal. Emotions were running extremely high in the area. The family of Griffin's partner had a reputation for being hard and they had made it quite clear that they had no intention of backing down in the face of intimidation. One of Joan's uncles got up and offered to shake hands with Griffin's nephew. "We know you had nothing to do with this," the uncle was conciliatory to Griffin's nephew. But the drug dealer refused to accept the peace offering and launched into a tirade of abuse and threats. He accused the victims and their relations of being "liars" and "rats". He phoned his uncle and told him to bring reinforcements along.

As everyone headed outside for a fight, the victim's family also called for help. Two cars raced up to the crowd. Christy and Collie Griffin jumped from one of the cars and directed their henchmen – who were armed with a hatchet, knife and baseball bat – who to attack and who to leave alone. Griffin's partner's father was held down by two men while his son, who had offered peace to Gary O'Reilly a few minutes earlier, was set upon. He suffered serious injuries, including a fractured skull and a smashed kneecap, in the ferocious onslaught and he was later rushed to hospital.

Extra Gardaí were immediately drafted into the area after the showdown, in a bid to calm the situation. A week later, detectives from Store Street arrested Griffin for questioning about the sex abuse allegations. Investigators knew that they needed to proceed with the charges as soon as possible to prevent the already volatile situation blowing out of control. Griffin was released without charge while a file was prepared for the DPP.

Griffin's thugs targeted the injured uncle again a number of weeks later. This time he was abducted by Griffin and his associates and brought to the Dublin Mountains. It was in a bid to impress on him the need for the victims to withdraw their allegations. But, despite the constant threat of violence and intimidation, the family and the victims were determined that they would make a stand. In the meantime the tension continued to build. On January 15, the Griffin family found themselves in more trouble with the law.

At 3pm that Wednesday afternoon, the undercover detectives watched from their hidden location as one of the gang's drug mules, Darren Kearney, arrived at Jackie Griffin's house with a rucksack. Twenty-seven-year-old Kearney, from nearby Oriel Street, was working as a gofer to pay off a €2,000 debt he owed Gary O'Reilly for cocaine. He spoke to Jackie Griffin who lived in the local authority house with her two sons – aged 18 and nine – and her Romanian lover. Officially she received Social Welfare and a small payment from Dublin Corporation for closing the gates, in a nearby public park. However, a secret trawl of her bank accounts by the CAB revealed that she had put over €100,000 through them in the previous six years.

Jackie Griffin told Kearney to go up the road to collect a package of cocaine which had been left at a pre-arranged spot. He was then to bring the package back to the house where she and her nephew were going to cut it up and package a number of orders. Kearney returned half an hour later and went in through the back door. A minute later O'Reilly, who had been supervising the collection from a safe distance, also arrived at the house and went inside. A few minutes later, the gofer left with the bag on his back. The officers then observed Jackie Griffin collect a weighing scales from a neighbour. There were no lookouts on the street. Five minutes later the drug unit and the divisional task force moved in.

As officers banged on the front door, others raced around the rear of the house where they met Jackie Griffin and her nephew running out the back door. They stopped Griffin but O'Reilly managed to vault a wall and make a run for it. As he did so, they spotted him throwing packages into gardens along his escape route. In the house detectives found cocaine dust scattered on tops and on the floor. They also discovered glucose powder which was being used as a mixing agent, scales and plastic bags. In the garden, they found rocks of cocaine valued at €80,000. Jackie Griffin was arrested but O'Reilly had managed to get away.

While one team was raiding the house, the officers in charge of the operation, Insp Jim Cannon and Det Sgt Steve Courage, were a short distance away arresting Kearney. Det Sgt Courage found a kilo of pure cocaine worth €100,000 in a cash box, in Kearney's bag. Forensic examination later identified O'Reilly's finger and palm prints on the box. The total value of the cocaine would have been in the region of €250,000, if it had been successfully mixed. The operation had cost Christy Griffin and his family over €300,000 in total.

At the same time other search teams raided premises connected with the family, including the base of the waste disposal company. They also arrested O'Reilly at the family home on Canon Lillis Avenue. He had just changed his clothes and placed them in the washing machine when cops burst in. Forensic tests later found that the clothes were covered in cocaine. The three were later charged with sections 3 and 15 of the Misuse of Drugs Act – possession with intent to supply – and remanded in custody.

In the meantime, the CAB investigation into the Sopranos continued. On January 30, Christy Griffin was arrested by Bureau officers. He was later charged on three counts of failing to make correct tax returns. In addition, he was served with a tax assessment for €530,000. Social Welfare officers attached to CAB then issued a demand for the repayment of a further €15,000 in social welfare payments which had been claimed under false pretences. Sandra and Francis O'Reilly, who were also questioned by the CAB, were served with a joint tax demand for €400,000. Over €150,000 was frozen in various bank accounts they controlled and they were ordered to repay another €135,000 in falsely claimed social welfare payments. Collie Griffin was also charged for failing to make tax returns and in October 2003 pleaded guilty to one of the charges. He was served with a tax demand for €170,000 and a demand for repayment of almost €15,000 in social welfare money. Jackie Griffin's accounts were frozen and €75,000 later handed over to the CAB. She also received a bill for €33,000 from the Department of Social Welfare.

In the months after the rape allegations, the tension had continued to grow between the two families and their supporters. Gardaí had increased their armed patrols in the vicinity of the homes of the two victims and their family members, in a bid to prevent an attack by Griffin's mob. Both sides openly threatened each other in the streets and there were a number of fights and stabbings, none of which were reported to the police. On July 9, 2003, Griffin was arrested by the detectives investigating the claims of his partner's daughter. The Director of Public Prosecutions had decided to proceed with a total of 11 charges relating to the rape and sexual assault of his partner's daughter. The DPP decided not to proceed with charges relating to the allegations of his partner's sister [Mary]. Griffin was formally charged before the Dublin District Court, with one count of oral rape in 1998, one count of rape in 2001 and nine charges of indecent assault on (Joan) on dates between 1993 and 1998.

The Sopranos had suddenly found themselves in the firing line of a law enforcement offensive coming at them on three fronts – the drug squad, the CAB and the sex abuse investigation.

* * * *

In January 2004, Jackie Griffin was jailed for six years after she pleaded guilty in the Dublin Circuit Criminal Court to possession of the cocaine with intent to supply. Judge Desmond Hogan said the fact that the cocaine, which was found in hard lumps, was being divided up and prepared for distribution in the presence of her nine-year-old son, was an additional aggravating factor. However he suspended the last 12 months of the sentence in recognition of her guilty plea and her co-operation with Gardaí. He took the same factors into consideration in exercising the court's discretion not to impose the presumptive mandatory minimum ten year sentence for possession of drugs worth over €10,000.

Griffin's defence counsel told the court that while her involvement in the distribution racket had been significant, her position was at the lower rung of a large network. Gardaí, however, later described her as being on the first or second rung of the organisation. Griffin wept as she was led away in handcuffs.

Local TD Tony Gregory praised the successful operation, pointing out that the Sopranos had a strangle hold on the community he served. Sinn Féin said nothing. However there was much annoyance when less than two years later, Jackie Griffin was given temporary release from prison to attend a cookery course. Darren Kearney also pleaded guilty and received a four year prison sentence, with the final year suspended. O'Reilly was still awaiting trial.

The exposure of Christy Griffin as a drug dealer wasn't necessarily a problem for his friends in the Republican movement. However the sexual abuse allegations were a totally different matter. The Provo godfather and his associates were said to have been "very angry" at Griffin when the claims first surfaced. He told the father of Griffin's –partner that he would never have had any dealings with the gang boss if he had known. He even suggested that the Provos might consider shooting Griffin. But the Provo OC's words were about as sincere as his organisation's claims of non-participation in serious crime. In any event the Republican's days as the OC of the Dublin Brigade were already numbered.

The Belfast-based Republican overlords had become seriously concerned by reports that their Dublin comrades were creaming off large amounts of "funding", which should have been lodged in the organisation's hidden accounts. By this stage, the Provos effectively controlled a huge VAT fraud operation, protection rackets which were disguised as security work, "donations" from drug dealers and the proceeds from the dockland theft ring. The OC had been able to build a fine detached family home in the much more upmarket suburb of

Rathfarnham, in South Dublin. He had decided to leave behind
the modest dockland neighbourhood where he had reigned
supreme. He also bought a holiday home in County Wexford
and a villa in Alicante in Spain where his pal, and former Dublin
OC, Dickie O'Neill was still based. As a result the Republican
movement found itself on the brink of a bitter internal feud in
the Winter of 2002, when the Northern command moved in
to punish their Southern comrades.

In November 2002, Kevin O'Neill, a brother of Dickie
O'Neill, was taken to a meeting with the IRA on the Border
during which he was shot in the legs. Around the same time,
drug dealer Sean Dunne was shot and seriously injured by an
IRA gunman at his home in Ratoath. Two other figures – one
an overweight conman and money launderer from Cork – were
also abducted for "interview". They managed to get away
uninjured when they told the Northerners everything they
knew about the rest of the rackets. The Dublin OC disappeared
for "debriefing", as did John Noonan. (*See Chapter Five.*) A
decision to shoot the OC was abandoned because of his wife's
powerful connections at the top of the Sinn Féin/IRA family
tree and the OC's record as a "good volunteer". The Northern
hierarchy were worried that if they made the wrong move it
would lead to a bitter split in the movement. Instead Griffin's pal
was "stood down", as were a number of other prominent Sinn
Féin and IRA members. Noonan later claimed in a magazine
interview that he had taken a conscious decision to retire from
the movement and look after his family. He implied that he had
sacrificed enough of his life for the cause.

The secret Provo purge had nothing to do with eradicating
serious crime in the organisation. It was designed to ensure that
most of the money from their various rackets found its way to its
intended destination – the coffers of the Republican movement.
They had no intention of giving up on such a lucrative source
of funding. However, they didn't want to harm Sinn Féin's
chances in the local and European elections, which were due
to take place in the summer of 2004. The solution was that a
number of other high-ranking IRA figures were sent to take
control of the day-to-day racketeering. The internal tension did

not affect Christy Griffin's situation and his gang continued to rob the container traffic from the docks, in conjunction with the Provos. But less than a week after his sister was jailed, the Gardaí gave him another major problem to deal with.

On the morning of January 26, Griffin organized the theft of a container load of Easter eggs, valued at almost €100,000, from the Freight Terminal in Dublin Port. The gang used a stolen truck and trailer unit to take the container. It was driven to Dunshaughlin Business Park in County Meath and parked beside another container which had arrived with €600,000 worth of smuggled cigarettes. The goods were destined for the Northern market. The stolen eggs and Griffin's associates were under surveillance and Gardaí later moved in and seized the two containers. A number of men were arrested and charged. A subsequent investigation by detectives attached to Store Street Garda Station traced the cigarettes to an Australian fraudster who had bought them in Europe on behalf of the IRA in mid-2003. The loss of the two precious cargos was a source of grave concern to the movement. It had stood to make a substantial profit from the deal.

On February 8, Special Branch officers arrested Griffin and two senior Sinn Féin/IRA figures as they met in the Eddie Rocket's café in Swords, to discuss the seizure. The two Provos were considered to be major players in illegal IRA financing, through robbery and smuggling operations. They had been sent down to sort out the mess left by the Dublin Brigade. One of the men was a 54-year-old from Galway, who also played the dual card of being involved in Peace Process negotiations on behalf of the IRA. He had previously been arrested with a large quantity of stolen computer parts but, in a bid to keep the Provos "on side", the Irish Government had instructed the Gardaí not to proceed with criminal charges against him. The second Provo arrested with Griffin was 59-year-old Peter Rodgers from Poleglass in Belfast. Rodgers had been jailed for life for the 1980 murder of Garda Seamus Quaid in County Wexford. He had been was released under the terms of the *Good Friday Agreement* in 1998.

Garda Special Branch officers and their colleagues in

Northern Ireland knew that both men were working for the highest levels of the Republican movement. The three were later freed without charge but the Gardaí had established a direct connection between a major drug trafficker and the Provos.

Two weeks later the Republican hierarchy summoned Griffin to a meeting in Belfast to discuss the seizures. Griffin returned to Dublin in one piece and it was back to business as usual.

Griffin's organisation got back on the rails, despite the disruption inflicted by the police. The gang continued to control drug trafficking and carry out armed robberies. An uneasy truce of sorts had settled in the ongoing feud caused by the sex abuse allegations. The case was repeatedly adjourned and Griffin made a number of attempts to pay off his victim. The sense of menace, however, was never far away. Griffin's closest sibling in the drug and robbery rackets was his brother Collie, a reformed heroin addict and a father of four children. Between 2004 and early 2005, Collie Griffin had been involved in a string of armed robberies around Dublin. At 7am on the morning of Thursday, May 26, 2005, Griffin and two other associates, 27-year-old Gavin Day Farrelly and 24-year-old Eric Hopkins left the inner-city in a stolen van. Their target was the post office at The Village Store, in the quiet North County Dublin village of Lusk. Shortly before 8am the post office took delivery of almost €50,000. Gavin Day Farrelly, from Lower Sheriff Street had been a member of the Sopranos gang for a number of years and was a close friend of Collie. Hopkins from Lower Rutland Street had been involved with Griffin for only a few months and had been involved in the gang's drug distribution. Neither of them had a criminal record.

As they drove up the M1 motorway, on the sun kissed summer morning, they reckoned that the job would be a pushover. Collie Griffin carried a loaded pistol and Farrelly, who was over six feet four, carried a sledgehammer, to smash in the security screens at the post office. On the way they changed vehicles and got into a stolen black Skoda. When they drove into Lusk, the gangsters had no idea that a major security operation was about to spring into action. Armed members of the ERU were waiting for them, in and around the post office. The gang's every move was being secretly monitored by the NSU. The man in charge of the operation was Detective Superintendent Dominic Hayes, of the National Bureau of Criminal Investigation. He would also lead the operation to shut down Marlo Hyland's crime empire.

Det Supt Hayes and his investigation team had been targeting armed robbery gangs around Dublin. They had established a network of reliable underworld informants. The controversial cop had been tipped off that Collie Griffin and his gang were planning to hit the post office. The plan was to intercept the raiders as they went into The Village Store. The post office was situated in the back of the supermarket. The ERU had deployed three cordon teams to cover the south, west and north of the building. One of the teams was concealed in a camper van parked outside the front door of the premises. Everything was in place, but the operation did not go as planned.

Griffin and his accomplices drove the Skoda up to the front of the building and watched for a few moments. When they arrived, the officer in immediate charge of the ERU teams, satisfied that the car was the gang's, gave the order to "move, move, move". At that same moment the robbery gang suddenly did an abrupt turnaround and drove to the rear of the building, along a lane. At the back Griffin, Hopkins and Farrelly jumped out of the car and went in through the back door. Farrelly was the first in the door and he began trying to smash down the protective screen at the front of the post office.

Just seconds before Farrelly arrived, two ERU officers, who had been disguised as builders, in hard hats and fluorescent jackets, had received an urgent radio message that the gangsters were on their way in. The two officers had rushed to the post office and showed the post mistress their identity cards. As she let them in through the security door, they'd told her that a raid was about to take place and that she and her staff needed to get down. This was the moment that Farrelly had arrived at the window and started flailing at it with the sledgehammer.

Inside the office the two ERU officers feared that the gang were about to start shooting. The smashing of the sledgehammer on the screen sounded like gunfire. One of the officers decided to go back out onto the floor of the shop and confront the gang. He first shouted: "Armed Gardaí on duty…armed Gardaí." And then he opened the door. He found himself facing Collie Griffin, who was holding a pistol in both hands, at chest level.

"Armed Garda drop the gun… drop the gun," he shouted at Griffin, who instead pushed the gun out to take aim. The ERU officer, fearing that he was about to be shot, fired two shots, hitting Griffin in the head and chest. The criminal slumped to the ground and died instantly.

In the same instant, Hopkins dashed over to his pal and appeared to be grabbing the gun.

"Armed Gardaí…drop the gun and get on the floor," the cop now shouted at Hopkins, who suddenly moved towards the officer in an aggressive manner. The ERU man believed Hopkins was about to shoot him. The officer fired one more shot, hitting Hopkins in the trunk and he fell back on to the ground. He died later in hospital.

As the third shot was fired by the ERU officer, his partner covered Farrelly, who was still hammering at the post office security screen. He was making so much noise that he didn't appear to hear the shooting. Farrelly was ordered to put the sledgehammer down. The most dramatic – and bloody – showdown between the Gardaí and Irish criminals in 15 years was over in less than 12 seconds.

For Christy Griffin and his family and the Hopkins family, it was a crushing tragedy. For the majority of the Irish public, however, there was little sympathy for the two criminals. They had gone out to terrorise innocent people and had paid with their lives. The ERU was applauded as heroes, especially the unnamed officer who had done the shooting.

The two deaths turned the north inner-city into a potential tinderbox. Griffin and his henchmen openly threatened to have Gardaí killed, in an act of revenge. Officers who knew his form took the threats seriously. All officers on duty in Central Dublin were ordered to be extra alert against any possible attack. Griffin's associates were found monitoring the activities of officers and, in one subsequent incident gang members had tampered with the brakes on a squad car parked outside the Bridewell Garda Station.

In the meantime, the tension between Griffin and the family of his partner's daughter intensified. 'Joan's' mother had returned to live with Griffin and had taken his side against her own daughter. A month after the Lusk shooting, her 15-year-old son – the rape victim's brother – called social services. The teenager complained that Christy Griffin was taking out his rage over Collie's demise by repeatedly beating him. As a result a care order was issued and the teenager was removed to live with his grandparents.

In the months that followed, and as the intimidation intensified, someone decided that Griffin should be murdered.

On October 7, 2005, a lone gunman called to the front door of Griffin's home in Swords. As the godfather was standing inside the door, the hit man, Gerard 'Batt' Byrne fired five shots at his target, hitting Griffin in the elbow before he ran off. Twenty-six-year-old Byrne was a well known serious criminal and a close friend of the rape victim's family. He had made no secret of the fact that he and a number of his associates were prepared to take on Griffin if he continued to intimidate his young victim and her family. Although Griffin knew the identity of his attacker, he refused to co-operate or even make a complaint about the incident to the Gardaí.

Two days later Griffin lost another important ally when his nephew Gary O'Reilly was jailed for four years. He had pleaded guilty to possession of the cocaine he was spotted throwing away during the Operation In-Law searches in January 2003.

Some weeks later, Gardaí were called to examine an unlocked stolen Ford Mondeo car, which had been parked in a housing estate in Swords. When they searched it, they found keys sitting on the dash and a 7.62 mm Israeli military assault rifle, in the boot. Three weeks later, on November 19, Baiba Saulite a Latvian mother-of-two had been shot dead by members of Marlo Hyland's criminal gang. At the time the discovery of the weapon was thought to have been linked to an earlier attempt to have the young mum shot. Detectives who later investigated the murder of Marlo Hyland, established a link between the stolen Mondeo and his gang. They found the original registration plate for the car in the grounds of an apartment block which was being used as a storage depot by Marlo's mob. However, it later transpired that the weapon and car had probably been supplied by Hyland and left for collection for use in a second attempt to kill Griffin, whose trial was finally set down for hearing in May 2006. Marlo had been associated with Paddy Doyle, who was involved in both Baiba Saulite's murder and the plot against Griffin.

As the case approached, 'Joan's' mother tried to convince her to withdraw the charges but her daughter refused. When the trial began, before Mr Justice Paul Carney in the Central Criminal Court, the mother was declared a hostile witness by the prosecution when she retracted her original statement and refused to testify against Griffin. Extra armed and uniformed Gardaí were drafted in, amid tense scenes in and around the Four Courts building in Central Dublin where the trial was being held. Associates of Griffin hung around the courtroom and the precincts of the court, openly intimidating and threatening the victim's family. There were a number of confrontations between the two sides and Gardaí had to continually intervene to avoid the situation deteriorating further. Members of Griffin's mob wore bullet-proof vests as they attended the court. At one stage, a number of drug addicts were present in the vicinity carrying blood-filled syringes and scissors.

Det Sgt Walter O'Connell and his officers seized the weapons from Griffin's associates and a number were barred from the court building. A member of the victim's family told me at the time: "There was about 20 of them [Griffin's associates] there all the time and some of them were going to inject infected blood into us so that we would have the HIV virus for the rest of our lives...it was a terrifying atmosphere."

As the trial progressed – and both the victim and Griffin testified – the jury became aware of the menacing atmosphere in the court. Griffin's flunkies were making serious efforts to intimidate them. At the end of the trial the jury was unable to reach an agreed verdict and the case was sent forward for a re-trial. After the case jurors requested a Garda escort from the precincts of the court, such was the level of intimidation and fear they felt.

Griffin's retrial on the rape and sexual assault was set down for hearing on December 11, 2006. In a last ditch bid to scupper the case, the gangster unleashed a spiral of violence that would end in murder. At 6am on the morning of November 5, a lone gunman got out of a car at Oriel Street in the inner-city area. He walked into a nearby street and fired three shots into the family home of Griffin's victim. Two shots were fired into the upstairs bedrooms and one into the downstairs sitting room. A few minutes later, the same gun man fired more shots into the house of another relative living nearby. This time two shots were fired through the sitting room window, one through the hall door and two into the owner's jeep. No one was injured in either incident, though the houses were occupied at the time.

The next night, November 6, a hand grenade was thrown into the rear garden of Griffin's home in Swords. It exploded, causing extensive damage to the rear patio door, the ceiling in the house and a paved area in the garden. Griffin was in the house with one of his children but they both had a lucky escape. Gardaí later reported that although Griffin recognized his attackers he refused to co-operate with the investigating detectives. About 30 minutes later a second grenade had exploded at the home of Griffin's nephew Danny O'Reilly – a director of the waste disposal company and a brother of Gary – in Lanesboro Park in Finglas causing extensive damage. No one was home at the time.

On December 11, a jury of six men and six women was sworn in before Mr Justice Paul Carney in the Central Criminal Court. Griffin, who was out on bail, pleaded not guilty. Mr Justice Carney said at the start of trial, in the absence of the jury, that it was his preference to hold the trial in Green Street Courthouse, which normally accommodated the anti-terrorist Special Criminal Court and had a strict airport-style security system in place. But it was unavailable and the only other option was move the trial to Cloverhill Courthouse, which had a similar high security regime. Cloverhill is situated on a campus holding Wheatfield and Cloverhill Prisons, near Clondalkin in West Dublin. In recent years the complex was used for a number of high profile gangland murder trials, where there were concerns over security. The judge turned down repeated objections from Griffin's defence team against holding the trial in Cloverhill. They claimed it was prejudicial to Griffin because it was on the same campus as two prisons and would therefore prejudice the jury.

Carney, who had an impressive record in his handling of some of the most difficult underworld cases in the Irish criminal justice system, was determined that the same atmosphere of intimidation and menace would not prevail, as it had at the previous trial in the Four Courts. He had been briefed by the Gardaí on the level of threat that existed and requested personal armed police protection for the duration of the hearing. A large force of armed police was allocated to the court building, to ensure that there were no ugly incidents. Arrangements were made to bring the victim and her closest family members to court each day, under armed escort. The jury was also to receive discreet protection.

To emphasiss his decision, the outspoken judge requested Det Sgt O'Connell to read out a garda security assesment. It would then be placed on the trial transcript, in the absence of the jury. The report noted that during the May hearing the jury: 'was aware of the continuous presence of the opposing factions in the vicinity of the court and was intimidated by their presence.' It stated that it was the belief of the investigating Gardaí that efforts were being made 'to intimidate the jurors'. The report also catalogued the number of shootings and violent incidents associated with the impending trial.

It continued: 'There is a grave possibility that incidents will escalate as the new trial date approaches. In an effort to keep control of this volatile situation armed detectives patrol the inner-city area around the clock and two uniform members are confined to a beat in the area where the two feuding families are residing.'

The Garda report also revealed that detectives believed there was a serious likelihood of intimidation and other violent incidents, in or around the court building, at the new trial. Carney remarked that people wearing bullet-proof vests would not be allowed into his court and declared: "So let us have no more nonsense about that."

Griffin's defence counsel, Martin Giblin SC, expressed his concern about "some matters in the report" such as the Gardaí's "beliefs". He contended, intelligence reports could be "highly unreliable". Mr Giblin said Griffin should be given an opportunity to test Garda information. He had constitutional rights and rights under the European Court of Human Rights. Griffin's counsel said he was, "alarmed at the suggestion that Gardaí believe that the last jury members were intimidated". He added: "I would like to have the right to question them about their observations."

Mr Justice Carney ruled that the trial would proceed.

The trial was also adjourned for a day so that medical testimony could be given. This was after it was claimed that the victim's mother was suffering from anxiety and was too ill to give evidence in the trial. The defence made submissions that the jury should be discharged as a result of her absence but this was also rejected by the judge.

On the third day of the trial, December 13, Griffin's victim 'Joan', now aged 21, took the stand. In her direct evidence she told prosecuting counsel, Deirdre Murphy, SC, that she was eight years old when Griffin and her mother began a relationship in 1993. He moved in with her family soon after the relationship started and they moved house a number of times. She said she was forced to call the accused "Da" and that he exercised authority over her. Her mother was working outside the home. 'Joan' recalled arriving home from school one day in the autumn of 1993 and getting into her night-dress, when Griffin had picked her up and rubbed himself against her body. When her mother arrived home from work that night, she went into 'Joan's' bedroom to kiss her goodnight. She said the accused also came in and kissed her and said he was "sorry" for what he had done earlier.

The next incident she recalled was around March 1994 after her mother went out and Griffin was baby-sitting. He picked her up and pushed himself against her, before kissing her and then said he was "sorry". She said he always said he was "sorry" after these incidents, which happened whenever her mother went out. 'Joan' told the court that when they moved to a bigger house in late Autumn 1997 "things got worse" with Griffin assaulting her after her mother went to the pub.

'Joan' became very emotional and physically sick as she gave explicit details of the nature of the abuse she suffered at the hands of the gang boss. The judge adjourned the hearing for the rest of the day after 'Joan' told him she was "going to be sick", shortly after the case had resumed following a 20 minute break at her request.

Later on that same night, Gerard 'Batt' Byrne walked with a friend from Sheriff Street to a store on Mayor Street. It was in the heart of the Irish Financial Services Centre (IFSC), the endless office blocks which had replaced the dereliction of the old dockyards. At 8.50pm, 'Batt' Byrne was standing talking to a member of the shop staff at the door when a gun man jumped out of a passing car. The assassin fired a single shot into the back of Byrne's head. As the underworld figure fell to the ground, the cold-blooded executioner fired another six shots into his victim's head, before running off. Gardaí had recently warned Byrne that they had intelligence suggesting that he was a target for murder. Despite having to give him this helpful advice, at the same time Byrne was also being investigated about his involvement in a campaign of intimidation against a female Garda based in Store Street Garda Station. Byrne and his associates had posted a mass card to the officer a month earlier, which was followed by a second letter addressed to the officer containing ammunition.

The feud between Christy Griffin and his enemies had taken a sinister twist. A major security operation, involving dozens of extra armed police, was ordered by Garda HQ. They intended to prevent a further escalation in the violence which had been unleashed on the streets of the docklands. Permanent uniformed, armed patrols and checkpoints, backed up by the ERU and helicopters, were deployed in the neighbourhood where both sides lived.

Some months after the murder, Byrne's family issued a statement to this writer about what they believed to be the reason for his death. It read:

'Gerard stood by what he believed in, he put his own life at risk by standing by a girl and her family. The young girl had been raped by her mother's boyfriend. Gerard had three contracts put on his head to stay away and he ignored these threats because he didn't believe in rape or abuse against children and women. On a number of occasions Gerard asked Griffin for a fist fight and Griffin wasn't man enough to do that. Gerard had been blamed for a lot of things to do with Griffin and Griffin knew it wasn't him (Gerard) who carried out all these attacks on him. Griffin says all of this about Gerard because he is trying to make a good man look as bad as himself. Gerard was no drug dealer, he didn't like drugs. Gerard was no angel and he certainly was no monster like Griffin, he would do anything to help you. Gerard stood by this girl because he had four sisters of his own and he wouldn't have liked this to happen to any of them. Gerard died because of this – for what he believed in.'

The following morning, on December 14, the murder received extensive TV, radio and newspaper coverage. Reports referred to how the murdered man had taken the side of a woman who had been raped by a criminal figure and that he was involved in a long running feud which had begun over a sexual assault. Griffin's defence team made an application to have the trial stopped claiming that the coverage was prejudicial to their client.

Senior counsel Martin Giblin told the court: "In my respectful submission, we have far exceeded the threshold in this instance; there is hardly any doubt that members of the jury have seen these reports and made the link between the rape of a minor and inner-city area; members of the jury will have made the connection and my client cannot get a fair trial. This has created a very substantial risk and the trial should be stopped."

However Mr Justice Carney said he was not prepared to stop the trial. He said: "The last time I sat in this court in a trial which went on for seven weeks in which every single day there were applications for discharge of the jury – three on some days – due to material in the media; I didn't discharge the jury and the matter has not been appealed. There is a great interest and concern in the media about crime, about gangland crime and sexual crime. A great deal of it takes place in the inner-city. I repose confidence in juries; defence bar seems very often not to repose confidence in juries; the Court of Criminal Appeal also. The Supreme Court reposes supreme confidence in juries. I am satisfied the jury is capable of acting on the trial and of following the directions of the judge. I am prepared to give the jury a strong warning."

When the hearing resumed, 'Joan' told prosecuting counsel that Griffin abused her when her mother was out. Her mother would go out at least one night a week and sometimes twice, depending on her mood. She said Griffin would say he was sorry after each assault and tell her that she shouldn't let him do it. She felt like "the evil one" but couldn't try to stop him because she was only a child at the time. She recalled she was looking at the television one night in the summer of 1998, in her mother's bedroom when he came in, turned off the television, and forced her to have oral sex with him. She said that Griffin ejaculated onto her clothes then made her sleep in the bed that night. Her mother was away for the night. She was 13 at that time and felt afraid of the accused. She washed her clothes the next morning, so that her mother "wouldn't see what was on them".

She recalled another night when her mother was away. She was 16 and the accused gave her permission to go with a male cousin and an aunt to a nightclub. It was towards the end of the year and he allowed her out on condition that she didn't tell her mother and was back home at a certain time. They went to The Vatican nightclub in Harcourt Street but her cousin wasn't admitted and remained outside. They walked home after the disco ended because they couldn't get a taxi. Griffin was in the house when she got back and she went to bed after changing into her pyjamas. She told Ms. Murphy that he got into the single bed beside her and then raped her. He then left the room and she couldn't remember if he said anything. She washed herself in the toilet and returned to bed. She said nothing happened between them after that night, other than the accused trying to kiss her. She had never consented to the behavior she described. Sometimes she said he bought her everything "obviously to keep my mouth shut".

The following day Mr Justice Carney, at the behest of the defence, asked the jury if it had been influenced by media coverage of "other events" the previous day and if it could deal with the case "exclusively on the evidence you hear in court and the legal directions given by the judge". He told the six men and six women that if necessary he had the power to sequester them in a hotel "without access to radio, television or newspapers" until the trial concluded.

After retiring for 15 minutes to consider the judge's query, the foreman announced: "We have all agreed we have not been influenced by the media." He added that none of the members were aware the case had been mentioned in the media and they were all satisfied they could try the case on the evidence given in court.

When her cross-examination resumed, 'Joan' told the court that Griffin had bought her a car and had also offered her up to €500 for sexual favours. "I was given the car to keep my mouth shut but he had a row with my mother and took it back," she said.

"If he was buying you all these things to buy your silence was he not taking a great risk in taking it back?" Mr Giblin suggested.

'Joan' agreed the car was bought so that she could get into the city centre from Swords for study, and to meet her friends and to get home again but said she couldn't remember anything about a row over insurance. She said that she couldn't even remember much about the car at all. She denied the defence suggestion that she told her mother she was withdrawing her allegations against the accused but said her mother had asked her to withdraw them.

On the morning of December 20, the hearing was adjourned after Griffin went to Beaumont Hospital, complaining of chest pains. He arrived in court after lunch and told his counsel that he had been given a prescription to deal with his muscular pain.

In his own testimony the godfather claimed that the allegations levelled against him were untrue and he could not explain why 'Joan' had made them.

"No oral rape, no rape and no sexual assaults ever took place," he claimed. Griffin said he thought he got on well with his victim after he began living with her mother. He said he bought her a car when she was 16 so that she could go to college and get home again. She was to get a part-time job to pay for the insurance but he sold the car after it was left lying for some months and he concluded she had no intention of going to college.

He also denied that he ever offered her money for sexual favours. "Her allegations have destroyed mine and my family's lives," he moaned. Griffin told prosecuting counsel during cross-examination that he was 23 when he began living with his partner and it felt strange at first being a father to children but he got used to it when he "got to know the kids". He denied the victim's claim that he had instructed her and her sibling to call him "Da" and said it was their idea. Her allegations were untrue and were made "to hurt her mother and to hurt me".

When the hearing of evidence concluded, the trial judge adjourned the closing stages of the trial until after the Christmas break because, he wasn't happy with the amount of time left to deal with the case before the holidays.

But there was to be no peace or goodwill over the festive season, as far as the feuding gangs were concerned. In the early hours of December 27, Stephen Ledden was sleeping on a couch in the front room of his father's home on Oriel Street. Around 12.20am, a man believed to have been an associate of Gerard Byrne, who was appropriately nicknamed 'Madser', walked quietly into the house. He went over to Ledden and shot him once in the back of the head as he slept. Despite the presence of armed Gardaí in the area, the killer managed to slip away into the night. It was later discovered that the avenger had mistaken Ledden for the man suspected of shooting Byrne a few weeks earlier. The blood feud had just claimed another life.

When the trial resumed, the prosecution and defence teams made their closing statements to the jury. That was followed by a lengthy and detailed charge by the trial judge on the issues of law. On January 17, the jury retired to consider its verdict and spent the night in a hotel. The following morning, after a total of five hours deliberating, the jury indicated that it had reached its verdicts.

The atmosphere was extremely tense as the jury filed into the packed and silent court room. They told Mr Justice Carney they had returned unanimous verdicts.

Christy Griffin was convicted on all counts.

He was ashen-faced as he heard the result. Despite his best efforts to thwart the case, the self-styled Tony Soprano was placed in handcuffs and remanded in custody.

Mr Justice Carney directed that Griffin be registered as a sex offender and that a Victim Impact Report be prepared for the sentencing hearing, which he set for April.

The conviction vindicated the young woman and her family who had suffered four years of hell in order to bring the gangster to justice. She was determined that Griffin would be exposed to the world and agreed to have him identified in media reports of the trial. She wanted her tormentor named and shamed.

On April 24, 2007, Griffin was brought before the court, flanked by armed police and prison guards, to hear his fate.

Detective Sergeant Walter O'Connell gave the court details of the godfather's serious criminal record and he listed the catalogue of violent incidents, shootings and bombings, including the Byrne and Ledden murders, which had resulted from Griffin being charged with the sex crimes. He also revealed how the gangster had twice refused to co-operate with Gardaí after he had been the victim of murder attempts. Det Sgt O'Connell said that as a result of the violence the inner-city neighborhood had been saturated with armed Gardaí and "but for this strong garda presence other killings would have happened".

Garda Niamh Shelly, one of the officers who had investigated the case, told the court that 'Joan' still feared Griffin and was suffering from loss of appetite and sleep deprivation, due to the ongoing fear. A psychological report showed that 'Joan' had been severely traumatized by the sexual abuse over a number of years and her continued fear of Griffin. Her greatest concern was that she had "lost her mother" due to her revelation of the abuse. 'Joan' told the psychologist that she looked forward to going to school to get away from Griffin and often asked to be allowed sleep-over in her grandmother's home to get away from the sex offender but wasn't allowed to do that. Her mother was distressed when she told her of the abuse but nothing happened. The psychologist also found that it never occurred to the victim to report the abuse herself directly to Gardaí as she "grew up in a society in which there was an ambivalent attitude to the Gardaí". The psychologist also reported that he found it difficult to separate her fear of Griffin and the effect of the abuse to explain her current level of trauma, which he described as "severe".

Griffin refused to stand when Mr Justice Carney addressed him to pass sentence. Even if he had stood in the dock Griffin's legs might not have been able to hold him up with the shock he was about to receive.

The judge sentenced him to life.

The gangster who had thought himself untouchable couldn't hide his anger and disbelief at the sentence – one of the toughest ever handed down to a sex offender by an Irish court. He kicked the wall in frustration.

The judge noted that the Court of Criminal Appeal – with which he had many public spates through the years – had started to uphold discretionary life sentences in cases of the "utmost gravity". He noted also Griffin's "multiplicity of convictions" which he described as "horrendous" and said that sentences of nine, six and three years in prison had not had any effect on him. The judge said: "Clearly this case is one of the utmost gravity in view of the age of the victim when the abuse began and the effects it has had on her as reported to the court in the psychological report so that a sentence of life imprisonment is justified." He refused an application by Griffin's counsel for leave to appeal the conviction.

As he was being led down to the cells, Griffin probably wished it was for selling drugs rather than for being a pervert. It was the ultimate ignominy for a guy who fashioned himself on Tony Soprano. Instead of taking a cell on a landing with his henchmen and associates, Griffin was placed in a segregation unit. It was reserved for sex offenders who were at risk of attack from other inmates. In an ironic twist the last episode of Griffin's favourite TV series was broadcast a month later.

After the trial, Griffin's victim spoke to this writer about her experience: "The abuse was terrible but after I went to the police there were so many times that I wanted to drop the case so that this violence would stop. I think it is a scandal that it took four years for this case to finish and that he could be on bail for that time to intimidate people and cause trouble. I am heartbroken that Gerard [Byrne] was murdered because of all this. He was a good man."

While Griffin's legal team immediately set about appealing the conviction, he began plotting revenge. Several members of the victim's family received death threats and Gardaí also uncovered a serious plot to attack one of the senior detectives involved in the case. In the meantime Griffin's lucrative drug rackets were taken over by another former associate. At the time of going to print – October 2008 – the armed police presence in Griffin's neighbourhood is a constant reminder that the war he declared is far from over.

In April 2008, 30-year-old father of two, Anthony Russell, one of Griffin's closest associates, was shot dead by two masked gun men as he sat drinking in the Ardlea Inn Pub in Artane. Russell, who was heavily involved in armed robbery and drug dealing, had been involved in Griffin's spiral of violence and murder. Russell was suspected of being the getaway driver for the Batt Byrne hit in December 2006. Investigators believe that his involvement in the blood feud was a contributory factor to his murder. It subsequently emerged that Russell had also been accused of circulating pornographic pictures of another criminal's teenage niece on his mobile phone. At the time of writing, at least ten individuals who were associated with the warfare have been officially notified by Gardaí that their lives are under threat from other criminals. Many of the hoods making the threats are themselves under threat.

In July 2008, the Court of Criminal Appeal heard Griffin's

appeal against his conviction. His legal team submitted a number of grounds for the conviction to be overturned, including the media coverage of the Gerard Byrne murder during the trial. Michael O'Higgins SC also stated that the acceptance of a Garda security report by Mr Justice Carney and the decision to hold the trial at Cloverhill courthouse, which he described as a "prison campus" with airport-type security, also added to the unfairness of the trial. He also argued that the trial had not been unfair because an important prosecution witness – Griffin's partner – had been unable, for medical reasons, to testify. She attended the two-day appeal hearing in support of Griffin.

Opposing the appeal, Deirdre Murphy SC, for the DPP, rejected the arguments and denied Mr Justice Carney had erred by not adjourning the trial because the victim's mother was medically unfit to give evidence. The court reserved its judgement until October 2008.

Despite being locked up for possibly a very long time, Griffin, like most other underworld godfathers, still runs his drug business from his cell. Detectives, who have been close to the various investigations into Griffin's operation, believe that he will continue to orchestrate violence on the streets of his old neighbourhood.

We haven't heard the last of Dublin's Tony Soprano.

NINE

MURDER INC

"An ancient city well studied in the art of war."

The motto engraved on the coat of arms for Limerick City was taken from an epic poem about the ancient City of Troy, written around the year 29 BC. The use of the motto can be traced back to the 17th Century when, after enduring a series of bloody sieges laid to it by the armies of Cromwell and William of Orange, the city at the mouth of the River Shannon was compared to Troy. The city fathers were acknowledging the hardships and slaughter suffered by its valiant citizenry in the many conflicts thrown at it throughout history. However this proud motto took on a new interpretation in the first decade of the 21st Century – thanks to elements of the city's population who were themselves well studied in a type of warfare, devoid of valour.

In 2003, senior detectives from Limerick were dispatched to meet the top brass of the UK's National Criminal Intelligence Service (NCIS) in London. The purpose of the visit was to provide a briefing on the activities of the feuding criminal drug gangs in the city and their extensive connections to organised crime in the UK. The Gardaí had discovered that the Limerick gangs had nurtured extensive contacts and logistical support in a number of English cities. The mobs had hired hit men in the UK and were also buying high-powered weapons and drugs from sources in London, Birmingham and Bradford in Yorkshire.

The Gardaí desperately needed assistance to break the

supply line to the battle-front on the streets of Limerick. NCIS chiefs had originally been sceptical about whether they should throw resources into investigating the UK connection to a criminal gang from a small Irish city. They didn't believe that the Limerick outfit could be so well organised and dangerous.

But they were astounded by the spine chilling story they heard, as the Garda officers detailed the ferocious murder machine they were pitched against. The Limerick detectives described a huge international drug conspiracy and a low-intensity urban war, where every type of fire power was being used, including AK 47 assault rifles, machine guns, grenades and bombs. The officers depicted a brutal world of blind tribal hatred. This had combined with pure evil and greed to create a lethal mix of savagery and barbarism. They told how kids in their early teens – who had been reared on hate – were involved in murders and attempted murders and how, at the same time, there had been several plots to literally massacre whole groups of opponents.

The officers gave details of the scores of shootings, stabbings, arson and bomb attacks, in which the intended victims had been seriously injured but had survived. Several other elaborate murder plots had been foiled by the over-stretched police. They even explained how they had uncovered a bomb making factory. The gangs had clearly shown they had no regard for innocent bystanders caught in the crossfire and there was a constant threat that the warring sides might turn their guns on the police.

By the time the Garda officers flew back to Limerick, the NCIS chiefs were convinced that a war was raging in the capital of Ireland's Midwest. They urgently began mobilising their surveillance and intelligence resources, to investigate the UK connection.

* * * *

Since the beginning of the new Millennium organised crime has exploded on the streets of Irish cities and towns. As the drug trade boomed, gangland executions spiralled to unprecedented levels, giving Ireland an unenvied reputation for one of the highest per capita murder rates in Western Europe. Amidst the mayhem, Limerick, the country's third largest city – with a population of 80,000 – earned the dubious title of the country's murder capital. It also had the highest rate of knife crime in Ireland.

In a four year period, from 2001 to 2005, 27 people were shot, beaten or stabbed to death in the city. And gangland murders accounted for most of the victims. By October 2008, a ferocious feud between two family-based criminal organisations that had raged since 2000 was responsible for 19 gangland murders in the city. In that same period Dublin, with a population 13 times larger than Limerick's, had recorded over 80 killings which could be connected to underworld feuding.

In January 2003, the situation escalated to such an extent that the Emergency Response Unit, the Garda's elite specialist weapons and tactics unit, was deployed to patrol the streets of the city. At the time, such a huge security operation, which also involved dozens of other armed police patrols, backed up by helicopters, had never been witnessed before in the Irish Republic. In the working-class estates worst hit by the violence, even unarmed police patrols had to be escorted by armed units for their own protection.

The two groups of heavily-armed, savage thugs had embarked on a mindless cycle of murder and mayhem. It gained the otherwise progressive, cosmopolitan city international headlines for all the wrong reasons. The activities of the warring clans prompted the cringe-inducing description in an international travel guide: 'Limerick is best seen through the rear view mirror!'

The city had worked hard to shed its image as the grim, poverty stricken, two tiered society which was so powerfully portrayed in Frank McCourt's novel *Angela's Ashes*. Since the birth of the Celtic Tiger, it had undergone a remarkable transformation and brought hope to many of those who had been denied opportunities in the past. Today it is a vibrant centre of culture, arts, education and industry. But the warring gangsters, who openly strut around the streets, wearing bullet-proof vests and driving armour-plated jeeps, are so far disconnected from civil society that they couldn't care less about the city's international image or reputation.

There is a dynamic to serious crime in Limerick that makes it unique. It is primarily a family affair, where loyalties and sides are decided along blood lines. So entrenched is the tribalism and blind hate, that just being related to one of the warring families is enough for a person to be considered a legitimate target by the other side. After each murder or serious attack, the offending side will always let the other know that it was responsible – although they are never so forthright with the police.

Inter-family feuds are not a new phenomenon and have been the scourge of everyday life in the working-class ghettos for as long as people can remember. In the 1980s, Limerick earned the rather uncomplimentary title "Stab City" – which has rankled with the decent, law-abiding population ever since – because so many petty feuds were sorted out with a knife.

Long before gangland erupted in 2000, the murder rate in the city was already alarmingly high. A 1995 report, based on Garda statistics, showed that between 1972 and 1991 Limerick had the second highest rate of homicide in the State. It had 44 deaths, recorded over the 20 year period. It ranked second only to the Cavan/Monaghan Garda divisional area on the Border, which had become a killing field as a result of the Northern conflict.

To the outsider the Limerick feuds are complex and labyrinthine. Vendettas are passed, like a family heirloom, from generation to generation. There is also a siege mentality and a predisposition for extreme violence among some of the fighting clans, which some local historians have claimed are traits genetically inherited from the city's warlike ancestry. The bloodlines of some of the participants in the ongoing violence can be traced directly to the British Army and the notorious Black and Tans – a vicious band of British Army psychopaths who were sent to stamp out the Irish War of Independence in 1920. The familial roots of some of the better known clans can also be linked to the most violent elements of the travelling community.

Across the country since 2000, the family names Keane, Collopy, Ryan, Campion, McCarthy and Dundons have become synonymous with bloodshed and violence. These families have produced a chilling breed of killers, devoid of any sense of humanity, compassion or fear. There is evidence that they are even prepared to murder their own, if the need arises. The Limerick families have become integral players in Ireland's Crime Inc. network. They are involved with practically every other underworld organisation in the country and supply hit men, weapons and drugs. In recent years most major criminal conspiracies exposed in this country have had some link to Limerick. By 2008 Gardaí had recovered up to seven firearms which forensics had shown were used in gangland shootings and killings in Dublin. These included the weapons used in the murders of John Daly and Baiba Saulite. It was clear evidence of the inter-connection between the mobs on both sides of the island.

The godfathers from the "Ancient city, well studied in the art of war" are feared throughout gangland. These violent madmen make even the Finglas and Crumlin mobs in Dublin look almost harmless by comparison. But there is one family in the midst of this rabble of cut-throats and psychopaths who have the ominous distinction of being the most ruthless and dangerous of them all. They are called the McCarthy/Dundons – a family firm that could best be described as Murder Incorporated.

From 2000, a complex blood feud has raged between the Keane/Collopy clan and the Ryans. Through the years this has developed into a war between the Keane/Collopys and the McCarthy/Dundons, who had an ambitious plan to wipe out all opposition and control one of the biggest criminal organisations in the country. In a subsequent trial for the murder of gang boss Kieran Keane, a senior detective explained the modus operandi of the McCarthy/Dundons: "The motivation was to eliminate those who stood in their way and those perceived to be their enemies with the objective of totally dominating Limerick City," Superintendent Gerry Mahon told the Circuit Criminal Court, as five members of Murder Incorporated – who had all been sentenced to life imprisonment – sniggered and laughed amongst each other, like a bunch of bold school kids.

One unfortunate person the gangland death squad "perceived" as an enemy was a totally innocent man called Brian Fitzgerald. The father-of-two-refused to allow the gang sell drugs in the night-club where he worked as head of security. As a result, Murder Incorporated showed that there were no bounds to its brutality and Brian Fitzgerald was callously executed. The crime horrified the people of Limerick, who had been silent witnesses to the madness which was dragging their city into a state of lawlessness and blood-letting.

The murder led to an unprecedented display of public revulsion when the people took to the streets of the city to hold a candle-lit procession. But to Murder Incorporated public opprobrium was irrelevant.

Brian Fitzgerald was to be the first casualty in what amounted to an attempted underworld coup.

* * * *

The spark that ultimately lit the Limerick powder-keg was the murder of a ruthless killer called Eddie Ryan in 2000. Ryan acted as an enforcer for brothers Christy and Kieran Keane. The Keanes had established a well-organised criminal empire in the Midwest region from the early 1990s. Christy Keane, who was described by Gardaí as "ruthless, extremely violent and highly strung", was the undisputed godfather. He ruled his patch with an iron fist.

Born in 1960, Keane ran a successful coal business which was a front for a much more lucrative industry. His gang controlled one of the largest drug trafficking networks in the country. The Keanes were also involved in prostitution, protection rackets, counterfeit money and documents, stolen goods and vehicles and the supply of firearms. Keane enjoyed close links with the INLA and other criminal gangs in Dublin, including those led by Declan 'Wacker' Duffy, Troy Jordan and John Gilligan. The contacts were made through horse dealing and sulky races. In Cork, he did business with the Flynn crime family and he had close links with the Provisional IRA and later on renegade IRA gangs. Keane also had extensive connections to criminals in Northern Ireland and the UK.

The Keane empire was based in St Mary's Park, a run down corporation estate in the shadow of St John's Castle, just north of the city centre. Also known as the Island Field, it became the Keanes personal fiefdom. Geographically the Island, which had once been used to billet invading armies and their livestock, was perfect as a territorial HQ. It was encircled by the Shannon and connected to the rest of the city by a single road. Strangers and cops entering the gangster's domain were quickly spotted. Eddie Ryan, who was a year older than Christy Keane, was an ideal enforcer.

Ryan had an awesome record for armed robbery and violence which dated back to when he was just 12 years old. He grew up in Hogan Avenue in Kileely, just across the river from the Island on the city's Northside. He was described as a vicious, extremely dangerous hoodlum who enjoyed inflicting pain. When Ryan was 17, he stabbed another local man to death in a row outside a city centre cinema and was convicted of manslaughter. After doing time for that crime and a number of armed robberies, the Kileely killer went to work for his old friend Keane.

Ryan collected "debts" and carried out "enquiries" of the very painful type, to uncover police informants or touts. In case anyone doubted his ability to inflict pain, Eddie Ryan also made no secret of his relationship with the Republican movement. The fact that he was so widely feared – or "respected" – by some of the city's most formidable hard men spoke for itself.

During the Christmas holidays of 1993, the relationship between Ryan and the Keanes was forged in blood and established the gang's brutal reputation. What began as a tragic road accident spiralled into a bloodbath. In the space of 72 hours the crime gang had been responsible for two murders and an attempt to massacre one entire family.

The previous February, Kathleen O'Shea, the partner of traveller Patrick 'Pa' McCarthy, had been killed when she stumbled out in front of a bread van being driven by Daniel Treacy, Christy Keane's nephew. A Garda investigation found that it had been a tragic accident and the van driver was exonerated. Afterwards the Keanes paid for the dead woman's funeral and gave money to McCarthy as a form of compensation.

But McCarthy, who was a chronic alcoholic, made the fatal mistake of continuing to harass the Keanes and the Treacys, putting the squeeze on them for more money. On December 28, 1993, in a drunken haze, McCarthy and his two brothers decided to go to Christy Keane's house for another row. At the front door they were by met Keane's other nephew and criminal understudy, 21-year-old Owen Treacy. Pa McCarthy made threats and demanded more money.

It was a tragic mistake.

As the commotion continued, Treacy was joined at the door by Christy Keane and a scuffle ensued. Eye-witnesses later told Gardaí that they saw Keane stab McCarthy through the heart. The injured man died in the back of his hiace van, as his brothers rushed him to hospital. Keane and his nephew were arrested for questioning about the incident a few hours later and released pending further investigations. 'Pa' McCarthy was buried on New Year's Eve.

After the funeral his brothers, sisters and other relatives gathered in Martin McCarthy's caravan. It was parked at the Cooperage Canal Bank on Clare Street, a short walk from the Island Field. The group drank cider and beer, as they huddled around a small fire under the light of a single candle. Ten adults and two sleeping children were crowded into the cramped space. Around 10.30pm, two of the mourners left. As they did so, two armed and masked men slipped from the shadows and challenged the young couple. They were told to go and keep their mouths shut while they had the chance.

Eddie Ryan and his accomplice then stood in the caravan door and began blasting the huddled group in front of them, with a shotgun and an automatic pistol. A total of seven shots were fired in what was a clear attempt to massacre the remainder of the McCarthy family. As police and ambulance crews arrived, Michael McCarthy was found lying on the floor. He had a gaping gunshot wound to the neck where a bullet had passed right through. He died before he got to hospital. His brother Joe had been hit in the back and leg and his sister Nora in the hip. Their cousin Noreen was also hit in the leg. Miraculously the two young children were uninjured.

Local Gardaí didn't have to look far for suspects. Eddie Ryan and his wife Mary, Christy and Kieran Keane and another gang member, Declan 'Darby' Sheehy were later arrested in connection with the cold-blooded outrage. There wasn't enough evidence with which to prosecute a case against Ryan or his accomplices, although detectives were satisfied that Ryan and Christy Keane were the gunmen.

A few days later, the godfather was charged with the murder of 'Pa' McCarthy because there were three eyewitnesses to the stabbing.

At the subsequent funeral of Michael McCarthy a local priest described the murders as "senseless and mindless". Although he didn't know it at the time, the clergyman was predicting the bloody future for several local criminals, including the men who had tried to wipe out the McCarthys. "Violence begets violence, leading inevitably to more suffering and more grief and more loss of lives," he said. Less than ten years later his prediction had become a paradigm for life in the city's seedy underworld. In March 1995, Christy Keane was tried for the murder of 'Pa' McCarthy but was acquitted after the witnesses proved to be unreliable.

It was only during the subsequent investigation into the McCarthy murders that Gardaí began to realise the full extent of the criminal empire controlled by the Keanes. However, smashing their criminal operation would prove extremely difficult. The butchery during the final 72 hours of 1993 was one of the worst cases yet seen in the Irish criminal underworld. Together, the Keanes and Ryan had made their mark and in the process they had ensured that the mob was protected by an impenetrable wall of silence.

In the meantime, their drug trade flourished. The money rolled in so fast that at one stage the Keanes were forced to store cash in wheelie-bins. In the latter half of the 1990s, the police launched a major investigation into the crime gang, codenamed Operation Coalface. It led to a number of significant drug seizures and resulted in the conviction of a handful of gang members but they failed to get the godfathers controlling it all.

The drug trade was booming in the mid–west by the end of the 1990's and it wasn't long before Eddie Ryan began organising his own lucrative distribution racket, much to the consternation of the Keanes. This was the real reason why the gang war exploded, although a number of ongoing petty feuds provided the catalyst for the outbreak of hostilities. Ryan joined forces with another drug dealer called Sean 'Cowboy' Hanley, who was also from Kileely.

Hanley got his nickname in the early 1980s when he began importing ponies from Welsh coal mines and selling them to children in Limerick. The two hoods, who were soon raking in a fortune, teamed up with a number of other significant players. This alliance would provide the nucleus for the notorious McCarthy/Dundon mob. They planned to overtake the Keane/Collopy organisation and become the biggest dealers in the region.

At the same time a bitter family feud was simmering between the family of Eddie Ryan's brother, John, and the Collopys, who were close friends of the Keanes in St Mary's Park. John Ryan was married to Christina McCarthy whose family were also from St Mary's Park. In 1982, two of her brothers were stabbed to death during a row with another local criminal Anthony Kelly. His brother, Mikey Kelly, happened to be one of Eddie Ryan's best friends.

John Ryan's involvement in the feud began when his brother-in-law accused one of Jack Collopy's children of causing damage to his car in St Mary's Park. The row led to an incident in the Moose Bar on Cathedral Street, during which Jack Collopy's wife was beaten up. That was followed by a brutal attack on Jack Collopy by John Ryan and one of his brothers-in-law. Collopy, an ex-soldier, was stabbed in the gut by Ryan and beaten over the head with an iron bar. He spent two weeks on a life support machine and had to learn how to talk again.

In another incident, one of Ryan's brothers-in-law, Pa

McCarthy (no relation to the McCarthys murdered in 1993), was shot in the back, as he drove his car near the Collopy's home. Three young children sitting in the back of the car narrowly escaped serious injury. Three members of the Collopy family were identified by McCarthy as the shooters and charged in relation to the incident. They were subsequently found not guilty in 1999.

The women in both families were blamed locally for fanning the flames of the feuds. The strong influence and involvement of the "gentler sex" in violence is also unique to Limerick. The situation was exacerbated through gossip and rumours, which were spread by both sides. The younger children from both camps were also poisoned by the senseless hate. When John Ryan's daughter had a schoolyard row with one of the Collopys, her father retaliated by firing shots at their home. Eddie Ryan and the Keanes had an unwritten agreement to remain neutral in the ongoing disputes, which were becoming a major problem. But it didn't bode well that Eddie Ryan was with his brother when the Collopy home was shot up.

In any event, the volatile nature of the former criminal partners meant that a power struggle between the two sides was becoming increasingly inevitable. By the summer of 2000, the bitterness had reached boiling point. A row broke out between Samantha Ryan, John Ryan's daughter, and Natalie Keane, Christy's daughter. Both fathers agreed that the only way to resolve the dispute was for an arranged fight between the two girls. After a half-hour of fighting Natalie Keane gave up. The 19-year-old had a piece of her ear bitten off and the victory went to Samantha Ryan.

On October 25, 2000, there was another row. This time it was between John Ryan's daughter and a niece of Christy and Kieran Keane at St Mary's secondary school in Corbally. The following day the girl's mother, Anne Keane, the wife of Christy's brother Anthony, called to the primary school in Bishop Street to collect her daughter. She met John Ryan's two daughters, Samantha and Debbie, and a fight ensued. Anne Keane was knocked to the ground, punched, kicked and then slashed in the face with a Stanley blade. The two women were subsequently charged with assault but the case never went to court.

Later that evening, a number of shots were fired through the front window of John Ryan's home, at the Lee Estate situated in the heart of Keane territory. He called Eddie who immediately went to the house to find out what was happening. Eddie Ryan said he would sort out the problem by visiting Christy Keane and his sidekick, Owen Treacy. Ryan told his brother he wanted "to give Christy a box".

The Ryans drove up to Treacy's house on Colmcille Street. Eddie Ryan was armed with a sawnoff shotgun. As they approached the house, Owen Treacy fired two shots, hitting their car. Eddie Ryan fired back, as he and his brother sped away. The car was then hit by more shots which shattered the rear window. What had started as an apparently innocuous row, had suddenly escalated into a shooting war. Eddie Ryan was determined to spill Keane blood. There was no longer any chance of reconciliation.

The war was about to begin.

On the afternoon of Friday, November 10, 2000, Christy Keane was waiting to collect his son outside the Ignatious Rice College on Shelbourne Avenue. Eddie Ryan and one of his sons were waiting for him. He was carrying a 9mm automatic pistol, under his jacket. When Keane spotted Ryan walking towards him, he opened his window to talk to his former partner. But Ryan was not in a talking mood and instead pointed his gun at Keane's head.

The weapon jammed, as he squeezed the trigger. Ryan tried to fire the weapon again and his son smashed in the windows of the car. Keane managed to drive off at speed down a pavement, sending children and parents scrambling out of the way.

Eddie Ryan had crossed the line. The Keanes knew that in their primitive world, where only the strongest survived, there was only one course of action for them to take.

Ryan also knew the consequences of what he had just started – that he would have to kill or else be killed himself. He was now at war with the Keanes.

Following the incident he left Limerick and went to stay

with his mistress in County Down. The following Sunday, he returned to Limerick for the funeral of his brother-in-law. As a mark of respect on the sad occasion, Ryan decided not to wear his bullet proof-vest when he went to the removal ceremony in St John's Cathedral that evening. After the ceremony, he spoke with his pregnant wife Mary before going to The Moose Bar at Cathedral Place with his son, Kieran.

The feared gangster arrived in the packed bar just before 9pm on November 12, 2000. Eddie Ryan sat at a table, just inside the front door beside Mary Reddan and her daughters Deirdre and Majella. Mary Reddan was the sister-in-law of Jack Collopy, with whom the Ryans and the McCarthys had been feuding. As Ryan entered the pub, Kieran Keane got a call on his mobile phone informing him that his target was in the bar. He had sent spies out to locate Ryan and was waiting for news. Keane was with his accomplice, a 19-year-old member of another crime family from St Mary's Park, when he got the tip off. The previous night his minions had stolen a getaway car for use in the hit, from a pub at Murroe, County Limerick.

Keane had recruited 23-year-old hood Paul Coffey, a close associate of the Collopys, who was unlawfully at large from prison, to drive the car. Keane armed himself with a .357 Magnum revolver. His henchman, who was sitting in the front passenger seat, carried a 9mm automatic pistol. The same magnum had been used in the gun attack on John Ryan's house on October 27. Kieran Keane instructed Coffey to drive to The Moose Bar. When they arrived, the killers parked in a yard across from the pub and Keane got out to make a phone call. A few minutes later he got back into the car and told Coffey to pull across in front of the pub for "a few minutes". As the car stopped, Keane and his accomplice pulled balaclavas down over their faces and got out.

At precisely 9.53pm the gunmen appeared inside the pub door. Eddie Ryan was sitting with his back to them. Keane shouted in his direction: "You bastard, come out ya bastard." Keane and his accomplice then opened fire in the direction of their former partner and friend. The gunmen fired 14 rounds at Eddie Ryan. Mary and Deirdre Reddan were also hit in the hail of indiscriminate bullets. The noise of the shots was deafening and terrified customers dived to the floor for cover. The attack was over in ten seconds.

The gunmen ran back to the getaway car. Keane shouted, "drive, drive" and Coffey sped away. As they left the scene, the killers fired seven more shots at the front of the pub showing no consideration for the innocent bystanders – many of whom would have been relations and neighbours. Luckily no one was hit in the fusillade.

Keane was delighted with his night's work. He kept shouting and cheering in the back of the car: "Eddie is dead, Eddie Ryan is dead; he's gone."

Coffey dropped the killers at a nearby house. Then he dumped the car on a deserted lane and set it on fire.

In the pub there was a stunned silence as the customers began to realise what had happened. The smell of cordite from the gun shots wafted in the air. Eddie Ryan had been hit 11 times, at point blank range. Two rounds hit him in the right shoulder, seven in the back and one each in the hip and left arm. The bullets travelled through Ryan's chest penetrating both lungs. Another shot ripped through his spinal cord. Forensic examination would later show that some of the bullets which hit him were specially designed for use by the German police, for shooting out car tyres.

Eddie Ryan slouched down in his seat. A customer ran over and asked Ryan where he had been hit. "Everywhere," gasped the underworld hard man, as he slipped off his chair onto the floor. Blood oozed from his wounds, as he gasped for his last breath. Seconds later Eddie Ryan was dead.

Mary and Deirdre Reddan had been seriously injured in the merciless gun attack. Mary Reddan was hit in the abdomen and lower chest and her daughter was also hit in the chest. Both women underwent emergency surgery for the life-threatening wounds. Mary Reddan was airlifted by helicopter to be treated at Cork University Hospital. Doctors later said the women had been lucky to survive.

Kieran Ryan had also been lucky. He was in the toilet when Kieran Keane walked through the door. If he had been with his father he would have been either killed or seriously injured. Kieran Keane would have considered that a bonus.

Gardaí knew that the feuding would result in more violence and death. Within a few days, they had established who had been involved in the murder of Eddie Ryan. On December 7, a large force of armed officers raided several houses in St Mary's Park. They arrested seven suspects. Among them were Kieran Keane, Philip Collopy and Paul Coffey. While he was being questioned, Coffey broke down and admitted his role in the crime. He gave detectives a detailed statement about the crime and who was involved. In his statements he claimed Kieran Keane and Philip Collopy were the gunmen. In the meantime, he was charged with murder and Gardaí were hopeful that he would become a State witness. However Coffey subsequently retracted his statement, because of intense intimidation and threats to his family. He was later sentenced to 15 years in prison after he pleaded guilty to Ryan's manslaughter. No one else was charged in relation to the crime.

The murder of Eddie Ryan sparked a major upsurge in violence. Over the following year there were to be at least 30 petrol bomb and gun attacks on John Ryan's house alone. And for each attack there was retaliation. In one incident, in May 2001, Owen Treacy's father Philip, a baker, suffered serious burns when two petrol bombs were thrown through the front window of his home in County Clare. Two associates of the Ryan family, 25-year-old Noel Price from Kileely and 19-year-old Michael Stanners of Delmege Park, were later charged with the attack. In May 2003, the two thugs were convicted of arson and were each jailed for 12 years. Price had more than 10 previous convictions which included an arson attack on the car of an off-duty Garda, assault, possession of a firearm and drugs offences.

Against the backdrop of the ongoing feuds, dark forces were coming together in an unholy alliance elsewhere in Limerick. The new force would push the gangland violence to crisis point. Like vultures, this malevolent mob lurked in the background, waiting for the right time to move in and clean up. The starting point was the Dundon family's return to Limerick in June 2000.

* * * *

When it came to producing hard, violent men, Limerick had always stood out from the rest of the country. But no one had ever seen the likes of the Dundons and their entourage of hate-filled thugs. These guys could only be described as a murder machine. As soon as they arrived in the city, the chaos began.

In 1982, settled traveller Kenneth Dundon married Anne McCarthy from Hyde Road in Prospect, a working-class ghetto on the southern side of the city. Dundon, who was born in 1957, was an extremely violent man. His first serious conviction was recorded in 1974 when he was sent to a young offender's prison for two years, for wounding with intent. Dundon and McCarthy married in Hackney, North London. In the same year he was convicted for assault, occasioning actually bodily harm. Those who knew him well said that his children had the worst possible role model in life.

From the time they were children, John, Dessie, Gerard and Wayne, gained a reputation for violence and were constantly in trouble with police. Like their father, they had no behavioural boundaries when it came to dishing out violence and committing crime. And following his example they terrorised the elderly and other vulnerable people who they targeted and robbed. They feared no one.

Wayne Dundon was a particularly dangerous individual, who had certainly earned the name of being a psycho. He never drank, smoked or took drugs. Wayne Dundon just liked to inflict pain and fear. He even gave his own mother a severe beating on one occasion. It resulted in her being hospitalised for three weeks. When he was 18 years old Dundon was jailed for four years for a series of robberies from elderly people. During one burglary, Dundon savagely beat a wheelchair-bound pensioner. When he was due for release the British Home Office considered him so dangerous that it took the extraordinary step of ordering his deportation from the UK and banned him for life.

When the Dundon boys arrived back to live in Limerick in 2000, they were the last people the place needed. They teamed up with their cousins, the McCarthys, including Larry

McCarthy Junior, James McCarthy and Anthony "
McCarthy. This was the genesis of the McCarthy/D
gang. The leader of the gang was 22-year-old Larry McC
Junior. The McCarthy/Dundons were notorious for double and even treble-crossing associates and even fella gang members. They also had long, unforgiving memories and grudges were never forgotten. Loyalty was an attribute that was alien to these thugs.

In fact their treachery was so notorious that behind their backs they were referred to as the "piranhas". The following is a description of them given by an experienced local detective who knew them best: "They are the most devious and dangerous bastards that we ever encountered in Limerick, which is saying something. They were called the piranhas because they would eat each other if they were hungry enough. They run with the hares and hunt with the hounds. Killing or maiming comes like second nature to all of them and they have absolutely no fear of the law. They carried out a campaign to intimidate and seriously injure a number of Gardaí and prison officers in the city."

"They are so dangerous that they would be shaking your hand one minute and then shoot you in the back, as soon as you turn away from them. They hold grudges for years. In one case the McCarthy/Dundons shot a man who had assaulted one of their aunts ten years earlier."

"They don't care about doing time or being shot and injured, although they would prefer to avoid both if they could. They accept the danger as part of everyday life, like it is an occupational hazard. It is fair to say that they brought a level of savagery not seen anywhere else in this country or indeed a lot of other countries."

The McCarthy/Dundons were very ambitious. As soon as they arrived back in Limerick, they began plotting their eventual takeover of gangland. In the early years of the feuds between the Ryans and the Keane/Collopys, they tended to stay clear of the action, although they did supply a number of firearms to the Collopys, for use against the Ryans.

Instead they focussed on building a large scale drug dealing network, in conjunction with Cowboy Hanley, Eddie Ryan's best friend. Hanley had a major influence over the gang and introduced them to other major players, who were also waiting in the background. The McCarthy/Dundons also had extensive criminal contacts in the UK which became an important part of their operation. In turn the McCarthy/Dundons joined up with members of the Casey family who were also involved in crime in that part of the city. Wayne Dundon had married a Casey, as did one of the McCarthy sisters.

As soon as they arrived in Limerick the intimidation – and shooting had started. Inevitably they came to the attention of the Gardaí. From the beginning the members of the extended family gang showed no fear of the police. The Dundons regularly set up ambushes for passing patrols and attacked officers. On September 5, 2000, Gardaí from Roxboro Road Garda Station, who were investigating the theft of circus horses, called to the Dundon's home at Hyde Road, to arrest Dessie Dundon – who was then aged 20. Wayne Dundon launched a savage attack on Detective Garda Pat Cox and his partner Detective Garda? Brian Lynch, as he tried to free his brother.

During the incident, Dessie shouted to Wayne to get him his knife so he could stab one of the arresting officers. Wayne Dundon dumped a concrete pillar cap and a bag of rocks on Detective Garda Pat Cox. The officer suffered serious injuries to his arm and shoulder, as he tried to protect himself. The officer was so badly hurt that he never worked in active service again. The brothers were arrested when reinforcements were called and later charged with assault.

A bitter and extremely complex series of feuds also broke out between the McCarthy/Dundons, the Caseys and another criminal family, the McNamaras. At one stage, the McCarthy/Dundons began feuding with the Caseys. Later, after they effectively kissed and made up, the McCarthy/Dundons and the Caseys went after the McNamaras. It led to a series of shooting incidents, assaults and even kidnappings. In one incident, John, Dessie and Wayne Dundon kidnapped a man associated with the McNamaras and threatened to kill him. He made a statement to the Gardaí about the abduction. Cars and houses were also attacked and set on fire, as Gardaí tried to quell the feuding.

Members of the McCarthy/Dundons, Casey and McNamara families were arrested and charged with various serious criminal offences including attempted murder, wounding, assaults, criminal damage, false imprisonment and issuing death threats. On one occasion when John Dundon was charged with assault, Gardaí objected to him getting bail on the grounds that if he was released they feared for the safety of a number of people living in the O'Malley Park area of the city.

In late 2000, local Garda Inspector Jim Brown, who was then based in Roxboro Station, set up an operation to put a stop to the ongoing feuding and mayhem. Brown, who had been one of the city's most respected police officers since he was first stationed there in 1978, believed it was only a matter of time before people were killed.

In June 2001, Larry McCarthy Junior and John Dundon tried to shoot brothers Martin and James Casey but hit an innocent passer-by instead. Eye-witnesses identified the pair and John Dundon was charged with that offence. Larry McCarthy's windows were then blasted in by members of the Casey faction and he too made a statement to police, in a rare acknowledgement of the law. Two Local Authority houses where the Dundons lived on Hyde Road were also burnt out.

By then several of the combatants were facing serious charges including criminal damage, assault and firearms offences. A lot of them had been remanded in custody to prison when their bail was refused which brought a degree of calm to the situation. However a local city councillor stepped in to make a joke of the criminal justice system. Michael 'Mikey' Kelly from Southill – a close friend of Eddie Ryan – helped in no small way to create the circumstances which sent Limerick's crime problem spiralling out of control.

A sinister individual, with a reputation for serious violence and crime, Mikey Kelly had done everything in his power to undermine the local Gardaí. Kelly liked to portray himself as an ordinary decent criminal, who had retired from a life as a violent brute and wanted to give something back to his beloved community. In reality, he was a killer, a protection racketeer and a blackmailer who had watched the film *The Godfather* too many times. Playing on that charade, he had topped the poll in the local elections in 1999, becoming an alderman – and a huge embarrassment to the establishment in the city.

At the height of the feuding Kelly established a "peace process" to bring about an end to the feuding, which he tried to claim was similar to the Northern Ireland situation.

The real motivation for his peace talks had more to do with getting his brother Anthony off charges connected with the violence. Anthony Kelly had also been involved in a bitter feud with the Caseys and he had been charged with shooting Paddy Casey in the head, with a Humane Killer. Kelly "brokered" the peace deal between all the combatants, in a clever bid to pervert the course of justice. As a result all those involved in the tangled feuds, who had given statements to the Gardaí and agreed to give evidence in the myriad criminal cases, agreed to shake hands and withdraw their evidence. Most of the related cases before the courts had to be dropped and the protagonists were released from custody including the Dundons.

Kelly then organised a number of choreographed press conferences for the local media, where the enemies posed for pictures and shook hands. The situation was extremely frustrating for the police who had put a huge effort into trying to stop the violence. Mikey Kelly continued a campaign of harassment and disruption aimed at the local Gardaí until his death from gunshot wounds in 2004. Kelly's untimely departure was shrouded in mystery – no one knows whether he committed suicide or was actually shot. As soon as the dust settled, the thugs continued shooting and intimidating each other.

The McCarthy/Dundons went back to making money and got involved in armed robberies. Twenty-seven-year-old John Creamer, a cousin of the Dundons, was involved in an armed robbery with his relations at a jeweller's shop in 2001. On October 11, when he went to collect his share of the takings, he was ambushed by his cousin John Dundon who was armed with a Mac 10 machinegun. Creamer, who had an extensive criminal record and a reputation for violence, was shot 14 times and was left with 28 entry and exit wounds in his body. He was hit in the head, neck, chest, left arm and leg. One of the bullets hit him in the jaw and travelled through his mouth taking a piece of his tongue and smashing his teeth in the process. He underwent 12 hours of surgery and was in intensive care for several weeks. It took him almost two months to regain consciousness but he defied science and eventually recovered. Doctors were astounded that he survived the attack. But despite his near death experience, and the fact that he could clearly identify his attacker, Creamer refused to co-operate with investigating Gardaí.

In late 2001 and early 2002, the McCarthy/Dundons began a terrifying campaign of intimidation aimed at a number of prison officers based in Limerick jail. The gang members had been in and out of prison on a regular basis, as a result of the feuding and other criminal activity, since arriving back in Ireland and had developed an intense dislike for the officers they had targeted. A hoax bomb was left at the home of one officer and shots were fired into the home of another. A prison officer's car was set alight with a petrol bomb and another car was destroyed with acid. John Dundon was again the prime suspect. He was later charged with over 20 offences, including assaults on three prison officers and threatening to kill a fourth in September and December 2001.

Three brothers from another family, who were also described as extremely dangerous psychopaths were closely associated with the Dundons. One of them, who was born in 1983, had become a murderer by the time he was just 19 and was even more volatile then the worst people in the McCarthy/Dundon clan. This man is suspected of carrying out at least four gangland murders in the city since that time. At the time of going to print, *Crime Wars* cannot name this hoodlum for legal reasons. This is how an experienced cop describes him. "[The criminal] would kill for anyone who would pay him and even the Dundons were afraid of him. We believe he was involved in several shootings and at least five murders since he was a teenager."

In the late 1990s, the Dundons' friends had been involved in a string of armed robberies in business premises and burglaries at the homes of elderly, vulnerable people living alone in isolated rural areas. The young killer had not yet reached his fifteenth birthday, when he was suspected of being part of a gang that had burst into the home of 68-year-old Patrick "Paud" Skehan at Bridgetown in County Clare, sometime late on the night of Holy Thursday, April 9, 1998. The helpless bachelor farmer, described by friends as a shy and intensely private man, was savagely beaten as he lay in his bed upstairs. Medical evidence would later show that the gang had smashed the old man's head several times, with a hard object, causing extensive brain injuries. A broken and blood splattered shovel handle was later found in the house. The elderly pensioner suffered several fractures to his skull and his nose was broken. They had then bound his hands and legs with TV cable.

Patrick Skehan was blindfolded, doused in petrol and hung upside down from the banisters of the stairs in his kitchen. When he was found by a neighbour, some 24 hours later, the farmer had been barely alive and was calling his dog 'Puppy'. He was dressed only in a shirt and underpants and his face was soaked in blood. The farmer survived on a life support machine for seven weeks but died on June 3rd.

The crime caused outrage and fear throughout rural Ireland. An associate of the McCarthy/Dundons, 28-year-old William Campion from Moyross in Limerick, was caught after forensic experts matched his shoes to bloody shoeprints found at the scene of the crime. In March 2000, he was convicted of murder and jailed for life. There was insufficient evidence to link anyone else with the crime.

As the Dundons drug dealing empire continued to expand, they were introduced to one of the main drug suppliers to the Limerick gangs. He was a man from a completely different background than that of his customers. Local businessman, Jim 'Chaser' O'Brien, was a farmer's son from Rawlinstown, Grange in County Limerick. Born in June 1963, O'Brien had a privileged upbringing when compared to the thugs he dealt with. He was educated by the Christian Brothers in Hospital, County Limerick and entered the bar trade after leaving school. He worked in a number of well-known pubs around the city and county and then bought his own premises, which he named 'Chaser O'Brien's' in Pallasgreen, on the Limerick-Tipperary Road.

Around the same time in the early to mid-1990s O'Brien's involvement in another less legitimate business – drugs – began to surface. O'Brien was a greedy man with a taste for the high life – he liked designer clothes, fast cars and glamorous women. By the new Millennium, he was identified by Garda intelligence as an associate of several well known criminals in the city, including the leader of the McCarthy/Dundons, Larry McCarthy Junior. As he prospered, he bought the Henry Cecil night-club and bar in the city centre.

O'Brien's main partner-in-crime was one Anthony Kelly a veteran criminal who Gardaí classified as a major godfather. Born in 1957, Kelly ran a large second-hand furniture business from his home town of Kilrush in County Clare. A multi-millionaire, with an extensive international property portfolio, he was a clever criminal who managed to remain one step ahead of the law, which is reflected in his criminal record – he has six previous convictions for larceny, assault and receiving stolen goods.

In 1984, he had been jailed for nine months for running a rather novel prostitution racket for the benefit of lonely bachelor farmers throughout County Clare. Kelly toured the back roads of his home county in an old van, which had once been used as a mobile bank, with a few "grand girls". Clients were entertained in the back of the "passion wagon" as Kelly drove them around the roads.

The businessman went on to be the target of several major Garda investigations through the years. In 1997, he was one of the first underworld figures in the country who was forced to pay a tax bill for over €1 million to the CAB. The estimate was based on his criminal activities. Kelly also had extensive underworld contacts in the UK.

For many years, Kelly had been living with a Limerick woman called Marie Cronin. In 1998 her criminal brother, who was an associate of Kelly and 'Chaser' O'Brien, was responsible for a particularly gruesome murder in the Henry Cecil, when he shot an innocent 20-year-old woman. Cronin had intended shooting his wife, Angela Collins. His subsequent trial was told that he had argued with his wife earlier in the night and head-butted her, before storming out of the club. Cronin returned a short time later, armed with a hand gun, which he aimed at his wife. As she tried to defend herself, the gun went off hitting Georgina O'Donnell in the eye. She died the following day and Cronin was jailed for life.

The alliance between the McCarthy/Dundons, Cowboy Hanley, Chaser O'Brien and Anthony Kelly was soon proving very successful. Nevertheless both O'Brien and Kelly were worried about the gang's propensity for extreme violence. The two 'businessmen' had managed to avoid being subsumed into the ongoing conflict between the Keane/Collopys and the Ryans. It is now known that the smarter godfathers had advised their partners-in-crime to cool things down. The criminal cartel had ambitions to take over the entire drug trade but that might not be possible if they kept attracting so much attention from the police.

On August 21, 2001, the McCarthy/Dundons and the Gardaí both had reason to be in celebratory mood – albeit for completely different reasons – when Christy Keane was nabbed carrying a sack load of drugs in the Island Field. The feared godfather, who had evaded the law for so long had been spotted by a vigilant Garda patrol. For several months The Island Field and the neighbourhoods affected by the simmering Keane and Ryan feud, had been saturated with extra armed patrols to prevent a bloodbath. When he spotted the cops, Keane made a run for it, still shouldering the heavy looking coal bag. When the officers caught up with him and searched the bag they found €240,000 worth of hashish. Keane, the clever hoodlum who had constructed a wall of silence around himself and his family through terror, was stunned that he had been caught so easily. It was a major victory for the police in the city. It would also provide a potentially lucrative business opportunity for the McCarthy/Dundons and their allies.

The same month had been a bleak one for the city. Five men were either beaten or stabbed to death, although none

of the murders was a direct consequence of the feud. One of
the victims was Brian Hanley the son of Cowboy Hanley, the
McCarthy/Dundon's partner-in-crime. Brian Hanley was on
bail at the time. Gardaí had caught him with over €1 million
worth of ecstasy a short time earlier. Cowboy and his son
were out drinking in Hassetts pub in Kileely, on the night of
August 25, when they became involved in a row with Eamon
and Sarah Craig.

The Hanleys later followed the Craigs to their home where
a fight ensued. Outside the house Sarah Craig stabbed Brian
Hanley in the chest, after he bit her husband's face. Hanley died
shortly afterwards. The grief-stricken drug dealer launched a
campaign of intimidation against the Craigs after the killing
and was given a jail sentence as a result. Initially Eamon Craig
took responsibility for the death but Gardaí had discovered the
truth. Before Sarah Craig went on trial, a gunman burst into her
home and held a gun to her head. Her life was spared when the
weapon failed to go off. She was subsequently jailed for four
years for manslaughter but the sentence was suspended by the
Court of Criminal Appeal.

Three days after Hanley's death, Christy Keane's 17-year-
old son Liam also found himself in trouble with the police – as
the prime suspect for stabbing 19-year-old Eric Leamy to death.
The row had started after Keane's friend, Jonathan Edwards,
was spotted kicking a puppy. The following day a friend of the
dead man, Willie Moran Junior, hit Edwards over the head
with an aluminium bar, seriously injuring him. While still in a
coma, Edwards developed pneumonia and died in hospital. In
a subsequent trial Moran was acquitted, on the grounds that
he was defending himself.

Liam Keane was charged with Eric Leamy's murder after
a number of people gave Gardaí statements saying they had
witnessed the attack. The case was to cause a national outcry
two years later, when it collapsed in the Central Criminal Court
in Dublin. All the witnesses had developed, what Mr Justice
Paul Carney described as "collective amnesia". The trial fell as
a result and the DPP had no choice but to enter a nolle prosequi
and drop the charge against the smirking Keane. A picture of

the crime lord's son giving the two fingers to the camera in the following morning's newspapers became an image synonymous with the underworld's attitude to law and order. However by then there had been a dramatic shift in the balance of power in Limerick.

On March 13, 2002, Gardaí got an insight into the inner workings of Chaser O'Brien's drug operation when they busted one of his most important employees. She was a Limerick grandmother called Ann Keane. When cops swooped, she had just handed over €500,000 worth of drugs to Gerard Dundon, the youngest member of the Dundon family, who was then aged 16. The investigation that followed – appropriately codenamed 'Hillbilly' – involved officers from the Limerick Division, who subsequently found large amounts of cocaine, ecstasy, cannabis and heroin.

The drug seizures were made after a raid on the house, near Newport in County Tipperary, which was being used as a major distribution centre for the gang. A pistol and a rifle were also seized. A ledger found on the kitchen table showed that in the previous nine months the gang had moved drugs worth over €1 million. Keane was subsequently jailed for six years and her partner, Brian Ahern, got three years. Dundon got a suspended sentence in recognition of his tender age. One of the conditions of the suspension was that he remained living in Waterford and did not return to Limerick. However, in 2004, the sentence was activated after he was convicted of assaulting a Garda. Dundon attacked the officer, after the young hood had been spotted acting suspiciously in Limerick.

In May 2002, Christy Keane was convicted of the drug charges by a jury at Limerick Circuit Criminal Court. The godfather had tried to pull every trick he could to avoid going to jail. On the first day of the trial, the presiding judge ordered one of Keane's henchmen out of court for acting in an intimidatory manner towards the jury. Several of his associates, including members of the INLA in Dublin, were present for the trial. Then Keane produced an incredible witness as part of his defence.

Daniel Braddish claimed that he had been carrying the sack load of hash when Keane's arrest took place. Braddish claimed that he had paid for the drugs with stolen money. When prosecution counsel put it to him that he was being paid to take the rap for Keane, he replied: "The State should reward me with money for owning up to this. I expect him (Keane) to go free because he is innocent."

The witness was laughed out of court.

On Monday, June 3, 2002, the court sentenced Keane to ten years. He was taken to serve his sentence in Portlaoise maximum security prison, in the company of the country's most serious gangsters. For the time being at least Keane's drug business was in safe hands. Kieran Keane took over the reins and he soon let everyone in town know that he was, quite literally, calling the shots. Two months later, John McCarthy, Eddie Ryan's nephew, narrowly escaped serious injury or death when his house was raked by an AK 47 assault rifle. One of the bullets just missed his nine year-old son. McCarthy's attackers, cousins Ross Cantillon (19) and Roy Woodland (20), were disarmed and arrested by a passing Garda patrol a short time later. The two young men, both of whom were pathetic victims of the culture of hate, had been sent on the murder mission by Kieran Keane. Woodland had already lost a leg, after being shot in cross fire and on another occasion he was stabbed in the head. Cantillon had also been seriously injured in a number of stabbing incidents. For their efforts they were each jailed for seven years in February 2003.

With Christy Keane out of the picture, the McCarthy/ Dundons and their associates stepped up their secret plans for an underworld coup. Their plan was not very complicated – they just needed to wipe out the main players in the Keane/ Collopy gang. By doing so everyone would be happy. Eddie Ryan would be avenged and much more importantly for them, the McCarthy/Dundons could control the entire drug trade in the region. But Murder Inc. was prepared to wait for the right time before making their move.

In the meantime, they turned their attention to a totally innocent man who had also attracted the evil eye of the malevolent mob.

* * * *

Most victims of gangland murders are euphemistically referred to in media reports as having been "known to the Gardaí". The term basically suggests that the executed person was involved in the criminal world and had incurred the wrath of his associates. In the vast majority of the 120 plus gangland-style murders recorded since the beginning of the new Millennium, the motives can be traced to feuds among criminal groups. A lot of the victims tend to have blood – and traces of illegal narcotics – on their hands too. As a result, the public don't tend to be very sympathetic. The prevailing feeling is that it is just a case of criminals killing criminals – so let them wipe each other out. But that attitude creates a level of tolerance to the problem which ultimately leads to the deaths of innocent people. Hidden among the long list of names are the identities of a handful of people who were totally innocent victims of the bloodshed – people who were caught in indiscriminate cross–fire, such as Brian Fitzgerald. The deliberate, cold-blooded destruction of someone who was just trying to do his job was nothing short of an act of terrorism. It was a dark omen of what was to come.

A criminal organisation, completely devoid of humanity, singled him out for execution, simply because he stood up to them. He refused to be bullied by the atavistic McCarthy/ Dundons. As a result of that, his decent life was snuffed out by Murder Incorporated.

Brian Fitzgerald was a big strong man, who was born in 1967 and raised in Limerick City. Although he had grown up and rubbed shoulders with a lot of the local criminal fraternity he had opted for a life of honest, hard work. He had three interests in his life– his family, work and rugby. Brian Fitzgerald was one of five children – three boys and two girls – born to Martin and Bridie Fitzgerald, when the family lived in St Mary's Park. They moved to the Lee Estate when he was 12. After leaving school Brian worked for Krups, the German household electrical appliance manufacturer for over ten years. It closed in 1998 with the loss of 500 jobs.

In 1995, he married his childhood sweetheart, Alice

McNamara and a year later they bought their first home, a semi-detached house at Brookhaven Walk. It was in the middle-class suburb of Corbally, on the northern outskirts of the city. Fitzgerald was totally devoted to his wife and two little boys, Aaron and Evan. After the closure of Krups, he worked as a doorman at clubs and pubs around Limerick, a job he was naturally suited to. He was six feet one inches in height, was a fitness fanatic and had been the Munster power-lifting champion in 1997. He rarely drank and was passionate about rugby. He regularly lined out for St Mary's Rugby Club and had played one season with Thomond Rugby Club.

He got a job as a bouncer at Doc's, a trendy city centre night-club. The club catered for 800 patrons and was hugely popular. Brian Fitzgerald soon moved up to the position of the club's security manager, heading a team of 13 staff. He became the public face of the club, the first person the public met at the front door. Brian took his job extremely seriously and enforced a strict no-drugs policy. Brian Fitzgerald didn't like the tradition of the menacing bouncer and insisted that his staff maintained an informal and welcoming demeanour.

His paramount concern was that young patrons were protected and safe while inside the club, both from themselves and others. He ensured that a member of staff, with basic medical skills was always present to look after people who drank too much. At the security manager's instigation, patrons who were seriously intoxicated were always sent home in a taxi from the front door. He didn't want drunken customers rambling off into the night, posing a danger to themselves and others. Fitzgerald also adopted a diplomatic, cool-headed approach when faced with trouble.

Many of the city's drug pushers had been discouraged from even trying to enter the night-club to peddle their wares. But that didn't deter the McCarthy/Dundons who saw the huge potential for business. Gardaí estimated that if a gang could establish themselves in Doc's, the drug trade could have been worth more than €30,000 a week. But Brian Fitzgerald was determined that that was not going to happen. As a result, he found himself on a one-way collision course with the most evil criminal gang in Ireland.

By the summer of 2001, the McCarthy/Dundons had already shown that they fully intended dominating the criminal landscape in Limerick. They were in the midst of a number of violent feuds with other families and had launched a campaign of intimidation against Gardaí and prison officers. They were robbing and shooting and the money was rolling in from the sale of drugs. Larry McCarthy Junior and his nasty relations considered themselves untouchable. Taking Doc's night-club would be a push over – they were wrong.

Larry McCarthy Jnr and John and Dessie Dundon had already been in Doc's on a few occasions, when they came to the attention of Brian Fitzgerald. As a street-wise, man-about-town, he knew who and what he was dealing with. In September, he told the three of them that they were barred. The dangerous thugs could not believe what they were hearing. They enquired if the security manager knew who he was fucking with. The courageous bouncer told them politely they would not be dealing drugs to patrons in his club. The matter was closed – and so was the front door.

From that moment, Larry McCarthy and John and Dessie Dundon began to intimidate and threaten Brian Fitzgerald. They would drive by the front door of the club at night, where the security manager was on duty, to let him know they were watching him. The gang could not, and would not forget the man who had stood up to them and decided to show him what they were capable of.

Around 12.50am on the morning of December 18, 2001 a gang member fired a shotgun blast through the front sitting room window of Fitzgerald's home. Three days later, at 11.30 pm on December 21, Larry McCarthy Jnr and John Dundon approached Brian Fitzgerald at Doc's to make sure he'd got the message.

"John Dundon made a gesture with his hand indicating that it was like a gun and said: 'Fitz, you're going to get it soon,'" the security manager told Gardaí in a statement about the intimidation. At the same time McCarthy gestured to Fitzgerald by running his fingers across his throat indicating that he was to be killed. The Gardaí decided to move quickly against the mob, who had already made their way to the top of the most wanted list in the city.

In January 2002, Larry McCarthy Junior was arrested and charged with making death threats against the security manager. John Dundon was also arrested. He was charged with over 20 offences, relating to his ongoing intimidation of prison officers and Gardaí. Both men were remanded in custody.

On February 11, 2002, McCarthy applied for bail in the High Court in Dublin. Gardaí objected and Brian Fitzgerald testified that he had feared for his life when McCarthy had threatened him in December. The court refused the application.

Larry McCarthy Jnr was incensed that Brian Fitzgerald had "the cheek" to get up in court and testify against him. The up-and-coming crime lord, who celebrated his 23rd birthday behind bars, was facing at least four years in prison if Fitzgerald's case was not dropped. On February 2, 1999, McCarthy had received a six year prison sentence after being convicted on a charge of violent disorder. The sentence had been suspended, however, as long as he stayed out of trouble. If he was convicted of the current charge, then McCarthy estimated that he would spend four and a half years locked up. He wasn't prepared to let that happen.

In the meantime, McCarthy and his associates made several approaches to a number of Brian Fitzgerald's friends, urging them to get him to drop the charges. The night-club security man told one of his friends that he wasn't interested in withdrawing his complaint. He was deeply angry that shots had been fired at his home, where his wife and children were sleeping. He was determined to make a stand.

The situation took a dramatic turn on April 23, 2002, when McCarthy appeared for a remand hearing before Limerick District Court. When the court was told that the Book of Evidence relating to the Fitzgerald case had not yet been completed, the court struck out the charge and McCarthy was free to go. The State however could re-enter the charges when the book was finalised. Over the next few days he left the country and began moving between the UK and Spain

The following morning, John Dundon was also released from custody – although not with the consent of a judge. He was due to appear before the Circuit Criminal Court in the city. Dundon was being transported to Cork Prison in the back of a taxi which was escorted by a Garda car. He was wearing handcuffs and the child locks were activated on the taxi doors to prevent him opening them. But Dundon had made arrangements with one of his pals. As the taxi stopped at traffic lights near King's Island the thug ran over and simply opened the back door. Dundon raced off and vanished. He later fled back to London and was not seen for over a year.

A few days earlier, Wayne and Dessie Dundon had been convicted of assaulting the Gardaí in September 2000. Wayne Dundon was sent down for two years and Dessie got nine months. For a short time Limerick was to get a reprieve from the scourge of the McCarthy/Dundons.

In the meantime Larry McCarthy Jnr kept up the pressure on Brian Fitzgerald to withdraw his complaint. McCarthy was extremely aggrieved that he had been forced to stay in prison for three months. During research for this book it was established that a friend of Brian Fitzgerald's had been acting as a double agent for the crime lord. He continually tried to scare the security manager by telling him stories of what he'd "heard" the McCarthy/Dundons were planning for him.

On September 16, McCarthy phoned Fitzgerald from England and demanded, again, that he withdraw the charges. Brian was at home with his wife Alice at the time and she later recalled that he had a lengthy conversation with McCarthy. It was followed up by a number of other calls from the gangster. At the time, the security man had confided to family members and some friends that the pressure was getting to him. It is now understood that McCarthy instructed Brian Fitzgerald to make a statement withdrawing his complaint. On October 4, the security man made the statement.

Brian Fitzgerald may have believed that his problems with Murder Inc had ended with that but he was wrong. He had crossed swords with a gang who would not forgive or forgot. Larry McCarthy Junior was not fully satisfied that the case would be dropped. He feared that Fitzgerald might change his mind and he would be arrested again. If the Gardaí provided protection for the bouncer, there was no way he could be got at. The young godfather wasn't prepared to take a chance. The gang's trade in drugs and firearms was working well and it would be bad for business if he had to go inside for over four years. A meeting was held among gang members, during which the fate of Brian Fitzgerald was decided. He was to be murdered in the early hours of November 29, 2002.

Investigating Gardaí believed that up to eight people – all either members of the McCarthy/Dundon gang or their associates – were involved in the conspiracy to murder the security man. English-born criminal James Martin Cahill was hired as the hit man. Overweight and completely bald, he certainly didn't look like the part of a gangland executioner. Cahill was born in Birmingham but had moved to Kilrush, Co Clare to live with an uncle when he was 15 years of age. November 29 was to be his twenty-eighth birthday.

Cahill was a serious criminal who had no qualms about killing another human being. He'd had violent tendencies from childhood and had been thrown out of a school after he seriously injured a teacher. In 1999, he was jailed for ten years for armed robbery and possession of firearms, with intent to endanger life in Galway. However, the Court of Criminal Appeal overturned the conviction on a technicality. For several years he had been associated with all those involved in the unfolding conspiracy. He would later claim that Larry McCarthy Junior offered him €10,000 to carry out the hit. John Dundon secretly returned from the UK to carry out surveillance on Brian Fitzgerald, along with his brother Dessie.

Jim 'Chaser' O'Brien organised the transport and other logistics for the 'hit', in conjunction with a 34-year-old Limerick criminal who was based in Dublin. The Dublin-based mobster, who is related to the McCarthy/Dundons, is classified as a major criminal figure by Gardaí. At a national level he is involved in drug trafficking and protection rackets. He has extensive links to several organised gangs throughout the Continent, the UK and Ireland, as well as renegade Republican groups. The godfather runs a security company as a front for his gangland activities. Described in Garda intelligence reports as "exceptionally clever", he has a controlling interest in the activities of the McCarthy/Dundons and uses gang members as hired guns for other murders.

James Martin Cahill would later claim in court that after a number of meetings with Chaser O'Brien, he was brought to Anthony Kelly's home in Kilrush the night before the murder. He alleged that Kelly had supplied him with the automatic pistol and a magazine full of bullets. He claimed Kelly showed him how to use the weapon and told him not to "mess it up". However Kelly was later acquitted by a jury because there was no corroboration to back up Cahill's story.

In the days leading up to the murder, John and Dessie Dundon drove Cahill out to Brookhaven Walk on a reconnaissance mission and to check out the CCTV security cameras Brian Fitzgerald had erected around his home. Dessie Dundon also pointed out the marked man to Cahill at Doc's night-club. Cahill walked past his target to have a good look at him.

But seven hours before the murder gang went into action they had a problem. Two days earlier on November 27, 2002, an associate of the Dublin-based criminal from Limerick had stolen a high-powered Ducati motorbike. It had been parked at an apartment complex at Morton Hall, Brews Hill near Navan, County Meath. The 22-year-old thief, from Mulhuddart in Dublin 15, had also been nominated to act as Cahill's driver in the Fitzgerald murder.

Around 8pm on the evening of November 28, security staff working at the Parkway Shopping Centre in Limerick had spotted the stolen motorbike and noticed that it had been hot wired. The Gardaí had been called and the bike was seized. Unknown to them, they had just thrown Murder Inc.'s plans into disarray. The original driver of the getaway bike had got cold feet and decided to pull out of the plot. Dessie Dundon then contacted another associate for a replacement motorbike. The same associate agreed to drive it for €10,000.

Around the time that his killer's first motorbike was being recovered by Gardaí, Brian Fitzgerald left for work as usual at around 8.10pm. The dedicated family man bathed his two sons, who were aged one and five, and stayed with them until they fell asleep. They were to be his last precious moments with his family.

Thursday night was student night at Doc's and it passed off without incident. Around 3.30am Brian Fitzgerald dropped other staff members home in his Opel Frontera jeep and then headed back to his wife and children.

Dessie Dundon had been lurking in the shadows near Doc's night-club, stalking his victim. He phoned Cahill to alert him that Fitzgerald was on his way. Cahill and the bike man were hiding in bushes near their target's home in Corbally. It was shortly before 3.50am when Brian Fitzgerald arrived home. As he jumped out of his jeep, Cahill and his accomplice came running towards him from the shadows.

Cahill was armed with a 9mm automatic pistol. As he ran, he tripped and twisted his ankle but he kept going. The doorman, who was on his guard, saw them coming and got ready to defend himself. He shouted at them: "Come on ye c***s, ye."

Cahill opened fire on his innocent victim, as he came towards him. Although Brian Fitzgerald was hit twice in the chest, he managed to make a desperate dash to safety.

His terrified wife Alice had heard the shots and her husband shouting at his attackers. She also heard glass breaking. She frantically tried to get her mobile phone to work to call the police but it wouldn't. She later told detectives: "I ran out to the kitchen and I got the phone off the wall and I rang the guards. I looked out through the panel in the door and I could see Brian in a struggle with a fella in a helmet. I could see Brian looking back at me. He was at the back of my car. I thought they were trying to take him away."

Brian Fitzgerald managed to get roughly 70 yards down the road, before he fell to the ground beside a car parked outside a neighbour's house. At that moment, Cahill caught up with his helpless victim. He took aim and shot him twice into the back of the head. Brian Fitzgerald was left lying face down in a pool of blood. Cahill then ran back to Fitzgerald's jeep and began searching inside. Detectives believed that the killers wanted the murdered man's mobile phone, to delete evidence of calls from Larry McCarthy Junior. It was also speculated that they had intended planting a gun and drugs in the jeep, in an attempt to have their victim accused of being a drug dealer himself.

At that moment Alice Fitzgerald believed her husband and childhood sweetheart had been abducted. As she looked out through the blinds on the sitting room window, she could see Cahill's associate standing just outside with his back to her.

"I knocked on the window; he turned around and looked in at me. I could see his face. He had shiny, dark, glassy eyes. If I had to go by his eyes, he had dark hair and I showed him the phone. The fellow was directly outside the window within feet of me. The second one, his upper body was leaning over the jeep."

When the accomplice saw Alice Fitzgerald at the window, he shouted to Cahill and they both ran down the road to where they had parked the stolen motorbike. Less than eight minutes later, the first Garda unit arrived at the scene. Initially the dead man's wife and the officers suspected that Brian had been kidnapped.

A half hour later, during a search of the area, a Garda found the body of the McCarthy/Dundon's latest victim in the beam of her torchlight. Brian Fitzgerald was pronounced dead at the scene, a short time later.

Within minutes of the shooting, the driver of the bike dropped Cahill to a getaway car. It was a Ford Mondeo supplied by Chaser O'Brien, which he had parked some distance away. The driver sped off and dumped the bike in a laneway situated off the Old Dublin Road near an area called Dillon's Cross. When he got there he set the bike ablaze and went to the home of a criminal associate, a short distance away. From there he called a taxi to get back to his home at the other end of the city.

At the same time, Cahill had driven back to Annacotty Village on the outskirts of the city where Chaser O'Brien lived. He then hid the murder weapon under bushes behind the Jackie Power memorial statue in the village. He showered and changed his clothes to get rid of forensic evidence in O'Brien's home at Willow Crescent. Chaser had organised transport to get the hit man back to Dublin, where he had arranged to meet the Dublin-based godfather. From there, he travelled to Belfast where he met with John Dundon and Larry McCarthy Junior. They later travelled on together to Birmingham, by ferry and road.

The brutal execution of Brian Fitzgerald shocked and outraged the people of Limerick. It also put the city's simmering crime crisis back on the national media agenda. The murder had also sent a shiver of fear through those involved in the security industry in the city, who had been trying to keep the clubs and pubs they were protecting crime and drug free. Who would dare stand up to the mobsters now that the outspoken one among them had been butchered? Murder Inc. was laying down a bloody precedent for the way they intended doing business in the future.

It didn't seem to bother the mob that they would be the obvious suspects in the case, given their history with the murdered man. The motive was as obvious as the one for the murder of journalist Veronica Guerin by John Gilligan. In their warped logic the gang had the same rationale as any other terror gang – they wanted the public to be afraid. This was only the first shot in the war they had been planning for several months.

The execution came as a deep shock to the local Gardaí, many of whom had been friends of Brian Fitzgerald. The fact that they were already in the process of investigating the threats made against him by the McCarthy/Dundons would make this investigation a lot more personal. One of his friends later remarked: "If he had asked for protection he would have got it, but I think he was too embarrassed because he had withdrawn his statement. Or else Brian just didn't realise what he was up against on his own."

* * * *

Gardaí launched the largest murder investigation seen in the region since Detective Garda Jerry McCabe had been gunned down by an IRA gang six years earlier. The Divisional officer,

Chief Superintendent Gerry Kelly immediately set up an investigation incident room in Mayorstone Garda Station. His senior officers, Superintendents Willie Keane and Gerry Mahon; Detective Inspector Jim Browne and Inspector John Scanlan; Detective Sergeants Tom O'Connor, Eamon O'Neill and Paddy O'Callaghan were to lead the investigation.

These men were among the most experienced and respected criminal investigators in the country. Detective Inspector Jim Browne, who had a formidable reputation for taking on the city's organised crime gangs, had personally investigated the death threats against the security manager. The two men had also been good friends. Over the following traumatic years, Chief Supt Gerry Kelly and his team kept driving the investigation forward, even at times when it appeared that they were getting nowhere.

Statistically the Gardaí in Limerick had an impressive record of solving serious crime and murder investigations. They didn't know it at the time but Brian Fitzgerald's execution was to be the first horrific crime in a virtual tsunami of bloodshed coming their way. A team of officers from the National Bureau of Criminal Investigation in Dublin were also deployed to the city. From the outset, the investigators did not have far to look for suspects. They had become well acquainted with the upsurge in violence that had accompanied the gangland emergence of the people who had threatened Brian Fitzgerald's life – the McCarthy/Dundons.

By the following evening, well placed, reliable informants had confirmed the involvement of the gang in the heinous crime. The first intelligence reports had revealed that Jim 'Chaser' O'Brien had hurriedly organised transport for two people out of Limerick, in the hours immediately before and after the murder. As a result of that information James Martin Cahill was identified. The investigation team also knew the identity of the man from Mulhuddart who had robbed the first motorbike intended for the murder. In turn that led officers to the identities of the rest of the gang.

By the time Brian Fitzgerald was laid to rest on December 2, the Gardaí had a clear picture of the gang behind the horror. But knowing the culprits and proving a case in a court of law were two different matters. Thousands turned out to pay their final respects to the night-club security manager. Fr Tom Mangan told mourners that Brian had paid the ultimate price for his beliefs. In his homily the clergyman summed up the feelings of the public: "For his beliefs Brian has paid a heavy price. Nobody deserves to die like that. How can an act like this achieve any benefit, any time, anywhere? There is no sense to it. But there are people in our society today who seem to make sense of this." The heart-break suffered by Brian's wife and family was incalculable. Less than a week after the funeral, there was more pain for his shattered family when his sister Susan was diagnosed with ovarian cancer. She died in January 2005. The reaction of five-year-old Aaron Fitzgerald to the death of his dad – from whom he had been inseparable – should have given the mobsters pause for thought. In order to explain the loss the innocent boy was told that the brightest star in the sky was his daddy. So in the weeks after his Dad's presence in his life had been replaced by sadness, Aaron waited for the stars to come out each night. When they did he searched for the brightest one, gave it a thumbs-up and called out: "Goodnight Dad."

The investigation into the murder quickly began to make progress. The sense of horror and revulsion – even among members of the criminal underworld – resulted in a huge amount of good quality intelligence coming into the incident room in Mayorstone.

A few nights later on December 11, a member of the McCarthy/Dundon gang, Englishman Philip Deane was sent to Ireland by Larry McCarthy Junior to dispose of the murder weapon. James Martin Cahill drew a map, to direct him to the spot where he had hidden the gun, near Chaser O'Brien's home.

A member of the public spotted Deane, as he dumped something in the waters of the Mulcaire River near the Salmon Weir Apartments in Annacotty. The police were contacted and the following day a Garda diver found the 9 mm pistol. It would prove to be a significant breakthrough in the case. Subsequent investigations revealed that the weapon had originally been de-activated in the UK. Weapons, which have had their firing mechanisms removed, are popular souvenirs among gun enthusiasts. However, this particular weapon, which had been re-activated, would eventually uncover a major gun-running operation, involving re-activated weapons, between suppliers in Bradford, Yorkshire and the Limerick mob. The same day detectives searched Chaser O'Brien's home at 10 Willow Crescent.

A week later, on December 19 the investigation team searched the home of Larry McCarthy Junior's lover, Louisa Higgins, at Byrne Avenue in Prospect and arrested her for questioning. McCarthy had been having a secret affair with the 22-year-old behind his girlfriend's back from when she was 17. The mobster was infatuated with Higgins.

During the search, detectives found seven hand-written letters which McCarthy had sent to his young lover. The letters, three of which were written while he was on remand in prison in early 2002, contained evidence of McCarthy's hate-failed obsession with Brian Fitzgerald. Forensic analysis of the documents revealed that the letters were all written by McCarthy Junior and his fingerprints were also uplifted from the paper.

In the letters to Higgins, McCarthy tried to portray himself as an innocent man but he could scarcely hide his contempt for the murder victim. One of the letters contained the following passage:

"Oh I better tell you why I'm here [prison]. Shooting? Murder? Robbery? No none of the above, for driving my own car and for threatening Brian Fitz in December 01 at Doc's 20th I think. I didn't say anything to the dope. I have been sent forward for trial on them both and refused bail. I can't apply for bail again until July. But I might have a chance in 4 to 5 weeks times to get out if not then I don't know what. They are still charges, but you know what they [police] are trying to do, 6 years!"

Another letter contained the remark: 'Doormen. I think I will kill all of them.'

McCarthy also referred to Brian Fitzgerald as a 'lying cunt'. In reference to the possibility that his suspended sentence would be activated he wrote:

'Even if I get six bells [years] does he [Fitzgerald] think I
will be happy when I get out? Because I don't fucking think I
will. I don't mind being in jail but it drives you mad when you
are here for something you didn't do. This is a joke that isn't
funny woman. Well not to me anyway!'

In another letter he revealed that he had been advised by
his partner Chaser O'Brien to get offside and continue making
money from their drug business:

'But u know yourself, if I take Jim's advice and stay away
from smelly Limk and just work away I will get loads of dosh
with him. But that bastard [Fitzgerald] is driving me crazy. He
is on my mind worse than you.'

In the dying days of 2002, the McCarthy/Dundons began
mobilising for war. Despite the intensive investigation now
aimed at them the mob pushed ahead with their plans for a
gangland uprising. In the days after Brian Fitzgerald's murder,
Gardaí made the disturbing discovery that the members of
Murder Inc. – posing as a 'sports team' – had travelled to
Florida to train in the use of firearms. During the previous
summer the 'sports team' had spent a week at a specialist gun
school, practising their marksmanship with a wide variety of
lethal automatic weapons. Most of Ireland's criminal gangs
now regularly take part in weapons training courses, mostly
in Eastern Europe. It is no coincidence that the accuracy of
underworld hit men – and the murder rate – has increased
dramatically since the gangsters discovered 'gun holidays'.

The heat from the police and the public's revulsion at the
Fitzgerald murder did not force the membership of Murder
Inc to keep their heads down. Just to prove the point, the
McCarthy/Dundons made their New Year resolution clear in
the opening minutes of January 1, 2003, when they gunned
down another innocent man.

Around 11.30pm on New Year's Eve, 39-year-old Sean
Poland returned to his home at Blackwater near Ardnacrusha
in County Clare, with his partner Joanne Lyons. The couple
who had spent the evening socialising in the Round House
Bar in Limerick city centre went home to ring in the New Year

together.

The block-layer and part-time used car salesman had no idea that he was being stalked by at least five members of the McCarthy/Dundon gang. Unlike Brian Fitzgerald, Sean Poland had not had any angry confrontation or run in with the mob. His problem was simply that he had the misfortune to come into contact with them in the first place. Poland came to their attention after he had sold a car to a gang member. The gang had decided they wanted to rob the cash back from him. This was a double-cross which was typical of the McCarthy/Dundons.

Among the car salesman's stalkers that night were at least three of the people identified as being involved in the security manager's execution a month earlier. In addition to that murder, one of the gang members had also been directly involved in the horrific attack on pensioner Patrick 'Paud' Skehan in 1998.

The couple were home a short time when the vultures moved in and Sean Poland answered a knock on the front door. When he opened it, one of the masked gangsters shot him without hesitation in the lower abdomen. The hoodlums stepped across their victim and stormed into the house. Inside they tied up Joanne Lyons and subjected her to a horrifying 40 minute ordeal, as they ransacked the house for cash.

They left with almost €1,000 from the car sale – ignoring the seriously injured man they had left lying at the front door. Joanne Lyons eventually managed to free herself and raise the alarm. By then it was too late for her partner.

In the first minutes of the New Year, Sean Poland died from his injuries before an ambulance crew could get to him.

The murder was another shocking example of the barbaric nature of the McCarthy/Dundons who had marked their territory by claiming the lives of two innocent victims, in the space of a month – worse was to come.

TEN

THE DOUBLE CROSS

The investigation of the Sean Poland murder was also the responsibility of the Gardaí in Limerick. And from the beginning the intelligence clearly pointed to the McCarthy/Dundons and their associates as the suspects for the crime. It was now clear to Chief Superintendent Kelly and his staff that they were dealing with a criminal gang who had no boundaries beyond which they would not go. Gradually the local force, although backed up by the NBCI, was being stretched to the limit. In the city's three Garda stations detectives were also investigating at least ten serious shooting and stabbing incidents, associated with the feuding alone. In addition there was a mountain of every day complaints and crimes to be dealt with on a daily basis. However, in Mayorstone Garda Station, which was now also the HQ for the Poland investigation, The Fitzgerald Investigation team were about to make a major breakthrough in the case.

Ongoing surveillance and intelligence gathering operations had focused the investigation team's attention on 28-year-old Philip Michael Dean the criminal who had been sent from Birmingham to dispose of the murder weapon. Dean was the youngest of six children. He came from a broken home and had been involved in petty crime all his life. His only legitimate activity was for a brief period when he had a small computer business which went bust. He had incurred 15 criminal convictions most of them for theft. Dean first met Larry McCarthy Junior in 2000 through Amy Harrison, his partner and the mother of his two children. It was an encounter that he would live to regret.

Against his will, he became one of the gang's logistics managers – transporting drugs, guns and gangsters between the two countries. In early January, the Fitzgerald murder investigation team received intelligence that Dean had been sent to Limerick to deliver a consignment of drugs for the McCarthy/ Dundons. On January 14, Detective Sergeant Eamon O'Neill and a team of armed officers intercepted Dean, as he drove into Limerick on the Dublin Road. When they searched the car they couldn't find any drugs. Instead they discovered a .32 semi-automatic pistol and a mini mag-lite torch which had been adapted to fire .22 ammunition. They also found a quantity of ammunition. Dean was arrested under the Offences Against the State Act for illegal possession of firearms and brought in for questioning.

Over the next few days in custody Dean, who had been working under duress for the McCarthy/Dundons, decided to come clean. He then made a number of startling revelations about his involvement in Murder Inc.

Dean gave officers a detailed account of his activities for the crime gang. He revealed his dealings and meetings with McCarthy Junior, Cahill, Chaser O'Brien, the Dundons, the Dublin-based gangster and Anthony Kelly from Kilrush. Most importantly he shared what he knew about the plot to murder the night-club security man. He revealed that it was him that had been sent by McCarthy Junior to dispose of the murder weapon in the Mulcaire River. He had been present during a number of discussions between gang members John Dundon, Larry McCarthy Junior and James Martin Cahill, after the murder.

Philip Dean then described making six trips from England to Limerick, between June and December 2002, to deliver guns and drugs for the gang. He had been given no choice but to work for the mob. They had threatened him and also kept his partner and children 'hostage' to ensure that he made the deliveries. He claimed that Larry McCarthy had threatened him with a "bullet in the back of the head" if he didn't continue working for the mob. McCarthy, who was notoriously miserly, preferred using fear instead of cash to get people to work for him. Dean had been paid a pittance for each run.

During the six month period in 2002, he had personally delivered hashish worth €500,000, 250,000 ecstasy tablets and two slabs of cocaine. He also smuggled in a total cache of 24 weapons including Mac 10 and Uzi sub-machine guns, automatic and semi-automatic pistols, converted torch guns and a large amount of ammunition. One of the weapons had been used to execute Brian Fitzgerald. Dean said that he had made the deliveries in person to O'Brien and other named members of the mob in Dublin, Newry, Tralee, Kilrush and Limerick.

Most of the information spilling from Dean could be corroborated and he said he was prepared to testify against the gang, on the condition that he and his family would be placed in the Witness Protection Programme. It was a stunning development for the police. If their witness testified in court there was a strong possibility they could convict the hierarchy of the country's most dangerous criminal gang for a very long time. It was decided to maintain absolute secrecy about Dean's admissions.

On January 16, Dean was brought before Limerick District Court where he was charged with three counts of possession of firearms and ammunition. He was remanded in custody to Cloverhill Prison in Dublin. For the time being at least the gang would not know that their delivery manager had been spilling the beans.

Dean's revelations had created a huge workload as detectives had to corroborate every line in his 25 page statement. In so-called supergrass trials, the criminal courts can only accept the corroborated evidence of a gang member. Testimony that cannot be independently verified is considered inadmissible.

Chief Superintendent Kelly and his staff were also involved in high-level discussions with the Garda HQ, the Department of Justice and the Director of Public Prosecutions in relation to the case and Dean's suitability for the WPP. Putting Murder Inc's entire boardroom behind bars was a tantalising prospect. However there was one piece of vital information which

Philip Dean had not been privy to. It related to the gang's most ambitious plot which was about to come to fruition.

* * * *

While the McCarthy/Dundon gang were building their power base, the bitterness between the Ryans and the Keanes had continued to fester. Early in 2002, Kieran Keane was jailed for three months after he head-butted Eddie Ryan's widow Mary on a street outside the local court buildings near St John's Castle. He shouted at her: "I got your husband. Now I'm going to get you". In March, Eddie Ryan's son, Kieran, stabbed Christy Keane's son, Liam, on a city street and was also charged. On other occasions members of the Keane and Collopy faction openly taunted their adversaries on the streets. One of their favourite jibes was: "The maggots are atin' Eddie." There had been several street assaults, shooting incidents and attempts to burn each other's homes.

On January 23, 2003, Kieran Ryan stood trial at Limerick Circuit Criminal court for stabbing Liam Keane. Even on the way to his trial, Ryan had been ambushed on the street and was left battered and bruised. When the hearing commenced Liam Keane, the injured party and principal witness, took the stand and was asked by the prosecution who had stabbed him. "Kieran Ryan. Kieran Ryan stabbed me in the back," he replied. Then he was asked could he identify his attacker. Keane looked around the courtroom, past his adversary who was sitting in front of him, turned back and blankly replied, "no".

The courts or the rule of law had no relevance in the tribal world of the Ryans or the Keanes. They were devout practitioners of the doctrine of 'an eye for an eye' and 'a life for a life'. With no formal identification of the defendant, Judge Carroll Moran had no alternative but to direct the jury to find Ryan not guilty. "It is a very sorry state of affairs that this should happen and if this is going to persist we are going to live in a state of social chaos and anarchy," the judge declared angrily.

Within hours Judge Moran's prophecy had become a grim reality. Between 10.30 and 11 o'clock that night Kieran Ryan, his older brother, 20-year-old Eddie Junior and their friend Christopher "Smokey" Costelloe were walking on Moylish Road in Ballynanty, on their way to the home of another friend. They were in high spirits, celebrating Ryan's escape from justice earlier in the day.

The three thugs would later claim that a van suddenly pulled up alongside them and two armed and masked men jumped out. They bundled the Ryan brothers into the vehicle and drove off. Costelloe had been left on the side of the road and reported the "abduction" to the Gardaí. If the Ryans had been kidnapped, then this was a major escalation in the feuding. The police immediately launched a huge manhunt.

As officers from across the city and surrounding divisions were being mobilised for the search, experienced detectives expected the worst. They believed that they would be searching for dead bodies. Over the next seven days, the Gardaí, backed up by scores of soldiers, searched the Cratloe Woods and Woodcock Hill area. It is situated just across the Clare border, outside the city. It was the most likely location where assassins could comfortably dispatch their victims, without the fear of being caught in the act. The Gardaí began to focus their enquiries on the most likely culprits – the Keane/Collopy gang. Several of their homes were searched and everywhere gang members went they were stopped, searched and questioned about the missing brothers.

As the days went by without any developments, fear and apprehension gripped the city as the people expected the worst. If the Ryans turned up dead it would be an unprecedented escalation of hostilities. Further bloodshed and mayhem would be as inevitable as night following day. Gardaí now also knew that the gangs had a lot of deadly firepower at their disposal. The Limerick feuds had again put the city at the centre of attention from the national and international media.

As the searches continued, a number of houses were shot at or petrol-bombed. There were serious street-fights between men, women and children, from both sides. The poisonous hate had again seeped into the school yard. There had also been a full scale riot between both sides at the city's gleaming new circuit court complex. Potential combatants began to openly wear bullet-proof vests, as if they were uniforms. They made no effort to conceal the fact that they were preparing for war. The tension in the city was palpable. Limerick had become a powder keg – and it was only a matter of time before the fuse was lit.

Only a handful of people knew the truth of what was really going on. The "abduction" of the Ryans would be remembered as one of the most devious double-crosses in Irish gangland history. It was an elaborate plot worthy of the darkest imaginings of a Hollywood script-writer.

Subsequent Garda investigations would reveal that the Ryans were never actually kidnapped. It was later established that the brothers had stayed in a mobile home near Thurles in County Tipperary, which belonged to a criminal associate of their father. Their host was also a close associate of Sean 'Cowboy' Hanley, who had taken the Ryan brothers under his wing after Eddie's death. The plan to avenge Ryan's murder had begun on the night Kieran Keane and his accomplice had sprayed the Moose Bar with bullets. Two years of plotting were about to reach their climax.

Behind-the-scenes, the McCarthy/Dundons had secretly agreed to join forces with the Ryans, through the involvement of Cowboy Hanley and Jim 'Chaser' O'Brien. The move also had the backing of the Dublin-based godfather. By pooling their collective resources, they could become one of the biggest criminal gangs in the country – and fabulously wealthy with it. But in order to achieve dominance they realised they had to wipe out the opposition – the Keanes and the Collopys.

It had been decided that hitting Kieran Keane or his lieutenants on the street was not an option. They were too careful and always on their guard. Just taking out one major player in the gang would not help shift the balance of power either. The gang would have to launch a surprise attack – and it would have to be spectacular. Something as elaborate as a kidnap ruse was the only way to outwit the Keane/Collopys and to catch them off-guard and so the Ryans were happy to oblige to being the bait for the deadly trap.

The McCarthy/Dundons had been careful not to allow themselves to be seen to be allied to the Ryans and their ancillary associates. In the past they had been on friendly terms with the Keanes and the Collopys, with whom they dealt in drugs and guns. But double-crossing them was not a problem – this was purely business. Murder Inc had been careful not to show the slightest hint of animosity towards their enemies. With the Ryans missing they contacted Kieran Keane with an offer he should have refused.

As detectives later tried to unravel the elaborate plot, they suspected that the McCarthy/Dundons had either told the crime boss that they were holding the Ryans hostage or had already murdered them. It is unclear whether they set up the "kidnapping" plot after being initially contracted to do so by Keane, who feared that one day Ryan's sons would kill him in revenge. What has been established is that Keane had agreed to pay €60,000 to the double crossing killers, in return for them getting rid of the two brothers.

On Wednesday, January 29, Dessie Dundon called to see Kieran Keane. An arrangement was made for Keane to meet the gang later that night and either witness the execution of the Ryan brothers or view their dead bodies.

Keane and Dundon arranged to meet the 'abduction gang' in the home of 21-year-old Anthony 'Noddy' McCarthy, at Fairgreen in the Garryowen area of the city, later that evening. Keane went to the meeting with his nephew Owen Treacy. Treacy would later claim he had no idea what the meeting was about, although that was unlikely given that he was a close confidant of his uncle.

Around 6pm, Treacy and Kieran Keane left Treacy's home at St Munchin's Street in Keane's blue Passat car. The crime boss employed an anti-surveillance techniques by taking a circuitous route around the city, driving up one way streets in the process, in order to lose any Garda tail that may have been on them. When they arrived at 'Noddy' McCarthy's around 7pm they met another gang member, 18-year-old Keith Galvin, a cousin of Larry McCarthy Junior. Galvin told Treacy and Keane: "The lads are inside."

In the sitting room of the house they met Dessie Dundon
and Noddy McCarthy. Noddy McCarthy suddenly produced
a .38 revolver and ordered the two men to get down on the
floor.

Keane and Treacy had walked into a death trap.

The gangsters grabbed the bag containing the agreed
€60,000. Dessie Dundon tied their hands behind their backs
and ordered them to sit down. Keane and Treacy were told
that if they played along they would be released unharmed and
everything would be "ok".

At the same time, two other gang members emerged from
the kitchen, wearing balaclavas. Treacy recognised one of them
as 31-year-old David 'Frog Eyes' Stanners. Dundon demanded
that Keane phone the two leading members of the Collopy
gang, brothers Kieran and Philip Collopy and arrange to meet
them "out the road". Philip Collopy had been arrested with
Kieran Keane, following Eddie Ryan's murder. Keane and
Treacy both refused. Despite being beaten and tortured, they
would not give in to the demand. They were both experienced
enough to know that their captors had one plan for all four of
them – murder. Hoods were then placed over their heads and
secured with duct tape.

After about an hour, Keane and Treacy were led out to a
waiting Nissan Micra car and pushed into the boot. Noddy
McCarthy drove the car and Galvin sat in the passenger seat.
The kidnappers brought their captives to a house in Roundwood
Estate, a middle-class area of Rosbrien, on the outskirts of the
city, which was owned by a relation of Galvin. They drove
the car into the garage of the house and ordered the uncle
and nephew to get out. Inside they were brought upstairs and
their hoods were taken off. The hostages were again ordered to
phone the Collopys and arrange to meet them on a country road
outside the city. The two men still refused to make the call.

Their captors had now been joined by 24-year-old James
McCarthy and by Christopher 'Smokey' Costelloe who had
'escaped' during the 'kidnap' of the Ryan brothers a week earlier.
Treacy overheard Dundon talking to someone on the phone.
"We've got them," said Dundon.

Ten minutes later the hostages were led down the stairs, at gunpoint, by Noddy McCarthy. They were brought out to a green Hiace van and pushed into the back where they were ordered to lie on the floor. Blankets were thrown over them.

Frog Eyes Stanners drove the van, with James McCarthy in the passenger seat and Smokey Costelloe in the back. Costelloe was armed with the gun that Noddy McCarthy had been using earlier. The van drove for around 35 minutes and eventually stopped on a lonely road, at an area called Drumbanna five miles outside Limerick City. David Stanners ordered Kieran Keane out of the van and pushed him to the ground. He stabbed Keane in the side of the head and then calmly shot the crime lord in the back of the head with a handgun. The gangland hard man collapsed onto the cold, wet road.

Costelloe and Stanners then turned their attention to Keane's terrified nephew and Costelloe began stabbing him in the throat. Treacy sliced the palm of his hand, as he tried to wrench the knife from his attacker's hand. Stanners grabbed the knife from Smokey Costelloe and continued stabbing Treacy.

Stanners stared into his victim's face and hissed: "This is the last face you are going to see." He stabbed Treacy several more times in the ear, neck and chest. In total Treacy suffered 17 serious stab wounds in the attack. Seriously injured, he fell to the ground and pretended to be dead. He heard James McCarthy shouting to the others: "Come on, come on, he's dead, he's dead."

The killers got into the van and drove back towards Limerick. They were convinced that the two men were dead. But their plan had backfired.

Before the attack, Treacy had managed to loosen the ties on his hands and when the van left he staggered to his uncle's side. He could hear Keane faintly breathing. Despite his appalling injuries, Treacy struggled to his feet and stumbled to a house up the road, to summon help. By the time help did arrive Keane was dead. An autopsy would later find that he died from a single gunshot wound to the head. He had also suffered six stab wounds near his left ear.

Owen Treacy was rushed to hospital, under armed guard,

where he underwent emergency surgery. The situation could have been a lot worse had the gang managed to lure the Collopys to the same spot. If their heinous plan had been successful, the road at Drumbanna would have been the scene of an unprecedented gangland slaughter.

As Gardaí rushed to the scene at Drumbanna, there was another dramatic development. Six hours later the Ryan brothers turned up at Athlone Garda Station. They looked remarkably unscathed considering that they were claiming that they had been held hostage for a week. Later that day the Ryans were the centre of attention at a very public street party in Kileely. The revellers drank cans of beer and posed for the crowd of press photographers and TV crews, who had come to cover this major gangland story of mystery and murder. Among the people celebrating were two members of the murder gang – James McCarthy and Smokey Costelloe.

Locally the Ryan brothers' story was greeted with scepticism – although no one dared voice their suspicions in the climate of fear that prevailed. Kieran Ryan stood smirking and laughing with his mates, while reporters asked him about what had happened to him and his brother.

"I got threatened not to talk to anyone. I don't know where I was held, I couldn't tell you. Our family had no hand, act or part in Kieran Keane's murder. We didn't do it," he said.

The killers decided to go into hiding and regroup when they learned that Treacy had survived the attack. They hung on to the hope that he would succumb to his injuries and die. There were recriminations between the gang about who had screwed up Treacy's murder. Meanwhile back at the city's Garda HQ, Chief Superintendent Kelly and his officers had the awesome task of trying to unravel the astonishing events of the past week.

Limerick's feuding had suddenly become a national crisis and the ongoing situation was discussed at Cabinet level. The Garda Commissioner of the day, Pat Byrne, sent scores of extra Gardaí from Dublin and Cork into Limerick, to prevent an all-out bloodbath and to assist in the complex investigation. In an effort to handle the mammoth workload, all leave for detectives in the city was cancelled. In the months that followed, fatigue and exhaustion was a common complaint, as officers worked 18 hour days.

For the first time ever, teams of the Emergency Response Unit were deployed to man checkpoints and mount foot patrols on the streets. A Garda helicopter was deployed on a semi-permanent basis to the city for several months and the Commissioner met with the Justice Minister to brief him on the unfolding events. He also visited Limerick with his deputies. At a press conference that afternoon, Chief Superintendent Kelly described the worsening situation as one of "utter madness".

Despite his critical injuries, Owen Treacy was able to identify his attackers. Detective Garda John Nagle visited Treacy in the intensive care ward of Limerick Regional Hospital three hours after the shooting. Although he was very seriously ill, he was coherent.

"Who stabbed you and who shot Kieran Keane?" the detective asked.

Treacy replied slowly: "Green Hiace". Then he whispered: "David 'Frog Eyes' Stanners, James McCarthy, Moyross and Smokey Costelloe."

Over the following weeks, Owen Treacy gradually recovered from his terrible injuries. He agreed to give the Gardaí a full statement of the events on the night of his uncle's murder. He could clearly identify six members of the abduction gang– Frog Eyes Stanners, Smokey Costelloe, James McCarthy, Dessie Dundon, Noddy McCarthy and Keith Galvin. Treacy was breaking from the accepted tradition among the gangs of never allowing the police to get involved in disputes.

But this was no ordinary situation.

The opposition were clearly hell bent on wiping out as many of the Keanes and Collopys as they could get their hands on. This was a plot to commit mass murder and Treacy's survival instincts told him to co-operate with the police.

As news leaked out that Treacy was going to recover and was prepared to testify against his attackers, the gangster was placed under 24-hour armed Garda protection. It was a rather awkward situation for a serious criminal but he knew the gang would make every effort to murder him before he reached the witness stand. In the hours after the murder, several members of the McCarthy/Dundon mob fled Limerick and went to the UK and Spain. Houses belonging to mob members and their families were burned. Chaser O'Brien was among a group of known criminals arrested for questioning, within hours of the murder. As soon as he was released without charge, he fled the country for Europe and never returned.

The Keane murder plot had seriously backfired for Murder Inc but this would in no way quell their ambitions. Both sides began to prepare for a further escalation in hostilities. While Treacy was under police protection, his gang were getting ready for an equally spectacular backlash – they planned to up the stakes and use bombs.

Within hours of the Keane murder, Gardaí realised that the same gang had been responsible for Brian Fitzgerald's murder. The detectives were making good progress in both investigations. By March 2003, the investigation into the events at Drumbanna had led to 34 people being arrested for questioning. This tally included the Ryan brothers and their Tipperary "host", who were quizzed about the alleged abduction. The file on the case eventually ran to over 5,000 pages, containing 720 individual statements.

The investigation teams had also focussed their attentions on the hit man James Martin Cahill. They were aware that he had been hired to do another murder. Philip Dean had told them about a meeting he had been at with Cahill and the Dublin-based godfather on January 12, 2003 – two days before Dean's arrest.

The godfather wanted Cahill to murder Declan 'Decie' Griffin the former criminal associate of PJ Judge. Griffin, who was a drug dealer and a controversial police informant, had tried to murder Larry McCarthy's cousin in a row over a woman. On November 3, Griffin had fired shots at the gangster's house. As a result the godfather took out a contract to kill Griffin. A few days after the murder of Brian Fitzgerald, Gardaí had arrested two suspected hit men from Northern Ireland. They had strong links with the Limerick mob and had been on their way to shoot Griffin. When the pair had been searched, officers found €16,000 in cash, a photograph of Griffin, a list of addresses for him and a Beretta pistol.

The Dublin gangster still wanted Griffin dead and in the January meeting had shown Cahill the addresses where Griffin lived and had also given him a picture of the victim. The hit man agreed to do the job for €20,000.

By the time he got round to doing the hit two months later, Cahill was being secretly watched by the Garda National Surveillance Unit. On the evening of March 21, a surveillance team spotted Cahill after he had taken delivery of an Uzi sub-machine gun. When the Emergency Response Unit moved in to stop him, Cahill tried to get away. He was arrested near Saggart in south County Dublin, after a short high speed chase.

The hit man was caught red-handed with the weapon and was taken to Kevin Street Garda Station in Dublin for questioning. While Cahill was being detained, detectives from Limerick interviewed him about Brian Fitzgerald's murder and put to him the allegations contained in Philip Dean's statement. Cahill denied everything. He was then brought before the Special Criminal Court where he was charged with possession of a firearm and ammunition. He was remanded in custody.

Just before Cahill's arrest, there had been more bad news for Murder Inc. The five members of the gang involved in Kieran Keane's murder were arrested in dawn swoops in Limerick and Tipperary. On March 23, three of them – James McCarthy, Frog Eyes Stanners and Smokey Costelloe – were formally charged with the false imprisonment of Kieran Keane and Owen Treacy. A week later, Noddy McCarthy and Dessie Dundon were also charged with two counts of false imprisonment.

The arrest and charge of six members of the McCarthy/ Dundon organisation, in such a short period of time, was a major victory for the police. Two of the people they now had in custody had also been involved in Brian Fitzgerald's murder. As a result of Cahill's arrest, the mob had good reason to be concerned for their collective freedom. The hit man then sent word that Dean had turned.

The McCarthy/Dundons confirmed this through their

extensive prison networks. Their former gofer, who was on remand, had been taken out of the general prison population. He was locked up in solitary confinement for his own safety. Dean's testimony could directly implicate Larry McCarthy Junior and Cahill in the Fitzgerald murder. Like Owen Treacy, he could prove to be very dangerous to all of them.

To encourage Dean to change his mind, McCarthy decided to target his family. On the night of April 9, the gang organised a petrol bomb attack which extensively damaged the couple's home in Handsworth in Birmingham. As a result of that incident, Dean's partner, Amy Harrison and their two children – who were aged three and five – were taken into the British Witness Protection Programme.

The day after the attack, Dean was jailed for three years when he pleaded guilty to the three firearms charges. In June, he was formally accepted into the WPP in Ireland. In the meantime the Gardaí kept up the pressure on the gangs. That same month, the five killers – James McCarthy, Frog Eyes Stanners, Noddy McCarthy, Dessie Dundon and Smokey Costelloe – were further charged with the murder of Kieran Keane and the attempted murder of Owen Treacy.

By the summer of 2003, at least 30 of the serious players in both gangs were in custody, awaiting trial on a variety of charges. These included nine men who were arrested during an all-out riot outside a fast food joint on the Ennis Road in May. The number of Limerick gangsters in custody caused serious headaches in the prison system. The authorities went to great lengths to keep the feuding hoods apart, to prevent a flare up behind bars.

Several shipments of drugs were intercepted and a large quantity of firearms was seized, as a result of the offensive. Detectives in the city then made a disturbing discovery when they received intelligence that the Keane/Collopy gang had been trying to acquire more bombs. Three months earlier, the Gardaí had intercepted members of the gang as they were transporting pipe bombs in a car from Dublin. Then, in early June, detectives learned of an advanced plot to plant a car bomb. It was in a bid to kill several members of the McCarthy/Dundon mob in one attack.

Detective Inspector Jim Brown's officers were tipped off that a shed behind a bungalow in the countryside at Mungret, County Limerick, was being used as a bomb-making factory. An undercover investigation had uncovered a link between the factory and members of the Continuity IRA. On June 3, a large force of officers, backed up by the ERU, raided the property. They recovered a large amount of bomb-making equipment, a machine gun, hundreds of rounds of ammunition, cocaine worth €30,000 and a cocaine packaging press.

The officers also found an under-car bomb which was about to be delivered to Limerick City. Army Bomb Squad experts later described the device as being capable of killing up to four or five people and injuring many more.

Four men were arrested and later charged in connection with the haul. Thirty six-year-old Declan 'Darby' Sheehy, a close criminal associate and friend of Kieran and Christy Keane, was found standing close to the device. Also arrested were 58-year-old Richard Smith and his 30-year-old son Sean, who were living in the rented house. They were originally from Brixton in London. The fourth man was 31-year-old Michael Scanlan, who had close links with the CIRA and the Keanes.

The Smiths gave Gardaí the names and confirmed the involvement of several criminals and terrorists in the operation. But they refused to testify in court. Richard Smith was later jailed for five years in connection with the find. Sean Smith, who admitted that he was to get €10,000 from the Keane/Collopys for delivering the bomb to Limerick, was sentenced to 12 years. Scanlan got five years and Sheehy was acquitted by a jury.

The arms seizure at Mungret also had a major impact on the Brian Fitzgerald murder inquiry and led directly to a major international operation. Forensic experts in the ongoing investigation had established that the murder weapon had been re-activated. The Uzi sub-machine gun seized from James Martin Cahill in March 2003 and the weapon found in Mungret were also found to have been re-activated. An analysis of other weapons which had been seized by Gardaí during the previous 12 months found another three such weapons. It was established that they were all coming from the same source and Gardaí tracked them to the UK. Detectives from Limerick travelled to meet with the chiefs at the National Criminal Intelligence Service in London. They requested help in tracking down the suppliers of the weapons to the two gangs.

As a result, an undercover surveillance operation was mounted by the Gardaí, in conjunction with Scotland Yard's anti-terrorism branch and the Lancashire Police. The murder hunt team had established a link between the McCarthy/ Dundons and Limerick ex-pat James Patrick Moloney, who was living in Bradford, West Yorkshire. Moloney had been supplying weapons to the McCarthy/Dundons and the Continuity IRA for several months. The firearms had then been transported to Ireland by Philip Dean, on the instructions of Larry McCarthy Junior.

The weapons came from two members of the Morecambe Rifle and Pistol Club on the Lancashire coast. Robert Naylor (49) and James Greenwood (56) were both gun enthusiasts who bought deactivated weapons as a hobby. But they used their skills to make easy money restoring the firing mechanisms in machine-guns and pistols and then selling them to criminal gangs.

On August 10, 2003, police arrested Moloney, Naylor and Greenwood after the gun enthusiasts delivered three automatic weapons to the Limerick supplier. Moloney, told police that he had intended selling the weapons to "people who might want to buy them". In the follow-up investigation another 40 reactivated weapons were recovered in Morecambe in November. The three men were subsequently convicted and jailed at the Old Bailey in November 2004. Moloney pleaded guilty and was sentenced to seven years while Naylor and Greenwood were jailed for ten and nine years respectively.

* * * *

Despite the extraordinary number of successes being scored against the gangs, as a result of the investigations in Limerick, there was no let up in the violence on the streets. On July 3,

2003, John Ryan was shot dead, as he laid patio stones for a friend in the front of a house in Thomondgate. He was shot four times by the pillion passenger of a motorbike and died a short time later in hospital. The two suspects for the attack were teenage members of the Keane/Collopy gang – they were aged 16 and 17. The next generation of killers were already being blooded. Later that evening it was the turn of the Keanes to throw a party similar to the one the Ryans had following Kieran Keane's execution.

Several members of the Keane family were arrested for questioning about the murder including Kieran Keane's widow Sophie and their 14-year-old son, Joseph. When Gardaí searched the teenager, they found a note in his clenched fist. It made for chilling reading and illustrated why there will never be peace between the warring clans.

The note contained a list of hand-written names. At the top was written: 'People who set up and killed my father, all will be dead by the time I am 32, now I am 14. That's a promise boys.' That was followed by the list of names headed by the word "scumbags". The list included the names of the main players in the McCarthy/Dundon gang, including the five men then awaiting trial for his father's murder. It also included the names of Larry McCarthy Junior, Anthony Kelly, Cowboy Hanley, Jim O'Brien, Keith Calvin and two members of the Ryan clan. The people who were in prison had a '?' beside their names while those still at large had a tick.

At the bottom of the note was written: 'Date 17/5/03. Time exactly at 1.47am. People with ? are locked up. The people with the tick will be got before the other six and all of them will be got before I am 32 because all of the people who are getting locked up will be out by then. They will be got by me or somebody else for my father, Kieran Keane's death.'

The note was signed off and addressed to his mother with the words: "I love you Mam.'

Two years later, Keane was saying goodbye to her.

Joseph Keane and two others, kicked 18-year-old Darren Coughlan to death in a case of mistaken identity on November 8, 2005. They thought he was another teenager aligned to the

McCarthy/Dundons. Their victim had nothing to do with crime and became another innocent victim of the madness. As a result, Keane and his 19-year-old cousin, Richard Treacy, were each jailed for six years for manslaughter. Their accomplice, Shane Kelly from Saint Mary's Park, who had also been investigated as part of the John Ryan murder, got seven years. As they were being led away to a waiting prison van, the three killers smiled and winked at their family and friends. Going to prison didn't seem to bother them at all.

On July 25, 2003, John Dundon was arrested by police in Manchester after they were tipped off about his whereabouts by Gardaí in Limerick. They had an extradition warrant for Dundon's return, to face a charge of threatening to burn a prison officer's home. A month later, he was flown back to Cork Airport where he was arrested by Limerick detectives and placed in custody. In the end he only spent a few months in prison for the charge. In the meantime the violence continued.

On August 21st Anthony Kelly was in the kitchen of his plush mansion, Cragg House, which stands high on a hill looking down on Kilrush. He was in the process of making tea around 11pm when a gunman fired several shots through the window, hitting him in the chest and arm. Despite his injuries, Kelly managed to call the Gardaí and he was rushed to hospital.

The following day, Gardaí appealed for information about the incident. When they were asked for a possible motive, Superintendent John Kerin was candid. "We are keeping an open mind as to who was involved in the shooting at this stage and we have not ruled out a link with the ongoing feud in Limerick," he said.

The man suspected of carrying out the attack had himself been shot by one of the Dundon brothers. The criminal blamed Kelly for supplying the weapon to Dundon and he wanted revenge.

After emergency surgery, Anthony Kelly recovered from his injuries. A month after the shooting Kelly was well enough to be arrested by detectives investigating Brian Fitzgerald's murder. He admitted to detectives that he knew Philip Dean and that he was a friend of Larry McCarthy Junior. However, he denied any involvement in the security manager's murder. He was released without charge while the investigations continued. In the meantime the McCarthy/Dundons were plotting another revenge attack. Twenty-three-year-old Michael Campbell McNamara was a member of the Keane/Collopy gang and had been centrally involved in the ongoing bloodshed. He was the boyfriend of Christy Keane's daughter. Campbell McNamara had been involved in a number of attacks on the McCarthy/Dundons, including setting fire to their houses. A grenade was found in a car which he had abandoned and he was arrested for questioning in connection with John Ryan's murder.

If Murder Inc had a check list for selecting a victim, then Campbell McNamara ticked all the boxes. The gangster was very careful about his movements especially after the McCarthy/Dundon crew had lured Kieran Keane to his death. Personal security was the top priority of every criminal in Limerick. On October 20, Campbell McNamara arranged to meet his friend Andrew Nolan to buy a shotgun. McNamara would only arrange such an appointment if he trusted the person he was dealing with. He had no reason to suspect Nolan. But he was wrong to trust him.

When McNamara arrived to meet Nolan at the Carew Park Estate, he walked into a death trap similar to the one that had claimed the life of Kieran Keane. Dillon had been forced to set up McNamara by three members of the McCarthy/Dundons. They took their victim away to Barry's Field, an area of isolated waste ground nearby. The three thugs then beat and tortured their victim and tried to force him to lure the head of the Collopy clan, Brian Collopy, to meet him. But Collopy was not so easily duped. His instincts saved his life.

The mutilated body of Michael Campbell McNamara was found the next day by a member of the public. His armed and legs were bound and there was evidence that he had suffered horrific torture before death. He had been stabbed at least ten times, in the back and chest. The young gang member was then blasted in the back of the head. That shot was followed by a second that was fired at point blank range at his pelvis and buttocks. The shot, which led to his death, caused horrifying injuries to his body. Nolan was subsequently jailed after he pleaded guilty to a charge of reckless endangerment. He told Gardaí who had forced him to lure Campbell McNamara to his death but there was no way he would become a witness for the prosecution.

A week before the murder of McNamara, Kenneth Dundon was also keeping up his family's reputation for savagery. He stabbed his wife's drug addict lover to death in a London flat. Anne McCarthy had started an affair with 50-year-old heroin addict Christopher Jacobs after they had met at a dole office, a few months earlier. Dundon would later claim that he became "angry" after his alcoholic wife spent a number of nights with Jacobs, in his flat in Hoxton, North London.

On October 2, Dundon had spotted his wife in a market and took her back to the Dundon family home near Bethnal Green in East London. Jacobs had tried to "rescue" his lover but Dundon threw him out on the street. The affair, however, continued and on the night of October 8, Dundon, wearing a balaclava, kicked in Jacobs' door, armed with a knife. In a blind, murderous fury he set about Jacobs, stabbing him repeatedly in the face and neck.

Jacobs suffered appalling injuries, including an 11cm deep wound to the left side of his face. It severed blood vessels and caused him to choke to death on his own blood. Anne McCarthy Dundon, who was in the flat at the time of the attack, identified her husband to the police and he was arrested hours later. He denied the murder and was freed on station bail, pending further police investigations. Dundon fled home to Limerick.

A month later the British authorities issued a European arrest warrant for Kenneth Dundon and he was posted on Scotland Yard's Most Wanted list.

* * * *

The trial of the five McCarthy/Dundon members for the murder of Kieran Keane began in Cloverhill court in Clondalkin, West Dublin on the morning of November 5, 2003. It had been due to commence in October before Mr Justice Paul Carney at the Central Criminal Court, sitting in Limerick. The trial had to be moved back to Dublin, however, when the court found it impossible to empanel a jury of 12 people from a total panel of 529 people summoned to attend the court. The sense of fear was plain to see. Jurors presented medical certificates for myriad medical problems but mainly for 'stress and anxiety' because of the seriousness of the case. Jurors clearly felt that the gangs could get to them. The failure to run the trial in Limerick was a major embarrassment to the State and a victory for mob rule.

The court in Cloverhill was deemed to be the most secure for the trial because it is attached to Cloverhill Remand Prison. There was tight security in and around the building. Arrangements were made to protect the judge and prosecution counsel. The seven men and five women of the jury were driven to the court complex, under armed escort. Everyone entering the court walked through electronic scanning equipment.

Throughout the 31 day trial, the five killers appeared confident and cocky, smiling and waving to family and friends in the court. They sneered across at members of the Keane family, including the murdered man's widow, Sophie Keane. The five gang members sat in a row beside each other, behind their five individual legal defence teams. They denied all the charges against them.

Owen Treacy proved to be a reliable and strong witness. He was not intimidated by the stares and threats being directed at him by the five men sitting in the dock. At one stage during Treacy's lengthy cross-examination, on November 13, 2003, John Dundon, who was in the back of the court room, approached Treacy's wife, Donna Treacy. In a loud voice he snarled at her: "I swear on my baby's life that when this is over I am going to kill Owen Treacy." Dundon didn't seem to mind that his threats had been witnessed by several Gardaí, as well as by the Keane and Treacy families.

Detectives immediately arrested John Dundon and took him into custody. Two days later, he was charged with threatening to kill Owen Treacy. He was remanded in custody. On the evening of Saturday, December 20, after two days and nights of deliberations, the jury found the five men guilty of murder, attempted murder and false imprisonment. Mr Justice Carney sentenced all five men to the mandatory life sentence for murder and deferred sentencing them on the remaining three counts until February 3, 2004.

Keane's widow, Sophie, took the stand in order to tell the court how the murder had affected her and her family. "They are animals," she said of the five men who had just been convicted. "My life stood still and my life was finished the day they took my husband's life." She was then asked by prosecuting counsel what her husband had done to deserve such a death. Before she could reply, one of his killers shouted: "He sold drugs and killed people. He killed Eddie Ryan."

As the five men were led away in handcuffs, to a convoy of prison vans, Noddy McCarthy shouted towards Treacy and the rest of the Keanes: "For every action there's a reaction – remember that. You'll be looking over your shoulder for the rest of your life boy."

James McCarthy snarled at Treacy, calling him a bastard.

The following February, the Central Criminal Court returned to Limerick, amid massive security, to pass sentence on the five men for the outstanding convictions. It was intended as a symbolic gesture to remind the gangs that the rule of law would not be intimidated or thwarted. Mr Justice Paul Carney sentenced the McCarthy/Dundon killers to 15 years each, on the counts of attempted murder and a further seven years each on the two false imprisonment charges.

As sentence was passed, the five men whooped with laughter, cheered and shouted threats at the Keanes. But Mr Justice Carney had a stark warning for the ebullient thugs and their clans. "Life sentences have already been imposed on each of the accused in this case. I wanted to say primarily to the friends and supporters of the accused on the outside that each of them will die in prison unless there is intervention in their cases by the Parole Board. The Parole Board is entirely independent, but it seems unlikely to intervene while the feud is a live issue. This should be borne in mind by the friends and supporters of the accused outside and the accused themselves."

A week later, Gardaí arrested Kenneth Dundon in Limerick. He was remanded in custody, where most of his family and friends were now residing. Dundon fought the British extradition all the way to the Supreme Court but was sent back to face trial in September 2005. He made legal history as the first person in Ireland to be extradited on an EU warrant. A year later, he pleaded guilty to the lesser charge of manslaughter and was jailed for a relatively lenient six years. Together with time already served on remand and remission, he was nearing the end of this sentence at the time of going to print.

The warring gangs had suffered considerable damage at the hands of the Gardaí by the time Kieran Keane's killers had been jailed for life. By Summer 2004, 25 of the major players in the gangs were serving lengthy sentences, for a variety of serious offences. The crack down by the police had brought about an uneasy peace and the murder rate had dropped – for the time being at least. Brian Collopy, who had taken over the reins in the Keane/Collopy mob, had even tried to organise a type of peace pact between the gangs. The constant police pressure had proven to be very bad for business. It was causing the gangland equivalent of a serious economic downturn.

* * * *

Despite the relative calm, the criminal gangs had not gone away. Wayne Dundon was still one of the most feared men ever to walk the streets of Limerick. In August 2004, the *Sunday World* reported how he was involved in a campaign of intimidation to drive families from their homes in the BallinacurraWeston area of the Southside of the city.

Dundon and his henchmen had approached an innocent family, who had nothing to do with crime, as they had put their parents' home up for sale. Wayne Dundon told them that if they didn't accept a bid from the gang – which was way below the market value of the property – then they would not be selling the house to anyone. When the owners refused, the house was fire-bombed and daubed with graffiti declaring: "The Keanes are scum."

Dundon also forced other families to move out and sell their houses to his family, for as little as €10,000. The "neighbours from hell" moved into the Ballincurra-Weston area after Limerick City Council had successfully evicted members of the McCarthy and Dundon families from Local Authority houses on the Northside of the city.

While the local Gardaí kept him at the top of their 'most wanted' list, Wayne Dundon had proved hard to catch. But then the psychotic thug walked himself straight into a lot of trouble and illustrated his malevolent nature.

On the evening of December 19, 2004, 18-year-old Ryan Lee was standing at the door of his uncle's pub, Brannigans Bar on Musgrave Street. Ryan worked as a bar man and was taking a quick break in the night air.

Wayne Dundon dropped off his wife and 14-year-old sister at the pub. Ryan told Dundon's wife that she could not bring the child into the pub with her – it was against the law. The girl protested and claimed she was over 18 but she had no ID to prove it.

Dundon then appeared beside the young bar man. "What's the problem?" he growled.

When Ryan explained, Wayne Dundon became aggressive. "It's her first night out, give her a fuckin' break," he demanded.

The bar man said it was against the law to have a minor on the premises late at night. In a subsequent interview with the *Sunday World*, he recalled what happened next:

"He stepped up close to my face and put his finger in the shape of a gun and said to me: 'Fuck you, you're dead.' He was really big and intimidating. Up close you can see the evil in his eyes. I thought that he was going to hit me there and then but he didn't. He said to his wife: 'Are you staying?' and grabbed his sister by the hand and took her back to the car. He kept staring back at me, even when he got into the car. He watched me for a short while and turned the car on the road and then he sped off so hard that the tyres spun on the road."

Exactly 28 minutes later, a man matching Dundon's description was picked up on the pub's CCTV cameras, arriving outside on a motorbike. Still wearing his helmet, he walked through the bar and in behind the counter. As he walked up the length of the counter, he looked closely at each staff member. Then he went into the front bar where Ryan Lee was pulling pints for the locals.

The gunman stood behind the bar and produced a large, long-barrelled handgun. He took aim and fired a single shot from close range. It hit the barman in the side of his left knee. The bullet travelled straight through his kneecap and out the other side, shattering it in the process. The gunman tried to go out through the front door of the bar but it was locked. Then he turned to go back out the way he'd come in.

On his way past his victim, who was lying on the ground in shock and pain, Dundon decided to fire another shot into him. This time the bullet hit Ryan's right hip, travelled through his groin and lodged in his left leg. As Dundon left the premises, the owner of the bar, Steve Collins, went after him. The gangster turned and fired a single shot at him. Ryan Lee was rushed to hospital where he underwent emergency surgery and remained hospitalised for two weeks. He was unable to walk for several months.

The attack was further evidence that the Dundon's had no regard for human life and didn't care who they shot. But Ryan Lee knew who had threatened him. Two days later, Gardaí arrested Wayne Dundon and brought him in for questioning about the incident. While he was being interviewed by Detective Gardaí Arthur Ryan and Brendan Casey, Dundon suddenly jumped up and launched an attack on the two officers. In the melee that followed, he smashed Detective Garda Ryan's jaw and also injured his colleague. Again Wayne Dundon showed no concern for the fact that the whole attack in the incident room had been recorded on tape.

Wayne Dundon was charged with assault and making threats to kill and brought before the local District Court. Gardaí objected to bail and insisted that Dundon be held in custody, pending his trial because of the danger he posed to his victim. When the court remanded him in custody, Wayne Dundon dropped his trousers and mooned at the judge. He was sent to prison where his father and brothers, John and Dessie, were already in residence.

A month later, in January 2005, John Dundon was jailed for four and a half years by the Circuit Criminal Court in Dublin, after he pleaded guilty to the charge of threatening to kill Owen Treacy. Judge Yvonne Murphy described the offence as a "grave crime" which represented "an offence against public justice".

Meanwhile Ryan Lee and his family were placed under armed police protection. Despite the fact that Dundon was in prison, he ensured his associates made every effort to force the bar man to withdraw his complaint. The intimidation scenario bore chilling comparisons to the experiences of Brian Fitzgerald before his murder. Threats were made to extended family and friends of the victim and there was also an arson attack on the bar.

On the night before the trial began in May 2005, a letter was dropped through the door at the home of Ryan Lee's girlfriend. It was addressed to Ryan's uncle Steve Collins, who was also about to give evidence in the trial. It read: "Steve, if you think it's over, think again. Look at all the people that are dead. Look, if you want to call it quits you know what to do. If not, we will attack you, your staff and your businesses… it's up to you."

Before the trial, Wayne Dundon's victim was informed by the prosecution that he could not in any way refer to the shooting incident in his direct testimony. This was because Dundon was appearing on a charge of threatening to kill or cause serious harm. Although there were ample grounds to suspect that Wayne Dundon was the actual shooter, it could not be proved so he wasn't charged with the offence. Throughout the six day trial at Limerick Circuit Criminal Court, he continuously sneered and sniggered across the courtroom at his victim and his family. In the end the last laugh was on Dundon when the jury found him guilty as charged.

Detective Sergeant Eamon O'Neill then gave evidence of Wayne Dundon's previous criminal record before Judge Carroll Moran. The experienced detective, who had been a police officer in the city for over 12 years, described Wayne Dundon as one of the most violent criminals he had ever come across in Limerick.

The court was also shown the CCTV footage of his attack on Detective Gardaí Ryan and Casey.

Judge Carroll Moran sentenced Wayne Dundon to ten years for the threats to Ryan Lee's life. He also imposed two concurrent three year sentences, for the assaults on the detectives.

The jailing of the Dundons was a source of considerable relief to both the Gardaí and the ordinary decent citizens of Limerick. It was also welcomed by the other hoods the psychos had in their sights. As a result of the convictions of Wayne and John, local wags gave the family a new nickname. They were now called the "Dum Dum Dundons" – they had finally been caught just because they couldn't stop themselves from mouthing off and threatening people.

* * * *

The investigation of Brian Fitzgerald's murder had remained a high priority for the Gardaí in Limerick. A huge file had been compiled around the admissions and statements of Philip Dean. Officers had spent hundreds of hours painstakingly corroborating every piece of information he had offered up. They had followed up hundreds of leads and their enquiries had helped smash an important arms smuggling operation. It had also led to the conviction of a number of significant players, including the actual hit man James Martin Cahill.

But then disaster struck.

Philip Dean was due for release from prison early in 2005. But in the meantime the intimidation and the enormity of testifying against a major criminal gang had eventually got to him. The gang had relayed threats to him through their contacts in the prison where he was being held. Gardaí had also learned of a plot to try and kill him. Despite the fact that both he and his young family were in the Witness Protection Programme, and he had been assured of being set up in a new life abroad, he told Chief Superintendent Gerry Kelly's officers that he could not go through with it. When Dean left prison, he and his family left the WPP. No one will ever know if the mob had made him an offer he could not refuse.

In the absence of a witness from inside the mob, the huge amount of evidence the investigation had compiled was nothing more than circumstantial. They didn't have enough of a case to charge the main players in the conspiracy. For several months, it appeared that one of the worst murders in Limerick's bloody history would remain unsolved. But then there was a rather unexpected development.

James Martin Cahill was becoming extremely edgy and paranoid, as he sat in his prison cell. Neither he nor the rest of the McCarthy/Dundon mob knew that Dean had decided to withdraw his evidence. They were nervously watching and waiting to see what the cops would do next. Cahill knew from the allegations contained in Dean's statement, which had been put to him while he was in custody in March 2003, that he was very likely to be convicted of the murder.

The hit man also began to believe that Murder Inc would see him as the weak link and make efforts to have him killed in prison. He knew the mindset of his fellow mobsters. They had no problem murdering anyone who posed a threat to them. It was a fact that the gang had people in every prison in the country. If they wanted, they could easily have Cahill dealt with. The hit man would be inside until at least March 2008. It would be at least another two and a half years before he was eligible for release for the firearms charge. After a while he could take no more and phoned the Gardaí in Limerick.

When the investigation team at Mayorstone Garda Station first received the call, in May 2005, they could scarcely believe it. It is a rather rare occurrence for the suspected hit man in an investigation to invite the cops to meet him. When two detectives met Cahill in Portlaoise Prison, he was obviously edgy and very nervous. His opening words were: "They are going to kill me." Then he informed the astonished officers that he was prepared to make a full confession and also testify against the rest of the gang. But before he named names he wanted a transfer to a more secure facility.

"I shot him and no one else. I want to get this out of my system. I want to get this out in the open," he said. Then he told the officers of how he had attended a meeting before the murder where he first heard of the plans to kill Brian Fitzgerald. He was to be paid €10,000, in two payments of €5,000 each.

The murderer claimed he had been shown how to use the firearm and was told by one of them to: "Put one in that c***'s head." Cahill then described how he pointed his gun at the back of Brian Fitzgerald's head and turned away as he pulled the trigger. He said his body was shaking as he carried out the killing.

Over the following weeks, Cahill made a number of statements in which he outlined in detail everything he knew about the murder of the night-club security manager. Cahill said he wanted to be taken into the Witness Protection Programme but was prepared to plead guilty to the murder, without any preconditions. He wanted to clear his conscience.

Cahill's admissions were an astonishing development. The detectives involved in the case already had a huge amount of evidence gathered which corroborated a lot of what the hit man told them. He confirmed much of what they already knew about the crime. There were a number of urgent meetings with the DPP to discuss the new developments. On June 16, 2005, James Martin Cahill was formally charged with the murder of Brian Fitzgerald.

Since he'd fled the country after the Fitzgerald and Keane murders, Jim 'Chaser' O'Brien, had continued to build a huge international drug trafficking operation. Operating between bases in Spain, Holland and Belgium, he began organising large scale drug and gun smuggling routes between the continent, UK and Ireland. Larry McCarthy Junior, who was then living between Spain and the UK, had also got involved in the business. In 2004, a major international investigation had been mounted into Chaser O'Brien, involving the Gardaí and their colleagues in Holland, Belgium and the UK. The Operations, codenamed 'Sword', 'Slue', 'Pub' and 'Lotje', focused on O'Brien and one of his closest sidekicks, 28-year-old Cecil Kinsella from Tipperary. In September 2003, Kinsella and Christopher Maguire, who was also from Clonmel, had been arrested with ecstasy and cocaine valued at over €1.8 million. Kinsella had also been caught with an automatic pistol, equipped with a silencer. When the two men got bail, they had skipped and joined O'Brien in Holland.

O'Brien had sent the two fugitives to run operations for him in the UK, where they'd teamed up with Larry McCarthy Junior. The 2004 international investigation revealed that O'Brien had extensive links with criminal organisations all over Europe and was involved in the smuggling of every type of narcotic, as well as firearms. O'Brien ran his operation from Antwerp, in conjunction with two criminals from Belgium and Holland. Over the period of a year, the multi-jurisdictional investigation had led to the seizure of huge amounts of cocaine, ecstasy, heroin and illegal cigarettes in four countries.

In the UK, Cecil Kinsella and McGuire had been tracked down and extradited back to Ireland to face drug and firearms charges. In July 2005, Kinsella was jailed for ten years for drug trafficking and possession of firearms. McGuire got six years for the same offences. On October 27, 2005, Chaser O'Brien was arrested by Belgian Federal Police, following a surveillance operation by Belgian and Dutch cops. He was detained under Belgian legislation for being the head of a criminal organisation. O'Brien was also arrested in relation to the large scale trafficking of ecstasy, cocaine and hashish. O'Brien, who had been living under the name Yam Kaminski, was also charged in connection with a seizure of a large amount of weaponry and explosives including four kilos of semtex. It was one of the largest organised crime investigations in Belgium's history.

At the same time, his two Belgian partners were also arrested. A cache of machine guns and pistols were seized at a premises controlled by one of the men, 52-year-old Redgy Tygat. Across the border, Dutch cops arrested O'Brien's other partner, one Edwin Kanters. When the police raided Kanters' home they discovered a major ecstasy factory. The criminal was in the process of packing a consignment of 300,000 ecstasy tablets which were destined for O'Brien's Irish associates.

The arrest of O'Brien was another serious blow to Murder Inc. He was subsequently convicted for membership of a criminal gang and jailed for three years for leading a criminal organisation. He was also jailed for another five years by a court in Antwerp for firearms, explosives and drug trafficking offences.

The ongoing enquiries into the smuggling of illegal firearms also turned the heat up on Larry McCarthy Junior, Police identified a flat in Hackney, East London where the Limerick hood was running a glorified gun warehouse, in conjunction with a number of other English gangsters. McCarthy was arrested with two others when police raided the flat and found a Mach II sub-machine gun, more than 750 bullets and 500 blank rounds.

In 2006, McCarthy was subsequently jailed for 11 years at Southwark Crown Court, after being found guilty of possession of a firearm with intent to endanger life and conspiracy to possess illegal weapons. The gang boss was classified as a Category A prisoner and sent to a maximum security prison.

* * * *

Two weeks after the arrest of 'Chaser' O'Brien it became obvious that there were more problems for Murder Inc, when Cahill pleaded guilty to the murder of Brian Fitzgerald in the Central Criminal Court on November 14, 2005. There was tight security for the hearing, as cops were all too aware that the rotund hit man was now a major target for one of the most dangerous gangs in Europe.

After entering his plea, the court was given details of how Cahill carried out the contract murder. Detective Sergeant Seamus Nolan from Henry Street Garda Station told prosecuting counsel, Mr Denis Vaughan Buckley SC, that Cahill was one of two assailants who had gone to Brian Fitzgerald's house at Brookhaven Walk in Corbally, in the early hours of November 28, 2002. They were wearing motorcycle helmets and waited for him in the bushes. Det. Sgt. Nolan described how the bouncer had struggled and shouted at the two men, before a number of shots were discharged and he fell to the ground injured. Cahill pursued his victim and shot him twice in the back of the head, as he lay on the ground. Alice Fitzgerald sobbed in the witness box, as she described how the murder had left her devastated.

"Brian was only one man in the world but he was all the world to me. Brian wasn't just my husband, he was my best friend. He was a major part of my life. We grew up together," she said, as she wept.

Brian's widow said that she and her husband did not have much, but they had worked hard for what they did have. "We had planned for a future with my two sons, a future that we won't see now," she continued.

Alice spoke of her husband's love of sport which he had passed onto his oldest son Aaron. After the murder, she had been forced to leave her job which she had held for 17 years as she was medically unfit for work. She was left to rear her young family on a widow's pension of €180 a week because her anxious children feared she would not return home if she went to work.

"There are days when I can't open my front door because of regular flashbacks. I can smell the smoke of the gunfire and the loud bangs I will never forget. I feel I will never again be safe or happy. I have not spent one night in my home alone," she added. Cahill apologised to the Fitzgerald family, through his counsel Mr Brendan Nix SC, for the appalling suffering he had caused them. Taking the witness stand the hit man told Mr. Justice Paul Carney: "I am willing to say that I will testify if a further case is coming."

In a pleading voice he asked that all the evidence and transcripts be kept on file in case he was unable to testify. "I feel my life is in danger in prison, not just from prisoners but from prison officers because of what I feel in this case," he said. "What I am trying to say is that I will testify against people. That's why I feel my life is in danger." Mr Justice Carney sentenced Cahill to a mandatory life sentence for the murder and remarked to the court: "I think I understand what the accused is saying". He said however, that evidence from the case would be returned to the Gardaí in accordance with the law. He directed that a transcript of the proceedings be placed on the court file.

As Cahill was being led away in handcuffs, and surrounded by armed detectives and prison officers, he turned and shouted:

"Ask him [Judge] to bring the killers to justice."

The plump, balding killer looked a pathetic sight as he was led to the waiting prison van. He looked agitated and scared and shouted to reporters: "I am going to be murdered in my cell tonight or in the next few days. Watch."

Cahill had every reason to worry. Back in Limerick, the gang violence had continued unabated. Between 2005 and 2006, another six men were shot, stabbed and kicked to death as a direct result of the feuds. At least 20 people had been injured. Gardaí made several arrests and seized firearms. Among those captured was an Egyptian national called Ibrihme Hassan, who had been sent from Dublin to carry out a contract hit in June 2006. He was arrested by undercover Gardaí in possession of a firearm before he got to his target.

In the meantime, the Fitzgerald investigation team compiled another bulky file for the DPP. They recommended charging up to seven individuals in connection with the murder based on the evidence of Cahill which they had been able to corroborate. They were also hopeful that they could convince Dean to change his mind and testify in the case.

On October 17, 2006, Anthony Kelly was the first man to be arrested and charged with the murder of Brian Fitzgerald.

Two weeks later Kelly applied for bail to the Dublin High Court. Detective Sergeant Seamus Nolan told the High Court that Anthony Kelly and an associate, Larry McCarthy Junior, had recruited Cahill for the murder of Brian Fitzgerald. He said Cahill was prepared to give evidence against the accused. He also revealed that Philip Dean had been placed in the Witness Protection Programme because of fears for his safety, after he gave police a substantial amount of information.

Detective Sergeant Nolan made a strenuous objection. He made a number of remarkable disclosures, which are not often heard in an Irish court, to support his case. He told the court that there was a fear that Kelly would leave the jurisdiction and would take serious steps to make sure Cahill did not appear to give evidence against him. "They are even more at risk of being murdered now that he has been charged," the officer said.

The detective said the accused had tried to sell his home

and that Kelly's furniture firms were a cover for a massive drugs and firearms importation business. He accused Kelly of being one of the country's biggest importers.

When it was put to Detective Sergeant Nolan, by Kelly's counsel, that his sister had offered a substantial €75,000 bond to secure his bail, the detective replied candidly: "I would object to €75 million. He drives a car which is worth in excess of €100,000 and has substantial interests in Morocco, Europe and China. I believe he is closely linked with criminals in this area. I believe Mr Kelly should not be granted bail. I do not think any assurance would ensure that he will turn up at court. I believe there is a substantial and real risk witnesses will be murdered, even within the confines of prison."

"From speaking to Mr Cahill himself, he clearly outlines the efforts made previously to assassinate Mr Dean [going] to and from prison. There was a female, I believe, noting his movements with a view to pointing him out so he could be shot. Consideration was given to using a rocket launcher to blow up the transport used."

Mr Justice Paul Butler said that he was not overly concerned about the flight risk but he was refusing bail on the grounds that the Gardaí had a genuine fear that witnesses would be interfered with.

On December 5, 2006, Dessie and John Dundon and a third man were also charged with the murder. There was tight security around Limerick District Court when the three arrived at the building, in a convoy of prison vans and ERU jeeps. Detectives armed with machine guns patrolled the area and marksmen had been placed on the roof. The three men – all of whom were already in custody – were officially remanded in custody.

Two weeks later the Supreme Court also rejected an appeal by Anthony Kelly seeking to overturn the High Court's refusal to grant him bail for the murder charge.

Even from behind the prison walls, the Dundons were dangerous men. A few weeks before they were charged with the Fitzgerald murder, one of the brothers had been linked to another horrific crime in which an innocent person had been executed. Gardaí investigating the murder of young Latvian mum, Baiba Saulite, in November 2006 believed that John Dundon had organised the weapon and the logistics for the crime, from his prison cell. He had contacted Martin 'Marlo' Hyland, who was an associate of the gang, and told him to arrange the killing. *(See Chapters Four and Five.)*

As soon as Cahill revealed that he was prepared to testify, the Dundons began hatching an extraordinary plan to ensure that he didn't. Such was the level of fear that the gang had the ability to get to the hit man, that he was moved to a landing by himself in another prison. All his food was specially prepared to ensure that it wasn't poisoned, after prison staff found rat pellets in the prison kitchen.

From their prison cells, Wayne and Dessie Dundon then set up an arms plot worthy of an international terrorist group. They wanted to buy an awesome arsenal of weapons, including assault rifles and rocket launchers. The weapons would be used to literally blow-up Cahill, as he was brought to court in a prison van. There was no concern, or even thought given, to the fact that prison officers, police and innocent bystanders could also be killed in a full-blown terrorist attack.

Two men, 27-year-old Glen Geasley from Ballincollig in Cork and 21-year-old Sean Callinan from Tullamore, were instructed to make contact with a UK gang and buy the weapons. Fortunately the Crime and Security Branch at Garda HQ got wind of the plot and launched one of the most sophisticated undercover stings ever witnessed in Irish crime fighting.

In February 2007, Geasley met two men – one of Asian descent – in London to discuss the deal. The two men had been introduced as arms dealers. Geasley told them that he worked on behalf of Wayne Dundon, who he described as a major criminal figure in Ireland. He told the two dealers that the gang needed "all the weapons for a war in Limerick", between Dundon's people and their enemies. One of the dealers showed Geasley a laptop, with a selection of pictures of different types of hardware they had available. It was accompanied with a price list. Geasley said he would get back to them.

Dundon's front man had no idea that the two so-called arms dealers were in fact specialist undercover agents from Britain's

Serious Organised Crime Agency (SOCA). Codenamed John and Raj, the SOCA agents had been enlisted by Garda HQ to set the trap. This was the first time such an operation was ever mounted. The officer in charge of co-ordinating the elaborate sting was Detective Chief Superintendent Tony Quilter.

In order to establish proof that Wayne Dundon was in charge of the conspiracy 'John' informed Geasley that he needed confirmation that he was, as he claimed, acting for the Dundons. He had been told that Wayne Dundon was the "decision man". It was arranged for the secret agent to visit Wheatfield Prison, where the deadly criminals were being held.

On April 5, 2007, 'John' was instructed to visit another inmate, Thomas Flood. John Dundon was in the visitor's cubicle next door. The agent handed over a copy of the *Irish Independent* which contained inserts from a London magazine, with further mobile phone contact details.

A few days later, the undercover agents were contacted by Geasley, with a shopping list for an awesome arsenal of firepower. There was enough weaponry on the list to equip a military unit. It detailed 24 weapons, including RPG 7 rocket launchers, AK 47 assault rifles, Uzi sub-machine guns, semi automatic pistols and a large quantity of high-powered ammunition. The agreed price was €60,000 in cash.

On April 20, 'Raj' contacted Geasley to say he had arrived in the Rochestown Park Hotel in Cork and wanted the cash before the shipment could be handed over. When Geasley arrived at the hotel he phoned Dessie Dundon on his mobile phone in prison. Dundon told his front man to get two sample weapons before the cash was handed over. The agent refused and demanded the full payment up front. Geasley agreed and later on, Stg£45,000, in used British and Northern Ireland bank notes, was delivered in a Tommy Hilfiger sports bag.

'Raj' then showed Geasley a mobile phone picture of the arms shipment, with that day's *Evening Herald* newspaper in the forefront. The weapons in the picture were a collection of firearms and a rocket launcher which Gardaí had seized from the Provisional IRA. At the same time 'John' was 20 minutes away at the Ibis Hotel on the main Cork to Waterford Road in a van with the weapons. When Callinan arrived, the undercover officer showed him the weapons in the van.

At that moment, the ERU surrounded the van and arrested Callinan. Simultaneously Geasley was also arrested and the cash was seized. In Dublin, the cells of the Dundons brothers were also searched and three mobile phones were seized. Murder Inc had been dealt another severe blow.

In February 2008, Geasley and Callinan subsequently pleaded guilty to three charges of conspiring with others to possess weaponry. Detective Chief Superintendent Quilter gave the court the background to the case. He told the court: "Geasley represented himself as an agent of a criminal organisation based in this country, running their empire from Irish prisons."

Judge Patrick Moran said he dreaded to think of the consequences if the extraordinary police work had not foiled the arms plot. Geasley was jailed for 12 years, with the final five suspended, while Callinan was jailed for six, with the final three suspended. There was much speculation at the time that the two had benefited from a secret plea bargain arrangement with the State, in return for guilty pleas. But it was accepted that both men were working on the orders of the Dundons. At the time of writing Murder Inc's gun-running plot is still officially an open case. Gardaí say they hope to bring others, "higher up in the organisation", before the court.

In a rather ironic coincidence, the Court of Criminal Appeal reduced Wayne Dundon's sentence from ten to seven years on the same day that the arms plot trial opened in Cork Circuit Criminal Court. The news that the hoodlum would be due for release, sooner than expected, was greeted with dismay in Limerick.

* * * *

On October 15, 2007, Anthony Kelly, the Dundon brothers, Dessie and John, and a fourth man – who cannot be named here for legal reasons – went on trial for the murder of Brian Fitzgerald before Mr Justice Peter Charleton at the Central Criminal Court. All four pleaded not guilty. Like the Keane murder trial, it was also held under heavy security in Cloverhill, which had become the favoured venue for hearing dangerous gang-related cases.

The jury of 12 men sworn to hear the case were told that the trial could last up to ten weeks. The Judge warned the jury that they should not read any crime reports whatsoever for the duration of the trial or news articles or colour pieces concerning the trial.

In his opening address, Senior Counsel for the State, Denis Vaughan Buckley, told the jury that the main prosecution witness was James Martin Cahill, who had pleaded guilty to committing the murder and would say that the four accused had taken part in the planning and execution of the offence.

The trial then heard evidence from Alice Fitzgerald who recalled the events of the night her husband was murdered. Neighbours also told of being woken by the shouts for help and gun shots. One neighbour said she heard someone shouting out, "Oh God no," which was followed by two or three shots, then a gap of around 30 seconds, before another two or three shots sounded. Another woman said she heard Brian Fitzgerald crying or shouting out: "Help me, I'm being shot at." On the ninth day of the trial, James Martin Cahill took the witness stand. Over the following six days he made some bizarre revelations that made him sound like he had gone mad. In his direct evidence Cahill told Mr Vaughan Buckley that Anthony Kelly gave him a gun and a clip full of bullets and showed him how to use it. He said he was asked by Larry McCarthy Junior to shoot someone who had "made a statement against him". He was offered €10,000 and agreed to do it for that amount.

Cahill said he had travelled to Dublin with McCarthy Junior to arrange the motorbike which was to be used in the attack. He described how, after several meetings with McCarthy he was driven to Kelly's house, where Kelly provided him with a gun and showed him how to use it. "He was clicking it back and showing me how to use it. The safety and that," he said.

Cahill claimed that Kelly talked to him as he was leaving. "He said he didn't want to know what we were doing but not to mess it up. He just said don't mess around." On the day of the murder, Cahill said he was in a car with Dessie Dundon when Dundon asked another one of the accused if he would drive the motorbike. Cahill told prosecuting counsel that Desmond Dundon pointed Brian Fitzgerald out to him, outside Doc's night-club in Limerick.

"I walked past him. I didn't take much notice of him. It was just he was a big lad," he said.

Both Dessie and John Dundon drove out to Fitzgerald's home with him one day to see where the CCTV cameras were located. The hit man said on the night of the shooting, he and another accused man hid in some bushes near the house, until Fitzgerald arrived home. Dessie Dundon phoned to tell them when the bouncer had left work. When Brian Fitzgerald's jeep pulled up, Cahill said he ran towards it and there was an argument.

"I shot him in the heart, then after a while I walked round and shot him in the head." He said he didn't know how many times he fired: "I just clicked it."

After the shooting Cahill and his accomplice drove to collect a red Mondeo they had been using. Cahill gave his helmet to the driver and left him to dispose of the motorcycle and the helmets. He said he left the gun and the cartridge of bullets in a hedge. He went back to Chaser O'Brien's house, had a shower and got changed out of the clothes he had worn for the murder. Then he was driven to Heuston Station in Dublin where he was met by the Dublin-based godfather and driven to Connolly Station to get the Belfast train. He said he booked into a hotel with McCarthy Junior, where they met John Dundon.

"Larry McCarthy was asking me did the shit run down his legs and everything and I said yes but it never."

They stayed in Belfast for a couple of days before travelling to England.

Cahill told Mr Buckley he couldn't remember whether they went to Manchester or Birmingham but he remembered meeting Anthony Kelly in a Manchester hotel. He denied that they talked about the murder on this occasion.

Under cross-examination Cahill told defence counsel that he thought he was going to be killed in prison. He said he had been afraid of being killed by the prison officers or by "politicals".

"I was in the cell in Portlaoise and they were talking above me. They were saying the murder victim didn't get a chance." Cahill said he was hearing screaming and voices in his head and they only went away when he told the truth about the things he had done in his life. He said the voices started when he was in solitary confinement while serving a five year sentence for possession of a machine gun which he said was to be used in a murder [of Decie Griffin] in Dublin in 2003, for which he was to be paid €50,000. He said the voices sounded like someone talking to him outside his head: "I was coming down the stairs in Portlaoise and I was getting some heroin off the lads and the voices were saying 'he's on camera'." He said the voices referred to him as a paedophile and a supergrass and sometimes seemed to be coming out of the television, answering him back and asking him questions. Cahill said he began seeing a psychologist in 2005: "I was afraid of seeing the psychologist because I was still getting the screaming. Stuff I had done when I was younger, abuse and stuff. I was getting flashbacks. I could see the murder in pictures."

He agreed with counsel for one of the accused that he had told the psychologist he often talked to himself. The hit man said he was very concerned to get the evidence right but got mixed up with another murder that had been planned: "I was getting everything jumbled up with the screaming and everything." During this period he wrote a 90 day "diary", covering the years 1997 to 2003. He detailed a wide range of criminal activity carried out by both him and others. He agreed with counsel that in the diary he had named around 100 other people involved in crimes, including drug trafficking, murder, arms offences and a trip to Germany to buy radio-controlled car bombs. However, he then said that some of this was what the voices had told him to write. Cahill said repeatedly that he was afraid the officers were going to kill him and on one occasion he had thrown boiling water on a prison guard because he thought he was going to attack him. He told Roger Sweetman SC, who was defending Dessie Dundon, that he'd made a statement to

Gardaí in September 2005 that Paddy "Dutchy" Holland and John Gilligan wanted his book of evidence to give to people in Limerick. He also claimed that he had told Gardaí he found a gun in Brian Fitzgerald's jeep on the night of the murder because of the screaming and it wasn't true.

Cahill could not be "one hundred per cent certain" who asked him to carry out the shooting or who was to pay him €10,000. He then said that no one had told him to shoot the night-club security man in the head. He could hear a voice saying "give him one in the head." Cahill said he had never fired a gun before, although he had fired a shotgun and a blank pistol in robberies. On the second day under cross-examination, Cahill told counsel for John Dundon that Larry McCarthy Junior had not asked him to shoot Fitzgerald.

Cahill agreed with John Dundon's counsel that he had shared a cell with an individual and had close association with another person who was "no friend of the Dundons". He also agreed that there had been an allegation that he stalked a brother of John and Dessie Dundon but denied that he had been hired to kill him. He further denied that he had been asked to shoot Brian Fitzgerald to "atone" for this. Cahill agreed with John Dundon's counsel that he had told a psychologist that he was hoping for a new life in Australia through the Witness Protection Programme if he testified. He added: "Where I can be safe".

Counsel told him that he had also told the psychologist that he intended to negotiate for a shorter sentence. Then, in an extraordinary series of admissions, Cahill revealed that he had abused at least six children in Ireland and the UK, including one nine-month-old baby. He also said he had abused a dog and had fantasies about abusing a horse and having sex with his mother. When defence counsel asked what kind of horse was in his fantasies he replied: "An ordinary little horse." Cahill told the jury that he had always told the truth and that he had told Gardaí about abusing children and had named names. However, defence counsel told him that, in the absence of the jury, the Gardaí had told the court that he had spoken of the abuse in such vague terms that they were under the impression that he had been abused as a child himself. The killer said he heard screaming in his head that sounded like his victims and it only stopped when he told the truth. Claims that he had previously made about being threatened by John Gilligan and Patrick "Dutchy" Holland were untrue. The voices in his head had told him to say it. He also revealed that he had refused to leave his cell to meet a consultant psychiatrist from the Central Mental Institution. The interview was conducted while the psychiatrist was standing in the door of the cell. Cahill was naked, wrapped in a blanket and sitting on a plastic blue mattress, on the floor. As Cahill continued with his bizarre testimony, he changed his story again. He stated that John Dundon was not present when Brian Fitzgerald was pointed out to him or when they had inspected the murdered man's house, as he had previously claimed. He said he could no longer be sure that John Dundon was present, although he could remember his brother, Dessie Dundon, being there.

Cahill told Anthony Kelly's defence counsel, Michael O'Higgins SC, that he had been hearing screaming in his head during the three days that he had been on the witness stand: "I got them when I was in my cell yesterday and when I was coming in the van."

He also said he had heard voices while he was giving evidence: "Not when I'm speaking. I was getting them the other day. Just speaking and you will be OK". On the fourth day of cross-examination by the four counsels representing the accused men, Cahill said he had been involved in six murder plots, both before and after the shooting. He denied that he had ever fired a handgun before the murder and insisted that Anthony Kelly had shown him how to use the gun for the shooting. Cahill said that he had been involved in five murder plots in Ireland and one in England but denied he had committed two murders in England, as he had told his psychologist in prison. He denied that his hand-written diary, which he called "My Life of Crime", showed that he was obsessed with guns.

Mr O'Higgins pointed out that in this account Cahill made numerous references to obtaining guns for people.

Cahill denied this: "I never got them for other people; I got them for armed robberies."

The defence counsel put it to Cahill, numerous times, that there was no three-hour window in his account of the night of the killing that would have allowed him to travel to Kilrush to get a gun from Kelly. He also said that it would have been impossible for Cahill to have met Kelly in Manchester in the days after the murder, as claimed in his testimony. O'Higgins said Cahill had a ticket to leave Belfast at 10.30pm on December 1, arriving in Liverpool at 6.30am, the following morning. However, Kelly was travelling from Hollyhead to Dublin on a sailing that was supposed to leave at 6.30pm on December 1. It was delayed until 3.15am on December 2, so, O'Higgins said, they would have literally been "ships passing in the night". Kelly's counsel said that Cahill's sister and brother had told Gardaí that Cahill was a compulsive liar. He then quoted from a statement made by the hit man's sister in which she said he had lied about every member of the family and had stolen from and betrayed them all in various ways.

Cahill denied he had exaggerated abuse they had received as children and that he had been known as "Billy Bull-hitter" in his home neighbourhood in Birmingham.

He agreed that he had been violent as a child and had been expelled from secondary school, after throwing a teacher down the stairs. He was sent to a special school after that, but according to his sister, had stolen from there as well. He also agreed that he had dealt drugs from jail, after developing a serious drug problem. O'Higgins told Cahill that he was not the changed man he claimed to be. In December 2005, after coming forward to admit to the murder, he threw boiling water in the face of a prison guard who Cahill said had "looked out for me".

Cahill denied that he had added sugar and soap to the water which would make the burning worse because the water stuck to the face. Cahill said he never used sugar for this purpose but "some times I use it on my cornflakes". The voices in his head had been telling him to attack the guard and he had not mentioned this to the prison governor because he thought he too was trying to kill him. On November 7, Mr Justice Peter Charleton directed the jury to acquit John Dundon of murder.

He explained that he had come to this decision after Cahill's comment during cross-examination: "I'm getting like voices and I don't want to convict someone in the wrong." The judge explained that Cahill had gone on to say that he did not remember Dundon being present when the murdered man was pointed out at his place of work, or on a visit to the victim's house before the murder. Cahill had also said that while Dundon was present at a house where the murder was discussed he was not present for the conversation. After John Dundon had been dealt with, the prosecution and defence teams made their closing statements.

In his subsequent lengthy charge to the jury, Mr Justice Charleton reminded them that they could only convict if they were satisfied beyond all reasonable doubt. If they did have a doubt then they must find in favour of the accused. He also reminded them that they could only accept the parts of Cahill's testimony which could be corroborated.

On November 15, the jury returned unanimous verdicts finding Anthony Kelly and Dessie Dundon not guilty of the murder. They found the fourth accused man (who cannot be identified for legal reasons at the time of going to print) guilty of the murder of Brian Fitzgerald. After the trial, John and Dessie Dundon were returned to their cells to continue the sentences they were already serving. The fourth man was sentenced to life. Anthony Kelly walked away from court a free man, arm-in-arm with his partner Marie Cronin.

Alice Fitzgerald was visibly upset as the verdicts were returned. She left the court opting not to give a victim impact statement.

The Gardaí and Brian Fitzgerald's family were disappointed with the result of the trial which turned out to be an anti-climax. The testimony of the hit man, in which he depicted himself as a perverted lunatic, was incapable of convicting anyone. But, almost five years to the day of Brian's murder, two of his killers had ended up behind bars serving life. The Gardaí were equally satisfied that another member of the murder gang, Dessie Dundon, was also serving life behind bars albeit, for a different killing. There was extensive independent evidence available to corroborate Cahill's testimony about his accomplice. The detectives involved were philosophical – their war with Limerick's criminal fraternity was far from over.

* * * *

After the trial Kelly's solicitor, Eugene O'Kelly, welcomed the verdict and stated his client's feelings: "Anthony Kelly is extremely relieved that his trial is now over. It has been a very long and difficult trial. He had proclaimed his innocence from the very beginning and he is very grateful to the jury for upholding his innocence." "The resentment is that he has been incarcerated for one year on the word of a self-professed perjuring, perverted killer, James Martin Cahill. The state was happy to rely on that uncorroborated, unsubstantiated evidence. This man's freedom has been denied to him for the past year, based on the rantings and ramblings of a demented psychopath," he added.

Kelly was clearly relieved that he was a free man again. But as he was leaving prison after a year on remand, his son and nephew were about to take his place.

Two days after the Fitzgerald trial ended, Kelly's son, Richard (20), and his nephew, James Kelly (26), pleaded guilty to possession of firearms and were each jailed for five and four years respectively. The cousins had been arrested with the two stolen sawn-off shotguns in the grounds of Kelly's Kilrush mansion in April 2007, while Kelly was in prison awaiting trial. Gardaí had secretly watched the two men retrieving the weapons from a hiding place beside Crag House.

Five months later, Anthony Kelly found himself in the eye of the storm again as Limerick's most dangerous gangsters spilled more blood – and reached a new low in the process. On the afternoon of April 5, 2008, Mark Moloney, an associate of the Keane/Collopy side was shot dead in a drive-by shooting in Garyowen. The attack was organised by the dreaded McCarthy/ Dundons. James Cronin, the 20-year-old son of Kelly's partner Marie, had taken part in helping to organise the vehicle used in the attack.

Within six hours of the shooting, James Cronin was shot dead by members of his own gang after he became upset about the murder. Murder Inc. was not prepared to risk Cronin suffering a crisis of conscience and talking to the police. It didn't seem to matter to the underworld madmen that they were putting themselves in direct conflict with one of their most important business associates. It showed that this deadly gang had become savages.

Two days after Moloney's murder, on April 7, Gardaí recovered Cronin's body from a shallow grave near the Caledonian Park area of the city. At the same time, a second young man who had also been with James Cronin at the time of the murder, gave himself up to Gardaí in Roxboro. He literally ran to the police because he suspected the gang was about to murder him as well because they thought he was a risk to them. It was an illustration of how paranoid the McCarthy/ Dundons had become about leaving "loose ends". Six of their most important members were serving life because they had been "sloppy". That was evident following the conviction of the gangsters involved in the Kieran Keane murder. They had openly squabbled with each other for "making a bollix" of the double execution.

Ger Dundon was later quizzed about the Moloney and Cronin shootings. As soon as he was released, he left the country with another associate and flew to Spain. In the meantime, associates of Anthony Kelly began to make enquiries about the killing of James Cronin.

On July 4, 2008, Ger Dundon was arrested by Gardaí as he was about to board a flight to Amsterdam at Cork Airport, using a false passport. He had returned from Spain but claimed that he needed the forgery because his life was still in danger. Dundon was arrested and charged with three counts relating to the possession of a false passport. On August 27, he was jailed for nine months after pleading guilty to the offence.

His defence barrister told Cork District Court that his client's use of a false passport was "motivated by fear for his life". There were some wry smiles in the courtroom as the barrister declared: "While growing up in Limerick, his family became embroiled in a dispute with another family. As a result he has received very little education and is unable to read or write... he has received numerous threats against his life and I understand that's why he got the false passport and wanted to get out of the country for a few days."

In pleading for leniency for the vicious thug the barrister said Ger Dundon's main concern was: "his family and he wanted to go back to school. He is currently unemployed and I believe that the reason for this is the constant threats to his life."

A few days later, John Dundon was released from Wheatfield Prison after serving just over three and a half years for making death threats against Owen Treacy. Just before his release the "Dum Dum Dundons" organised to have a bullet-proof vest delivered to the prison so that he could wear it from the moment he stepped outside. As soon as he got out, he caught a flight and went on a "holiday".

But Limerick, and the rest of the world, has not heard the last of Murder Incorporated.